Julian Gold

Object-oriented Game Development

ADDISON-WESLEY

An imprint of **Pearson Education**

Harlow, England • London • New York • Boston • San Francisco • Toronto • Sydney • Singapore • Hong Kong
Tokyo • Seoul • Taipei • New Delhi • Cape Town • Madrid • Mexico City • Amsterdam • Munich • Paris • Milan

Pearson Education Limited
Edinburgh Gate
Harlow
Essex CM20 2JE
England

and Associated Companies throughout the world

Visit us on the World Wide Web at:
www.pearsoned.co.uk

First published 2004

ISBN 0 321 17660 X

British Library Cataloguing-in-Publication Data
A catalogue record for this book is available from the British Library.

Library of Congress Cataloging-in-Publication Data
Gold, Julian.
  Object-oriented game development / Julian Gold.
    p. cm.
  Includes bibliographical references and index.
  ISBN 0-321-17660-X (pbk.)
   1. Computer games–Programming. 2. Object-oriented programming (Computer science)
  I. Title.

  QA76.76.C672G65 2004
  794.8'151–dc22

                                                          2003062857

10 9 8 7 6 5 4 3 2 1
09 08 07 06 05 04

Typeset in 9/12 pt Stone Serif by 30
Printed and bound in Great Britain by Biddles Ltd, King's Lynn.

The publishers' policy is to use paper manufactured from sustainable forests

To Sienna

Contents

10 Game development roles **367**

10.1 The cultural divides 367
10.2 The programming team 368
10.2.1 Programming roles 369
10.2.2 Recruitment 373
10.2.3 Programming production phases 373
10.3 The art team 375
10.3.1 Art roles 375
10.4 The design team 379
10.4.1 Design risk management 379
10.4.2 Design personnel 383
10.5 Putting it all together 384
10.6 Summary 385

11 Case study: Cordite **387**

11.1 Technical analysis 387
11.1.1 Low-level file management 388
11.1.2 Object streams 391
11.1.3 Collision 393
11.1.4 Scripted behaviour 395
11.1.5 Objects 398
11.1.6 Human control 401
11.1.7 Particles 404
11.1.8 And so on 412
11.2 Summary 414

Appendix: coding conventions used in this book 415
Bibliography 417
Web resources 419
Index 421

Acknowledgements

The following bright and kind souls are implicated in the writing of this book.

Sam Brown, Peter Bratcher, Adrian Hirst, Graeme Baird and Beverley Shaw at Six By Nine Ltd – I pestered you with my ideas until you either agreed with me, shot them down, or lost the will to argue back. What else are friends for?

Emma: you proofread this stuff and didn't have a clue what you were reading. You corrected my overenthusiastic, dodgy English (*sic*), and fear of your incorrect apostrophe wrath kept me on the straight and narrow. Well, mostly anyway! Thanks also for putting up with my antisocial hours of typing when eating, drinking and not being grumpy were in order.

Introduction　　1

1.1　What is this book?

There's a better than 50% chance that you have picked this title off the shelf in a bookshop and are wondering if it's going to be another one of those 'secrets of the inner circle' type of titles. You know, the ones that promise to tell you unspoken truths on how to write really cool games but in reality offer up a rehash of a manual you may already have for free anyway. I should know, I've bought a few of them in the past, and if you haven't experienced the disappointment getting to the end and thinking 'Is that it?' I don't recommend it. I certainly hope that this isn't such a book, that it offers some useful insights that you can't really get from anywhere else, and that when you finish it you're a little wiser than you were.

The goal of this book is to discuss a pragmatic approach to computer game development. It borrows some of the traditional philosophy of developers and adds a smattering of software engineering principles, team-oriented processes, project management and a dash of what passes for common sense around this business. Although there have been many fine books written on each of these topics – some used as references for this title – to my knowledge this hasn't been done in the context of games before, certainly not in any great detail and with any non-trivial technical content relating to a broad set of disciplines, so it is my hope that this book has something unique to offer.

I would hope to persuade and enlighten some of my audience to do things as I would do them. However, I also expect some or even all of you to take issue with some of the things I discuss and solutions I present in the book. I can't put forward hard and fast answers to either technical or management issues, because if it was that easy to come up with them, we would all be doing it, wouldn't we? Rather, I intend to establish a few simple broad principles and then present some solutions to the related problems which are 'good enough', in that doing them is better than not doing them.

1.2 But why?

Currently, as we begin the twenty-first century, commercial game development is at a crossroads. As I type this, three new game platforms are launching or queuing up for launch in Europe: Sony's PlayStation™2, Nintendo's GameCube™ and Microsoft's X-Box™. These consoles represent another quantum leap in gaming technology; irrespective of their actual abilities, both the expectations of the public and the corporate hype that will fuel them will leave the world asking for ever prettier, ever more complex, ever more involved and subtle or realistic gaming experiences.

This would be manageable if the timescales of projects could grow to match their scope. In an industry where working overtime is already normal hours, there soon will be a need to redefine the day as thirty hours if games are to be delivered on time and on budget without disappointing the increasingly particular public.

How can we square this circle? Clearly adding more hours to the day isn't going to happen, so we shall need to fall back on the usual management consultant cliché of working smarter, not harder.

This book describes, in short, ways of working smarter so that we can continue to excel, push our technological envelopes and manage the growing complexity of developing gobsmacking entertainment titles for the next-generation platforms.

1.3 Who am I?

I have spent the past ten years working in the games industry for both small and big players. Prior to that, I have a strong academic mathematical background with a BSc in astronomy. I spent a few years writing image-processing software in FORTRAN for the Royal Greenwich Observatory in England, before starting in the video games business in 1993. Having experienced development for PC and a plethora of consoles as a programmer and then a lead programmer, it is my somewhat counterintuitive experience that the same – or at least similar – mistakes are made, irrespective of company size or financial security. This strongly suggests that it is the *process* that needs attention rather than the acquisition of staff or other resources.

1.4 Who are you?

This book is intended for game programmers, though it is not exclusively about programming. This is simply because game development today is a synthesis of several disciplines:

- programming
- art
- design
- music.

Not to mention the management of all of these.

It's a programmer's daily job to liaise not only with other programmers but also with those in the other disciplines. In short, very little that any one individual does in the course of development happens in isolation, so it would be a mistake to consider programming without specific reference to the other practices. For brevity, but with little loss of generality, I'll stick to the holy trinity of programming, art and design in this book.

So, you're a programmer. Or you manage programmers. Or you simply work with programmers on a day-to-day basis: a producer, perhaps. You are probably working in a team and almost certainly in a commercial environment. Whilst it's great fun to develop software in leisure time with your friends – and this book will still hopefully prove of some use if you are doing so – many of the philosophies and practices that we'll examine arise because of the way that commercial pressures affect the development process. Similarly, if you are the sole programmer/artist/designer/musician/teaperson, then you are not the direct target but you may still gain benefit from a read through the book.

1.5 So what will you read about?

This book's content can be divided into two main areas. The first will concern the major issues (as I see them) involved in the commercial game development process. This will be done at a level that is abstract enough to be generally useful but pragmatic enough to be applicable to a real-world situation. In fact, it is intended that the content remains as abstract as possible, since there is no way I can know the specific technical problems you will need to solve.

The second area is game programming, or rather game software engineering. I'll talk about choice of language for development and the implications of this choice. I'll also look at the high-level design process and how it translates to source code. I'll discuss a way to analyse and approach cross-platform development. And finally we'll start applying the results to develop some specific game systems.

If you're a lead programmer or a technical producer, you'll probably want to concentrate on the process sections. If you're a programmer aspiring to senior or lead roles, you'll probably find the other sections focusing on development more useful. But feel free to pick and choose, as they can be read in isolation with a minimal amount of cross-referencing.

So without further ado, let's start.

1.6 A brief history of games

Though it is beyond the scope of this book to provide a detailed history of computer games, it is well worth looking back to review some of their evolution, and particularly to look at how development methodologies have changed over time and who is developing them.

1.6.1 The time that land forgot

Computer games are older than many people may think. Indeed, games such as chess and checkers have occupied (and continue to occupy) the efforts of many academic and corporate researchers worldwide. (In fact, if there is a game played by humans, then there is almost certainly a computer equivalent.) The development of such gaming technology probably goes back to the 1950s, when electronic computers – more often than not the playthings of the military, who wanted them for ballistics calculations and such like – were becoming available to civilian educational establishments and commercial enterprises. Samuel Jackson's checkers algorithm is a prime example of the progress of software technology driven by games. Written around 1956, it is optimal in that if it can win from a given situation, then it will. Checkers is one of the few games that is considered 'solved'.

More surprisingly, the first graphical video game appeared in 1958, when William Higinbotham, a researcher at the Brookhaven National Laboratory in New York, used a vacuum tube system to produce a very simple tennis game with a small blob for a ball and an inverted 'T' for a net. Being entirely hardware-based, the game was lost for ever when the system was dismantled a few years later.

Typically, the development of gaming technology remained a broadly academic discipline, since hardware was grotesquely large and just as expensive and unreliable. Indeed, it would remain so until the 1970s, when the mass production of semiconductors became feasibly cheap.

If the hardware was impractical and unreliable, then the accompanying software was equally so. Computer languages have evolved from literally setting binary switches or wiring plug boards, to punched cards, to having a program – be it a compiler, assembler or interpreter – that can translate near-English text into the required binary instructions. Until relatively recently, programming was done at a binary or near-binary level, which made the development of complex algorithms and systems painstaking, time-consuming and error-prone.

In 1962, Steve Russell, a researcher at the Hingham Institute in Cambridge, Massachusetts, came up with Spacewar, a two-player game featuring missile-firing spaceships (see Figure 1.1).

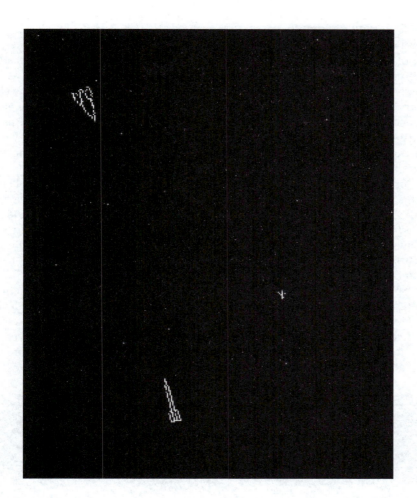

Figure 1.1
Spacewar: the mother of
all video games?

By 1969, when Russell had transferred to Stanford University, Spacewar had become a huge hit with visiting engineering students, one of whom was Nolan Bushnell. Bushnell was working at a theme park while studying electrical engineering and he thought it might be an idea to try to use a computer in an amusement arcade. He spent his spare time designing a commercial version of Russell's Spacewar, which he called Computer Space. In 1971, Bushnell's game became the world's first coin-operated computer game. Bushnell went on to found the Atari Corporation, which was to dominate video game technology for over a decade.

1.6.2 It's all academic

Meanwhile, in the late 1960s, what we know as the Unix operating system grew out of what started as a multiuser gaming environment at AT&T Bell's labs in California. Though Unix is not usually associated with games, there was one massive side effect that would affect games a decade down the line: the development of the C programming language. The intention was to create a language that could be used portably to write operating systems. Whilst the goal of portability was achieved only partially, the C programming language would eventually become the staple of the games programming community. But there was a lot of water to run under the bridge before that happened.

In the early 1970s, Intel produced the first commercially available single chip with a modern central processing unit (CPU) architecture, the 4004. With the onset of this very large-scale integration (VLSI) technology, it was starting to become possible for small computing devices to be manufactured cheaply and sold to the public. A number of games consoles became commercially available, usually supporting very simple games such as Pong – a descendant of Higinbotham's tennis game – on cartridge-based read-only memory (ROM) (see Figure 1.2).

So it was still the territory of hardware manufacturers to develop the fixed content. But as the techniques for manufacturing silicon semiconductor devices evolved at break-neck pace, it became possible for people to actually have their own computers at home. Machines such as Sinclair Research's ZX80 paved the way for the (better-off) consumer to purchase a computer for their leisure use. And almost all early computers came with a version of BASIC.

Figure 1.2
Pong. Anyone for tennis?

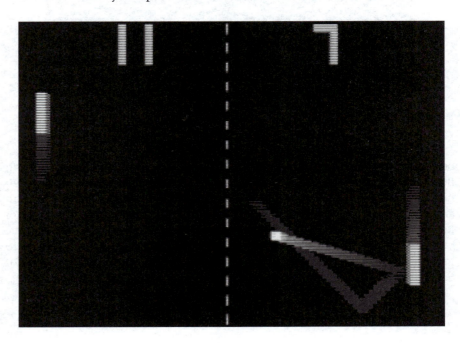

BASIC was never destined to become a game development tool. Most versions were interpreted and therefore too slow to perform the sort of number crunching required for chess and checkers and to update graphics smoothly in (say) a Pong-type game. But its simple and accessible syntax was to provide a springboard for a generation to learn some of the principles of programming. For some, this might have been enough in itself; but many were not satisfied with the speed and facilities offered by their computer's BASIC, so they started using the PEEK and POKE commands to modify data to produce custom graphics and even to write machine instructions. I fondly remember spending hours typing pages of DATA statements in, usually to some disappointment or frustration as a typing error trashed my unsavable work.

The computer games business became serious when those who had persevered with their home micros got hold of the second-generation systems: machines such as the Atari 800, the Commodore 64, the BBC Micro and the Sinclair Spectrum. These machines supported advanced versions of BASIC, but, more importantly, assemblers would become available, which allowed programmers to ditch the BASIC operating system and program the CPU directly. Cassette tape storage meant that software could be distributed in a sensible fashion. And so the games industry was born.

1.6.3 My! Hasn't he grown?

Over the course of the 1980s, game titles grew in scope and complexity. Starting from Pong *et al.*, games evolved from simple block sprites to the wire-frame three-dimensional environment of David Braben's Elite. The public wanted more; programmers were learning and becoming more ambitious. Game technology started to grow correspondingly in size and complexity.

Initially, it had been possible for one individual to take a game idea, write the code, draw the graphics, write the music and generally take charge of all the aspects of game development. Typical project timescales were from one to six months. As the games grew in scope and sophistication, two issues became apparent.

First, it might take two or more people to complete a game in a specified time. Maybe this would be two coders, or maybe a coder and a specialised artist, but some permutation of skills and people. Not too surprisingly, it would turn out that two people could not do twice the work of one, irrespective of how the tasks were divided up. In any case, commercial game development was becoming a team sport.

Second, as the software techniques became more complex, assembly language became quite an inefficient way to implement the algorithms. Assembly programming is a time-intensive skill. Another pressure on assembly language was the desire of the games companies to produce the same game for several platforms. Assembly language is largely machine-specific, so the conversion[1] process usually meant an entire rewrite.

---

1 'Conversion' meaning making a game work near-identically on two systems, as opposed to 'porting', which implies simply making a program implemented on one machine work on another.

What was really needed was a language that was fast enough to run game code smoothly but that was also portable, so that large portions could be written as machine-independent chunks to speed up the lengthening development process. Enter the C programming language, written initially for Unix, itself spawned by game development. Suddenly it all made sense. By the time the 16-bit consoles (SNES, Sega Megadrive) and 32-bit home computers (Commodore's Amiga and Atari's ST) were on the market, C was gaining favour as a pragmatic compromise for commercial development.

It was a strange synthesis. C is, like BASIC, a high-level language. But the similarities stop there. C is a compiled language, and in the 1980s the compilers – especially for the 16- and 32-bit targets – produced poor output code. More importantly, C is a structured language written by academics for writing operating systems (as opposed to BASIC, which is an unstructured teaching language, and any assembly language, which has no concept of structure). The transition for many game programmers would be difficult, and there was a lot of very poor C being written.

1.6.4 From bedroom to boardroom

Not that this was apparent to the consumer. The 1980s were a golden time for game development, with sales of games on the 16- and 32-bit platforms making fortunes for some and the development environment starting to move out of the bedroom and into more formal offices, giving corporate respectability to the industry. Much was being promised. How much would be delivered? I would argue that, with a few exceptions, the games industry underperformed in the 1990s, a victim of its history and partially of its own success. It is also my contention that it is easily fixed, that is if changing hearts and minds is ever easy. To see how, I'll start by examining the game development process, as it exists today, in detail.

1.6.5 Summary

Game development has a curious mixture of academic and industrial influences in its family tree. It has grown from a specialist subject of interest mainly to computer scientists into a mainstream, mass-market, multimillion-pound business. Riding – and eventually significantly driving – the development of consumer electronics, it has gained importance and credibility both as a business venture and as a discipline worthy of academic study.

The game development process

2

2.1 Philosophy

To begin with, let's discuss some of the important principles that govern not only software development but just about any creative process. They may seem trivial or obvious, and I hope that they do. If they are obvious, then we all agree on them. Presuming then that our logic is sound, we cannot fail to agree with any consequences derived deductively from them.

2.1.1 Context

Let me start with an analogy borrowed from science but applicable in any field. Ultimately, almost all of modern physics can be described by three equations, called the laws of quantum electrodynamics (QED). Here they are, in their full tensor notation, for completeness:

$$L = -\frac{1}{4} F^{\mu\nu} F_{\mu\nu} - \overline{\Psi} \Upsilon^{\mu} \frac{1}{i} \partial_{\mu}\Psi + e\, \overline{\Psi} \, \Upsilon^{\mu} A_{\mu} \Psi$$

Now it turns out that these squiggles are very useful for determining the properties of photons – particles of light – but not at all useful in working out how much beer you can drink before you feel very ill indeed. This is surprising, since both these phenomena are consequences of QED. It's just that one (the beer) is very much further removed from the other (the photon).

So what is this metaphor telling us? Well, it's basically saying that, as well-meaning and correct as one particular system is, there are places where it works, places where it still works but you could never tell, and ultimately maybe places where it does not work at all.

This is a useful lesson: as well as having a system or philosophy, we need to have some knowledge of how applicable that system or philosophy is to a given situation.

That's a bit abstract; so let me make it more concrete. Mr Jones[1] has worked in the Gooey widget factory for ten years, starting as a lowly floor sweeper and

---

1   All characters and situations contained in this story are only marginally fictional and have had their names changed to prevent litigation.

rising to office manager. He knows that it takes ten minutes for a worker to make a widget from the time the raw materials are placed in their hoppers to the moment the formed components pop out of the press, on to the conveyor belt. Therefore, it stands to reason and simple arithmetic that in an hour a single person can make six widgets. Ergo, in an hour ten people can manufacture 60 widgets, and consequently the workforce of exactly 100 widget makers can, in a ten-hour day, make a whopping 6000 widgets, assuming no mechanical failure.

Sure enough, that's what his factory has done – more or less – in the time he's been there. Furthermore, if there is suddenly a huge demand for widgets, then he knows he can scale up production by adding a widget maker and widget-forming machine, or by the existing staff working longer hours.

Under Mr Jones, Gooey has prospered. But Mr Jones gets bored, and eventually he decides to answer that advertisement he saw in the paper. Another local company, The Gadget Factory, is looking for a person with management skills to oversee a software development house writing bespoke graphical user interface components for a multitude of clients. Well, in short, he applies, gets the job and utilises his well-founded management practices at The Gadget Factory. Six months later, it folded due to staff expiring on late shifts.

You see, what Mr Jones failed to appreciate was that although you can make six widgets in an hour and so you can make 12 in two, it was not the case that if you can make one gadget in an hour, then you can make two in two hours. There was a context – a range of validity – where Mr Jones's management practices, as correct as they were, were just not very useful.

So our first broad principle is this:

> Every principle or practice has a range of validity. There are places where it is useful and places where it is not useful, irrespective of how true it might be.

It is certainly not true that you can apply simple scaling principles to software development: increasing staff hours or numbers will not result in a proportionate change in output, and under some circumstances it can even result in a fall in productivity. This is due partly to human nature and partly to the nature of software development as a creative process. It is a common failure of management to assume that managing humans is a single skill or, conversely (and just as disastrously), that it is all about the technicalities of developing a specific product.

2.1.2 Iterate!

Iteration will be a common theme throughout this book. It is as powerful a development paradigm as a programming tool, and it is fundamental to almost all creative processes. Put simply, we expect our game to start simply, maybe even from nothing whatsoever, and over the course of time to evolve into something more rich and complex. At times, the process may go backwards – we may scrap or rewrite pieces entirely – but for most of the cycle we expect to see growth and evolution.

So what? you say. Well quite a lot, I say. The point is that it's considerably more difficult to write a complex system in one step than it is to write a simple system that exhibits the required behaviour roughly and then evolve towards the complete requirement in small steps. It's how Mother Nature does it, after all. As I'll discuss later, this powerful notion will allow us to control the progression in quality of all components of the development process – programming, art and design.

Iteration is so fundamental that it is probably impossible to avoid it. Over the course of most products, we'll end up doing then redoing pieces of code, or graphics, or levels. But there is a big difference between simply letting it happen and formally embracing it, putting structures and practices in place to make iteration work for us in some way. A wise saying comes to mind: What cannot be avoided should be welcomed.

Our second development axiom is therefore this:

Start small. Get bigger through small, incremental steps.

2.1.3 Not all statistics are damned lies

If I throw a die a few times, then I am typically more surprised if the same number turns up every time than if different numbers turn up. Generally, we expect there to be some variation in the results of repeated tasks. For example, if I draw ten circles freehand, then it is very hard to make them indistinguishable from each other. In statistics, the relevant term is the 'expected value', the one that has the highest probability of appearing. It is just that – the *most likely*. It doesn't preclude other values appearing.

Yet I am continually amazed at how often developers expect one algorithm, one model, one design, one level, whatever, to be the expected value – exactly what is required. I have no doubt that there are genuinely talented individuals who can, time after time, hit the nail on the head while blindfolded, so to speak. But for the remainder of us mortals, there is a more useful pattern that helps to guide our creativity.

For any skill that you currently have, if you use it a few times, the results will – like the circles – not be identical. Some will be better than others (more circular). Some will be poor, some will be average and some will be good. Generally, as a skill is exercised over a period of time, the percentage in the poor, average and good buckets change. When you start using your skill, most of your hits will be in the poor and average buckets. Typically, with practice and development, the fraction of poor will go down, the fraction of average may drop slightly less and the fraction of good will increase. It would be quite uncommon to produce all poor or all good.

This restates the well-known phases of learning:

- *Unconscious incompetence*: I didn't even know I couldn't do it.
- *Conscious incompetence*: I'm aware it's not how I'd like it to be.
- *Conscious competence*: If I make the effort, I can get the desired result.
- *Unconscious competence*: I don't even have to try and it works out.

What can we learn from this progression? Clearly, if we are asked to use a given skill once, whether it turns out poorly, average or well will depend largely upon our intrinsic skill and experience levels, but there are no guarantees. The more we exercise the skill, the more likely we are to hit the good zone.

Given only a single sample, there is also no opportunity to assess *relative* merit – it may be difficult to define poor, average and good, with no standard to compare with. It will be much easier to assess 'poorest', 'OK' and 'best'.

Hence axiom three:

Avoid presenting single solutions to critical tasks.

2.1.4 Don't do it again

Since we are now expecting a natural variation in the quality of work that we present, we shouldn't feel too embarrassed about the times when we do screw up. We can screw up individually, or a whole bunch of us can get together and screw up cooperatively – the same principle applies. And that's OK so long as we're realising we're screwing up and we're willing to ask the question: how can we prevent this happening again?

Unfortunately, it isn't always easy to know that you've messed up. Here's an example from a project I worked on. Artists were producing models for us and saving their work on to a common network drive. The models and their associated textures were then built into a single resource file and imported into the game. As well as building the models, our artists also had to attach null nodes into the models – points from which we would hang stuff such as cameras and weapons.

On occasion, the number of nulls in a model would be changed and the previous model on the network drive overwritten. It would then be imported into the game, where, after an unspecified amount of time, something would attempt to access a non-existent null and the game would crash. A programmer would then spend an hour or three struggling to find out why the game hangs with the poor debugging tools and long resource rebuild times. The artists were unaware that this went on. Ask them today how things went on the project and they'd say it was fine.

This was a terrible way to work! Without going into the specifics of what went wrong, we needed a team member to point out what was going wrong to all sides and help us find a way to fix it. The moral is:

If something does not work, stop doing it and replace it with something that does.

And its corollary:

Acknowledge your mistakes. Learn from them, and ask yourself: how can I prevent this happening again?

2.1.5 Do it again

Making mistakes is part and parcel of the creative process. As we discussed earlier, it's an almost vital part of tuning our medium- and long-term development strategy to prune out redundant avenues of exploration. As long as we're not profligate in our research, and we make the conscious structural efforts to avoid or minimise the mistakes of the past, we'll improve our chances of delivering our future products on time and within budget.

But rather obviously, making mistakes is only part of the story. Unless we do (quite a lot of) stuff right, we're not going to make any progress of any real form. We would hope that, along the way, we are learning from the things we do right, and that – where appropriate – in the future we'll continue to do it. Thus:

> If something works, keep doing it.

Whatever it was that worked really well, write it down, get it made into a huge poster and make sure everyone walks past it on the way to their desks. The continual reinforcement of good practice can only benefit your business.

2.1.6 Don't do it again (again)

If you collect up the things you do wrong and the things you do right, you end up with experience. This is a precious resource for an individual, and an even more valuable quantity for a development company. If a developer loses its entire staff after the end of a project – and it happens – then the company's ability to deliver within constraints the next time is seriously compromised. This isn't a situation we would invite. We would hope ideally to gain experience of an aspect of development only once and to reuse that experience – in appropriate contexts – in the future. There are several ways to interpret and implement reuse, and we shall look at them in detail later.

> Avoid repeating things you do wrong. Avoid having to redo things you've already done right.

2.1.7 See it from all sides

Humans being what they are, there is a deep tendency for programmers to exhibit the symptoms of 'baby duck syndrome': sticking rigidly and valiantly with the things we learn first, despite the fact that the world is changing about us. Being flexible and open-minded is not easy, and taking on new ideas and concepts without prejudice is harder still, but it is a requirement of existence, never mind video game development. We become better workers – and easier-going people – when we are able to weigh up the pros and cons of several options and decide which to take in a more objective fashion.

> Weigh up the pros and cons for *all* the potential solutions to a problem. Avoid being dogmatic.

2.2 Reality bites

There is still an aura of glamour about the game development business. Many people conjure up images of young entrepreneurs devoting their lives to sitting in front of a keyboard typing, only stopping to wrap their latest Ferrari around a lamp-post on their way home from another champagne-soaked party. There is a little truth to this image, but by and large the game development community is populated with people who would not look out of place in any branch of computing, earning maybe a little less in salary, topped up with occasional bonuses. In fact, even the Ferrari drivers can find the industry a tough place in which to make a profit. Here's a brief look at why.

2.2.1 Hard cash

So you want to write games? Games development in the twenty-first century is an expensive business. Currently in the UK, an average title will take well over £1m to develop, and this figure could easily top £2m soon. It is no longer the domain of the bedroom coders and artists, attracting graduate- and postgraduate-level programmers and film-industry-quality artists and animators.[2] Projects have grown in time from perhaps a few weeks from start to end in the 1970s to, on average, between one and two years from concept to shrink-wrap. There is no typical team size, but, as a rule of thumb, four to six programmers, six to eight artists and two designers (plus production staff) is not uncommon.

With such a large fraction of costs being spent on salaries, one of the ways that developers have limited the costs from spiralling out of control is by preventing project timescales from increasing proportionally with the scope and complexity of a product. When you factor in the likelihood that a product may have to be developed on several platforms simultaneously, it is easy to see that the pressures on development teams tend to increase rather than decrease or even stay roughly static. With many teams already working long hours, there will soon be no alternative *but* to work smarter.

For many independent developers, the problems are considerably worse. The economics of starting and running a small business that generates no income for the best part of two years force many to the receivers before they get to mastering. More worryingly, the majority of start-ups that go under fail on their second product, because when they presented their original demos to the publishers they had that code and art to build on. For their next game, they start from scratch.

Getting a good publishing deal is a must, but sadly this is beyond the scope of this book. However, companies with an enlightened way of working will stand a better chance of impressing a potential publisher than those who don't, so I hope that if what you read here makes sense and you take some of it on board, then you have the edge over your competitors when going for that contract.

---

[2] Design is a more eclectic affair, with no currently acknowledged formal discipline backing it.

This book is primarily about programming, and the games community has a different feel to it from other branches. It definitely comes across as a less rigorous place, where there is less need to follow the rather restrictive disciplines that a traditional suit-and-tie software engineering environment might enforce. In the next section, I'll look at how that has come about and what impact it has had on development.

2.2.2 The Hacker's Charter

Games programming started as an almost amateur affair, with titles being put together in people's houses by one or two friends using poor tools and working stupidly long hours for the love of what they did. The lack of formal training, lack of discipline, lack of a structured language in which to write their code and lack of a robust supporting toolset to help the development process led to some abysmal coding practices. What is worse, they led to an inverted snobbery that somehow this was The Way to develop games. This has led to what I call the 'Hacker's Charter', the notion that what games programmers do is different to what other programmers do and therefore anything is justified. So, in this section, we'll look at how (or even whether) games software development differs from other software development.

Every piece of software that is written has an associated set of priorities. For example, it is much more important that an online banking system is secure than that it runs quickly. It is much more important that a nuclear power station's monitoring system does not crash than that it has pretty graphics. It is much more important that my bat responds to my controls in Pong than that there is a speech-simulated scoring system. So here at least is a common thread for all programming disciplines: for every application or library or even code fragment, a programmer is assessing how to achieve subtasks by considering a set of priorities.

Indeed, for almost every line of code that a programmer writes, there is often a choice of expression: integer or floating point? Single or double precision? Pointer or instance? Pass-by value or reference? Recursion or iteration? And so on.

What the programmer chooses should be influenced by the priorities of the task at hand. So if the priority is to be really accurate, then only double precision will do. If it has to be lightning fast, then maybe it should be floating- or even fixed-point integer. If it has to be robust, then only allow pass-by value (no invalid addresses to cope with) and use pre- and postconditional status checks in every procedure and function.

What priorities do games have? That is too general a question. The priorities of a text-based adventure such as NetHack will differ from the requirement of Quake 3 in some respects. However, to be devil's advocate for a while, let's choose the following relatively common priorities:

- *Speed*: the game has to run at 50 Hz (60 Hz NTSC). In other words, I must be able to update the state and draw the world in 1/50 of a second or less.

- *Control*: the object I'm controlling must respond (perceptibly) immediately to my changing the physical controller state – whatever that might be.
- *Robustness*: the game should never crash, especially if that would result in the loss of a player's efforts.

How appropriate, then, is the hacker's claim that these represent unique development priorities for entertainment titles?

Robustness

'Speed, control then robustness' might be a typical programmer's assessment of the top three priorities for the title. However, it will almost certainly not match your quality assurance (QA) department's priorities. If your game crashes, then there is not a shadow of doubt that the game will be returned to you with an A class bug, irrespective of how well it performs in the other categories. In fact, it is considerably more important for games to be rock-solid than other types of software, for two reasons.

First, it is uncommon for games to have intermediate releases to fix problems found belatedly on released titles. Software patches are released occasionally, but these are the exception rather than the rule.

Second, many games run from read-only media – a CD, DVD or cartridge – and it is therefore impossible to patch them once released anyway.

It is undesirable to risk getting a name for unreliable software. This applies to all kinds of software, not just games, but it doesn't fit at all well with a business model that means you need to shift over 100 000 units just to break even. It is therefore totally reasonable to argue that – viewed from a commercial standpoint – all software titles have robustness as their number-one priority. So, we've found something in common between all strands of software development: basically, we don't want to get the customer angry.

Speed

The requirement that games run at 50 Hz (or 60 Hz) is perhaps a little strong. It's certainly true for some genres, but as the limits of consoles are pushed by sheer game complexity, the one-frame update is usually relaxed to two frames. The goal of the constraint is not to achieve a particular speed, but rather that the graphics can be refreshed smoothly. The practical implication of the constraint is that we limit the number and complexity of objects in our game and get them doing as little as possible (but no less) to satisfy the requirements of their behaviour, as well as making sure that the data-processing side of our game is efficient.[3]

These are hardly alien concepts to the world of software development. It is naive to think that games are the only software systems that require fast data processing. For example, telephony applications need to multiplex and demulti-

---

3   Being 'optimally efficient' is just one pie-in-the-sky delusion inspired by the Hacker's Charter. All non-trivial software can be optimised *ad infinitum*, given enough time, energy and inspired thought.

plex a vast number of audio streams in real time to avoid signal degradation. The sort of code that performs this is every bit as optimal as inner-loop game code, every bit as time-critical as game code, and maybe more so.

Indeed, it is difficult to think of many situations where developers would not attempt to make sections of code run faster, where this would significantly improve performance, not compromise other priorities and where the program fragment in question is at all worth optimising. (A full and seminal treatise on all aspects of optimisation is given in Abrash, 1994).

I was once in conversation with a proponent of the Hacker's Charter, who suggested to me that video games were to the software industry what Formula One is to the automobile industry. Whilst that might sound very impressive, it turns out to be a poor analogy. Formula One cars are built at extraordinarily high cost for a few highly skilled individuals to drive with both financial and physical risks undertaken to achieve high placing in a competition, and with a view to consequent monetary gain and sporting achievement. The commercial risks are very high and pay off for only a minority of manufacturers (witness Ferrari's dominance of Formula One over the years, with McLaren usually second).

On the other hand, developing games software is a business venture that requires high-volume sales to achieve profitable status and so becomes a balance between commercial factors and design ideals. Risk levels need to be low to moderate because the one- to two-year lag between initial concept and shrink-wrapped product will be filled with zero real income, and sales will need to fill that void.

To correct the original metaphor, commercial games development is probably more akin to mass-producing a sports car than Formula One vehicles. However, the analogy has limits, and since neither I nor my opponent understands much of the details of vehicle manufacture and research, it is probably not worth pursuing further.

Control

The requirement that control be perceptibly immediate is a vital prerequisite for so-called 'twitch' games, or indeed any situation where a potential opponent – human or otherwise – can act or react in a similar space of time. Again, this is hardly a unique constraint. Imagine a fly-by-wire aircraft control system that did not service its controllers frequently enough, and then ask yourself if you would fly with that airline.

Commercial realities

Thus far, no mention has been made of what is undoubtedly the highest priority of all in a commercial development environment: delivering on time within budget. That this is considered a management issue rather than a development issue is again due to the legacy of the game development process rather than being intrinsic. It should be noted that many or even most commercial endeavours, be they software, hardware or otherwise, overspend and deliver late. There is no magic wand to wave.

Nevertheless, a team that has delivering on time and within budget as a primary development goal will generally cost less and take less time than a team that does not. Historically, the game development process has had a producer or management acting as a control valve on the developers to constrain their worst excesses – the tendency of team members (programmers in particular) to 'go off on one' and spend disproportionately large amounts of time on non-critical tasks. There are two competing pressures here – the aforementioned desire (primarily of management) to meet the scheduling requirement, and the need to push the envelope of technology in what is a dynamic and competitive marketplace.

Clearly there are some compromises to be made. A team could spend an indefinitely long time developing technology, adding features and optimising, but that would be commercial suicide. It would also be quite dangerous to release a partially completed game, but exactly *how* risky would depend on how complete the game was and how closely it was meeting its other development priorities. (This raises the interesting question of how we decide whether a game is complete; we shall look at this issue more closely in a later chapter.) Given that there needs to be a trade-off between development time and content, it would be preferable if that balancing act were a part of the project plan rather than the imposition of constraints on the team.

Many development teams are not used to factoring such considerations into their plans (and some teams are even happy to work without a plan). The Hacker's Charter would have us believe that game development is a serendipitous affair and any attempt to limit the process suppresses creativity. This is quite incongruous with the reality of commercial software production, and it is no surprise that many games developers – both small and large – are struggling to meet the increasingly sophisticated requirements of the marketplace.

2.2.3 So why are games different?

You may be tempted to think that the argument presented here is that games development is no different to any other sort of software development, but there are differences and they will inevitably have a bearing on how we approach the various phases of the product lifecycle. Here, I'll take a brief look at what actually makes developing commercial games software different from other programming disciplines.

Open-ended design

We can draw a distinction between games that are 'original', in that they create a game world that defines its own rules and mechanics, and 'simuloid'[4] games, which are adaptations of an existing activity – e.g. chess and soccer. In the latter case, customers would be understandably disappointed if some key feature had

---

4 I coin the term 'simuloid' to describe a game that looks like a simulation of some real-world activity but has had adaptation to make it playable as a video game. For example, no soccer title simulates ball physics, because that leads to an almost uncontrollable playing experience.

been omitted, whereas in the former there is greater scope for control of content. In both cases, we can distinguish three sets of features (see Figure 2.1):

1 *Core*: the set of features and mechanics that define the title and distinguish it from other titles. A game comprised simply of core features would not hang together and would not constitute a commercially releasable product.
2 *Required*: the set of features that make this a playable and internally consistent title. A game consisting of core and required features is of releasable quality. However, it lacks the polish that would make it a commercially competitive product.
3 *Desired*: the set of features that make it a polished, rounded and complete-feeling game. For example, visual candy or hidden levels.

Whilst it could be argued that (again) these feature sets are common to all branches of software development, games – especially non-simuloid – have an unprecedented amount of control over the feature sets. This ability to redefine the scope of each of these classes – removing features from one or perhaps shifting them into another – is unique in the scale in which it can take place.

Heuristic content

Because a game is typically more than the sum of many independent real-time systems, often of moderate to high complexity, it is occasionally difficult to predict exactly how it will look and feel until the systems are in place. Prototyping is useful, but often this determines only *viability*, not *playability*. It is relatively common to have to amend content on the fly, or even remove it altogether, simply because it results in an uncontrollable or dull game. Concepts such as 'boring' and 'difficult' are, of their nature, highly subjective. What is unchallenging or dreary for a hard-core gamer may be entertaining and taxing for a less experienced player. This requirement to balance core content with the intended user is somewhat atypical for software development, certainly to the degree of prevalence in games programming.

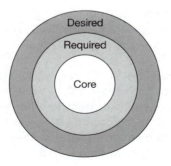

Figure 2.1
Classification of game features.

Artistic content

Many other flavours of software contain artistically rich imagery, but games out-strip all other kinds by a huge margin. The quantity of 2D – still images, full-motion video (FMV), texturing, special effects, etc. – and 3D models sets games aside from any other kind of software targeted at a mass audience. And whilst this content is usually generated by artists, the impact on games program-ming is significant: the mechanism by which a model or image moves from an art package to being an active game object is one of the most crucial pieces of the development jigsaw and will be looked at in detail in forthcoming chapters.

Control methodology

Most games have a control system that is quite different from other software applications. For console games – whose host comes with a control pad having maybe ten buttons and one or two analogue joypads – this is particularly so, and much work will go into controlling what can often be a rich and complex system with a particularly limited control set. As stated before, it is a high prior-ity that game response to control input should be as close to perceptually instantaneous as possible. Accordingly, user-interface design may be quite differ-ent from a standard (PC-style) application.

Complexity reduction

At the time of writing, the 2.66-GHz PC has recently come on the market. The Apple G series offers similar performance levels. This is an unprecedented amount of processing power, several orders of magnitude more than any sensi-ble developer can assume as a target machine. At the current time, the bottom line is that a game should be playable on an Intel Pentium II 200 MHz. This is, in a sense, annoying, since we don't get the opportunity to write all the cool algorithms we can now use with all those floating-point operations (FLOPs) at our disposal. But it is an old story, and one of the benefits of the Hacker's Charter is that it has encouraged the ability to make complex, CPU-guzzling algorithms work on low-end machines.

Of course, it is all smoke and mirrors, but no less of an achievement for that. For example, making a realistic (and enjoyable) vehicle simulation run on a 33-MHz CPU is a great accomplishment, and it is this challenge of reducing the complexity of a problem whilst minimising the loss to the gamer's experi-ence that makes game development as addictive as it is.

2.2.4 Conclusion

It is evident that, like all software, games have a set of priorities that dictate devel-opment strategies, choice of algorithm and programming paradigms. There are many genres of game, and they will typically differ in the set of priorities they observe. However, none of the constraints is unique in the sense that no other software discipline observes them or at least something similar. It could be argued that what makes game development unique is the synergy of constraints, the particular combination of requirements for the development. Whilst this might be true, any other combination of constraints is just as unique, so in essence games development is no more unique than any other strand of software development.

The essence of the Hacker's Charter is that developing computer games is different from developing other sorts of software and so does not benefit from the structures and disciplines that have evolved elsewhere in the computing industry. This turns out to be bunkum, and damaging bunkum at that! Just as efficient code exploits structure to improve performance, so efficient development practices exploit structure to reduce development time and increase production efficiency. If game development is to avoid becoming prohibitively expensive and time-consuming, then the Hacker's Charter must be put to rest once and for all. In the next chapter, I'll look at the techniques I consider to be fundamental to drag game software development kicking and screaming into the twenty-first century.

2.3 Summary

- Practices have a range of validity, outside the bounds of which they are of limited use. Knowing these bounds is as important as the practices themselves.

- Software development teams do not scale. Adding team members can actually hurt productivity.

- Iteration is an intrinsic part of the software development process. We can – and should – exploit it to our advantage.

- No problem has a single solution, and all solutions have pros and cons. Never present a single solution for a given problem.

- Teams and team members that learn from their mistakes perform better next time around.

- If you don't need to do it more than once, don't.

- Game development is a business, not a hobby. Its goal is to make money for the company; great games are a by-product of that.

- The Hacker's Charter has adversely affected the development, management and production of games.

Software engineering for games

3

Many books have been written on software engineering, and it would be pointless simply to regurgitate their contents here. Instead, we can apply our context principle and consider the question of what software engineering practices we can borrow to make games development more efficient. First, we should be clear about what 'more efficient' means. The central problem is that games are getting more complex and resource-hungry but the team size and project timescales are not expanding accordingly. So we are looking for those software engineering practices that can reduce project timescales and make better use of team members.

In this chapter, we will discuss some of the problems associated with software engineering in the games industry, and their solutions, and then discuss the most useful techniques and how to apply them in practice.

3.1 The peasants are revolting (or why the Hacker's Charter is bad for developers)

The Hacker's Charter is a huge obstacle to putting in place any sort of structured process. It is frighteningly widespread, almost ubiquitous. A naive optimist may hope to reverse this trend locally, perhaps by example. 'If I can show how much more efficient it is to do these things than not do them, then they will almost certainly take them on board' could be the sentiment, which is fine except in so much as it does not work. The problem is that it is not possible to stand by and spectate – it requires active participation and support from all team members. Clearly, if there is any initial resistance – and there will be! – then the practices (at best) will fail due to passivity and (at worst and most likely) will fail due to active resistance.

The best chance you have is to start a company with these practices built into the working ethos and then enforce them rigorously from day one. You would ideally recruit a team of like-minded, or at least open-minded, individuals who can implement the practices. However, this will be a realistic proposal for only a minority of cases. Most of the time, there will already be a team of programmers with varying skills and attitudes, and somehow we must persuade them to adopt our practices.

It is obvious that tough but fair management is required. Teams need to understand that these practices are being implemented not as some crusade of pedantry but as a means of generating profit, and that they *are* the rules. However, there is a hidden problem.

3.2 The lords are revolting (or why the Hacker's Charter is bad for management)

You see, it is not only programmers who subscribe to the Hacker's Charter; you will very often find management buying into it too. The reasons are legacies of the 1980s, when bedroom programmers were turning round software titles in next to no time. During the explosion of development that occurred in that decade, there were many cowboy outfits that promised much to publishers but delivered very little. Trust between publisher and developer became undermined; at the same time, the legal issues surrounding deliverables were tightened in order to prevent those errant developers haemorrhaging money.

As a direct result of the growing mistrust, developers were encouraged to show significant progress at project milestones to reassure their backers that work was indeed being done. The term 'significant' implies 'visible', largely because the management in publishers is generally not technically minded and may not be hugely computer-literate. Rather like Mr Jones in The Gadget Factory in Chapter 2, its evaluation of how things are produced may just not be applicable in the software business.

This illustrates a clear ignorance of the software development process, because although (by the *Iterate*! principle) we are supposedly starting small and getting larger, we also acknowledge – and carefully encourage – the possibility that from time to time we can scrap what isn't working (*Don't do it again*). Or, indeed, we may be writing (say) a memory manager that reduces fragmentation: no visible result, improved performance after an overnight soak test, perhaps, but it is uncommon for publishers to watch a game for that long to see nothing untoward happen.

Clearly, these practices violate the *Context* and *Don't do it again* axioms of development. The usual result is that teams are forced to produce visual results – flash graphics – at the expense of all the other priorities of the game, possibly including robustness, controllability and even speed. This usually takes place in the period before milestones; worse still, some time may have to be spent after the milestones, unpicking the changes that were made, before development can progress.

All this leads to a false belief in what can be achieved in a particular amount of time. Programmers have been happy to work outrageous hours to achieve superficial visual deadlines, resulting in a false sense of progress and even a complete change in the emphasis of the game.

In short, the Hacker's Charter, which originated in a cottage industry development environment, has infiltrated larger-scale commercial development and dominated development practice. Consequently, it has set an unrealistic base-line that has been taken on board by management, to the detriment of the products and their profit margins. Since the ultimate objective of any commercial enterprise is to continually increase its profitability or stock value, it is clear that if you are working for a company exhibiting these modes of behaviour, then there is something very rotten in the state.

3.3 Stopping the rot

Having been presented with a bleak diagnosis, be reassured that the prognosis is still reasonable. Development is, by its nature, a synthesis of both risky and dependable strategies, and it is in the management of the strategies that we seek to improve the situation. As stated earlier, the discrepancies between the goals of development teams and management, and a general lack of trust between them, are a major source of concern, and it is to this that we shall turn and seek ways of improvement.

3.3.1 From bedroom to office

The transition from game programming as a bedroom hobby to a large-scale commercial venture was very rapid, arguably too rapid for its own good. As project sizes grew, there came a point when one or two individuals just could not turn them around in a realistic timescale. Individuals who were unused to working in teams, sometimes with unfamiliar people, would bring programming practices that were suited to only one person – themselves. The metric for recruitment was not how team- or product-oriented candidates were, but simply how technically proficient they were: usually in the form of a demo. For a while, the demo scene became a major target for acquiring programmers and artists, but many companies subsequently discovered that a good demo coder is not necessarily a good game programmer. So what makes a game programmer? It is up to employers to define the role of programmers within their corporate environment. Defining exactly what skills are required for a professional game programmer is the first stepping-stone to stopping the rot.

A programmer's lot

It goes without saying that a game programmer should be able to program. Nevertheless, on closer inspection it is a bit more of an open-ended issue. For example, if you are seeking a C++ programmer, do you consider a very competent C programmer? How about a Java programmer?

While these are pertinent questions that form the core of many an interview, they are not the whole story. A programmer does more than program in their day-to-day course of work. Here is a (non-exhaustive) list of the sort of tasks a programmer will perform during the course of a project:

- contribution to the overall design and plan of the project;[1]
- bottom-up and top-down analyses of the respective parts of the problem domain;
- scheduling of the respective components as a result of the analyses;
- implementation and maintenance of appropriate algorithms in a fashion compatible with the goals and priorities of the project;
- monitoring of progress of their tasks;
- liaison with art, design, music and production as required;
- liaison with the lead programmer;
- participation in technical review;
- occasional support of other programmers.

Clearly, there is quite a bit more to the role of programmer than simply programming. Communication skills, design skills and even production skills are required for a programmer to perform their daily duties effectively. Candidates will vary in their abilities to perform any one of their tasks, and it is therefore an employer's responsibility, having employed a candidate, to provide any extra support and training required to improve their skills in these areas.

The more observant of you may have noticed a dirty word in that last sentence. The concept of 'training' is often laughed at in the games industry, at least as far as programming is concerned. There is an attitude that games programming cannot be learnt, that it is simply in the blood – yet another hangover from the Hacker's Charter. Technical proficiency – writing the fastest, smallest, most gee-whiz code – has been valued over and above other skills that a programmer can bring to the team and the company.

The training need not be formal. It can be an initial induction followed by occasional but regular support by lead and head programmers (and no doubt in the other disciplines). Nevertheless, before training can be introduced into the workplace, there is something that has to be put in place: a set of clear working practices to support the list of duties.

3.3.2 Working practices for programmers

The company should invest some time in creating a working practice definition for each role it defines within the organisation. It should be thin enough to be unintimidating but comprehensive in its scope. Generally, it's best to leave out the justifications for why the practices are the way they are, lest you end up with a *War and Peace*-size document that people can still take issue with. It should be unambiguous in its statement that 'this is how we do things', and it should be enforced by senior staff and management as firmly and as fairly as possible.

There are many subscribers to the Hacker's Charter who will not take at all well to this document and its enforcement, or indeed to any attempt to for-

---

1 I define a 'design' as a description of technical content; a 'plan' is how one intends to go about implementing that design.

malise working practice. Though not unique to the games industry, they are very prevalent, and they represent one of the biggest challenges facing commercial game development. These individuals – usually exceptionally talented on the technical side of development – believe (among other things) that their programming is an articulation of their creativity and that any attempt to formalise it is tantamount to suppression of their freedom of expression. To be fair, there is a grain of truth in this: it takes effort to learn new systems, and that effort could presumably be deployed elsewhere, sometimes with beneficial effect. Nevertheless, the practice of *laissez-faire* programming is better suited to individual R&D projects than to team-based development, and there are few commercially successful disciplines in the world – not just in software but in any profit-driven creative discipline of sufficient maturity – that do not have a working practice policy. The author can find no justification why the games industry should be any different.

This poses a dilemma for an employer, illustrated by the following joke:

Patient: Doctor, please help. My husband thinks he's a chicken.
Doctor: My word, that's awful. How long has this been going on?
Patient: About three years.
Doctor: That long? Why didn't you see me sooner?
Patient: Well, we really needed the eggs.

Many employers are happy to put up with proponents of the Hacker's Charter because they are often technically gifted and prolific. The lack of skills in other areas (the communication and design and support sides) is overlooked or tolerated, usually to the long-term detriment of the studio and the products, because on the surface there is no better alternative. The skills are difficult to replace because at present the demand for highly skilled technicians hugely outstrips supply.

Conversely, the scarcity of sufficiently competent games programmers in the labour market is such that any individual who can show the requisite technical skills and does not otherwise fluff their interview stands a considerably better than even chance of employment.

As a consequence, most games companies have recruited one or more 'chickens' and have become dependent on their 'eggs' ever since.

This is not to suggest that their eggs are not tasty and nutritious. Or, to collapse the metaphor, that they do not produce competent or even more than competent software. It is the impact they have on the development culture of the team and the studio that is at issue. 'Chickens' require sensitive but firm management if they are to be prevented from perverting company objectives in favour of their own.

3.3.3 Software standards

A component of many working practice policies is a software standard, a set of rules and conventions governing how code is produced and evolved. This is an area that can spawn religious wars about minor technical details, so it needs to be handled with some sensitivity. It is true that many projects have, in the past, been completed successfully without the need for a team or a studio to agree on a set of standards. It is also true that most large developers adopt one, most commercial libraries are written with one, and many teams end up agreeing on one.

It is important to keep the issue in proportion. Software standards are only a part of development, and a small part at that. Creating over-proscriptive and pedantic standards probably does more harm than good: it becomes difficult for programmers to memorise a huge volume of rules, it is correspondingly difficult to enforce a large policy, and there may well be a case that such an emphasis on presentation detracts from the substance of what is being presented.

A standard is simply a beginning point, a place where a professional team (and your studio is just one big team) agrees on how it's going to do things. Having agreed upon this, it should be pointed out that it is a programmer's professional responsibility to follow the standard (except in a few circumstances when it makes more sense not to). Most will. You may be unlucky enough to have a 'chicken' in the company who objects to either a particular standard or standards in general. If this is the case, then you should be concerned: if they object to something as simple and commonplace as having to follow a software standard, then they are more than likely to be a source of agitation with weightier matters.

As mentioned above, particular standards comprise a topic that generates heated and technical debate. One thing if any is apparent: you cannot create a standard that will please[2] all of the people all of the time. Or to put it another way, for every individual there will be some feature of the standard they don't like. Such is (professional) life. It is useful to divide individual elements of a standard into those that are made for a specific purpose, e.g. enforcing good practice, a particular naming convention, and those that are apparently arbitrary, e.g. do we use Kernighan and Ritchie-style braces

```
void SomeFunction() {
}
```

or the more modern style

```
void SomeFunction()
{
}
```

which is largely a matter of personal taste and habit.

It is important to be pragmatic when it comes to the enforcement of software standards. No one is going to enjoy pernickety policing where minor deviations from the standard are pointed out in copious numbers. Most conscientious pro-

---

2   'Please' meaning 'be acceptable to' in this context.

grammers will deviate from a standard that is not their adopted or habitual standard some of the time, so it is best to simply hope for (say) an 80% hit rate. We can then decide which aspects are solid (you *must* do it this way) and which aspects are flexible.

Context is important here. It is usually of greater importance to enforce a policy more rigorously in shared or public code than in private or implementation code, though it should be borne it mind that any healthy development philosophy will propagate useful or generic pieces of specific private code into the public shared area. In other words, private code should be written as if it is going to be public some day.

Getting over the hurdle of there actually *being* a software standard is simply the first obstacle. However it is approached, there is still the debate over the content of the standard to come. There is almost a law in development circles that says that the intensity of the debate about an issue of policy is proportional to some positive power of how far you try to spread the debate. In more concrete terms, it is trivially easy to create a standard yourself; it is mildly awkward to create a standard for your team; it is difficult to create a standard for a studio; and it is very difficult to create a policy for a set of geographically separate studios. In general, it is also harder to set a standard when a studio has been up and running for some time than it is to impose one at day one. So there is a strong motivation to keep decision making as local as possible and to make the decisions as early as possible. For this reason, the most efficacious method of introducing a software standard can be divided into two stages:

1 Decide what the *abstract* goals of the standard are. For example, many standards require that a programmer prefix global variable[3] names with 'g_'. The abstract version of this is to require that global variables are named in a clear and consistent way that distinguishes them from local and module-scoped variables. A set of these abstract goals taken together becomes the large-scale software standards policy.

2 Allow each team to implement the standards policy in a way that they agree on. In the case of the example above, some teams may decide to use the 'g_' convention for globals, others may prefer just a 'g' prefix, while others may still prefer a module identifier prefix – '<MODULE NAME>_'. These should be agreed on (if necessary) at the start of a project if possible.

It is then up to the teams to police their own standards in the way they see fit. As far as management policy should be considered, it is part of a programmer's job description that they follow the standards agreed by the team they are working in. Deliberate failure to do so should be treated in an analogous fashion to a programmer who refuses to write any code. No team should be allowed to be an

---

3 Not that I am suggesting that your code should contain global variables. They are the spawn of the devil and should be avoided.

exception. It is difficult to defend the plea of *'They're* not putting "g_" in front of globals, so why should we?' If that is allowed to stand, the chickens will really run the roost.

Often, a studio runs an anarchic system for a while and then realises that the code it is producing is just not of a professional standard: there is confusion about inconsistent naming, no one can tell the difference between pointers and instances, global variables and local variables clash causing unpredictable behaviour, etc. Introducing a standard to a project that has been running for some time often has programmers performing days of boring multiple search and replaces and rebuilds, ending up with an identical-looking game and a heap of frustration with the whole standards business. This is clearly an undesirable state of affairs, and the only sane way to avoid it is by a change-as-you-go policy: it's still search and replace, but it happens during the normal course of development so that programmers are still progressing the code base. It is still not ideal and, as stated earlier, it is always easier on everyone involved to set the standard sooner rather than later.

So what would the content of a software standard policy be? There will be a distinction between features that are common to all relevant languages and those required for a specific language. Since we have not discussed the issues around choice of language yet, we defer the presentation of an actual policy to that section.

3.3.4 Good working practice

A software standard is a start, but no more than that. Over and above that, there are other working practices that help a professional and their manager to monitor their work throughout the course of a project. These techniques are discussed at programmer level in McConnell (1993) and at production level in Maguire (1994).

3.3.5 Good programming practice

All computer languages currently in use for game development have idiosyncrasies that catch out the inexperienced or unwary programmer. Often, it is a mistake made once and never made again. Just as often, it is a recurrence of a previous mistake, albeit in a slightly different form. Many of the common – and subtle – pitfalls are well documented in books, e.g. Maguire (1993), Myers (1995) and Myers (1997). What is evident from such books and personal experience is that the learning of a computer language does not stop at mastering the syntax – not even nearly! An employer should therefore seek to continue the education of its staff.

A well-stocked library is an essential component of this ongoing education process. Making a title such as Maguire (1993) a required part of an induction process for a new employee can be a good start. Similarly, a good-practice document that distils the important elements of both books and experience into a series of short 'try to do this, try to avoid that' bullet points is well worth considering (but keep it separate from the coding policy).

However, the tendency is for the programmer to read these, get sucked into work and subsequently never find the time to further their reading. If we are to make the education of staff an ongoing process, it is therefore desirable to make learning part of the corporate culture.

This is not such a huge step. The predominant learning mechanism in the industry is by osmosis: programmer A talks to programmer B and passes on a snippet of information, or B reads some source code. The main problem with this is that we are as likely to pass on poor practices as good ones, so although we do need to encourage osmosis, we also need to be actively supporting the process. There are two ways of accomplishing this (and other) end: *peer review* and *paired tasks*.

Peer review

It is a good idea generally for a team to take a day once in a while to review the work they have done so far. An ideal time for this is just after a milestone. This prevents the review process breaking the flow of development. Peer reviews need to be as informal as possible; there's nothing much worse than participating in a witch-hunt[4] and the emphasis of the process should be on:

- ensuring that what has been implemented corresponds to the design (and ascertaining any reasons for departing from the design);
- disseminating broad implementation details to the team;
- sharing programming paradigms with the team;
- monitoring individual skill levels and performances;
- re-evaluating the next stage in the plan: has anything changed since the initial design that has generated extra requirements, or even invalidated certain areas?
- what is working? What is not working?

In essence, the review should be a positive process from which everyone can gain. So although the feel should be informal, there needs to be some structure imposed. Here is a suggestion for how the process should be handled:

- Decide on a review date. Book a meeting room for the whole day. Large teams may need several days, or alternatively create several parallel mini-reviews where subteams handle certain parts of the source tree.
- Decide what code is to be reviewed. As the code base grows during development, it will become impractical to review it all. Typically, review the larger systems, the newer systems, and those systems earmarked for modification in previous reviews.
- At least 48 hours before the review day, make sure all programmers have a copy of the relevant source code. A printout is preferable, since the best time to look over code can often be on the bus or train home or in the bath.

---

4 Being a witch during a witch-hunt springs to mind.

Fan-fold printout is preferable to A4 laser copy because you can see long lines in entirety and there's no need for stapling so page order is preserved.

- On the review day, get each programmer to present the design for the module he or she is reviewing, then its implementation. Keep each presentation as short as possible: no line-by-line dissertations. The team should then discuss any issues arising, including where the code is going in the future.
- After review day, any necessary changes should be made. It may be necessary to rerun the review if significant alterations or additions are required. Otherwise, the lead programmer can approve the modifications.

Special mention is required for a review held at the end of a project. Often called a 'post mortem', it is perhaps surprisingly the most important review of all. If you hold no other reviews, hold this one. The good news is that there is usually more time to spare during a product's ramp-down phase, so finding a day – or possibly more – can be easier and well worth the effort. Several important issues (over and above those mentioned previously) need resolving at the end of a product:

- Is this a one-off product or could/will there be a sequel? How much – if any – of the code base can be used in the sequel?
- Has the product spawned 'core' technology: components that can be reused in other products?
- Again, the most important issues: what went right, what went wrong, and how would we do it differently if given the opportunity?

Paired tasks

A problem with the peer-review process is that it is a discrete process: it only happens once every few weeks or months, meaning that there is often a large bulk of source code to review. It may be preferable to make reviewing a more continuous process, and one way to achieve this is to pair up programmers on significant tasks in the project. There are two ways of making this work:

- one of the pair – usually the more senior – is appointed to a 'reviewer' role; or
- each of the pair is jointly responsible for reviewing the other's code.

Which of these two methods to adopt will depend largely on the distribution of experience within the team.

Making two people jointly responsible has a number of benefits and costs, which we shall examine here.

Pros

- Critical tasks become less prone to slippage because of an individual becoming ill, going on holiday or even resigning. This loss of specialised skills is one of the banes of the business (and is, of course, a consequence of the Hacker's Charter).

- Code designed, written, maintained and policed by two programmers can be considerably more robust.
- It provides an effective way of implementing ongoing training and staff assessment if a trainee is paired with an experienced programmer.

Cons

- Two paired programmers do 'less' work than two individual programmers working on separate tasks. The quotation marks suggest that although a smaller volume of code is produced per working day, the code may be more bug-resistant and that therefore time may be saved in the long run.
- It is not clear who watches the watchers. Monitoring and supervising the pairs may require effort in itself if dysfunction becomes evident.

Interestingly, since the peer-review and paired-task methodologies are not mutually exclusive, the author suspects it may be beneficial to run both systems, thereby annulling the opposed pro/con features (as well as reinforcing the independent pros and cons).

3.3.6 Code reuse

The Hacker's Charter generates a diverse and destructive mythology in its wake. What is amazing – and equally infuriating – is when intelligent programmers who subscribe to the charter transform the personal statement 'I don't know how to do it' into 'It can't be done'. Amazing because these individuals are happy to solve other problems of considerably greater intractability. Amazing because not only do they make the statements, but they can also provide a rich framework of supporting 'evidence' as to why 'it can't be done'.

Code reusability is one of the issues that provokes the strongest reaction from charter proponents. They will claim that it can't be done, and if it can be done then it isn't worth doing, and if it *is* worth doing then it probably isn't reusable. Disingenuous philosophies such as these present an almost impenetrable barrier to what is a difficult software engineering discipline.

It is tempting to attribute this to the history of game development, but it turns out that while there is truth in the idea that the attitude is a hangover from the 1970s, it is not the whole story. Speak to many of the seasoned developers still battling away in the industry today, and you will realise that their livelihoods once *depended* on having reusable code.

Working as freelance programmers from home with amusingly short turn-around times, their bottom line was that if they did not deliver, they were not paid and so did not eat. In order to shorten the development period, they spent some time coding their keyboard readers, sprite renderers and other commonly used code segments. It is interesting that this pragmatic strategy was being used at the same time as the Hacker's Charter was evolving. Clearly, it shows that making code reusable was simply a question of attitude, not of technical difficulty.

Today the issues are similar. Though most employed programmers are not living hand to mouth, with projects (and hardware architectures) becoming larger and more complex the cost of development is continuously increasing. It is the author's assertion that code reusability will become a more and more important priority of development teams, and the difference between the companies that are profitable and those that fold will be in how and whether they manage the issue.

Now we do need to be a little careful here. Today's game architectures are considerably more complex than those of the 1970s, and what worked then may not work very well now. Most games are considerably more than a few input routines and a few sprite drawers, and it could – and has – been argued that reusable code can form only a small percentage of the final product. This is far from the truth, mainly because reusability, on closer examination, is a little more complex than it appears initially.

To start with, we can define more than one flavour of reusability. (Note that at this point we do not imply any particular reuse mechanism – it could be anything from cut-and-paste of code to libraries.) These classes of reusability may coexist and even overlap within a project or set of projects:

- *Functional reuse*: software development would be a tedious and error-prone process if we could not write functions or subroutines to perform tasks that are required in several places. When we take a piece of code and place it in a function that we call multiple times, we are performing one of the simplest kinds of reuse that there is.
- *Horizontal reuse*: a piece of software is reused horizontally if it is specifically intended to be shared by a number of projects being developed simultaneously. Horizontally reused software entities have a typically short lifespan in that they are not intended for use in future developments (though they may end up so through either deliberate policy or inertia.)
- *Vertical reuse*: a piece of software is reused vertically if it is intended for use in current and future products. Vertically reused software needs to be rather more future-proof than horizontally reused software and is, in general, quite a bit more difficult to write.[5] Pragmatism dictates that the software has a well-defined shelf life – a number of titles it will be used in – before it is re-engineered or replaced.
- *General reuse*: a piece of software that is intended to be reused both horizontally and vertically is said to be reused generally. It is a little more difficult to write a generally reusable system than a horizontally or vertically reusable system.
- *Engine reuse*: often, a system (or set of systems) can be comprehensive enough to support the majority of game functionality. Such a code base –

---

5 The difficulty comes in avoiding writing systems that are so general that they are awkward to use and suffer performance degradation, or too specific to be useful in more than one product.

often referred to as an engine – can form the basis of many products. For example, Epic's *Unreal* engine is a licensed first-person viewpoint renderer that integrates an object-oriented scripting system.

- *Pattern reuse*: very frequently we find ourselves writing pieces of code that look almost identical to others we wrote earlier, maybe with only semantic differences. Many languages provide a mechanism for reusing these code snippets: C and assembly have their preprocessor macros; C++ has a power-ful template paradigm on top of its C heritage. Patterns are a currently popular topic in the C++ development community and are discussed in detail in such books as Gamma *et al.* (1994).

- *Framework reuse*: similar to pattern reuse, frameworks are systems that do little or nothing in themselves but provide a paradigm from which to hang functionality. For example, an application may not have much more than an abstract application type and an abstract data model type, but it guides the development of an application in a logical and consistent way.

- *Placeholder reuse*: not all software written is intended for release. Often we write a simple version of something to get the ball rolling and replace it with a production version later on when it makes sense to do so. Just because we don't release it doesn't mean we throw it away. If it was useful as a placeholder in one project, then it will be useful as a placeholder in another project.

- *Component reuse*: sometimes we write code for one project that later turns out to be reusable in another. A set of files that can be lifted out of one project and placed in another with minimal integration work is termed a 'compo-nent'. Components should be as simple as possible and should not be dependent on resources that are not common to all projects (dependencies increase the size of the component and thus reduce their reusability, draw in features that may not be wanted or may even cause compile and run-time issues within their new environment, and increase compile and link times). For a detailed treatment of component development, see Lakos (1995).

- *Copy-and-paste reuse*: in some circumstances, we may want to avoid making two discrete systems dependent via a reusable element even though they require the same functionality. In this case, we may be tempted to create a private function or object, test it, then copy it from one file and paste it in the other. This is fine, but there are a couple of gotchas that should be heeded. First, there is the increased maintenance. If we need to add extra functionality in one place, then we may need to propagate it to all the places where we pasted. Second, if we find a bug in one copy, then we can be sure it exists in all the other copies and we need to be very sure that we've changed all the instances before proclaiming the bug as 'fixed'. Clearly, copy-and-paste reuse is applicable only for small and relatively simple systems – the larger the element, the greater potential for hidden problems and for addition of non-generic behaviour. If the component does something non-trivial, then it will be a candidate for sharing publicly and we start introducing the dependencies we tried to avoid. We can make our lives easier by ensuring that these reused elements are 100% private – they appear in no public code, are not externally accessible and are mentioned nowhere in interfaces.

So there are several ways to develop reusable code, from the humblest macro to the most powerful template libraries. What they all have in common is the following question at their root:

Will we need this more than once?

It's an easy question to ask and it isn't all that hard to answer. Indeed, answering 'yes' in as many cases as possible tends to lead to projects that even in the worst-case scenario of 'canning' can be happily cannibalised for many features that would otherwise draw valuable time from the team.

Hacker's Charter proponents may argue that it is difficult[6] to write reusable complex systems, and that it is pointless writing simple ones. Experience tends to show the contrary: indeed, the more complex the system, the better is the case for reuse (though other factors will be taken into account as well). As for simple systems, they tend to be what complex systems are built out of. Besides, the word 'simple' is misleading. Consider, for example, the requirement of storing objects in a linked list. This is a fairly atomic operation and certainly very common. To write a linked list module every time one is required would be a particularly risky way to develop: the probability of creating new bugs in every implementation is very close to 1. It makes much more sense to write a list module, test it thoroughly – once! – and reuse it (by some mechanism) where it is needed.[7]

The core myth

Central to the resistance to writing reusable systems is the belief that it takes longer to write a reusable entity than a bespoke one. There is certainly some truth in this assertion, though again the implication is that because it takes longer it therefore takes prohibitively longer. It is difficult to justify this view on any timescale longer than the duration of one product. Clearly, if the code we are writing already exists and has been incorporated into a previous product, then it takes no time at all to write and test. So even if we accept the notion that it takes longer to develop the reusable software, we can consider the extra time as an investment and be happy with that.

However, the author thinks this is a little conservative and offers the proposition that writing reusable code is a skill that improves with practice. The more experienced the programmer, the smaller will be the difference between the development time for non-reusable code and that for the reusable code.

---

6 Prohibitively difficult is what they imply.
7 Though often the reuse mechanism will depend on the context in which the list will be used.

Exactly what the time difference will be depends upon many factors and probably cannot be generalised. For small systems, the difference will be small. For large systems, it will depend on the proportion of reused functionality from small systems to the amount of specific functionality and new reusable functionality required. In other words, design is critical to creating large reusable systems.

How to write reusable code

So far, we have established that writing reusable code is both fundamentally required if development is to be an economic process and certainly possible, if only because there are so many ways to do it. That does not mean that it is trivial to implement, and it requires developing the attitudes and skills of programmers who have become used to more focused development strategies.

The simplest way of achieving this end is to set specific reusability targets at the outset of the project; in other words, one of the project priorities is to produce a set of reusable systems, in whatever sense the reuse is implied. Exactly what – if anything – these systems are will depend on the design phase of the project. Typically, at the start of the development lifecycle, we will have a design document that in general should not be treated as complete or even comprehensive. The technical design process will translate the design into a set of core mechanics that form the foundation of the game, and a top-down analysis then yields a set of systems that will be required to implement the core behaviours.

During the course of this top-down analysis, it will be possible to identify systems with reuse potential.[8]

However, this will pick out only the vertically reusable components:[9] to find the horizontally reusable parts (in those studios where more than one project is developed simultaneously), it will be necessary to broaden the scope of the search and involve other teams. In general, communication between teams can benefit all parties, and it is therefore useful to involve at least the lead programmers of all the development teams in some of the proceedings of the technical design. The author recommends a design summary meeting after the major details have been thrashed out, at which the horizontally reusable components can be identified.

Summary

- Reusability has a broad scope, from writing single functions to creating entire architectures.

- Reusable systems rarely happen by accident. They may need designing and planning on a team-, studio- or company-wide scale.

---

8 And, indeed, a corresponding bottom-up analysis will yield a number of existing reusable systems that can be incorporated at little or no cost.

9 In the weaker form of the term 'component'.

- Writing reusable code is an acquired skill that needs to be fostered.
- It need not hurt development time to create a reusable system where appropriate.

3.3.7 Dependencies: the curse of Hades

One of the major obstacles to code reuse is when you cannot take what you want without having to take stuff that you don't want, stuff you don't need or stuff that will actually cause you problems. Much of what we'll talk about in this section will boil down to eradicating, or at least minimising, dependencies between classes, components and other levels of the hierarchy.

Dependency is insidious. The more you allow it to creep into your code, the less reusable your systems become. Remember that dependency is transitive: if A depends on B and C depends on B, then C also depends on A. Or to put it another way, dependencies are difficult to sweep under the carpet. In the long run, it is easier to write and maintain reusable systems if you keep the dependencies at bay, and people are more likely to reuse your code and be able to understand your code if they have one or two components to consider rather than a bunch of interlinked spaghetti.

However, there are dependencies and there are Dependencies. Within the context of C++ development, let's enumerate the major types of dependency we will encounter in the following subsections. We'll say that two components – a single cpp/hpp file pair – are dependent on each other if there exists any sort of dependency between A and B or B and A.

Strong dependency

A strong dependency exists between components A and B if A.hpp must include B.hpp to compile and link successfully:

```
// B.hpp
#include "A.hpp"

class B
{
    A m_A;
};
```

Hard dependency

A hard dependency exists between components A and B if A is strongly dependent on B and B is dependent on A:

```
// B.hpp
#include "A.hpp"
```

```
class B
{
public:
    B();
    B( int i );

private:
    A m_A;
};

// A.hpp
class B;

class A
{
public:
    A( int i );
    B Foo();

private:
    int m_iData;
};

// A.cpp
#include "A.hpp"
#include "B.hpp"

B A::Foo()
{
    return( B(m_iData) );
}
```

Weak dependency

A weak dependency exists between components A and B if A.cpp needs to include B.hpp to compile and link successfully:

```
// B.hpp
class B
{
public:
    B();

private:
};
```

```
// A.hpp
class B;

class A
{
public:
    A( int i );
    B Foo();

private:
    int m_iData;
};

// A.cpp
#include "A.hpp"
#include "B.hpp"

B A::Foo()
{
    return( B(m_iData) );
}
```

Soft dependency

A soft dependency exists between A and B if A uses only pointers or references
to B:

```
// A.hpp
class B;

class A
{
public:
    A( B * pB );

private:
    B * m_pB;
};
```

In terms of seriousness, these dependencies order themselves this way (from
most to least damaging):

1   hard
2   strong
3   weak
4   soft

It is usually possible to move at least one step down this order: given a system with hard dependency, a variety of software engineering techniques can be used to turn it into a strong dependency, and so on. Sometimes, though, a hard dependency is exactly what is wanted – for example, to optimise the communication between classes in the components – so it would be quite wrong to suggest that all dependencies can and should be reduced in strength. Nevertheless, it is unusual to require a hard dependency, and if you end up creating one – by accident or by design – it may be worth re-evaluating the components to see if a cleaner implementation can be engineered.

Often, the dependency is quite unnecessary and may result from accidental or legacy inclusion of a header file. Tools exist that detect whether header files that are included are actually required – for example, Gimpel Software's PC-Lint. But usually, a casual inspection can weed out the totally unnecessary ones: the ones where the classes, types and free functions declared in the header are unused.

Then there are the cases where we refer to objects by pointer, reference or as a return type or typedef only. Again, if the header file has been pulled in, it can easily be pushed out and replaced with a forward reference. Remember, it's not just a better design when you do this: it compiles and links faster too.

```
// All these just need a forward reference to MyClass.
class MyClass;
void Foo( MyClass * pClass );
void Foo( MyClass & aClass );
void Foo( MyClass aClass );
MyClass Foo();
typedef std::stack<MyClass> MyList;
```

For the remainder of the dependencies, you can try a number of techniques.

Strength reduction

The idea with strength reduction is to replace strongly binding relationships with less binding ones. Inheritance is the most strongly binding: not only do you need the declaration of the inherited class to implement it, but also once you've done it then you can't undo it, i.e. inheritance graphs are static by nature. There is, however, a distinction between public, protected and private inheritance. Private inheritance hides the inherited class and is more akin to ownership. Protected inheritance falls somewhere in between.

```
#include "Base.hpp"

class Derived : public Base
{
};
```

Next most strongly binding is ownership, which is only slightly less strong than inheritance, and most closely resembles private inheritance. To grant ownership, you still need the header file declaring the owned class, and once you've decided what the owned class will be, there's no going back.

```
#include "Owned.hpp"

class Thing
{
public:

private:
    Owned m_Owned;
};
```

Least binding of all is reference. You don't need a header file to use a reference: just forward declare the class. There are two types of referencing in C++, one confusingly called a reference and the other called a pointer. Of the two types, reference is the stronger binding because a reference can be set only once during construction:

```
class Referred;

class HasReference
{
private:
    Referred & m_pInstance;
public:
    HasReference( Referred & aThing )
    : m_rInstance(aThing) // Can't be changed after this.
    {
    }
};
```

Pointers are the most flexible of the bindings (and, consequently, the hardest to manage). They can be set and reset at will, and they provide much of the flexibility in design and richness that C++ offers.

```
class Referred;

class HasPointer
{
private:
    Referred * m_pInstance;
```

```
public:
    HasReference( Referred * pThing )
    : m_pInstance( pThing ) // Changeable anytime
    {
    }
};
```

By replacing a more strongly binding relationship with a weaker one, we can reduce the interdependency of components. So, for example, we may consider replacing ownership with holding a pointer:

```
#include "Owned.hpp"

class Thing
{
private:
    Owned m_Owned;
};
```

→

```
Class Owned

class Thing
{
private:
    Owned * m_Owned;
};
```

There are a couple of (small) penalties to pay for this strength reduction: a slight drop in performance for that extra dereference, and the need to use dynamic memory management.

Notice that there is an intimate connection between the strength of a relationship and the requirement to include a header file. Reducing the strength of relationships often goes hand in hand with speeding up compile and link times too. But before you go away and start chopping away at your inheritance graphs and replacing instances with pointers, bear in mind that:

● If you want to in-line public or protected functions in a class, you will need to include the header irrespective of the strength of binding. Private in-lines can – and should – be defined in the cpp file.
● Weakened bindings do not necessarily result in better code: it's possible to compromise designs by strength reduction for the sake of it.

Refactoring

Maybe we can't get rid of the dependency entirely, but perhaps we can make our less derived classes more reusable by pushing the dependency into sub-classes. For example, consider the pair of classes shown here:

This has a dependency (implied by the ownership) that says all objects have animations. But hold on! I have a type of object that never gets animated, so why do I need all the other stuff – the header *and* the interface – that goes with being animated? The refactored design is shown here:

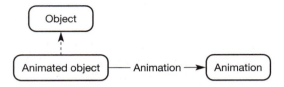

Dependency localisation

The trick here is to take all the dependencies that exist in a number of classes and lump them all into a single component that encapsulates them all. This is often called a 'utility' or 'toolkit' component.

Consider a rendering system that consists of the renderer itself, a scene graph package for the high-level tasks, and a file system for loading and saving data – in this grossly oversimplified case, models and textures. One way to organise this is shown in Figure 3.1.

Both models and textures can be read from a stream defined in the file system. Thus, both the scene and renderer components are dependent on the file component even though conceptually they bear no relation. Though we can't do much about the presence of any dependency between the scene system, the renderer system and the file system – we do want to be able to load stuff, after all – remember we are trying to weaken those dependencies as much as we can. So we consider removing the direct coupling, which requires file system header files, and replace them with calls to dumb toolkit functions, as shown in Figure 3.2.

This is a much cleaner design at the scene and renderer level – all signs of files and streams have been encapsulated in the toolkit package. By localising

Figure 3.1
Strongly coupled
components.

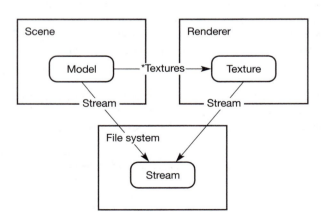

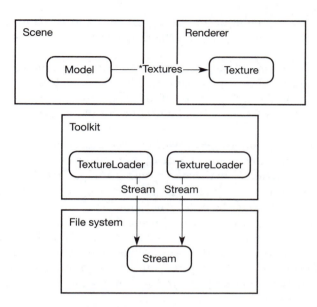

Figure 3.2
A less strongly coupled
design.

the dependency, we have simplified the design and also made maintenance less of a chore by keeping all the unpleasant code in a single component. In game code, we will mix scene, renderer and toolkit classes to get our desired result, but the mishmash of unrelated classes – and hence the lack of reusability – has been moved to where it can do less harm.

When you write code, think about the dependencies you are creating. Are they necessary? Can you weaken them? Can you remove them altogether? I'll wager a pile of doubloons that you can.

3.3.8 Reuse granularity

Another important parameter to consider when developing reusable systems is the *granularity* of reuse. A component – a single source and associated header file – is the smallest possible reusable unit and, in general, can be reusable if it requires no external resources to compile and link. Some components bind together to form what is often referred to as a subsystem. A bunch of header and include files form a single cohesive unit that can be imported into other programs. Extending this concept, a complete package is the next level of reuse.

The key question is this: is there a relationship between the size – the number of components – of a potentially reusable system and the likelihood that it will actually be reused? This is not a simple question to answer, but the answer is almost certainly 'maybe'.

Consider the case of a single component. If it compiles and links with no inclusion and linkage of external resources, then we are clearly dealing with a potentially highly reusable component. This is weakened only slightly with the inclusion and implicit linkage to standard library files. (The weakening is due to the rather annoying habit of 'standard' libraries to be anything but.) When it comes to multicomponent packages, there are two schools of thought:

- The component must be entirely self-contained: no linkage to external systems is allowed, other than to packages that reside at a lower level in the system.
- The component can depend on a broadly static external context composed of standard libraries and other, more atomic components.

In the case of the first philosophy, we often need to supply multiple files to get a single reusable component, because we cannot rely on standard definitions. For example, each component may have to supply a 'types' file that defines atomic integral types (int8, uint8, int16, uint16, etc.) using a suitable name-spacing strategy. If we subscribe to the belief that more files means less reusable, then we slightly weaken the reusability of single components to bolster the larger ones. We should also note that it is quite difficult to engineer a system that relies on privately defined types and that does not expose them to the client code. Systems that do so end up coupling components and have a multiplicity of redundant data types that support similar – but often annoyingly slightly different – functionality.

On the other hand, systems written using the latter scheme are better suited for single-component reuse, with the penalty that common functionality is moved to an external package or component. It then becomes impossible to build without that common context.

As a concrete example, consider a library system that has two completely self-contained packages: collision and rendering. The collision package contains the following files (amongst others):

```
coll_Types.hpp
Defines signed and unsigned integer types.

coll_Vector3.hpp
Defines 3D vector class and operations.

coll_Matrix44.hpp
Defines 4x4 matrix class and operations.
```

Note the use of package prefixes (in this case `coll_`) to denote unambiguously where the files reside. Without them, a compiler that sees

```
#include <Types.hpp>
```

may not do what you intend, depending on search paths, and it's harder to read and understand for the same reasons. Similarly, the renderer package has the files

```
rend_Types.hpp
```
Defines signed and unsigned integer types.

```
rend_Vector3.hpp
```
Defines 3D vector class and operations.

```
rend_Matrix44.hpp
```
Defines 4x4 matrix class and operations.

In terms of the contents of these files (and their associated implementations), they are broadly similar, but not necessarily identical, because one package may make use of functionality not required by the other. Indeed, there is a reasonable software engineering precedent to suggest that in general types that look similar (e.g. `coll_Vector3` and `rend_Vector3`, as in Figure 3.3) may have a completely different implementation, and that in general a `reinterpret_cast` is an unwise or even illegal operation. Usually, though, the files implement the same classes with perhaps some differing methods.

Some difficulties arise immediately. What does the remainder of the renderer and collision package do when it requires the user to pass in (say) a three-dimensional vector?

```
class coll_Collider
{
public:
    // ...
    void SetPosition( const ??? & vPos );
};
```

If it requires a `coll_Vector3`, does the user need to represent all their 3-vectors using the collision package's version? If so, then what happens if the renderer package exposes the following?

```
class rend_Light
{
public:
    void SetPosition( const ??? vPos );
};
```

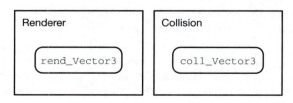

Figure 3.3
Stand-alone components.

The multiplicity of definitions of (near) identical types that are exposed in the interface of the package means that the classes are much harder, if not impossible, to reuse safely. We can get over the immediate difficulty by using an application toolkit component, as we discussed earlier, to provide classes or functions to convert between the required types. But this doesn't really solve the longer-term problem of reusability.

So instead, let's assume the user defines their own vector class. Now, whenever they need to call `coll_Collider::SetPosition()` and `rend_ Light:: SetPosition()`, they must convert their vector to the required type. This implies knowledge of how the library systems work and – one way or the other – tightly couples the code modules: exactly what we were trying to avoid!

So let's adopt the following rule:

Never expose an internal type in a public interface.

There are still problems to solve, however. Since libraries have a habit of expanding, there is a distinct possibility that the various vector libraries will, over time, converge as they grow. While a basic vector class may be considered a trivial system to implement, a mature module that has been debugged and optimised is almost always preferable to one that has been copied and pasted from elsewhere or written from scratch. Indeed, this is one of the major motivations for reuse – to avoid having to reinvent the wheel every time you need something that rolls.

In the light of the evolutionary, incremental, iterative nature of software systems, it becomes difficult to pin down what a 'simple' system is. A colleague once quipped to me that a linked-list class was elementary: 'We all know how to write those' he suggested, and indicated that list classes were candidates for copy-and-paste reuse.

On closer inspection, a list class is far from simple. There are many choices to make that dictate the usefulness, robustness and efficiency of a list. To name a few:

- Singly or doubly linked?
- Direct or indirect entries (direct elements contain the linkage data, indirect elements are linkage plus a reference to the stored data)?
- Static head and tail nodes?
- Nul-terminated? Or even circular?
- Dynamic memory allocation?
- Shallow and/or deep copy?
- Single-thread and/or multi-thread access?

A well-written list class would seem to implement less than trivial functionality. Proponents of independent components counter this by suggesting that since each component requires different functionality from their own variation of list class, there is no point creating a dependency on an external module, and introducing methods that are not used just wastes memory. However, consider the usage diagram in Figure 3.4. Despite modules A and B supporting different list functionality, by the time we get to linking the application we've effectively included all the methods of an entire list class and have redundant methods to boot.[10]

A further reason why we may get nervous is the difficulty in maintaining a set of disparate near-identical systems that may well have evolved from one or several common sources. If we find a bug in one version, then we have the onerous task of fixing all the other versions. If we add a feature to one version (say, the rend_Vector3), then do we add it to the coll_Vector3 too? If the class is private (not mentioned or has its header included in a public interface), then probably not. However, if the new functionality is in some way non-trivial (perhaps it's a hardware optimisation for the arithmetic operations), you would actively like to benefit from the new methods in many other places simply by altering it in one.

In other words, there is a principle (less strong than a rule) that the common components are trivially simple systems (for some suitable definition of 'trivial') and that the more orthogonal the various versions of the component are, the better. These somewhat arbitrary constraints tend to weaken the power of the independent component system.

These difficulties can be contrasted with those encountered by adopting a shared component strategy. In this scheme, we remove the separate (private) modules and import the services from another place, as in Figure 3.5.

This is certainly easier to maintain – changes and bug fixes are automatically propagated to the client systems. However, its strength is also its weakness. If it is a genuinely useful sharable component and it is reused in many places,

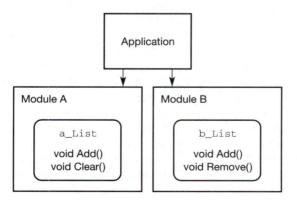

Figure 3.4
Illustrating method usage.

---

10 We can avoid the generation of unused methods using templates. Only the used functions will be instantiated.

Figure 3.5
Shared component.

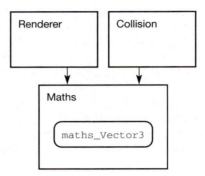

then any changes, however trivial, to the interface and even some of the implementation could force the recompilation of all the dependent subsystems. In a large game system, rebuilding everything may take up to an hour, even on a fast machine. Multiply this by the number of programmers forced to wait this time because of what may be a trivial change and it is easy to appreciate why it is desirable to avoid the dependency.

We can mostly avoid the dependency – or at least the negative consequences of it – by ensuring that the header file (i.e. the interface and some of the implementation) of the shared component changes infrequently, if ever. This is feasible for a mature component – one that has grown, had its interface refined and problems eradicated, and been used for some amount of time without issue. How could we obtain such a component? One possibility is to start with a system with independent components; the particular subsystem can be matured, logically and physically isolated from all the others. When it is considered ready, it can be placed into the common system and the various versions removed.

This hybrid approach removes some – but not all – of the pain of maintenance. Perhaps the simplest – but not the cheapest – solution to this dilemma is offered by a few commercially available version-control packages, such as Microsoft Visual SourceSafe. The sharing capability of this software allows exactly what is needed: several packages to share a single version of a component they depend on, with optional branching facilities to tailor parts of the shared components to the client package's needs.

Now, you *are* using a version-control system aren't you? Please say 'yes', because I've worked for companies that said they couldn't afford such luxuries, and the results were less than profitable. If you are serious about engineering your software components, then consider upgrading to one that supports sharing and branching. Otherwise, the hybrid solution works quite nicely.

3.3.9 When not to reuse
If it is possible to choose to reuse code, then it is logically possible that we may opt not to reuse it. Not all code is reusable and even potentially reusable systems

or subsystems should not necessarily be reused in any given context. It is therefore wise to look at the sorts of circumstances that may make it disadvantageous to reuse.

Prototyping code

Not all code is destined to make it to release. Some code may never even get into the game. If the project required a prototyping phase to prove concept viability, then a lot of suck-it-and-see code will have been written, and this should be marked as disposable *from the day the first character is typed*. What is important is the heuristic process involved in creating the prototype, and it is much more important to reuse the *ideas* than their first – usually rough and ready – implementations. Indeed, to do so can often become a bugbear for the project, whose entire future development is dictated by the vagaries of the first attempt.

It may be frightening to discard perhaps two or three months of toil. The tendency to avoid doing so is what might be described as the 'sunken cost fallacy'. Experience shows that keeping it can cause more problems than it solves, and it is usually the case that a rewrite produces a better, faster and cleaner system than the original.

Past the sell-by date

A lot of code has an implicit lifetime, beyond which it will still work happily but will prove to be technically inferior to any competitors. Vertically reusable systems need to be designed with this lifespan in mind. As a rule of thumb, graphical systems have the shortest lifespan because, typically, graphical hardware capability changes faster than less visible (literally and metaphorically) components. For example, a scripting language may work well – with additions and modifications – for many products over the course of several years. Programmers need to monitor the systems and their lifespans, and either ditch them entirely or cannibalise them to create a new system when appropriate.

3.4 The choice of language

ANSI C has become the adopted standard language of video game development, alongside any required assembly language for optimisation of critical systems. C has the advantages of a structured high-level language but still retains the ability to access and manipulate memory in a low-level byte or bit-wise fashion. Modern C compilers generate reasonably efficient code – though there is some variability in the range of commonly used toolsets – and the language is mature and stable.

So is the language issue settled? Not a bit of it. First and foremost, a development language is a tool, a means to an end and not the end itself. Each language has its own weaknesses and strengths, so it is a technical decision as to which language should be used to achieve which end.

For some tasks, only assembly language will suffice[11] because it requires access to particular hardware details beyond the scope of the high-level languages to provide; because maybe you're squeezing the last few cycles from a highly optimised system; or because, occasionally, there is just no support for high-level languages on the processor. Writing assembly language is a labour-intensive process, taking about half as long again to create and test as higher-level code. It is also usually machine-specific, so if large parts of the game are written in assembly, then there will be considerable overhead in parallel target development. Therefore, it is best saved for the situations that demand it rather than those we want to run quickly.

Modern C compilers do a reasonable job of producing acceptable assembly language. For non-time-critical systems this is fine; the code runs fast enough, and portability – whilst not always being the trivial process Kernighan and Ritchie may have imagined – is relatively straightforward. The combination of structured language constructs and bit-wise access to hardware makes the C language very flexible for simple to moderately simple tasks. However, as systems become more complex, their implementation becomes proportionately complex and awkward to manage, and it is easy to get into the habit of abusing the language just to get round technical difficulties.

If computer games tend to increase in complexity, then there will come a point – which may already have been reached – where plain old ANSI C makes it difficult to express and maintain the sort of sophisticated algorithms and relationships the software requires, which is why some developers are turning to C++: an object-oriented flavour of C.

It's hard to tell how widespread the usage of C++ is in game development. Many developers consider it to be an unnecessary indulgence capable of wreaking heinous evil; most commonly, others view it as a necessary evil for the use of programming tools in Microsoft Foundation Classes (MFC) on the PC side but the work of Satan when it comes to consoles; and a few embrace it (and object orientation, hereafter OO) as a development paradigm for both dedicated games machines and PC application development.

For the computing community in general, the advent of OO promised to deliver developers from the slings and arrows of outrageous procedural constructs and move the emphasis in programming from 'How do I use this?' to 'What can I do with this?' This is a subtle shift, but its implications are huge.

3.4.1 The four elements of object orientation

In general, an object-oriented language exhibits the following four characteristics:

1 *Data abstraction*: an OO language does not distinguish between the data being manipulated and the manipulations themselves: they are part and parcel of the same object. Therefore, it is obvious by looking at the declaration of an object what you can do with it.

---

11 In production code at least, placeholder code can be high-level.

2 *Encapsulation*: an OO language distinguishes between what you can do with an object and how it is done. The latter is an implementation detail that a user should not, in general, depend on. By separating what from how, it allows the implementer freedom to change the internal details without requiring external programmatic changes.

3 *Inheritance*: objects can inherit attributes from one or more other objects. They can then be treated exactly as if they were one of those other objects and manipulated accordingly. This allows engineers to layer functionality: common properties of a family of related data types can be factored out and placed in an inherited object. Each inherited type is therefore reduced in complexity because it need not duplicate the inherited functionality.

4 *Polymorphism*: using just inheritance we cannot modify a particular behaviour – we have to put up with what we get from our base type. So an OO language supports polymorphism, a mechanism that allows us to modify behaviours on a per-object-type basis.

In the 1980s and 1990s, OO was paraded – mistakenly, of course – as a bit of a silver bullet for complexity management and software reusability. The problem was not with the paradigm, which is fine in theory, but with the implementations of the early tools. As it turned out, C++ would require a number of tweaks over a decade (new keywords, sophisticated macro systems, etc.) and has become considered as a stable development platform only since the 1997 ANSI draft standard.

However, even being standard is not enough. The use of C++ and OO is an ongoing field of research because developers are still working out exactly what to do with the language, from simple ideas such as pattern reuse through to the complex things such as template meta-programming.

Stable it may be, but there is still a profound hostility to C++ in the games development community. There are any number of semi-myths out there relating to the implementation of the language that have a grain of truth but in no way represent the real picture. Here's a typical example: C programmers insist that C++ code is slower than C because the mechanism of polymorphism involves accessing a table. Indeed, as we can see from Table 3.1, polymorphic function calls do indeed take longer than non-polymorphic – and C procedural – function calls.[12]

Table 3.1

Type of call	Actual time (s)	Relative times (s)
Member function	0.16	1.33
Virtual function	0.18	1.5
Free function	0.12	1

---

12 Timings made on a 500-MHz mobile Intel Pentium III laptop PC with 128 MB RAM. Measurements made over 100 000 iterations.

However, take a look at a non-trivial system written in C, and chances are you will find something resembling the following construct:

```
struct MyObject
{
/* data */
};

typedef void (*tMyFunc)( MyObject * );

static tMyFunc FuncTable[] =
{
    MyFunc1,
    MyFunc2,
    /* etc */
};
```

Tables of functions are a common – and powerful – programming tool. The only difference between real-world C and C++ code is that in the latter the jump table is part of the language (and therefore can benefit from any optimisation the compiler is able to offer), whereas in the former it is an *ad hoc* user feature. In other words, we expect that in real-world applications, C++ code performs at least similarly to C code executing this type of operation, and C++ may even slightly outperform its C 'equivalent'.

To be a little more precise, we can define the metric of 'function call over-head' by the formula

$$\text{overhead} = \frac{\text{function call time}}{\text{function body time}}$$

where the numerator is how long it takes to make the function call itself and the denominator is how long is spent in the function doing stuff (including calling other functions). What this formula suggests is that we incur only a small relative penalty for making virtual function calls if we spend a long time in the function. In other words, if the function does significant processing, then the call overhead is negligible.

Whilst this is welcome news, does this mean that all virtual functions should consist of many lines of code? Not really, because the above formula does not account for how frequently the function is called. Consider the following – ill-advised – class defining a polygon and its triangle subclass:

```
class Polygon
{
public:
    Polygon( int iSides );
```

```
    /* … */
    virtual void Draw( Target * pTarget ) const = 0;
};

class Triangle
{
public:
    Triangle() : Polygon(3) { ; }
    /*…*/

    void Draw( Target * pTarget ) const;
};
```

Many games will be drawing several thousand triangles per frame, and although the overhead may be low, it must be scaled by the frequency of calling. So a better formula to use would be this

$$\text{total overhead} = \text{call frequency} * \frac{\text{function call time}}{\text{function body time}}$$

where the call frequency is the number of function invocations per game loop.

Consequently, we can minimise the moderate relative inefficiency of virtual function calls by either

- ensuring that the virtual function body performs non-trivial operations; or
- ensuring that a trivial virtual function is called relatively infrequently per game loop.

This is not to proclaim glibly that whatever we do in C++ there is no associated penalty as compared with C code. There are some features of C++ that are prohibitively expensive, and perhaps even unimplemented on some platforms – exception handling, for example. What is required is not some broad assumptions based on some nefarious mythology but implementation of the following two practices:

- Get to know as much as you can about how your compiler implements particular language features. *Note*: it is generally bad practice to depend in some way upon the specifics of your toolset, because you can be sure that the next version of the tool will do it differently.
- Do not rely on the model in your head to determine how fast code runs. It can – and will – be wrong. Critical code should be timed – a profiling tool can be of great assistance – and it is the times obtained from this that should guide optimisation strategy.

Just as it is possible to write very slow C code without knowledge of how it works, it is possible to write very fast C++ using knowledge of compiler strategy. In particular, the ability of OO design to make the manipulation of complex data structures more tangible leads to code that is better structured at the high level, where the mass processing of information yields significantly higher optimisation ratios than small 'local' optimisations (see Abrash, 1994).

Since C is a subset of C++, it is very hard to make out a case to use C exclusively; indeed, it is often a first step to simply use the non-invasive features that C++ has to offer – such as in-line functions – while sticking to a basically procedural methodology. Whilst this approach is reasonable, it misses the point: that OO design is a powerful tool in the visualisation and implementation of software functionality. We'll look at a simple way to approach object-oriented design in the next section.

3.4.2 Problem areas

There are still some no-go (or at least go rarely or carefully) areas in the C++ language.

'Exotic' keywords

Obviously, if a compiler does not support some of the modern esoteric features, such as

- namespace
- mutable
- explicit
- in-place static constant data initialisers
- general template syntax (`template<>`)
- templated member functions
- template arguments to templates: `template<template <class> class T>`

then you really ought to avoid using them. Luckily, this is not difficult and one can write perfectly viable systems without them.

Exception handling

As mentioned earlier, exceptions are to be avoided in game code because some console compilers simply do not implement them. Whilst it is quite acceptable to use them in PC tool development, their use in games makes relatively little sense. If your compiler does implement them, then bear in mind that they can gobble CPU time and do strange things with the stack. Better to avoid them altogether and pepper your game code with assertions and error traps (see Maguire, 1993).

Run-time-type information

Again, run-time-type information (RTTI) may not be available on all platforms or compilers, even if they aspire to be ANSI-compliant. But even if it is, there is the hidden cost that any class that you want to use RTTI with needs to be poly-morphic, so there can be a hidden size, run-time and layout penalty. Rather than use RTTI, roll your own system-specific type information system with embedded integer identifiers:

```
class MyClass
{
public:

    // Classes needing simple RTTI implements
    // this function.
    int GetId() const { return s_iId; }
private:
    // Each class needs one of these.
    static int s_iId;
};

int MyClass::s_iId = int( &s_iId );
```

Since RTTI is intimately related to the `dynamic_cast<>()` operator, do not use dynamic casting in game code. However, the other casts

```
static_cast<>()
reinterpret_cast<>()
const_cast<>()
```

are free of baggage and can (and should) be used where required.[13] Aside from the space cost of RTTI (potentially four bytes in every class instance that has no polymorphic interface), there is also a computational overhead. That's because RTTI works with strings, and string compares can sap cycles from your game.

Multiple inheritance

This is an area to be traversed carefully rather than avoided. Multiple inheri-tance (MI) sometimes turns out to be the best theoretical way of implementing a behaviour. Other times, inheritance is just too strong a binding and a similar effect can be achieved without invoking MI. Also, the implications of using MI as implemented in C++ can often lead to complicated issues involving virtual base classes and clashing identifiers.

---

13 And used in preference to the much-abused C-style cast.

In short, MI can look neat on a diagram but generate messy and confusing code. There is also a (small) performance hit when using MI (as opposed to single inheritance). This is because inheritance is implemented using *aggregation* (Figure 3.6). Classes are simply made contiguous in memory:

```
class A
{
    /* stuff */
};

class B : public A
{
    /* more stuff */
};
```

When it comes to MI, the inherited classes are aggregated in the order they are specified, meaning that the physical offsets to the two child classes are different, even though they should logically be the same (Figure 3.7):

```
class A
{
    /* stuff */
};

class B
{
    /* more stuff */
};

class C : public A, public B
{
    /* yet more data */
};
```

Figure 3.6
Aggregation of class data
(single inheritance).

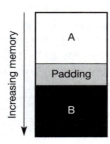

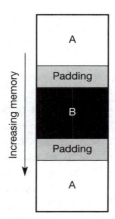

Figure 3.7
Aggregation of class data
(multiple inheritance).

Logically speaking, a class of type C can be considered to be of type A or type B. Since A comes first in the aggregation, this involves no extra work, but if we try to convert a C to a B, then the pointer requires amending by the size of an A plus any padding for alignment. It is this that makes MI more expensive.

So, the reality of MI is that it can be more expensive, depending on how the object is treated. The expense is limited to the occasional addition of a constant to a pointer – a single instruction on most CPUs and a single cycle on many. This is a negligible cost compared with (say) a divide (typically about 40 cycles on some systems).

3.4.3 Standard Template Library

When we learned C, our first program probably contained a line that looked rather like this:

```
printf( "Hello World\n" );
```

I'll also wager that a good deal of code today still contains `printf` or `scanf` or one of their relatives. Generally, the C libraries – despite their vagaries – are very useful for a limited number of tasks, and all compilers on almost all platforms – even the consoles – support them.

C++ has had a chequered history when it comes to supplying standard libraries. Originally, the equivalent of C's input/output (IO) functions `iostream`, `istream`, `ostream`, `strstream`, etc. – were supplied but were not at all standard. Now it turns out that these objects are less efficient than their less OO cousins and consequently aren't much use for game code. Nevertheless, it took a long time for vendors to consistently support the functionality.

Thanks to the ANSI committee, the stream library is a standard part of a C++ distribution these days, and it now comes as part of a larger set of objects called the Standard Template Library (STL). We'll discuss general use of templates in the next subsection, but some of these objects are very useful indeed and C++ programmers ignore them at their peril. However, STL is a two-edged blade, and it is worth examining it in a little detail to make a balanced assessment of its usefulness.

First, the 'Standard' part of the name is a bit of a misnomer, because although the interfaces are (very nearly) identical between compiler vendors and other public domain authors, the internal details vary wildly. Some STL implementations are rather more efficient than others, and one should be careful not to rely blindly on things being fast when developing for several platforms.

Second, STL has a serious image problem. It is not particularly user-friendly. As anyone who has opened an STL header file can testify, the actual code is formatted poorly, almost to the extent of impenetrability. Web searches in a quest to find out how to use it result in trawling through equally impenetrable help files and documents, and even buying a book can leave the programmer bemused enough to write off STL as impenetrable.

Now, the Hacker's Charter has encouraged a culture of 'If I didn't write it, I won't use it', so it is difficult to encourage use of any library code, let alone C++ template systems that sell themselves short. Yet it remains the case that if one makes the effort to get over the initial conceptual barriers that STL raises, then it can become as or even more useful – in specific circumstances – as `printf()` and friends are to C programmers.

What STL supports

STL provides a bunch of type-safe container classes that hold collections of objects in interesting ways: dynamic arrays, lists, queues, double-ended queues (deques), stacks, heaps, sets, hash tables, associative maps, trees and strings are all supplied with STL free of charge with every compiler that supports the C++ ANSI standard. Coupled with some careful typedef-ing, one can swap the containers arbitrarily, more complex containers can be constructed using the simpler ones, and all these classes can have custom memory managers added on a per-instance basis that efficiently allocate and free blocks using one's own algorithms.

There is little doubt that this is useful – and powerful – functionality that comes for free and is robust and portable, and there is surely a place for STL in every programmer's repertoire.

3.4.4 Templates

C++ templates are a powerful construct that combine preprocessor-like macro flexibility with the safety of strong type checking. It is a relatively straightforward way of writing virtually the same piece of code for an arbitrary and previously unspecified number of data types, without the risk of introducing cut-and-paste errors. At the extreme, templates provide a mechanism to perform complex operations through meta-programming, and therefore it is suggested respectfully that no C++ programmer write off using templates lightly.

There are several flipsides to templates, though. First, they are supported almost exclusively via inclusion in a project. This means that the entire implementation – sometimes complex and involved – needs to be included in a compilation, leading to significantly higher compile times. Changes to files in the template include graph will force these compiles more frequently than you would wish. From a commercial point of view, it's also undesirable to make your algorithms public for everyone to see (and potentially abuse).

Second, the mechanisms (there are several) that compilers use to instantiate template classes are less than lightning quick. This means that significant use of templates can lead to increased compile times (again!) and now increased link times too.

Third, if you use a lot of template classes, or a few template classes with lots of different types, then you can start to bloat your application with many copies of virtually identical code segments. On console architectures with limited memory, this could prove to be a significant contribution to the code footprint.

Fortunately, for at least some classes there is a solution. Many container classes are used for manipulating pointer types, and if many of these are being used then we can fall back on our C programming friend, the void pointer, to reduce the size of the bloat. Here is an outline of a simple pointer list class:

```cpp
template<class TPTR>
class PtrList
{
public:
    // All methods inline'd.
    inline PtrList()
    {
        ASSERT( sizeof( TPTR )==sizeof( void * ) );
    }

    inline ~PtrList()
    {
    }

    inline void AddHead( TPTR pItem ) { … }
    inline void AddTail( TPTR pItem ) { … }
    inline int  Size() const { … }

    // etc.

private:
    // Use a list from (say) the STL.
    std::list<void *> m_VoidList;
};
```

In the above example, we have used a list class from the STL to hold a collection of generic pointers. Note that because this is still a class based on a supplied parameter, we have preserved the type safety of templates, one of their major advantages over macros.

By in-lining all the methods of the class, we ensure that – to the best of our ability – there is no additional memory or execution overhead for using this wrapper class. For example, consider the `AddHead()` member function:

```
template<class TPTR>
inline void PtrList<TPTR>::AddHead( TPTR pItem )
{
    ASSERT( pItem != NULL );

    m_VoidList.push_back( pItem );
}
```

Calls are simply forwarded to the encapsulated container in this fashion.

Writing a class in this way will ensure that the compiler only ever instantiates one version of the complex system – the `void *` version – irrespective of how many types the template is invoked with.

Type conversions

C++ allows us to define a way to overload – provide a custom implementation of – just about any behaviour. In general, this can lead to confusing code that does not behave as it ought to; in particular, type conversions can not only hide complex operations but also invoke those operations considerably more frequently than desired.

There are, in fact, two ways of implementing type conversions: one through operator overloads, the other via conversion constructors. The operator version basically creates a user-defined cast that says, 'If you have one of these, do this sequence of operations and you will end up with one of those':

```
class Banana;
class Apple
{
    /* … */

    // This method turns an apple into a banana.
    operator Banana() const;
};
```

The other variant is a constructor taking a single argument of a type. For example – preserving the fruity theme:

```
class Pear;
class Fig
{
public:
    // Converts a pear to a fig.
    Fig( const Pear & );
};
```

Both of these constructs give the compiler an opportunity to invisibly perform type conversions and generally to bloat the code with potentially unnecessary function invocations. The good news is that you can prevent this overzealousness by one of two methods:

1 Do not use conversion operators and avoid single-argument constructors.[14] If you need to convert from one type to another make sure it is in a fashion the compiler cannot make use of:

```
class Durian;
class Rasperry
{
public:
    // Non-compiler  usurpable conversion.
    Durian ToDurian() const;
};
```

2 If you have single-argument constructors that can't be gotten rid of easily, and your compiler supports it, prefix them with the relatively new keyword 'explicit':

```
class Quince;
class Kumquat
{
    explicit Kumquat(const Quince & );
};
```

3.5 A C++ coding policy

Now that we have pinned our colours to the mast and declared that we shall be developing predominantly in C++, we can be a little more explicit about our coding policy. Once we have declared the policy, we can then illustrate it with a definite example, which will be used in all code samples (except where indicated otherwise) throughout the rest of the book.

---

14 Copy constructors are fine though.

3.5.1 General

● *New projects*: programmers should agree on the conventions required by the policy. The conventions should be followed in all shared project code.
● *Existing projects*: if the project has an existing set of conventions, then they should be followed. If the project has several localised conventions, then the local conventions should be observed.

In all other circumstances, the programmers should agree on the conventions required by the policy. They should then be applied incrementally.[15]

Library code – code that is shared or reused by some mechanism – should be written according to a policy that is applied consistently across all common code, paying particular attention to interfaces.

3.5.2 Policy specifics

A policy detail is a requirement that needs to be fulfilled by a particular standard. While teams are free to choose exactly what that standard is (allowing for the restrictions detailed above), the standard must be to some extent self-documenting and applied consistently by all team members in all non-pathological situations.

Naming conventions

● However we choose to name our variables, members and functions, it should be ANSI-compliant. For example, naming single-character identifiers by prepending an underscore (e.g. _x) is illegal under the latest ANSI C++ standard, which requires that these names be reserved for compiler use.

  Justification: your code may not compile on some platforms simply due to their naming of compiler-specific private identifiers.

● The policy should distinguish between identifiers at global, module, class and local scopes.

  Justifications:
  ● All sorts of problems can occur when names with different scopes clash:

```
int x = 0;

void f()
{
    int x;

    // What you want?
    x = 2;
}
```

---

15 The process of search and replace when coercing code into a new set of conventions is time-consuming and tedious and shows no external progress, which can often affect morale adversely. It is far easier and better to change code as you go along, as systems are modified and added.

- Global variables and functions can severely limit reuse potential by binding modules together. We want to highlight the places where the binding takes place so we know what we're dealing with when it comes to cannibalisation.
- The policy should distinguish between the public interface of a class and the private or protected implementation details.

  Justification: it's useful to know by looking at a member function whether we can call it as a user or an implementer.

- The policy should distinguish between pointer types and instances.

  Justifications: C++ distinguishes pointers and instances semantically via the `*`, `.` and `->` operators. It's useful to know which we can use. It's also quite important because we can safely pass pointers as function arguments but we can't always safely pass instances. Also, pointer types that are typically `new`'d need to be `delete`'d on destruction. Distinguishing pointers reminds us to do this and avoids memory leaks, which can cause nasty problems over the course of time.

- The policy should distinguish between preprocessor symbols and other identifiers.

  Justification: preprocessor macros can have unusual side effects: for example, `max(x++,y)` will increment x more than once. Disguising macros as variables or functions can therefore cause all sorts of pain.

- The policy should distinguish between namespaces and other identifiers.

  Justification: name spaces are designed to avoid identifier clashes. Naming them similarly to classes or other identifiers rather weakens their usefulness.

Code layout

- The policy should specify a suitable layout for braces and scope indentation.

  Justifications: people get used to seeing code layout patterns as well as semantic conventions, so keeping a consistent format makes maintenance and learning a touch easier. Using indentation to indicate logical flow of control is so useful – and commonplace – that most editors support automatic context-sensitive indentation.

- The policy should specify a layout for class declarations.

  Justification: keeping public and private/protected data and methods physically separate makes classes easier to take in at a glance.

- The policy should decide on a size for tabs, and editors should be set to convert tabs to spaces. The editor should use a non-proportional font.

  Justification: keeping code and spacing similar on a variety of machines and monitors becomes easier.

- The policy should specify a layout for source and header files, including some concept of ordering and sectioning.

  Justifications: keeping related things together makes them easier to find – you know where to look; C/C++ is very sensitive to order of declaration and definition, so a policy that enforces an order makes it easier (most of the time) to write code that compiles soon after writing.

C++ specifics
- Source files should have the suffix .cpp, header file .hpp.

  Justification: distinguishing C++ source and header files from C source and header files is important!
- All libraries should have namespaces.

  Justification: namespaces help to prevent identifier name clashes. Since libraries are shared between projects, they will be the major cause of symbolic conflict.
- The keyword 'using' should never appear in a header file in a namespace context.

  Justification: the keyword effectively nullifies the namespace, and since a header cannot know which other headers – and namespaces – it will be included along with, the chance of identifier name clashing is increased.
- All code should be 'const' correct.

  Justifications: 'const' allows compilers the opportunity to perform some local optimisations on code; more importantly, it enforces a logical structure that dictates what should and should not be modified. Subverting that can cause code abuses, confusion and obfuscation.
- Class data members should be private.

  Justification: public data members violate encapsulation – our ability to change implementations without changing interfaces; protected data members are public to classes that inherit them, so encapsulation is violated simply by derivation.
- No data at file scope should have external linkage: *No globals!*

  Justification: global variables unnecessarily bind modules together, and because they can be read from and written to arbitrarily, they make control flow harder to predict.
- Source files should include their respective header file as the first inclusion.[16]

  Justification: a header file should contain all the information – including references to other header files – required to declare their contents.

---

16 An exception: in some PC development environments, the use of precompiled headers can vastly increase the speed of a build, and it is required that the include file associated with the precompiled header be included before all others.

The actual implementation of this policy as used in this book is presented in Appendix A.

Summary

- The Hacker's Charter hurts development, production and management.

- A programmer has a number of roles other than programming.

- Code reuse is possible. It is an acquired skill, and it does not happen by accident.

- Dependencies make reuse harder and inflate compilation and link times. Make every effort to minimise them.

- Object orientation provides a good paradigm for writing reusable code, but it also gives the opportunity to vanish over the dependency event horizon, so to speak. Put simply, it is possible – with effort – to write good (reusable, robust, efficient, encapsulated) code in C++; it is just as easy or maybe easier to write bad code in C++ than in C.

- We distinguish between a coding policy and a standard – an implementation of the intent of the policy. Decide on the policy, and allow teams to define their standard.

Object-oriented design for games

4

Object orientation can – like most software engineering techniques – be taken to a ridiculously thorough level. Given that we have established some amount of flexibility in both technological and game-play content, we should be looking to borrow salient features from OO design that allow us to visualise and manipulate the logical structure of our software without necessarily committing us to any particular strategy.

Most of the commercially available OO design tools are capable of generating source code as well as providing a visible representation of our classes. Though these tools prove useful as a concepting medium, the author considers them to be of limited use: their layout algorithms often require dedicated input from the user to make them clear, not to mention aesthetic; they do not respond well to heuristic or *ad hoc* development strategies; and they do not always respond well to fine-tune editing of the source files. Overwhelmingly it is the graphical functionality that is useful in these packages. The ability to reverse-engineer an object diagram from a set of existing header files is a powerful tool, but if we are starting from scratch, wish to create a diagram for a design document and aren't too bothered about automatic source code generation, then it may be a better investment to use a general-purpose diagramming package such as Microsoft's Visio®.

4.1 Notation

A number of formal notation systems are in use by software engineers. They all share certain common elements, so we shall distil out these collective components and use a related but simpler notation for them.

4.1.1 Classes

We shall use bubbles to denote class declarations (not instances). For example, this denotes a declaration of a (concrete) class called 'Sprite':

It's the equivalent of the C++ code

```cpp
// File: sprite.hpp
class Sprite
{
public:
private:
protected:
};
```

An abstract class – one that cannot be instantiated – is denoted by a shaded bubble, shown here:

4.1.2 Relationships

There are two significant types of relationship that can exist between classes: *inheritance* and *ownership*.[1] Inheritance (sometimes termed an 'is a' relationship) is indicated by a dotted arrow drawn between the derived class and the base class, with the head pointing to the base object (implying that the derived is dependent on the base), as shown here:

The equivalent source code is as follows:

```cpp
// File: shape.hpp
class Shape
{
public:
    // Just to make me abstract.
    virtual ~Shape() = 0;
};

// File: circle.hpp
#include "shape.hpp"
```

---

1 There are other relationship types, such as uses in the interface and uses in the implementation, but these are not considered here.

```
class Circle : public Shape
{
public:
    Circle( float fRadius );
    ~Circle() { ; }
};
```

The ownership relationship – sometimes called 'has a' – is indicated by a solid arrow drawn between the owner and the owned in the direction of the owned class (again, implying dependency, although a weaker one than 'is a'), as shown here:

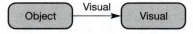

Note that the relationship has an associated name. The name string has a syntax that indicates the multiplicity of the owned object, as shown in Table 4.1.

No inference should be drawn as to how the owned entity is stored. For example, if A 'has a' B, then we may write:

```
// File A.hpp
class B;
class A
{
private:
    B * m_pB;
};
```

or

```
// File A.hpp
#include "B.hpp"
```

Table 4.1

Syntax	Meaning
Name	Has exactly 1
*Name	Has 0 to N
#Name	Has 1 to N
Name[k]	Has exactly k

```
class A
{
private:
    B m_B;
};
```

with the choice of how we choose a particular implementation governed by factors such as how big B is, what it is dependent on, whether B is a base class for a hierarchy of subclasses, etc.

4.2 The design process

The bubble-and-arrow notation system allows us to move away from specific implementation details to a generalised, more conceptual overview of our software designs. By working in the problem domain rather than the code domain, we can postpone certain types of implementation decision that would otherwise distract us from the design process. So we now need to be able to translate the – potentially still hazy – ideas we have in our head into some classes and relationships.

4.2.1 Phase 1: brainstorming

The idea is to start with some vague notion of what we want to do and move towards a concrete representation of it. Brainstorming is an important step in this process (and in many other areas, too), but it is not always done very well. Though this may be because different people have different takes on solving particular problems, usually it is because we all tend to apply a certain amount of self-censorship to the things we contribute to a public forum. Questions such as 'Is this relevant?' or 'Will they think I'm dumb?' tend to block the free flow of concepts. This is a hurdle that needs to be cleared because often, the ipsitive assessment – the one you make of yourself – is clouded by any number of contributory and not necessarily accurate judgements. The idea is to get people to contribute the things at the top of their head when they think about the problem: often, this will generate random noise as a simple by-product of human psychology.

Consequently, the brainstorming sessions should be as non-judgemental as possible, and there should be no (or little) censorship or even evaluation of ideas until later on. The team should be encouraged to generate a significant number of concepts related to the design, and the vast majority of them should be written down. Each concept should be limited to a single word or phrase that will represent a class, be it abstract or concrete. At this stage, we keep the granularity larger than the simple data types: we don't mention characters, integers or floats/doubles, since these are typically implementation details.

Case study 4.1: a car

We'll start with a simple notional breakdown of a car that might appear in a game. Though much detail will be required for a working implementation, we are concerned at this stage with big brushstrokes, and we'll evolve and refine the design as we progress through the various phases of the process. So here's a non-definitive list of top-of-the-head car-related concepts:

Car, wheel, engine, gearbox, automatic gearbox, door, bonnet, clutch, radio, fuel tank, suspension, brakes, exhaust, tyre.

4.2.2 Phase 2: prune the tree

At the end of the first phase, the team should be bled dry of ideas. There will be a whiteboard full of word and concept associations, and this now needs to be knocked into shape. Too many ideas will end up with a spaghetti diagram that is hard to follow; too few will not solve the problem at hand. The simplest place to start is to remove anything that is obviously irrelevant or unhelpful. Care should be taken here, as something that appears to be unrelated could actually turn out to be very useful when the mist starts to clear. So stick to removing the obviously out-of-place concepts.

Once the irrelevant things have been removed, it is best to remove the redundant. These are ideas that are duplicated, and if you did Phase 1 properly these will have been left in place. Again, some care should be taken not to remove things that look similar but turn out to be different in some important respects.

Case study 4.1 (cont.)

We can immediately remove the following irrelevant items:

- *Radio*: though there are undeniably several subclasses of radio, unless they form a vital part of the game play it is wise to omit them.

- *Doors*: if drivers can get in and out of cars, we may wish to keep doors. Also, if the cars can be damaged then we may want doors to flap open and even rip off entirely. Otherwise, it is hard to see them being anything other than a graphical nicety.

- *Bonnet*: ditto the case with doors.

- *Fuel tank*: although the size of a fuel tank determines how far the vehicle can travel, we are assuming for the purposes of the design that the car has an infinite amount of fuel. It's a game, not a driving simulator.

Interestingly and importantly, these decisions are made on the basis that we know what the features of the simulated concepts are. In other words, we are following a definite design. Whilst it is possible to keep open as many possibilities as we can, our OO models will be simpler and less expensive on the code side if we can *a priori* filter out unnecessary detail.

Now we have rejected the obviously superfluous, what else can we do? Well we notice that the word 'gearbox' appears twice, suggesting some common functionality that can be factorised. We would like to generalise automatic and manual shifts into one manageable class with subclasses implementing specific behaviours. So we can replace both gearboxes with the one abstract concept, 'transmission'. Note that because clutches are present only in manual systems, they can now be hidden as an implementation detail of the subclass and the gearbox class now need appear only once as a common property of manual and automatic transmissions.

Our concept list has now been pruned to:

Car, wheel, engine, transmission, automatic transmission, manual transmission, gearbox, clutch, suspension, brake, tyre.

4.2.3 Phase 3: draw the bubbles and lines

Now we take each of the remaining concepts and put bubbles around them, thereby creating a set of classes that currently have no relationships. Then they need to be moved around and the appropriate relationships drawn in, along with the names of ownerships and their multiplicities. There may be more than one way to do this. If there is, then it is often best to carry on with one way to see if there are any undesirable repercussions. Then backtrack and try it the other way, noting what changes. You'll then be in a position to determine the relative merit of either method.

Case study 4.1 (cont.)

Figure 4.1 shows our first stab at diagramming the relationships between the classes we've talked about.

Notice that many parts of the car may need to know about what other parts are doing, so they all point back to the car object. This is not always desirable – in principle, an object should exist in its own right without reference to other non-related

Figure 4.1
Class diagram for a
basic car.

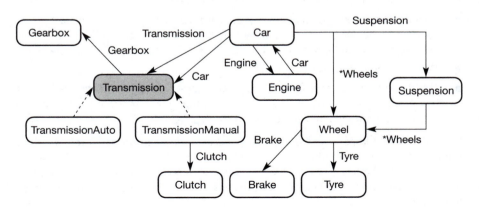

objects – but it does allow us to break up a large, monolithic task such as 'update the car' into smaller 'update the component parts of the car' tasks. What would happen if we wanted to (say) use the transmission component in a truck? Then we would abstract the concept of 'car', as shown here:

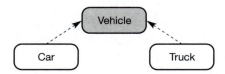

and adjust all the appropriate 'car' pointers to 'vehicle' pointers.

4.2.4 Phase 4: validate the design

The whiteboard diagram should now be nice and clean, and it should be possible to start with a class and ensure that it can gain access to all of the data it will need in order to perform its function. This will involve tracing the relationships carefully, and adding new relationships and maybe even new classes to ensure that the squiggles on the board reflect the logical relationships between the concepts you wrote down earlier.

Case study 4.2

Here is a top-of-the-head brainstorm of the classes required for a simple renderer. I'll evolve the design as we progress through the phases:

Renderer, Transform, Texture, Screen, Camera, Font, Image, Display, Mesh, Model, Frame, Position, Rotation, Viewport, Triangle, Polygon, Quad, Animation, Palette, Colour, Light, Ambient, Directional, Spotlight, Shadow.

I've decided not to include the following classes:

- Animation, since that is a system complex enough to merit its own design.
- Shadows, because they are beyond the scope of the renderer we are designing, and even if they weren't we really ought not to attempt shadows without a working renderer.
- Font, as we can certainly add a font later using textures.

We can also remove the redundant items:

- Image, as it is interchangeable with Texture.
- Display, as it is the same as Screen.

We can also strike the Polygon concept, mainly because most renderers deal with triangles and quads, not *n*-sided primitives. It also turns out to be quite hard to come up with a satisfactory structure for supporting arbitrary primitive types – virtual functions are too inefficient because primitives are quite low-level and there are therefore lots of them in a typical scene, which rather knocks inheritance of a primitive abstract type on the head.

This leaves us with the following associations:

Renderer, Transform, Texture, Screen, Camera, Mesh, Model, Frame, Position, Rotation, Viewport, Triangle, Quad, Palette, Colour, Light, Ambient, Directional, Spotlight.

Their relationships are shown in Figure 4.2.

Figure 4.2
Class diagram for a
basic renderer.

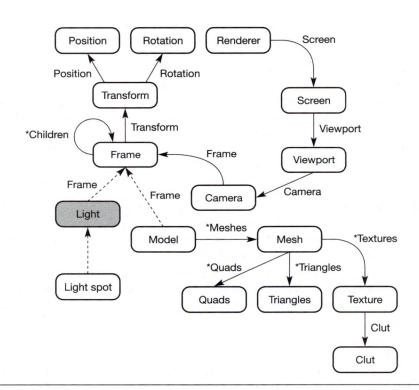

4.3 Patterns

Patterns were made popular in the 1990s by the 'Gang of Four' (GoF) book (Gamma *et al.*, 1994). They represent the logical relationships between classes that just keep appearing in your software, irrespective of whether you are writing spreadsheets, missile-guidance systems or resource managers.

Patterns are, at the very least, interesting, and more often than not they are extremely useful. Often, you're sitting there trying to work out how to get functionality from one class to be utilised by another without violating encapsulation, or how to construct mechanisms to perform complex functions, and a flick through the GoF book is all you need to gain the required insight. But this is only half the battle – we still need to implement the pattern, and writing useful pattern code still takes a bit of thought and effort. This section looks at a few of the useful patterns and shows how they can be implemented with a reasonable degree of generality and efficiency.

4.3.1 The interface

Also known as 'protocol', 'compilation firewall', 'pimpl'

The first pattern we'll look at is both simple and important. Remember earlier we were concerned about dependencies in common components? When a common component's header file changed, all the dependent source modules had to be recompiled. Any action, adding a method, changing an implementation detail or indeed the implementation, will trigger this rebuild. It's an irritating and schedule-consuming waste of time. Can we do anything about it?

The short answer is 'Yes, we can'. However, the solutions (they are similar in philosophy) are not applicable to all classes. Let's look at the solution methods before discussing their merits.

Interface

In Java, there is a specification of an interface – a set of functions that a class that supports the interface must supply. We can do a similar thing in C++ by defining a dataless class that consists of pure virtual functions.

```
// Foo.hpp
class Foo
{
public:
    Foo();
    virtual ~Foo();

    virtual void Bar() = 0;
    virtual void Pub() = 0;
};

// Foo.cpp
#include "Foo.hpp"

Foo::Foo()
{
}

Foo::~Foo()
{
```

```
// Always put an empty virtual destructor in the
// cpp file.
// Being virtual, it won't be inlined anyway, and
// some compilers have problems with virtual
// destructors defined within headers
}
```

Since there is no implementation to change, the only condition that might trigger a cross-package rebuild of many modules would be the addition or removal of a method. For mature interfaces, this is considerably less likely than for an 'in-progress' module.

Now the trick. Define an instantiable class that uses the Foo interface. Call it FooImpl to indicate that it's an implementation of an interface:

```
// FooImpl.hpp
#include "Foo.hpp"

class FooImpl : public Foo
{
public:
    FooImpl();

    /*virtual*/ void Bar();
    /*virtual*/ void Pub();
private:
    int m_iData;
};

// FooImpl.cpp
#include "FooImpl.hpp"

FooImpl::FooImpl()
: Foo()
, m_iData(0)
{
}

void FooImpl::Bar()
{
    m_iData = 1;
}

void FooImpl::Pub()
{
    m_iData /= 2;
}
```

Let's assume for the moment that we have some way of creating a `FooImpl` that is internal to the component. What we get back is a pointer to a `Foo`, which has an identical virtual interface. We are free to modify `FooImpl` as we please, because external modules only ever include `Foo.hpp`. The only snag is that since we never see FooImpl.hpp, we have no way of creating a `FooImpl` on the client side. The solution is to have a manager class do the allocation for us:

```cpp
// FooManager.hpp
class Foo;

struct FooManager
{
    static Foo * CreateFoo();
};

// FooManager.cpp
#include "FooManager.hpp"
#include "FooImpl.hpp"

/*static*/
Foo * FooManager::CreateFoo()
{
    return new FooImpl();
}
```

Pimpl

The name of the pattern is a contraction of 'pointer to implementation'. Instead of defining member data in the header file, we gather the data into a structure that we place in the source file and forward declare a pointer to this structure as the only member of our class:

```cpp
// Foo.hpp
struct FooImpl;

class Foo
{
public:
    Foo();
    ~Foo();

    void Bar();
    void Pub();
private:
    FooImpl * m_this;
};
```

```
// Foo.cpp
struct FooImpl
{
    int m_iData;
};

Foo::Foo()
: m_this( new FooImpl )
{
}

Foo::~Foo()
{
    delete m_this;
}

void Foo::Bar()
{
    m_this->m_iData = 1;
}

void Foo::Pub()
{
    m_this->m_iData /= 2;
}
```

The interface method is cleaner but requires the extra manager or utility component to create the instances. The pimpl method requires no virtual functions; however, there is an extra dynamic allocation for every instance new'd (and a corresponding dynamic deallocation on destruction), and the m_this-> notation is slightly unpleasant.

In the end, both solutions are essentially the same: in the interface method, the m_this is logically replaced by the implicit pointer to the class's virtual function table. Both use indirection to decouple their interfaces from their implementation. So a similar analysis will work for both cases.

The first thing to notice is that neither system has any data in its header, so we cannot in-line any functions. This is doubly so for the interface method because, except in very rare circumstances, virtual functions cannot be in-lined.[2] Also, since both systems require indirection, there is a performance penalty for creating a class in this way.

---

2 A function that is declared in-line virtual will be in-lined if, and only if, it is invoked explicitly via the class::method() notation and there are no uses of references or pointers to base classes calling that method.

What this means is that the interface is unsuitable for 'light' classes that have high-performance requirements. For example, a vector class would not be a good candidate for interface abstraction. However, a renderer or manager class whose methods support non-trivial functionality (i.e. the overhead incurred by the indirection is small compared with the amount of time spent in the function) may well be suitable. If many other components will be dependent on ours, then there is some motivation to protect those clients from the evolutionary tos and fros of interface design and, more importantly, implementation details of which class behaviour should be independent.

4.3.2 Singleton

A singleton is a class that logically has only a single instance in any application. It is a programmatic error to create more than one of these, and the implementation should prevent a user doing so. There are several ways to achieve this, and in this section we'll evaluate their merits and the value of the pattern.

Introduction

First, what sort of classes are singletons? Well, what do we have only one of? How about a display? That is a better candidate, though some systems may support multiple monitors. Since it is conceptually possible to have more than one display, chances are that it is not a clear-cut choice for a singleton. A 3D model is also not a good candidate – most games will have more than one! However, if we keep all the game's 3D models in one place (perhaps along with other data), then we have a system that there is logically only one of – after all, if there are several repositories, where do the models go? And in the end, we would need to keep a repository of repositories, so the repository is a *fundamental* singleton.

In general, this reflects a pattern: large database objects that oversee a set of controlled objects are natural singletons. Many other possibilities exist, though.

Implementation

Back in the bad old days of hack-and-hope C programming, we might have declared a singleton as a global object, thus:

```
#include "ModelDatabase.h"

struct ModelDatabase g_ModelDatabase;
```

Yikes, a global variable! Anyone can read or write it from anywhere. Perhaps, a little more safely, we can write;

```
#include "ModelDatabase.h"

static struct ModelDatabase s_ModelDatabase;
```

and we can control access to the model database via a suitable API:

```
void modeldb_Initialise();
void modeldb_Terminate();
void modeldb_LoadModel( const char * pModelName );
void modeldb_FreeModel( struct Model * pModel );
```

So far, so good. There is one instance of a model database in the module. However, nothing prevents the user creating one of their own. If it controls access to some set of system-wide resources, that might create all sorts of undefined havoc.

Also notice the Initialise and Terminate calls. At some suitable points in the game, we need to call these. When we graduate to C++, we get the opportunity to call these automatically via constructors and destructors:

```
#include "ModelDatabase.hpp"

namespace
{
    // Data declared in here is private to this module.
    ModelDatabase s_ModelDatabase;
}

ModelDatabase::ModelDatabase()
{
    // Do what we did in modeldb_Initialise().
    Initialise();
}

ModelDatabase::~ModelDatabase()
{
    // Do what we did in modeldb_Terminate().
    Terminate();
}
```

We're still stuck with the fact that we can create any number of model databases. And now that there is a physical object rather than a procedural interface to interact with, the user needs to get hold of the single instance. We solve these (linked) problems with the following structure:

```
// ModelDatabase.hpp

class ModelDatabase
{
```

```
public:
    // There's only one of a static object - just what
    // we need!
    static ModelDatabase & Instance();
    // ...
private:
    // Private ctor and dtor!
    ModelDatabase();
    ~ModelDatabase();
    static ModelDatabase c_Instance;
};

// ModelDatabase.cpp
#include "ModelDatabase.hpp"

ModelDatabase ModelDatabase::c_Instance;

/*static*/
ModelDatabase & ModelDatabase::Instance()
{
    return c_Instance;
}
```

We can now access the instance in this fashion:

```
#include "ModelDatabase.hpp"

int main( int argc, char ** argv )
{
    ModelDatabase & aDb = ModelDatabase::Instance();
    //...
    return 0;
}
```

The private lifecycle (constructor and destructor) of the class prevents users from creating instances. The only instance that can be created is the c_Instance static member – and since it is a member, its constructor and destructor can be called in member functions. *Voila*!

A variant of this approach is to declare the static instance of the singleton *inside* the Instance() function:

```
/*static*/
ModelDatabase & ModelDatabase::Instance()
{
    static ModelDatabase anInstance;
```

```
        return( &anInstance );
}
```

The bonus here is that the instance is not constructed until the first time
`Instance()` is called. C++ has added an invisible code block to construct the
object the first time the thread of execution enters the code block, and it uses
the standard library call `atexit()` to schedule calling the destructor. One problem with this variant is that (at least currently) some compilers have trouble
with the private constructors and destructors, to the extent that you may have
to make them public, thus weakening the intent of the pattern.

   This is a common way of implementing singletons. It will work for a large
number of applications, but the pattern of implementation has a flaw or two.
First, the single instance is constructed at file scope. Regrettably, C++ has no
rules about the order of construction – if another object at file scope in another
module requires ours and the model database has not yet been constructed,
well, whatever happens is not good. Similarly, our class can fail to initialise correctly if it depends on another system not yet constructed. Second, by
constructing a static instance, we allow for only a single behaviour of the singleton. What would happen if we wanted – or needed – to allow the user to
subclass the singleton? For example, supposing we wanted to change the behaviour of the database depending on a variable read at run time from an
initialisation file. Then it makes sense to have a pointer to an instance instead
of an object itself:

```
// ModelDatbase.hpp
class ModelDatabase
{
public:
    // as before
private:
    static ModelDatabase * c_pInstance;
};

class ModelDatabaseFast : public ModelDatabase
{
    //...
};

// ModelDatabase.cpp
#include "ModelDatabase.hpp"
#include "IniFile.hpp"

ModelDatabase * ModelDatabase::c_pInstance = 0;
```

```
/*static*/
ModelDatabase & ModelDatabase::Instance()
{
    if ( c_pInstance == 0 )
    {
        if (IniFile::GetString( "modeldb" )== "fast" )
        {
            c_pInstance = new ModelDatabaseFast;
        }
        else
        {
            c_pInstance = new ModelDatabase;
        }
    }

    return( *c_pInstance );
}
```

That solves that problem. However, we have a new one (no pun intended!) – we have dynamically allocated the object on the heap and will have to delete it at some point around program termination. I say 'at some point' because in a non-trivial application many classes will delete resources at shutdown and we need to avoid deleting objects twice or not at all, or accessing an already deleted resource in a destructor.

We could add a static `Terminate()` method, but it could be a thorny issue as to when we call it. We'd really like it to be called at global scope because most systems will have purged their resources by then. Can we arrange that? Well, yes we can. We can use the STL's template class `auto_ptr`, which I summarise here:

```
namespace std
{
    template<class T>
    class auto_ptr
    {
    public:
        explicit auto_ptr( T * pItem );
        ~auto_ptr() { delete m_pItem; }

            T * operator->() { return m_pItem; }
    private:
        T * m_pItem;
    };
}
```

The important part is that destructor: the pointer is deleted when the `auto_ptr` created with it goes out of scope.

We can plug this into our singleton class:

```
// ModelDatabase.hpp
#include <memory>

class ModelDatabase
{
private:
    // Since the destructor is private, the template
    // class needs permission to delete it. There is
    // no violation of encapsulation, though.
    friend class std::auto_ptr<ModelDatabase>;
    static std::auto_ptr<ModelDatabase> c_InstancePtr;
};

// ModelDatbase.cpp
#include "ModelDatabase.hpp"

std::auto_ptr<ModelDatabase>
    ModelDatabase::c_InstancePtr(0);

/*static*/
ModelDatabase & ModelDatabase::Instance()
{
    if ( c_InstancePtr.get() == 0 )
    {
        c_InstancePtr = new ModelDatbase;
    }

    return( *c_InstancePtr.get() );
}
```

So have we finally arrived at our 'perfect' singleton? Well, not quite. We can still have problems with the order of destruction of file-scope objects and, frustratingly, there is no simple solution to this.[3]

---

3   One solution is to specify an integer order of destruction of singletons. A management API then uses the standard library function `atexit()` to schedule the deletions in the required order.

In use

Singletons can reduce the amount of unnecessary dependencies that creep into your code. Consider the model database class existing in the object framework shown here:

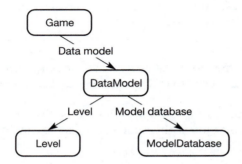

If we're in the Draw() routine in the Level class, here's a snippet of the code we might need to use:

```
// Level.cpp
#include "Level.hpp"
#include "Game.hpp"
#include "DataModel.hpp"
#include "ModelDatabase.hpp"
#include "Renderer.hpp"

//...

void Level::Draw( Renderer * pRenderer )
{
    ModelDatabase & aModelDb =
        g_pGame->GetDataModel()->GetModelDatabase();
    Model * pSkyModel = aModelDb.GetModel( "sky" );
}
```

Notice that we have to go to the top of the inheritance hierarchy (Game), then descend all the way down to get the class we require. To do this, we need to include files that may have little or no other relevance to us, which increases coupling, compile and link time and decreases reusability.

Contrast the same code using a singleton:

```
// Level.cpp
#include "Level.hpp"
#include "ModelDatabase.hpp"
#include "Renderer.hpp"
```

```
// ...

void Level::Draw( Renderer * pRenderer )
{
    ModelDatabase & aDb = ModelDatabase::Instance();
    Model * pSkyModel = aDb.GetModel( "sky" );
}
```

Since we don't own the model database, we are not responsible for creating it or destroying it, we don't need to cache references to it and we reduce coupling to auxiliary classes.

Before we get too carried away with ourselves, though, we should perhaps reflect on the fact that much the same effect can be obtained using a C-style procedural interface

```
void Level::Draw( Renderer * pRenderer )
{
    Model * pSkyModel = modeldb_GetModel( "sky" );
}
```

which is a little more readable. The singleton only really improves on this by the ability to have polymorphic behaviour determined at run time. If you do not need this, then there may be a convincing argument about using a procedural interface rather than a singleton.

There is a related pattern that is a hybrid of the singleton and the procedural interface. Its technical name is a *monostate*. This is slightly misleading, since there may be no state (i.e. dynamic member data) associated with the class. The implementation looks like this:

```
class ModelDatabase
{
public:
    static Model * GetModel( const char * pName );
    static void Initialise();
    static void Terminate();
private:
    static std::list<Model *> c_Models;
};
```

Other than being pure C++, there is little reason to favour this over a procedural interface. There are some very minor annoyances – a user can create an instance of this class, though they can't do much with it. Typically, it's poor form to write a class and then actively prevent polymorphic extension, and I would suggest that monostates are poor compromises.

A generic implementation?

After writing a few singletons, you'll notice that you get a bit bored with writing the near-same `Instance()` function every time (our current application has at least five singletons and is growing). Can we write a template to automatically generate a singleton? Well, the answer is a qualified 'yes'. Here is an example template:

```
template<class T>
class Singleton
{
public:
    static T & Instance();

private:
    Singleton();
    ~Singleton();
};

template<class T>
T & Singleton<T>::Instance()
{
    T anInstance;

    return( anInstance );
}
```

Certainly, that saves our fingers from typing unnecessarily repetitive characters. To create a singleton, we need to declare only:

```
class ModelDatabase { /*...*/ };

Singleton<ModelDatabase> s_ModelDatabase;
```

Excellent – except for one thing. It is the Singleton<ModelDatabase> that there is exactly one of, not the ModelDatabase. The user is free to create any number of additional instances other than the specified one. The definition of a singleton was that there could be only a single instance by definition. What we have created is, alas, not a singleton.

4.3.3 Object factory

The object factory allows us to address a shortcoming of C++. We'd like to be able to write

```
class Object { /*...*/ };
class Rocket : public Object { /*...*/ };
class Npc : public Object { /*...*/ };
```

```
Type aType = Rocket;

// Allocates a rocket.
Object * pObject = new aType;
```

but (alas) the language does not support type semantics in this way. The object factory pattern applies when you have a hierarchy of objects that need to be created dynamically. Typically, you do not know ahead of time exactly what types of object, or how many, you will create. For example, you could be creating objects based on the contents of an external script file.

A simple – and common – approach to writing a factory is to create an enumerated type that represents the different flavours of object you can create:

```
// Object.hpp
class Object
{
public:
    enum Type
    {
        NPC,
        ROCKET,
        DUCK,

        // New types above here.
        NUM_TYPES
    };

    // This is the 'factory'.
    static Object * Create( Type eType );
};

// Object.cpp
#include "Object.hpp"
#include "Rocket.hpp"
#include "Duck.hpp"
#include <cassert>

/*static*/
Object * Object::Create( Type eType )
{
    switch( eType )
    {
        case NPC   : return new Npc;
        case ROCKET: return new Rocket;
```

```
            case DUCK  : return new Duck;
        default:
            // Handle the error.
            assert( !"Object::Create(): unknown type" );
            break;
    }
}
```

Common this may be, but there are two big problems with this method, and both are related to the enumeration Type. First, if we are loading and saving the integer values of the type, then the application that writes them must be synchronised with the game that reads them. This may involve sharing the Object.hpp include file, which may or may not be possible or convenient.

Even if it is possible and convenient, there is a bigger problem: maintenance. In order to add a class to the factory, we need to update the enumeration. That means editing the header file of the base class. And that forces a rebuild of the base class and all of the subclasses. Ouch! We'd really like to be able to add classes at will without recompiling the project.

Note also that the Object.cpp file includes all the headers of all the subclasses. As the number of subclasses grows, this becomes a compilation and linking bottleneck – much thrashing of disk to be suffered. Clearly, we need to do better than this.

First, those enumerations: bin them! If you can afford the hit, replace them with string constants: although string compares are relatively inefficient next to integer comparisons, the act of creating an object is relatively expensive compared with either, and if your game is manufacturing many classes every frame, you may need to have a really hard look at your architecture.

```
// Object.hpp
class Object
{
public:
    static Object * Create( const char * pType );
};

// Object.cpp
#include "Object.hpp"
#include "Rocket.hpp"
#include "Npc.hpp"
#include "Duck.hpp"
#include <cassert>
#include <cstring>

/*static*/
```

```
Object * Object::Create( const char * pType )
{
    if ( !strcmpi( pType, "rocket" ) )
        return new Rocket;
    else if ( !strcmpi( pType, "npc" ) )
        return new Npc;
    else if ( !strcmpi( pType, "duck" ) )
        return new Duck;
    else
    {
        assert( !"CreateObject() : unknown type" );
    }
    return 0;
}
```

Note the use of case-insensitive compares: life is just too short to track down bugs due to case issues.

This removes the dependency on the Object.hpp header file. Now we can add a manufactured class, and only the implementation file need change. We can weaken the dependencies further by moving the factory to a separate component:

```
// ObjectFactory.hpp
class Object;

struct ObjectFactory
{
    static Object * CreateObject( const char* pType );
};

// ObjectFactory.cpp
#include "ObjectFactory.hpp"
#include "Object.hpp"
#include "Rocket.hpp"
#include "Npc.hpp"
#include "Duck.hpp"

/*static*/
Object * ObjectFactory::CreateObject( const char *pType )
{
    // As before.
}
```

We are still left with a compilation and linkage bottleneck due to these includes, and we are still a bit worried about all those string compares. What can we do about these? Quite a bit, as it happens. We need to alter things a little, but don't worry: it's for the better.

We move from a hard-coded (compile-time) set of objects we can make to a run-time set. Each class that requires being manufactured in a factory is obliged to register itself at startup. When it does so, it supplies its name and a pointer to a function that manufactures an object instance. We store these in an associative map, such as the STL's `std::map`. Storing the entries in this data structure will greatly increase the efficiency of the look-up process. (Note that because all object classes are registered with a single instance, an object factory is a good candidate for being a singleton.)

```
// ObjectFactory.hpp
#include <map>
#include <string>

class ObjectFactory
{
public:
    typedef Object * (*tCreator)();

    // Note that we need to associate strings, not
    // char *s because a map requires strict ordering:
    // the keys must define the operators < and ==.
    typedef std::map<std::string,tCreator> tCreatorMap;

    bool Register(const char *pType, tCreator aCreator);
    Object * Create( const char * pType );

    static ObjectFactory & Instance();

private:
    ObjectFactory();
    ~ObjectFactory();

    tCreatorMap m_Creators;
};

// ObjectFactory.cpp
#include "ObjectFactory.hpp"

// Ugly macro for brevity.
#define VT(t,c) tCreatorMap::value_type((t),(c))

using std::string;
```

```
bool ObjectFactory::
Register( const char * pType, tCreator aCreator )
{
    string str = string(pType);
    return m_Creators.insert(VT(str,aCreator)).second;
}

Object * ObjectFactory::Create( const char * pType )
{
    tCreatorMap::iterator i =
        m_Creators.find( string( pType ) );

    if ( i != m_Creators.end() )
    {
        tCreator aCreator = (*i).second;
        return aCreator();
    }

    return 0;
}

// Rocket.cpp
#include "Rocket.hpp"
#include "ObjectFactory.hpp"

// Another macro to save printing space.
#define OF ObjectFactory::Instance()

namespace
{

Object * createRocket()
{
    return new Rocket;
}

// This code ensures registration will be invoked at some
// time before entering main().
bool s_bRegistered =
    OF.RegisterClass("rocket",createRocket);

}
```

One further point is worth making: this implementation can be made generic very easily via the use of templates:

```
// GenericFactory.hpp
#include <map>
#include <string>

template<class T>
class GenericFactory
{
public:
    typedef T * (*tCreator)();
    typedef std::map<std::string,tCreator> tCreatorMap;

    bool Register(const char *pType, tCreator aCreator);
    T * Create( const char * pType );
    static GenericFactory<T> & Instance();
private:
    // Much as before.
};

// Implementation goes here.

// ObjectFactory.hpp
#include "GenericFactory.hpp"
#include "Object.hpp"
typedef GenericFactory<Object> ObjectFactory;
```

Unlike the singleton pattern, the object factory pattern generalises very nicely. By using a registration method rather than a static compile-time implementation, we can decouple the created data types from each other as well as from the factory.

4.3.4 Manager

A common pattern is when a number of similar, hierarchically related classes exhibit some collective, intelligent behaviour. This is often quite difficult to code and results in a rather un-object-oriented structure: objects that need to be aware of other, similar objects. This often results in increased complexity in otherwise simple objects, and it may even lead to significant coupling between classes.

In such situations, a manager class can help sometimes. It takes responsibility for creation, deletion and – more to the point – the cooperative (synergistic) behaviour between the classes it manages. A manager is a hybrid pattern. First, it is a very likely candidate to be a singleton. Second, since it may well be able to create and destroy families of classes, it will behave like an object factory. Figure 4.3 shows A typical manager pattern.

Figure 4.3
Class diagram for an
abstract manager.

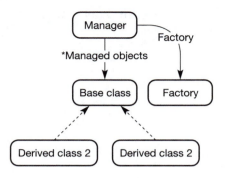

4.3.5 Visitor/iterator

Looking at the manager pattern above, we can see that the controlled objects will be stored in some kind of container class: an array, list, or more exotic animals such as hash tables or binary trees. Whichever we choose – which will depend on how the manager needs to access the contained objects – will be a private encapsulated detail of the manager's implementation. Consider a ThingManager that manages a bunch of classes called Things. Assume we have a dynamic array class that expands (and maybe shrinks) according to the storage requirements:

```
class Thing;
class ThingManager
{

public:
    void AddThing( Thing * pThing );
    // etc

private:
    array<Thing *> m_Things;
};
```

This is fine, so long as we don't need to give anything outside of manager some access to the Things. Do we then add the following line?

```
class ThingManager
{
public:
    const array<Thing *> & GetThings() const;
    // as before
};
```

Consider the following code that uses Things (which have a `Print()` method, for argument's sake):

```
const array<Thing *> & Things = aManager.GetThings();
for( int j = 0; j < Things.size(); ++j )
{
    Thing * pThing = Things[j];
    pThing->Print();
}
```

Fine, that works – until we have the bright idea that storing Things in a hash table is a much better approach because we do a lot of name- or ID-based look-up:

```
class ThingManager
{
public:
private:
    hash_table<string,Thing *> m_Things;
};
```

Now we're a little bit stuck. We may have written a lot of random-access code that plays with arrays of Things, and now that code is useless. The exposure of the Thing array has poked a great big hole in our encapsulation, and now that we've changed the manager – as is our wont – we're faced with maintenance when we really wanted to get a move on.

In general, anything that exposes how your implementation works to the outside world, which should not really care, is not a good thing. Note that we don't have to expose an internal type: only something that behaves like that type!

```
class ThingManager
{
public:
    int GetNumberOfThings() const;
    const Thing * GetThing( int n ) const;
};
```

is nearly as bad, as it still has the smell of an array.

How, then, do we access internal data in a way that's independent of how the data are stored in the manager class? That's where visitors and iterators come in.

Visitor classes

Visitors are controversial. They can turn into a maintenance bottleneck, which can easily defeat the benefit gained by using them. For this reason, they are best used in limited circumstances, particularly when the controlled classes are in a shallow hierarchy (i.e. there are only a few well-defined concrete subclasses).

To start with, let's look at the visitor pattern when dealing with only a single class. We'll stick with our Things for this. Then we'll look at how to extend the concept to larger hierarchies.

Visitors are the modern-day equivalent of enumerator-like callback functions, as seen all over the place in Windows SDK and DirectX. For example, we may write the manager class in pseudo-code, thus:

```
class ThingManager
{
public:
    typedef void (*tThingCb)( Thing *, void * );

    void VisitThings( tThingCb aThingCb, void * pUser )
    {
        for_each pThing in m_Things
        {
            aThingCb( pThing, pUser );
        }
    }

private:
    Collection<Thing *> m_Things;
};
```

The problem with this is that only one parameter is supplied to pass in context information, and that parameter is the nasty typeless `void *`. That can lead to all sorts of fun and games, not to mention bugs. For instance, what happens if we need to pass two pieces of context information into the callback? Then we might be forced to write

```
struct Context
{
    int iData1;
    int iData2;
};

Context * pContext = new Context;
pContext->iData1 = //…
pContext->iData2 = //…
aThingManager.VisitThings( MyCallback, pContext );
delete pContext;
```

which is not exactly performance code and can easily result in memory leaks or worse.

Consider the alternative:

```
class ThingVisitor
{
public:
    virtual void VisitThing( Thing * pThing ) = 0;
};
```

In itself, it does nothing. But – by the power of inheritance – we can define our subclass like this:

```
class MyThingVisitor : public ThingVisitor
{
public:
    MyThingVisitor( int iData1, int iData2 )
    : m_iData1( iData1 )
    , m_iData2( iData2 )
    {
    }

    void VisitThing( Thing * pThing )
    {
        pThing->DoSomething(m_iData1,m_iData2);
    }

private:
    int m_iData1;
    int m_iData2;
};
```

Now we can write our visitor call as:

```
class ThingManager
{
public:
    void VisitThings( ThingVisitor & aVisitor )
    {
        for_each pThing in m_Things
        {
            aVisitor.VisitThing( pThing );
        }
    }
};
```

What we've effectively done here is add a new virtual function to the ThingManager from the outside. Clearly, this is a powerful paradigm. We have extended the functionality of the manager without rupturing the encapsulation of the class.

It gets a little more fiddly when there is a hierarchy of managed objects. Here's a subset of a real example taken from the project we're currently working on. A class diagram will set the scene succinctly (see Figure 4.4).

Our LightManager supervises the creation, destruction and use of a number of lights, each of which can be one of several flavours – here, limited to two – point and directional. This gives us a choice of how to store the lights within the manager class: either we store the different types of light in separate collections, or we maintain a single heterogeneous collection of all lights. We choose to do the latter as it simplifies what follows.

As part of the lighting calculations, we need to be able to determine which lights affect which objects in the world, as to light every object with every light would degrade performance and not be visually correct. Since the light manager should not be required to know of the existence of objects in the world, it is therefore the duty of the objects themselves to work out which lights affect them. We decided to use the Visitor pattern to implement this. The difference here is that different types of light need to be treated differently by the objects. The LightVisitor looks like this:

```
class LightVisitor
{
public:
virtual void VisitPoint( PointLight * ) = 0;
virtual void VisitDirectional( DirectionalLight * ) = 0;
};
```

Figure 4.4
Light manager
framework.

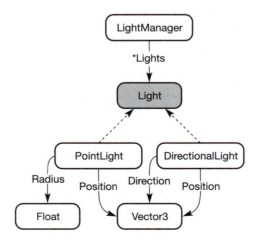

Now we have a problem: the visitor loop looks like this

```
for_each pLight in m_Lights
{
    aVisitor.Visit???Light( pLight );
}
```

We don't know what type of light pLight is, so we don't know what method to call. To get around this, we use the technique of double dispatching. Since each light type intrinsically 'knows' what type it is, the light itself can call the required method.

```
class Light
{
public:
    virtual void AcceptVisitor( LightVisitor & ) = 0;
};

class PointLight : public Light
{
public:
    void AcceptVisitor( LightVisitor & aVisitor )
    {
        aVisitor.VisitPoint( this );
    }
};

class DirectionalLight : public Light
{
public:
    void AcceptVisitor( LightVisitor & aVisitor )
    {
        aVisitor.VisitDirectional( this );
    }
};
```

Our visiting loop then looks like this:

```
for_each pLight in m_Lights
{
    pLight->AcceptVisitor( aVisitor );
}
```

There is an obvious drop in efficiency when using a polymorphic visitor: two virtual function calls per iteration. Nevertheless, this is not the primary problem. The issue is that if we add a new light subclass, then we need to update not only the base visitor class with a 'VisitNewType' method but all the subclasses too. Ouch!

The caveat is therefore this: visitors are powerful, but if they operate on heterogeneous collections whose inheritance graphs have a habit of growing, then they can cause a lot of maintenance to be undertaken.

Iterators

An iterator can be viewed as a generalised pointer. How does that help us? Well, suppose our Thing manager could return a pointer to the first Thing and an end-of-Things pointer:

```
class ThingManager
{
public:
    pointer FirstThing();
    pointer EndOfThings();
};
```

Then to step through the collection of Things, we write:

```
pointer p = aThingManager.FirstThing();
while( p != aThingManager.EndOfThings() )
{
    Thing * t = *p;
    t->Print();
    ++p;
}
```

Notice that the generalised pointer supports incrementation (++) and dereference (*),[4] just like a vanilla pointer. However, a plain pointer supports iteration this way only if the Things are contiguous in memory. A generalised pointer can hide how the elements are ordered in RAM, just so long as ++ gets the next pointer, and * accesses the referenced object. Iterators come with a guarantee: they will visit all the valid elements in a collection. They are, however, free to do it in any order they see fit. This is just what we want: as long as our collection of Things supports iterators, we can avoid exposing clients to the gory implementation details.

---

4 It is almost always preferable to use ++p as opposed to p++. The latter needs to return the value before the increment, therefore it has to construct and cache it. Since this happens many times, it can accumulate to a big waste of cycles.

How might we implement a generalised pointer? The first thought that occurs is virtual functions, and many textbooks on C++ data structures present such schemes. However, historically this implementation strategy has fallen out of favour because of the computational overhead of vtable indirection. Template containers make a much more efficient iterator.

STL shows us how to do this. All of its container classes define a type called `iterator`, which does all – and more – of what we need above. Using a typedef or two, we can easily expose the required interface:

```cpp
#include <vector>

class ThingManager
{
    typedef std::vector<Thing *> tThingList;
public:
    typedef tThingList::iterator iterator;

    iterator FirstThing()
    {
        return( m_Things.begin() );
    }

    iterator EndOfThings()
    {
        return( m_Things.end() );
    }

private:
    std::vector<Thing *> m_Things;
};
```

In our client code:

```cpp
ThingManager::iterator itThing = aManager.FirstThing();
ThingManager::iterator itEnd   = aManager.EndOfThings();
while( itThing != itEnd )
{
    (*itThing)->Print();
    ++itThing;
}
```

It's a bit syntactically yucky. If – as STL does – the iterator defines the method operator->, then we can write

```
itThing->Print();
```

without the * and the (required) brackets.

Note that we don't have to use STL containers. We can write our own collections – as efficient or robust as we need – and supply iterators for them. In doing so, don't be tempted to nest classes:

```
template<class T>
class container
{
public:
    class iterator
    {
        // …
    };

    //…
};
```

The iterator may need to be a friend class of the container, which is a pity because you can't forward reference nested classes. Usually the resulting code leaks encapsulation. The best way to define it is:

```
template<class T>
class container_iterator
{
    // …
};

template<class T>
class container
{
    friend class container_iterator<T>;
public:
    typedef container_iterator<T> iterator;
    // …
};
```

In conclusion, visitors and iterators can help us out of the problem of violating encapsulation in a contained system. Visitors are powerful but can be problematic if applied to the wrong sort of system. Iterators are lower-level entities, generalised pointers that have a negligible efficiency penalty but result in somewhat verbose source.

4.3.6 Strawman

The Strawman is almost certainly the simplest of all patterns and is unusual in that it defines – explicitly or implicitly – absolutely no behaviour whatsoever. 'What use is it, then?' I hear you ask. Well, it exists mainly to carry *type information*. Suppose we have a package that requires the user to pass in a pointer (or reference) to a user-defined class. That pointer will then be returned later to the user so that they can perform some operation on it. What would the signature of the function that passes the pointer in look like?

```
// MyClass.hpp
class MyClass
{
};

// package_TheirClass.hpp
void package_TheirClass::RegisterPointer( ?? pYourData );
```

The package can't know anything about your classes:

```
void package_TheirClass::RegisterPointer( MyClass * );
```

If it does, then you've done it wrong because you're binding systems that don't otherwise need to know about each other. The solution is to use a Strawman, a class with no insides.

```
// package_Type.hpp
class package_Type
{
public:
    package_Type() {}
    virtual ~package_Type() {}
};

// package_TheirClass.hpp
class package_Type;

class package_TheirClass
{
public:
    void RegisterPointer( package_Type * pType );
};
```

```
// MyClass.hpp
#include "package\package_Type.hpp"
class MyClass : public package_Type
{
public:
    // Your operations here.
};
```

If this is a bit too abstract, let's look at a real-life example. One project had a
package to handle game controllers. These game controllers could come in various flavours: joypad, keyboard, mouse, etc. The package defined a polymorphic
handler class that accepted different types of input data:

```
class ctrl_InputHandler
{
public:
    virtual void HandleJoy( ctrl_Joypad & aJoy, ??? );
    // Other controller types handled similarly.
};
```

The idea is that the client writes their own input handler to do whatever they
require it to do. However, there are a couple of things we needed to specify:
something about who was using the controller, and something about what was
being controlled. This was done by using two Strawman classes:

```
class ctrl_User
{
public:
    ctrl_User() {}
    virtual ~ctrl_User() {}
};
```

```
class ctrl_Target
{
public:
    ctrl_Target() {}
    virtual ~ctrl_Target() {}
};
```

The handler class now has member functions of the form:

```
void HandleJoy( ctrl_Joy & aData,
                ctrl_User * pUser,
                ctrl_Target * pTarget );
```

At the game level, we had a player owning a controller and using it to move a cursor to drive it around the screen (Figure 4.5).

The game's input handler code looked something like this:

```cpp
// GameInputHandler.hpp
#include "controller\ctrl_InputHandler.hpp"

class GameInputHandler : public ctrl_InputHandler
{
public:
    void HandleJoy( ctrl_Joy& aData,
                    ctrl_User * pUser,
                    ctrl_Target * pTarget );
};

// GameInputHandler.cpp
#include "GameInputHandler.hpp"
#include "Player.hpp"
#include "Cursor.hpp"

void GameInputHandler::HandleJoy( ctrl_Joy& aData,
                                  ctrl_User * pUser,
                                  ctrl_Target * pTarget )
{
    // This upcast is fine because we know what
    // the final user type is at the game level.
    Player * pPlayer = static_cast<Player *>(pUser);

    // Similarly, at this level that target is always
    // the cursor.
    Cursor * pCursor = static_cast<Cursor *>(pTarget);

    // Code to do things with players and cursors…
}
```

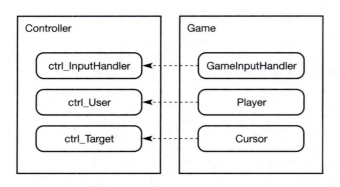

Figure 4.5
The game subclasses of the abstract component classes.

4.3.7 Prototype

A prototype is similar to a factory, in as much as it creates new object instances. However, it does this not by taking some type identifier and returning an associated class, but by cloning itself:

```
class PrototypeBase
{
public:
    virtual PrototypeBase * Clone() = 0;
};

class Prototype1 : public PrototypeBase
{
public:
    // Cloning without copying makes no sense!
    Prototype1( const Prototype1 & that )
    {
        // …
    }
    // Note the use of the 'covariant return type'
    // rule now supported by most C++ compilers: a
    // virtual function that returns a base class
    // pointer or reference
    // with an override in a subclass can declare its
    // return type to be the subclass type.
    Prototype1 * Clone()
    {
        return new Prototype1( *this );
    }
};
```

Another factory-like class then uses the prototype thus:

```
class PrototypeFactory
{
public:
    void SetPrototype( PrototypeBase * pBase )
    {
        delete m_pPrototype;
        m_pPrototype = pBase;
    }

    PrototypeBase * Create()
    {
        return( m_pPrototype->Clone() );
    }
```

```
private:
    PrototypeBase * m_pPrototype;
};
```

The prototype is useful because it can be used to set default values in a dynamic way:

```
PrototypeFactory MyFactory;
Prototype1 * pProto1 = new Prototype1( 10 );
MyFactory.SetPrototype( pProto1 );
PrototypeBase * pInstance1 = MyFactory.Create();

Prototype1 * pProto2 = new Prototype1( 20 );
MyFactory.SetPrototype( pProto2 );
PrototypeBase * pInstance2 = MyFactory.Create();
```

Here's an example of a prototype system in action. We have a game in which a player has a weapon that can shoot various types of bullets (see Figure 4.6 for some lines and bubbles). This translates into the following code skeleton:

```
// Weapon.hpp
class Bullet;

class Weapon
{
public:
    Bullet * CreateBullet();
    void SetBulletPrototype( Bullet * pBullet );

private:
    Bullet * m_pBulletPrototype;
};
```

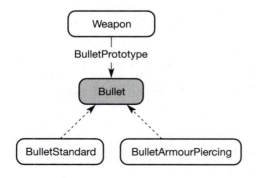

Figure 4.6
Class diagram for weapon and bullet management system.

```
// Weapon.cpp
#include "Weapon.hpp"
#include "Bullet.hpp"

void Weapon::SetBulletPrototype( Bullet * pProto )
{
    delete m_pBulletPrototype;
    m_pBulletPrototype = pProto;
}

/*virtual*/
Bullet * Weapon::CreateBullet()
{
    return( m_pBulletPrototype->Clone() );
}

//---------------------------------------------------------

// Bullet.hpp
class Bullet
{
public:
    Bullet();
    Bullet( const Bullet & that );
    virtual Bullet * Clone() = 0;
    // and other methods.
private:
    // some data fields.
};

//---------------------------------------------------------

// BulletStandard.hpp (BulletArmourPiercing is similar)
#include "Bullet.hpp"
#include "maths\maths_Vector3.hpp"

class BulletStandard : public Bullet
{
public:
    BulletStandard();
    BulletStandard( const BulletStandard & that );
    BulletStandard * Clone();
private:
    maths_Vector3 m_vPosition;
    // and other fields
};

//---------------------------------------------------------
```

```
// BulletStandard.cpp
#include "BulletStandard.hpp"

BulletStandard::
BulletStandard( const BulletStandard & that )
: Bullet( that )
, m_vPosition( that.m_vPosition )
{
}


/*virtual*/
BulletStandard * BulletStandard::Clone()
{
    return( new BulletStandard( *this ) );
}
```

Now the player (say) can change the type of ammo their weapon shoots by writing:

```
Weapon * pWeapon = GetWeapon();
pWeapon->SetBulletPrototype( new BulletStandard );
```

4.3.8 Russian doll

The aim of this mini-pattern is to eliminate global-like objects, by which we mean real globals (which are anathema) or singletons (which are tolerable but not aesthetically satisfying).

I was tempted to call this pattern a Trojan horse, but that had certain negative connotations. However, the idea is much the same – allow an object type to hide encapsulated details of other objects from a system that it passes through on its way into another system further down the hierarchy. The bypassed system therefore remains oblivious – and therefore independent – of anything contained in the object itself (the 'Trojans', if you will).

We will call the global-like objects 'services' and consider a non-horizontal object hierarchy where the objects all depend on a selection of those services, a bit like that shown in Figure 4.7.

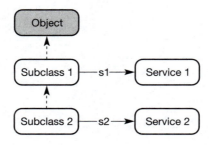

Figure 4.7
The 'Russian doll' pattern works well for object hierarchies that look like this.

Let's look at how the constructors of the subclasses might appear:

```cpp
// Subclass1.cpp
Subclass1::Subclass1( Service1 * pService1 )
: m_pService1( pService1 )
{
    /* Service1 assumed to be private */
}


// Subclass2.cpp
Subclass2::
Subclass2( Service2 *pService2, Service1 *pService1 )
: Subclass1( pService1 )
, m_pService2( pService2 )
{
}
```

Notice that the deeper the hierarchy gets, the more arguments the constructors need. Long argument lists aren't just ugly; they are also a fertile source of mistakes because of things like automatic type conversion. Furthermore, notice that Subclass2 gets to see a Service1 pointer even though it never uses or cares about it. To create a Subclass2, we'd write something like:

```cpp
// Things.cpp
#include "Service1.hpp"
#include "Service2.hpp"

//...
Service1 * pService1 = Service1::Instance();
Service2 * pService2 = Service2::Instance();
Subclass2 * pThing = new Subclass2(pService1, pService2);
```

Those global-like objects have a habit of popping up everywhere and getting passed around everywhere. We can tame this sort of creeping disease quite simply by using a container class – a Russian doll:

```cpp
// ServiceProvider.hpp
class ServiceProvider
{
public:
    Service1 * GetService1();
    Service2 * GetService2();
```

```
private:
    Service1 * m_pService1;
    Service2 * m_pService2;
};
```

Now we can write our constructors like this:

```
// Subclass1.cpp
#include "ServiceProvider.hpp"

Subclass1::Subclass1( ServiceProvider & rServices )
: m_pService1( rServices.GetService1() )
{
}

// Subclass2.cpp
#include "ServiceProvider.hpp"

Subclass2::Subclass2( ServiceProvider & rServices )
: Subclass1( rServices )
, m_pService2( rServices.GetService2() )
{
}
```

No more growing argument lists, and only the classes that actually require particular services need request and use them.

Case study 4.3: patterns in practice – the 'state manager'

Having talked quite abstractly about patterns, we'll now demonstrate their use in a case study. We'll discuss in detail the development of a state manager for a game (or indeed any other sort of application).

First, what (in this context) is a state? It is a single mode of behaviour that determines what the game is doing at any one time. For example, the game may be playing a cut scene, in a menu hierarchy, running the main game or paused. Each of these behaviours we call a state; Figure 4.8 shows some state classes. As always, we start by factoring out common behaviours: what is there that is similar to all states?

Looking at the examples above, we can infer that there is a concept of time passing (a cut scene plays or the game evolves): the state can be updated with respect to time. How do we measure time? In a game, we can either count elapsed frames or measure actual elapsed time. Which is better? That's another argument, which we'll deal with in a later chapter. For now, let's just assume we have a type `Time` that represents the elapsed interval since the last update.

Figure 4.8
Examples of state
subclasses.

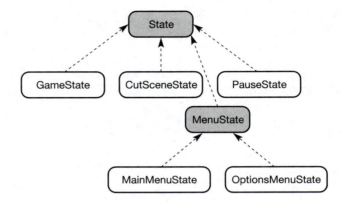

What else is common to state? We'd certainly like to be able to see some visual difference between states, so we'd like to Draw what's going on. Again, for argument's
sake, we'll assume we have a Renderer class that can draw stuff:

```
class state_State
{
public:
    state_State();
    virtual ~state_State();

    virtual void Update( Time dt ) = 0;
    virtual void Draw( Renderer * pRenderer ) const = 0;
};
```

Note that the Draw member is declared const: it shouldn't modify the state. What
else can we say about states? Well, our application will, at some point, have to
change state. Zero or one state will be outgoing and another one other will be incoming. These states may require initialisation and clean-up operations, so to this end we
extend the interface by adding two virtual methods, OnEnter() and OnLeave():

```
class state_State
{
public:
    state_State();
    virtual ~state_State();

    virtual void Update( Time dt ) = 0;
    virtual void Draw( Renderer * pRenderer ) const = 0;
    virtual void OnEnter() { ; }
    virtual void OnLeave() { ; }
};
```

We have avoided passing the outgoing and incoming states as parameters into these member functions, even though that might give more power and flexibility. Why? Because at this relatively low level, binding states to each other makes it harder to write a higher-level state that is as autonomous as it needs to be. If we really need to implement this sort of behaviour, then we can still do so further down the class hierarchy.

The sequence of operations involved in a state change is detailed in this code fragment:

```
void ChangeState( state_State *pFrom, state_State *pTo )
{
    if ( pFrom != 0 )
    {
        pFrom->OnLeave();
    }

    pTo->OnEnter();
}
```

Simple enough. (Of course, production code would be more robust – what happens if pTo is NULL? Nothing good, that's for sure, so the validity of the parameters needs to be asserted on entry.)

Now, a more awkward question: who owns the states? Who is responsible for creating, deleting and using states? The most obvious candidate is the application itself, as shown in Figure 4.9.

But – as ever – 'obvious' is not necessarily best. Anyone can create and destroy states arbitrarily, and that can lead anywhere from crashes – immediate or latent – to memory leaks, and we would like to avoid these if possible. This is just the sort of situation where a manager can help, centralising the point of creation and helping us to enforce the correct transitions from state to state.

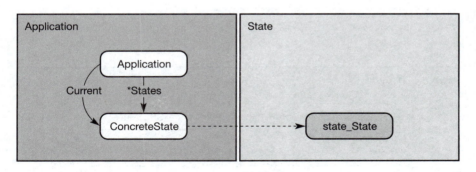

Figure 4.9
The application subclasses of the abstract state class.

```
class state_StateManager
{
public:
    state_StateManager();
    ~state_StateManager();

    void SwitchToState( state_State * pState )
    {
        if ( m_pCurrentState != 0 )
        {
            m_pCurrentState->OnLeave();
        }

        m_pCurrentState = pState;
        m_pCurrentState->OnEnter();
    }

private:
    state_State * m_pCurrentState;
};
```

The revised layout is shown in Figure 4.10.

Fine. But now we have another problem: the state manager is now creating the states that are required to make our application tick. How do we avoid coupling the state manager to our particular application manufacturing concrete states? Sounds like a job for a factory:

```
class state_Factory
{
public:
    state_State * CreateState( /*???*/ ) = 0;
};
```

Figure 4.10
The application implements concrete versions of the abstract state class.

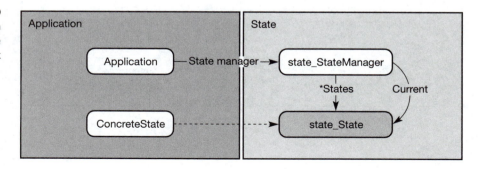

This is illustrated in Figure 4.11. Now, about that comment in the parameter list of `CreateState()`. Although an enumerated integer would suffice to describe the various states required, we have seen that this results in a highly coupled and therefore dependent set of modules that will force rebuilds left, right and centre. So let's avoid that and use names to uniquely identify states.[5] We're not dealing with inner-loop code that needs to run lightning quick – the application changes state relatively infrequently, so the occasional string compare won't hurt at all.

```
class state_Factory
{
public:
    state_State * CreateState( const char * pName ) = 0;
};
```

This forms the basis of our state management system. There are still some details to thrash out, though. Remember our state change pattern 'leave current, enter new'? Sometimes we might need to have a more complex behaviour, because we shall want to change behaviour of the state we are entering depending on what state we are leaving. Earlier, we rejected putting this sort of behaviour into the state class to keep the design simple and clean. Now we can see that it is the job of the state manager to control the transitions between application states. So we make that `SwitchToState()` method virtual, allowing the application to subclass and override to get the required specific behaviour (Figure 4.12):

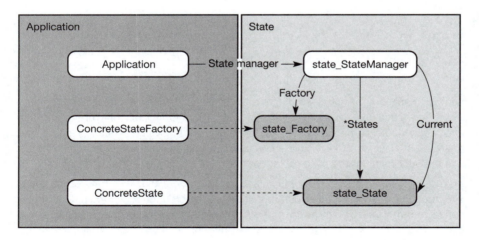

Figure 4.11

State manager with factory.

---

5   For the sake of sanity, ensure case-independent comparison of names.

Figure 4.12
Custom state
management.

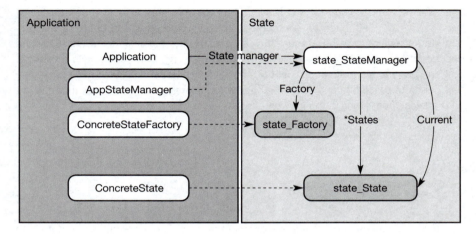

```
class state_StateManager
{
public:
    state_StateManager();
    virtual ~state_StateManager();

    virtual void SwitchToState( state_State * pState )
    {
        /* As before */
    }

private:
    state_State * m_pCurrentState;
};
```

Another inspection of our class diagram might suggest that the state manager class might be a candidate for a singleton. Quite so! There is logically only one state manager – why would we need more? – but since it is hard, nay impossible, to inherit from a singleton (what with those private constructors and destructors), it is important that it is the subclass, not the base class, of state_StateManager that is a singleton.

In fact, the manager is not the only class in the system that is a natural singleton. The state subclasses themselves are unique, so the creation functions passed to the concrete state factory can return the singleton instance rather than new'ing a subclass. This hugely reduces the likelihood of memory leaking, being multiply deleted, or other related horrors.

```
// ConcreteState.hpp
#include "state_State.hpp"
```

```cpp
class ConcreteState : public state_State
{
public:
    static ConcreteState & Instance();

    void Update( Time dt );
    void Draw( Renderer * pRenderer ) const;

private:
    // …
};

// ConcreteState.cpp
#include "ConcreteState.hpp"
#include "ConcreteStateManager.hpp"
#include "ConcreteStateFactory.hpp"

namespace
{

state_State * createState()
{
    return( &ConcreteState::Instance() );
}

bool registerState()
{
    ConcreteStateManager & aSM =
        ConcreteStateManager::Instance();
    state_Factory * pSF = aSM.GetFactory();

    return( pSF->Register( "Concrete", createState ) );
}


}

/*static*/
ConcreteState & ConcreteState::Instance()
{
    static ConcreteState anInstance;

    return( anInstance );
}
```

In engineering the state package in this fashion, we have established a paradigm: the way a system works. Take a look at how the application's main loop might be written:

```
Time t1 = GetTime();
Time dt = 0;
for(;;)
{
    ConcreteStateManager & aSM =
        ConcreteStateManager::Instance();

    state_State * pState = aSM.GetCurrentState();
    if ( pState != 0 )
    {
        pState->Update( dt );
        pState->Draw( pRenderer );
    }
    Time t2 = GetTime();
    dt = t2 - t1;
    t1 = t2;
}
```

We have a simple main loop, and a set of decoupled, largely independent states that can benefit further from inheritance to propagate common behaviours to state subclasses. This illustrates the benefits of moving to a pattern-driven, object-oriented programming methodology. Although a similar state system could, in principle, be written in C, the semantics of C++ make the code clear to understand, extend and maintain.

We'll return to the state management system later when we discuss adding actual data and graphics to the model.

Case study 4.4: graphical user interface

There isn't a game on the planet that doesn't have a user interface (UI), a method for taking changes in a controller and translating that into actions and responses in the game. This suggests that UIs are eminently abstractable, but we need to be a bit careful here because modern UIs usually come with complex graphical representations and we should be watchful to abstract only the generic behaviour common to all interface systems, lest we end up with specific behaviour at too low a level for reusability.

The graphical bit

For historical and habitual reasons, we'll assume that the basic package name for the GUI graphical bit is called 'view'. In order to keep the view package clean and simple, we need to avoid references to particular platforms and particular ways of drawing things. We'll make an assumption first: all graphical elements are represented by 2D rectangular areas. This isn't necessarily the most general way of storing region data, and it is possible to use non-rectangular regions for a truly universal representation. Nevertheless, whatever shape we choose, it will be bounded by a rectangle. For a few shapes, the rectangle will be a less efficient bound, but for the current purpose rectangles will do fine.

We'll look at the representation of the rectangle soon. But let's define the class that drives the whole GUI system – the View. A View is a rectangular region of screen that knows how to draw itself. It also supports the notion of *hierarchy*. A View can have child Views: when you perform an operation on a View, you implicitly affect all of its children as well (Figure 4.13).

This translates naturally to code that might look something like this:

```cpp
// File: view_View.hpp
#include <list>
#include "view_Rectangle.hpp"

class view_View;
typedef std::list<view_View *> tViewList;

class view_View : public view_Rectangle
{
public:
    view_View();
    virtual ~view_View();

    virtual void Render()const = 0;

    void AddChild( view_View * const pChild );
    void RemoveChild( view_View * const pChild );
    void RemoveAllChildren();
```

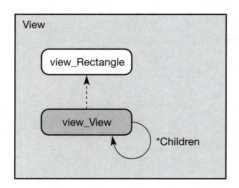

Figure 4.13
Basic view classes.

```cpp
private:
    std::list<view_View *> m_Children;
};

// File: view_View.cpp
#include "view_View.hpp"
#include <algorithm>

// Function objects that perform per-view tasks.
struct ViewDeleter
{
    inline void operator()( view_View * pView )
    {
        delete pView;
    }
};

struct ViewRenderer
{
    inline
    void operator()( view_View const * pView ) const
    {
        pView->Render();
    }
};

view_View::view_View()
: view_Rectangle()
{
}

view_View::~view_View()
{
    // Delete all child views.
std::for_each( m_Children.begin(),
               m_Children.end(),
               ViewDeleter() );
}

/*virtual*/ void view_View::Render() const
{
    // Base class must render all child views.
    std::for_each( m_Children.begin(),
                   m_Children.end(),
                   ViewRenderer() );
}
```

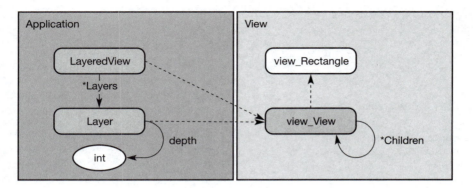

Figure 4.14
Using the `view_View`
class.

Notice that the `Render()` method is pure but implemented. This keeps the `view_View` class abstract, as at this level we don't define so much what we do as how we do it. This has a subtle repercussion on how we define the base rectangle. The key question is 'How do we represent a 2D position on the view?' Consider a game that uses a type of view called a *layered view*. This defines a precise order of drawing for a series of controlled views called *layers*. Each of the layers has an associated integer depth and the layers are rendered in order lowest to highest (Figure 4.14).

(You are permitted to either shudder or marvel at the recursivity here: a layered view is a view that contains layers that are also views, ergo they can be layered views.)

Now, consider how we might define the concept of position for a View. In the base system, an *x* and a *y* ordinate suffice. However, in the layered system, the depth is required to define a position uniquely. This suggests that making the concept of location abstract is essential to a generic representation (Figure 4.15).

Now it becomes the job of the view subclasses to redefine the concept of position should it be required. Each view supports a factory method, a virtual function that manufactures the correct type of positional descriptor.

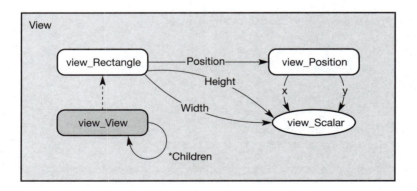

Figure 4.15
Adding position to the
rectangle.

```cpp
// File: view_Types.hpp
typedef float view_Scalar;

// File: view_Position.hpp
#include "view_Types.hpp"

class view_Position
{
public:
    // Public interface omitted for brevity.

private:
    view_Scalar m_x;
    view_Scalar m_y;
};

// File: view_Rectangle.hpp
#include "view_Position.hpp"

class view_Rectangle
{
public:
    // Public interface omitted for brevity.

private:
    view_Position * m_pPosition;
    view_Scalar     m_Width;
    view_Scalar     m_Height;
};

// File: view_View.hpp
#include "view_Rectangle.hpp"

class view_View : public view_Rectangle
{
public:
    virtual view_Position * CreatePosition()
    {
        return new view_Position;
    }

    // Remainder omitted for brevity.
```

```
private:
};

// File: LayeredView.hpp
#include "view_View.hpp"

class LayeredPosition : public view_Position
{
public:
    // Public interface omitted for brevity.

private:
    int m_iDepth;
};

class LayeredView : public view_View
{
    // Class body omitted for brevity.
};
```

There's one more issue to cover: drawing the view. Notice that we provided an abstract method

```
virtual void view_View::Render() const = 0;
```

to do our rendering. It is a bit annoying that we cannot pass a parameter in to say what we are rendering to, and how. Of course, if we did that, then we could start to eat away at a generic representation. So how do we pass in context information without resorting to specific implementation details? We use a Strawman object. Recall that this is an empty class used to supply type information only. In this example, we are passing in an arbitrary context, which the concrete rendering method will know how to convert into something useful:

```
// File: view_Context.hpp
class view_Context
{
public:
    view_Context();
    virtual ~view_Context();

private:
};

// File: view_View.hpp
```

```
class view_Context;

class view_View
{
    // As before, except -
    virtual void Render(view_Context *pContext) const=0;
};
```

Now, supposing that our application has a `render` package that defines a renderer class:

```
class rndr_Renderer
{
    // Lots of funky graphics stuff
};
```

Then we can define the application renderer thus:

```
class Renderer
: public rndr_Renderer
, public view_Context
{
};
```

which allows us to pass renderers directly into the application views:

```
void MyView::Render( view_Context * pContext )
{
    rndr_Renderer * pRenderer =
        static_cast<rndr_Renderer *>( pContext );

    // Draw the view.

    // Important and easily forgotten call to render the
    // child views.
    view_View::Render( pContext );
}
```

A couple of points. First, if you are still mistrustful of multiple inheritance, you can get a functionally (but not syntactically elegant) equivalent class by using single inheritance and embedding a renderer instance member with accessors:

```
class RenderContext : public view_Context
{
public:
    rndr_Renderer & GetRenderer() { return m_Renderer; }
```

```
private:
    rndr_Renderer m_Renderer;
};
```

Second, we need to rewrite the function object that does the rendering in view_View.cpp, given that we have added a parameter:

```
class ViewRenderer
{
public:
    // 'explicit' stops the compiler trying to convert
    // contexts to ViewRenderers at the drop of a hat.
    explicit inline
      ViewRenderer( view_Context * pContext )
    : m_pContext( pContext )
    {
    }

    inline
    void operator()( view_View const * pView ) const
    {
        pView->Render( m_pContext );
    }
}

/*virtual*/
void view_View::Render( view_Context * pContext ) const
{
    std::for_each( m_Children.begin(),
                   m_Children.end(),
                   ViewRenderer( pContext ) );
}
```

The input system

Now we want to define how player input data are managed. Note that this system is most definitely *not* a controller system. It is an *adapter* component that takes data from an external controller system (the specifics of which are intentionally not detailed here) and converts them into a form that is usable by the package and allows them to be passed to the appropriate subsystem.

The atomic class is naturally called Input and is an abstract object (Figure 4.16). However, there is one item of data that we associate with all flavours of input data, and that is an owner tag. This allows us to distinguish where the data came from, and it should be unique for every potential source of input data. We'll use an integer tag field here, though others are feasible.

Figure 4.16
The input object.

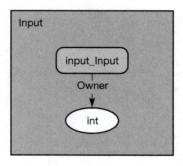

So far, so simple. Assuming that we subclass `input_Input` to give us a concrete object, we then need a mechanism to propagate the associated data to some sort of handler. A C-like solution would be to add a type field to the input data and then switch that on to pass on the correct data:

```
void HandleInput( input_Input * pInput )
{
    switch( pInput->eType )
    {
    case IT_JOYPAD:
        handleJoypad(((InputJoypad *)pInput)->m_Data);
        break;

    case IT_KEYBOARD:
        handleKeys(((InputKeyboard *)pInput)->m_Data);
        break;

    // etc

    default:
        break;
    }
}
```

This isn't a very flexible system. Adding controller types is a pain – the switch statement can become large and unwieldy and, as we've seen before, enumerations are generally a bit of a bind and a compilation bottleneck. Ideally, if we wanted to extend an enumerated type, we might like to express it thus:

```
enum Thing
{
    ZERO,      /* = 0 */
    ONE,       /* = 1 */
    TWO        /* = 2 */
};
```

```
enum ExtendedThing : public Thing
{
    THREE,      /* = 3 */
    FOUR,       /* = 4 */
};
```

But since this isn't allowed, and it could have horrendous side effects if it were, then it's better to abandon enums in favour of our flexible friend polymorphism.

The idea is to have a separate object that the application defines and that handles the various types of input that the application is interested in (and nothing else). This prevents the clogging effect of low-level monolithic systems. The object that provides this functionality is called an InputMap. A base InputMap supports a single virtual function, HandleInput:

```
class input_InputMap
{
public:
    virtual void HandleInput( input_Input & anInput )
    {
    }
};
```

Which does precisely nothing. The cunning bit takes place in your subclasses, where you provide the overloads of HandleInput that do your bidding:

```
class MyInput : public input_Input
{
    // Class body omitted for brevity.
};

class MyInputMap : public input_InputMap
{
public:
    virtual void HandleInput( MyInput & anInput )
    {
        // Do something groovy.
    }
};
```

The hope is that when you call HandleInput with an object of type MyInput, then your 'Do something groovy' code gets executed. Sadly, that hope is in vain. What actually happens is that `input_InputMap::HandleInput()` is called. Why? Because C++ can't do the doubly polymorphic thing – you want it to call the right function depending not only on the type of input map but also on the type of input. In the lingo, only the static type of arguments can be used to select the function to call (at compile time), not the dynamic type (at run time like you need).

Thankfully, there are work-arounds. One possibility is to use `dynamic_cast` to see whether type conversions exist, but this leads to inefficient code that is effectively just a type with a switch – the solution we rejected a while back. The solution we'll use here is called 'double dispatching'. We add an extra virtual function to the Input class called Dispatch:

```
class input_InputMap;

class input_Input
{
public:
    // As before.

    virtual void Dispatch( input_InputMap * pMap ) = 0;
};
```

Within your own subclasses of input, you then implement Dispatch as follows:

```
class MyInput : public input_Input
{
public:
    void Dispatch( input_InputMap * pMap )
    {
        pMap->HandleInput( *this );
    }
};
```

This basically turns a dispatch based on two values into two single dispatches, and it works a treat. That's because within `MyClass`, the type of `*this` is known at compile time (it's always `MyClass`), so the compiler always generates exactly the right call.

An `InputMap` can – and should – support as many types of input subclass as you need. If you fail to provide a `HandleInput` for a particular input class, then the base class (do-nothing) `HandleInput` is automatically invoked, so you can either flag an error or ignore the data.

Figure 4.17 summarises the input components.

```
class MyInputMap
{
public:
    void HandleInput( MyInput & anInput );
    void HandleInput( InputKeyboard & anInput );
    void HandleInput( InputJoypad & anInput );
};
```

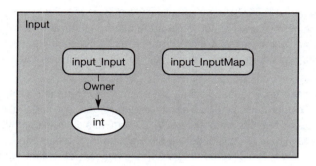

Figure 4.17
Input component
summary.

The GUI bit

Now that we have defined a basic graphical element – a View – and a way of passing input data around, we can combine these elements into an interface package.

So what do we want the GUI package to do? Well, it must support the concept of menus and gadgets (or controls). Notice that both of these elements should respond to user input. However, we also want to classify the in-game state as part of the interface. That requires either thinking of the game as a menu (not very elegant, intuitive or useful) or separating out the entity that receives input behaviour into a property class (Figure 4.18).

Notice here how the packages enforce the separation of the visual representation from the data representation: menus and gadgets have references to their views. This is a sign of a well-ordered system, as it allows the decoupling of how it looks from what it does.

We've added a new type of input map at the GUI level. This input map 'knows' which menu and which gadget it belongs to, so that when a gadget gets input that instructs it to (say) lose focus (i.e. move from being the active gadget to being inactive and change the active gadget to be another one), it can invoke the required functionality in the menu.

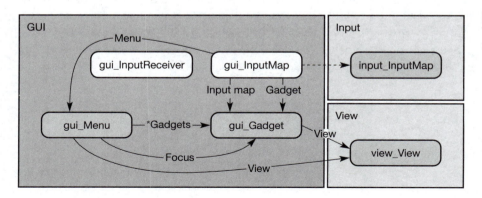

Figure 4.18
The GUI classes.

Strictly speaking, this isn't ideal, allowing lower-level objects (gadgets) to talk to higher-level objects (menus). Also note an implicit circularity (menu has a gadget, gadget has a menu via the input map) and an explicit circularity (gadget has an input map, input map has a gadget). Can we get rid of these traits? More importantly, should we?

Let's deal with the latter question first. We should be concerned if the reusability of our classes is compromised by their relationships to one another. If classes A and B are mutually dependent but we only need A, then there's clearly a potential problem if B must come along too. In this case, we have abstract classes – Menu and Gadget – that must be reused. The design tells us that the concept of a menu without a gadget is impossible. However, the *raison d'être* of a menu is to have gadgets (and if we really need a menu with no gadget, we can subclass to create a 'null' gadget). Conversely, the idea of using a gadget without a menu is bogus. So in the end, although our design is not purist, there is no problem with it as it stands.

Nevertheless, it's an interesting exercise to try to remove the circularities. One way that leaps out is to replace the references one way with dumb data. Instead of having pointers to gadgets (say), give gadgets integer IDs and refer to them that way. This is, in fact, the preferred solution of most GUIs.

Finally, let's look at adding the input-receiving behaviour to the game as we stated above. We need somewhere to inherit or own the behaviour class, and a state class (as discussed in preceding sections) is a very good candidate. Indeed, there are apparently close ties between the state system and the GUI system, and it is tempting to devise the sort of scheme shown in Figure 4.19.

This is a temptation that is well worth resisting. By linking packages at such a fundamental level, we are heading towards the sort of monolithic code systems that we would like to avoid. By keeping systems small and light, we increase the probability of reuse. Looked at another way, there is no necessarily logical or conceptual connection between states and views, so why should we create one?

That's not to say that states shouldn't own views. Quite the reverse. We want to reuse the View package in the game. All that we're saying is that the dependency should be at a higher level than the View and State packages live at, because we might not always want or be able to use views with states. We might create a new package – called Framework, say – that binds the packages at a higher level, as in Figure 4.20.

This is considerably better: we don't impact on the reusability of State and View classes and we create a new, higher-level package that is reusable in its own right.

Figure 4.19
A poor way to associate states and views.

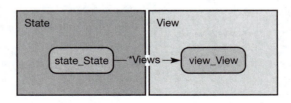

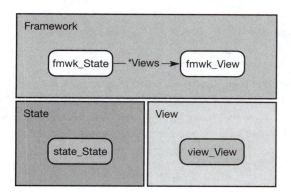

Figure 4.20
A better way to associate
states and views.

So let's assume that there is a class called `GameState` that updates and draws the
game. Figure 4.21 shows how the classes might relate. This works exactly as
required and shows the advantages of factoring common functionality and postponing
the binding of packages to higher levels.

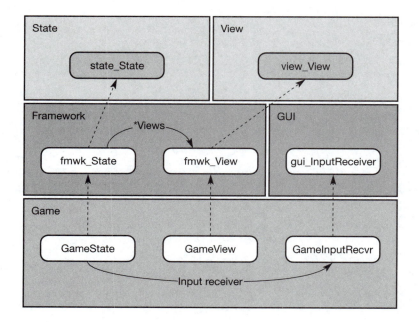

Figure 4.21
The intermediate
Framework component
avoids logically or
physically binding the
View and State
components.

4.4 Summary

- Object orientation fits well with game development.

- C++ may not be the most object-oriented of languages, but it is a good compromise between the speed and power of C and the more 'correct' languages out there.

- GoF patterns have their uses but they also have their costs in terms of both efficiency and impact on the surrounding architecture. Use with care.

The component model for game development

5

5.1 Definition: game engine

> A series of modules and interfaces that allows a development team to focus
> on product game-play content rather than technical content.

This chapter is about game engines. Or rather, it is about avoiding game engines.
Game engines, as we may infer from the above definition, tend to be monolithic
procedural systems, and since this book is banging on about the object-oriented
development of architectures, you can safely assume that the author doesn't think
too highly of them (or at least the monolithic procedural ones).

5.2 Motivation

There are, of course, some really famous and commercially successful game
engines. ID Software's Quake engine, (the appropriately named) Monolith's
Lithtech and Epic Software's Unreal engine are prime examples of well-written
modern game construction systems. They all offer just about everything you'd
need to write a game (though there are applicability issues that depend on your
target genre).

However, this isn't the place to review specific engines. Rather, we are going
to question the usefulness of the concept of an engine and consider the benefits
instead of writing games aided by software components.

5.2.1 Your engine has stalled

So what have I got against game engines? Well, first off, there is that habit they
have of being monolithic. Suppose there's a game engine that has really good
non-player character (NPC) behaviour control, and you'd like to use that in
your game. Can you do it? Chances are you can't. You see, the monolithic
nature of the engine means that the NPC control system uses at least the basic
definitions of the engine, and the artificial intelligence (AI) itself may depend
on extracting information from the environment that the engine itself supports

– for example, line-of-sight calculations might refer to the portals the graphics system uses to prune visible data.

Now what that means in practice is that I cannot use one part of the game engine – the NPC AI – without taking another – the environmental system. Now, what's the betting that the environment system comes with strings too? Perhaps the rendering API? Too bad that our game already has a renderer.

This is our dependency demon from previous chapters rearing its ugly horned head again. This time it's busy gobbling precious RAM and making life more complex than it needs to be. This is illustrated beautifully in Figure 5.1.

This isn't just a matter of losing memory, though. If the engine gains ownership of system hardware, then your objects can be locked out. And the reverse is true, of course: the game engine may fail because you have allocated a resource that it needs, even if that resource is in a part of the engine you do not use. If you have the luxury of being able to modify engine code, then you may be able to fix this problem. However, this is frequently not the case.

For these reasons, it is really very difficult to write a game engine to please most of the people most of the time. The best engines are limited in scope: first-person shooter engines, extreme sports engines, and so on. Which is fine if your company is continually churning out the same sort of game over the course of several years, but the moment you diversify it's back to the drawing board for a new game engine.

5.2.2 The alternative

We really, really, really want to take a big hammer to the idea of an engine and break down the monolith into a series of components. The ideal is to turn the relationships in Figure 5.1 into those shown in Figure 5.2.

The first big change is (as promised) that we've hit the engine with our hammer, and broken it down into two packages: one for rendering, one for AI. There is no logical or physical connection between these packages, and why should there be? Why would renderers need to know anything about AI? And what interest would the AI have in a renderer? (Suggested answers: absolutely no reason whatsoever, absolutely none.)

Figure 5.1

Duplication of code and functionality within an application when using a game engine.

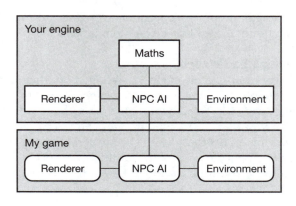

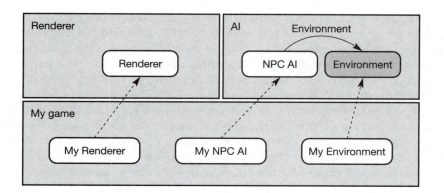

Figure 5.2
Game architecture using
a component philosophy.

Now, we can't break the relationship between the NPC AI and the environment the AI must traverse. However, we can move the complexity to where it belongs – in the game code. OK, I can hear you grumbling at that, so let's back up a little. The idea is to keep everything that is specific to your game environment in the game and to move everything that is generic about environments into the AI package's environment component. Nothing is stopping us from adding a whole bunch of toolkit routines and classes to the AI package that do a lot of common mathematical or logical operations; and we can declare virtual functions in the abstract environment base class that we implement in our concrete environment.

Let's generalise this to define a component architecture. This is a set of independent packages that:

- implements toolkit classes and functions for general common operations;
- declares concrete and abstract classes in such a way as to define a template for how the game classes should be organised.

So far, so grossly simplified. However, it illustrates the point that we have taken a strongly coupled engine and converted it into a series of loosely coupled or even independent building blocks.

Consider, then, the possibilities of working with a component architecture. Writing a game becomes a matter of choosing a set of components and then gluing them together. Where the components define abstract, partial or just plain incorrect functionality, we can override the default behaviours using the help of our friends polymorphism and inheritance. Instead of facing the creation of an entire game engine from scratch, we – in effect – create a bespoke one from off-the-shelf building blocks that can be made into just what we need and little or no more. No need to put up with redundant systems and data any more. No more monolithic engines. Product development time is reduced to writing the glue code, subclassing the required extra behaviour and writing the game. Welcome to a brave new world!

Before we get too carried away, let's apply the brakes ever so gently. The preceding paragraph describes the goal of component-based development. In reality, there is still a lot of hard work, especially in writing those subclasses. However, bear in mind that if written with sufficient care and attention these subclasses become reusable components in themselves. Can you see now why the component model is appealing?

Notice that the component architecture model remains open – it is not geared to write a particular type of game; it remains flexible because behaviours can always be overridden when required; and if a component runs past its sell-by date, it's only a small system to rewrite and there's no worrying about dependency creep because there are no – or, at worst, few – dependencies.

All right, enough of the hard sell. Let's look at how we might go about creating a component architecture. Because this is – as stressed above – an open system, it would be impossible to document every component that you could write, but we'll deal with the major ones in some detail here:

- application-level components
- containers
- maths
- text and language processing
- graphics
- collision
- resource management
- Newtonian physics
- networking.

5.3 Some guiding principles

Before we look in detail at the components, we shall discuss some basic principles – philosophies, if you will – that we will use in their architecture. These principles apply to game software in general, so even if you don't buy the component architecture model wholesale, these are still useful rules to apply.

5.3.1 Keep things local

Rule number 1 is to *keep things as local as you can*. This applies to classes, macros and other data types; indeed, anything that can be exported in a header file. To enforce this to some extent, we can use either a `namespace` for each component or some kind of package prefix on identifier names.[1] Keep the namespace (or prefix) short: four or five characters will do (we use upper-case characters for namespaces).

---

1 There may even be an argument for using both prefixes and name spaces. The reason for presenting a choice is that there are still compilers out there that don't like name spaces.

The first practical manifestation of this is to stick to C++'s built-in data types wherever possible:

```
int, char, short, long, float, double
```

and any unsigned variants of these (should you need them). This is in preference to creating type definitions such as:

```
typedef unsigned char uint8;
```

You may recall from previous chapters that definitions such as these are frequently overused with little justification for their existence. If you need these sort of constructs, make sure they are included in the name space and keep them out of public interfaces:

```
namespace COMP
{
    typedef unsigned char uint8;
}
```

or

```
typedef unsigned char comp_Uint8;
```

Remember that macros do not bind to name spaces and so should be replaced by other constructs (such as in-line functions) where possible, prefixed with the component identifier or perhaps removed altogether.

There is a balance to be struck here. If we were to apply this locality principle universally, we would end up with components that were so self-contained that they would include vast amounts of redundancy when linked into an application. Clearly, this would defeat the object of the exercise. So, for the moment, let's say that there's a notional level of complexity of a class or other construct, which we'll denote by C_0, below which a component can happily implement its own version, and above which we're happy to import the definition from elsewhere. Using C_0 we can define three sets:

- S_- is the set of classes whose complexity is much less than C_0.
- S_+ is the set of classes whose complexity is much greater than C_0.
- S_0 is the set of classes whose complexity is about C_0.

Now although these are very vague classifications, they do give us a feel for what goes into our components and what needs to be brought in (see Table 5.1).

The idea behind the vagueness is to give you, the programmer, some flexibility in your policy. For example, suppose a component requires a very basic

Table 5.1

S_-	S_0	S_+
Integral types …	Containers, vectors, matrices …	Everything else

container (implementing addition, removal and iteration only, say). Even if our policy says containers are imported, simple ('diet', if you will) containers can be defined within our component (and if we've written our containers using templates, then the size of redundant code is exactly zero bytes).

To summarise: by keeping appropriate C++ constructs local to a component you will improve the chances that this component can exist as a functional entity in its own right without the requirement to pull in definitions from elsewhere.

5.3.2 Keep data and their visual representations logically and physically apart

This is an old principle in computer science, and it's still a good one. When we bind any data intimately with the way we visualise those data, we tend to make it awkward if we decide to change the way we view the data in the future. Consider an explosion class. In the early phases of development, we may not have the required artwork or audio data to hand, yet we still wish to present some feedback that an explosion has occurred. One way of doing this might be to simply print the word 'BANG!' in the output console with a position. Here's some abridged sample code to illustrate this:

```cpp
// File: fx_Explosion.hpp
#include <stdio.h>

namespace FX
{

class Explosion
{
public:
    void Render()
    {
        printf( "BANG! (%f,%f,%f)\n", … );
    }

private:
    float m_Pos[3];
};

}
```

We have introduced a dependency between an explosion and the way we view it. When the real artwork finally arrives, we're going to have to change that rendering function even though the explosion has not physically changed. It is always a good idea to keep the simulation and your visualisation of it separate. That way, you can change the representation with the object itself being utterly oblivious. This general principle is shown in Figure 5.3.

The base class `Object` is a data holder only. Apart from a polymorphic method for rendering, nothing more need be specified regarding its visualisation:

```
class Object
{
public:
    virtual void Render( /*?*/ ) {}
};
```

(We haven't specified how we're going to render yet, and it's superfluous to this discussion for the moment, hence the commented question mark.)

Each object that requires to be viewed is subclassed as an `ObjectVisual`, which contains a pointer to a visual. This abstract class confers some kind of renderability on the object, though the object instance neither is aware of nor cares about the details:

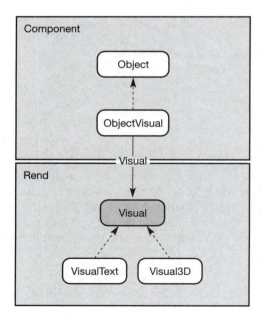

Figure 5.3
Keeping object data and their visual representation separate.

```
class ObjectVisual : public Object
{
public:
    void Render( /*?*/ ) const
    {
        m_pVisual->Render( /*?*/ );
    }
private:
    REND::Visual * m_pVisual;
};
```

The purpose of this principle will become apparent when we consider the historical precedents. In a previous era, with target platforms that were not so powerful, the luxury of having separate functions to update an object and then to render it was often avoided. Code for drawing the object and refreshing its internal state was mixed freely. And, of course, this made changing how the object was viewed next to impossible in the midst of development. By keeping the visual representation separate from the internal state of the object, we make life easier for ourselves in the long run. And we like it when it's easier, don't we?

Let's just sum this principle up in a little snippet of code:

```
class Object
{
public:
    void Render(/*?*/) const
    {
        m_pVisual->Render(/*?*/);
    }

    virtual void Update( Time aDeltaT );
private:
    REND::Visual * m_pVisual;
};
```

Note that the `Render()` method is kept `const` as it should not modify the internal state – when we need to do that, we call `Update()`. This allows us to maintain frame-rate independence – the update makes no assumptions about how long it takes to draw a scene, and we can call it as many times as we wish before calling `Render()` and still get a scene that is visually consistent with the internal state.

5.3.3 Keep static and dynamic data separate

Like separating state and visual representation, this principle makes code maintenance simpler. However, it can also greatly improve code performance and can reduce bloating with redundant data.

The principle is very simple at heart. If you have an object that controls a number of sub-objects, and you want to update the parent, then that involves updating all of the child objects as well. If there aren't too many children, then the cost may be negligible, but if there are lots of objects or the objects have lots of children, then this could become costly.

However, if you know that some of the children are static, then there's no need to update them, so we can reduce the overhead by placing the data that do not change in a separate list.

So that, in a nutshell, is how we can make our code more efficient. Now here's the way we can save data bloating. By recognising the existence of static, unchanging data and separating them from the dynamic data, we can confidently share those static data between any number of objects without fear of one object corrupting everyone else's data (see Figure 5.4).

We'll see this sort of pattern time and time again, so we should formalise it a little. We make a distinction between an *object* and an *object instance*. The former is like a template or blueprint and contains the static data associated with the class. The latter contains the dynamic data (see Figure 5.5).

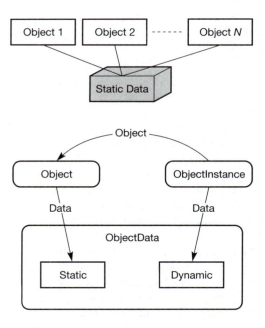

Figure 5.4
Many objects referring to a single static dataset.

Figure 5.5
Separating static and dynamic data using instancing.

The equivalent code is shown below:

```
// File: Object.hpp
class ObjectInstance;

class Object
{
public:
    ObjectInstance * CreateInstance();

private:
    StaticData m_StaticData;
};

// File: ObjectInstance.hpp
class Object;

class ObjectInstance
{
public:
    ObjectInstance( Object & anObject );
private:
    DynamicData m_DynamicData;
    Object & m_Object;
};
```

Notice that the `Object` contains a factory method for creating instances. This method can be polymorphic in hierarchies, and the object classes can easily keep track of all the instances of that object in the game.

That's all pretty abstract – the `Object` could be anything (including a Game Object, a class that gets a whole chapter to itself later on). So let's take a relatively simple example – a 3D model.

We'll assume we have some way of exporting a model from the artist's authoring package, converting that to some format that can be loaded by our game. This format will consist of the following data: a hierarchy description and a series of associated visuals (presumably, but not necessarily, meshes of some kind), as shown in Figure 5.6.

Notice that the abstract `Visual` class can represent a single or multiple `Visual`s using the `VisualPlex` class (which is itself a `Visual`). This is another common and useful pattern. Now we can think about static and dynamic data. Suppose we have an `Animation` class in another component. This will work by manipulating the transformation data inside the hierarchy of an object, which means that our hierarchy data will be dynamic, not static. Also, consider that our model might be *skinned*. Skinning works by manipulating vertex data

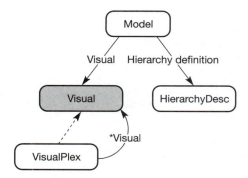

Figure 5.6
Object diagram for the
Model class.

within a mesh – which is the `Visual` side of things. In other words, the `Visual` can be dynamic too. So we consider separating out the static and dynamic data in these classes into *instances*, and in doing so we create a new class – the `ModelInstance` shown in Figure 5.7.

We use factory methods to create instances from the static classes, as illustrated in the following code fragments (as ever, edited for brevity):

```cpp
// File MODEL_Model.h
namespace MODEL
{

class Hierarchy;
class Visual;
class ModelInstance;

class Model
{
public:
    ModelInstance * CreateInstance();
```

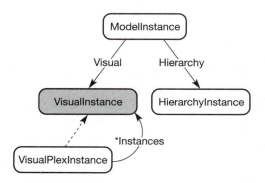

Figure 5.7
Object diagram for the
ModelInstance class.

```cpp
private:
    Visual * m_pVisual;
    Hierarchy * m_pHierarchy;
};

}


// File MODEL_Model.cpp
#include "MODEL_Model.hpp"
#include "MODEL_ModelInstance.hpp"
#include "MODEL_Visual.hpp"
#include "MODEL_Hierarchy.hpp"

ModelInstance * Model::CreateInstance() const
{
    VisualInstance * pVI =
        m_pVisual->CreateInstance();
    Hierarchy * pHier = m_pHierarchy->CreateInstance();

    return new ModelInstance( pVI, pHier );
}


// File:MODEL_Visual.hpp
namespace MODEL
{
class VisualInstance;

class Visual
{
public:
    virtual VisualInstance * CreateInstance() = 0;
};

}


// File:MODEL_VisualPlex.hpp
#include "MODEL_Visual.hpp"
#include "MODEL_Array.hpp"

namespace MODEL
{
class VisualPlexInstance;

class VisualPlex : public Visual
{
```

```
public:
    VisualInstance * CreateInstance() const
    {
        return new VisualPlexInstance(*this);
    }

private:
    array<Visual *> m_Visuals;
};

}


// File:MODEL_VisualPlexInstance.hpp
#include "MODEL_VisualInstance.h"
#include "MODEL_Array.h"

namespace MODEL
{

class VisualPlex;

class VisualPlexInstance : public VisuaInstance
{
public:
    VisualPlexInstance( VisualPlex const & );

private:
    array<VisualInstance *> m_Visuals;
};

}

// File:MODEL_Hierarchy.hpp
namespace MODEL
{
class HierarchyInstance;

class Hierarchy
{
public:
    HierarchyInstance * CreateInstance() const
    {
        return new HierarchyInstance(*this);
    }
};

}
```

5.3.4 Avoid illogical dependencies

Boy, am I fed up of seeing code that looks something like this:

```cpp
#include "FileSystem.h"

class Whatever
{
public:
    // Stuff…
    void Load( FileSystem & aFileSys );
    void Save( FileSystem & aFileSys );
    // More stuff.
};
```

Remember: the idea is that the class should contain just enough data and ways to manipulate those data as necessary, and no more. Now, if the class is related to a file system, then there may be a case for these methods being there, but since the vast majority of classes in a game aren't, then it's safe to assume that they are unjustified in being class members.

So how do we implement loading (and maybe saving)? We delegate it to another object (Figure 5.8).

Rather than create a dependency between component (or package or class) A and element B, we create a new element, AB, which absorbs that dependency. Not only does this keep A and B clean and simple to maintain; it also protects users who need the services of A or B from needing to include and link with the other.

With specific reference to serialisation, for each class that requires the ability to be loaded (or saved), we usually write a loader class to decouple the object from the specifics of the input or output classes.

Figure 5.8

Avoiding the binding of components A and B by creating a third component, AB.

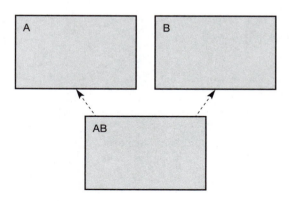

5.3.5 Better dead than thread?

Modern computer and console operating systems almost ubiquitously provide some sort of facility for running concurrent threads of execution within the game. This is a powerful paradigm, but – as always – with power comes danger. Often, less experienced programmers are lured into making such pronouncements as 'Wouldn't it be really cool if, like, each game object ran its AI on a separate thread? Then the objects would just run autonomously, and I could use the threading API to control how the AI was scheduled so I don't overrun frames and …'

Well, my opinion is: 'No, it would not be cool'. If you catch yourself saying something like that in the previous paragraph, step back and take a deep breath. I offer you two very good reasons why you should avoid the use of threads in your game wherever possible:

● The technicalities of thread synchronisation will cause you major headaches, obfuscate code, make debugging difficult and significantly impact development times in the wrong direction.
● If you are considering multiplatform development, then the threading facilities will vary widely from machine to machine, making it difficult to guarantee identical behaviour on the various versions of the game.

In most circumstances, it is both possible and desirable to avoid using threads, and it is easier to not use them than to use them. In other situations, you may find that a thread is required, for example in a network manager that needs to respond to asynchronous events on a socket. However, in these situations the 'threadedness' of the component should be utterly hidden from the user. All the unpleasantness with mutexes (or other flavours of synchronisation object) should be encapsulated logically and preferably physically within the component. A pollable interface should be provided so that any of the asynchronous stuff that may have occurred since the last update can be queried; effectively, a threaded component becomes a message queue that can be interrogated at will when the game dictates, rather than when the kernel decides that it feels like it. In this way, you localise the problems of thread synchronisation and keep control of your code.

5.4 Meet the components

It's now time to look at what goes into making components. The discussions won't be about how to implement the specifics of each component. Instead, we'll discuss something much more powerful: the architectural issues lying behind the component design.

5.4.1 Naming conventions

Within the component architecture, we shall make extensive use of name spaces to (i) group logically and physically related entities and (ii) prevent identifier name collisions. Now – incredibly – some compilers out there still can't handle namespaces, in which case you will have to fall back on the prefixing of class names with component tags. Physically, the components will reside in a subdirectory called 'components' (rocket science, huh?), and a component lives in a single flat subdirectory of that. Files within that directory are named COMPONENT_FileName.Extension.

5.4.2 The application

The application component is extremely simple. We can assume confidently and almost universally that an application will have the following three discrete phases of execution:

- initialisation
- main loop
- shutdown.

The class therefore practically writes itself:

```
namespace APP
{

class Application
{
public:
    virtual bool Initialise() = 0;
    virtual void Terminate() = 0;
    virtual void MainLoop() = 0;
};


}
```

The user's concrete subclass of `APP::Application` can then be used to hang global data from (with, of course, the requisite access control). It is also a good – if not the prototypical – candidate to be a singleton.

Now let's go a step further with the application class: we can add internal state management and user interface components to it (like MFC does, only elegantly). We have already met the state manager and the GUI components in earlier chapters, and they can be built into the application class wholesale because they are entirely generic:

```
// File: APP_Application.hpp
namespace STATE
{
    class StateManager;
}


namespace GUI
{
    class ViewManager;
}


class Renderer;


namespace APP
{

class Application
{
public:
    Application();
    virtual ~Application();

    virtual bool Initialise() = 0;
    virtual void Terminate() = 0;
    virtual void MainLoop() = 0;

    virtual bool Run()
    {
        Time aDeltaT = /* Get elapsed time */;
        bool b = m_pStateMgr->Update( aDeltaT );
        m_pViewMgr->Render( m_pRenderer );

        return( b );
    }

private:
    STATE::StateManager * m_pStateMgr;
    GUI::ViewManager * m_pViewMgr;
    Renderer * m_pRenderer;
}


}
```

We shall have more to say about applications when we look at cross-platform development in a later chapter.

5.4.3 Container components

Where do containers fit in the grand scheme of things? They are extremely common data structures, and it's essential to have a library of various types to hand. But (you may ask), what about the STL, which provides containers for free? Why go to the trouble of creating a core component?

The simple answer is: power and control. STL is big and unwieldy. Its scope is much greater than just the container classes it supports, so to use it simply for that purpose is the sledgehammer/nut scenario. Also, more practically, STL can seriously hurt your compilation and link times, and one of the goals of the component system is to make things go faster.

Nevertheless, it does no harm and quite a lot of good to keep the container classes STL-compatible. There are all these STL algorithms, functors and operators out there to use that will magically work with your own containers provided they support a subset of the public interface's methods and type definitions. Here, for example, is an example of an array class, kept broadly interface-compatible with STL:

```
namespace CONT
{

template<class T> class array;

template<class T>
class array_iterator
{
    friend class array<T>;
private:
    T * m_pItem;

public:
    inline array_iterator() : m_pItem( 0 ) { ; }
    inline array_iterator( T * pItem )
    : m_pItem( pItem ) { ; }

    inline array_iterator( const array_iterator & that )
    : m_pItem( that.m_pItem ) { ; }

    inline
    bool operator==( const array_iterator & that ) const
    { return( m_pItem == that.m_pItem ); }
```

```cpp
    inline array_iterator &
    operator=( const array_iterator & that )
    { m_pItem = that.m_pItem; return( *this ); }

    inline T & operator*()
    { assert( m_pItem != 0 ); return( *m_pItem ); }

    inline
    bool operator!=( const array_iterator & that ) const
    { return !operator==( that ); }

    // Postfix increment.
    inline array_iterator operator++(int)
    {
        assert( m_pItem != 0 );
        T * pNow = m_pItem;
        ++m_pItem;
        return( array_iterator( pNow ) );
    }

    // Prefix increment.
    inline array_iterator & operator++()
    {
        assert( m_pItem != 0 );
        ++m_pItem;
        return( *this );
    }
};

//-------------------------------------------------------

template<class T>
class array_const_iterator
{
    // Much the same as above but const-correct.
};

//-------------------------------------------------------

template <class T>
class array
{
```

```
public:
    /*
     * Constants/typedefs/enums.
     */
        enum { GROW_FACTOR = 2 };

        typedef array_iterator<T> iterator;
        typedef array_const_iterator<T> const_iterator;
        typedef T data_type;

    /*
     * Lifecycle.
     */
        array();
        array( int iInitialSize );
        array( const array<T> & that );
        ~array();

    /*
     * Polymorphism.
     */

    /*
     * API.
     */

        T & operator [] (int n);
        const T    & operator [] (int n) const;
        int size() const;
        bool empty() const;
        int capacity() const;
        void resize( int iNewSize );
        void reserve( int iSize );
        void clear();

        void push_back( const T & anItem );
        void push_front( const T & anItem );
        void pop_front();
        void pop_back();
        void insert( iterator i, const T & anItem );
        void erase( const iterator & iPos );
        void erase( const iterator & iStart,
                    const iterator & iEnd );
```

```
        void remove( const T & anItem );
        void remove_at( int iIndex );

        iterator       begin();
        const_iterator begin() const;
        iterator       end();
        const_iterator end() const;

        T       & back();
        const T & back() const;

        T       & front();
        const T & front() const;

        array<T> & operator=( const array<T> & that );

private:
    /*
     * Helpers.
     */

    /*
     * Data.
     */
        int     m_iNumItems;
        int     m_iNumAllocated;
        T     * m_Items;

}; // end class
```

The implementation can be kept clean, simple and efficient, yet STL's algorithms can be used seamlessly (and because it is interface-compatible):

```
#include <algorithm>

// An array.
CONT::array<int> aSomeInts(10);

// A function object
struct MyFunctor
{
public:
    // Some compilers will only inline code
    // if the data declarations are made first.
    int m_iCount;
```

```
public:
    inline MyFunctor()
    : m_iCount(0)
    {}

    inline void operator()( int & n )
    {
        n = m_iCount++;
    }
};

std::for_each( aSomeInts.begin(),
               aSomeInts.end(),
               MyFunctor() );
```

The array class still has quite a rich interface – there is a lot of control over size, and the array can grow when data are added for example. In some cases, even this is overkill when all that is required is an integer-indexed array of fixed size but (unlike a C array data type) that has controlled access,[2] so we have a set of 'fast, fixed-size' container classes denoted by an _ff postfix:

```
namespace CONT
{

template<class T,int N>
class pocket
{
public:
    // Types.
    typedef T data_type;
    typedef pocket_iterator<T> iterator;
    typedef pocket_const_iterator<T> const_iterator;

    // Lifecycle.
    pocket();

    // API
    void Clear();
    void AddItem( const T& Item );
    void RemoveItem( const T & Item );
    void RemoveAt( int iIndex );
    int  GetSize() const;
```

---

2 Many of the most hideous bugs I have met are manifestations of writing data past the end or before the beginning of an array. There is, therefore, great benefit from controlling access to a standard array.

```
    T &  operator[]( int n );
    const T & operator[]( int n ) const;
    bool Full() const;
    bool Find( const T & Item ) const;
    T *    Get( const T & Item ) const;
    int  GetIndex( const T & Item ) const;

    iterator       begin();
    const_iterator begin() const;
    iterator       end();
    const_iterator end() const;

private:
    T   m_aItem[ N ];
    int m_iIndex;
};

}
```

The most commonly used container classes in the component system are as follows:

- arrays
- lists
- queues
- hash tables
- set
- bit set
- stack
- heap
- string.

Your container component should ideally support all these types as well as their _ff variants, if appropriate. When writing them, it is important to try to minimise the number of dynamic memory operations they make, for two reasons. First, they are typically expensive operations and they may be invoked frequently. Second, data scattered in memory will almost certainly cause data cache misses, and iteration over the controlled elements will be slow because of this.

As an example of designing with this in mind, consider the hash table container. A common way to implement this is as follows:

```
template<class Type,class Key>
class hash_table
{
```

```
public:
// Interface.
private:
    enum { NUM_BUCKETS = 31 };
    std::list<Type> m_aBuckets[ NUM_BUCKETS ];
};
```

This open hashing system is technically superior in performance to a closed system (where we insert a new colliding element in the next available space in a fixed-size table), but those list classes can scatter nodes randomly in memory and the actual performance will be desperately poor, as I found out to my surprise and horror when writing a high-level collision management component.

5.4.4 Maths component

There are three tiers of maths components: low-level, intermediate-level and high-level classes. Low-level classes comprise:

● 2D, 3D and 4D vectors
● 2×2, 3×3 and 4×4 matrices
● quaternions
● random numbers
● transcendental functions.

Intermediate-level classes include:

● general vector class
● general *mxn* matrix.

High-level classes comprise:

● complex numbers
● interpolators
● integrators.

We'll examine these in turn. The low-level classes essentially support data types, and these will be used extensively by other components. They will therefore need to be high-performance classes: no virtual functions, no heavy memory management, and no flexible data representations. We have already implied this by separating out the 2D, 3D and 4D vectors and matrices. Though it is initially tempting to write a totally generic vector or matrix class using templates and then specialise for both stored data type and dimension, this isn't a good choice. Consider the constructor of a generic *n*-dimensional vector:

```
template<class T,int N>
inline Vector<T>::Vector( T v[] )
{
    for( int j = 0; j < N; ++j )
    {
        m_v[j] = v[j];
    }
}
```

That for loop is particularly inefficient, and it will appear in many places in the vector class implementation. In some places (the example above is one of them), it can be replaced by more efficient constructs, but generally it is unavoidable. The only recourses are to use some nasty template trickery to effectively write:

```
template<class T,int N>
inline Vector<T>::Vector( T v[] )
{
    m_v[0] = v[0];
    m_v[1] = v[1];
    //...
    m_v[N] = v[N];
}
```

(the details of which are opaque and may not be supported over all toolsets), or to relax the requirement to specify the dimension as a template parameter and write separate Vector2, Vector3 and Vector4 classes (and similarly for matrices). We'll go the latter route for the moment. Here's the 2D class body:

```
// File: MATHS_Vector2.hpp
namespace MATHS
{

template<class T>
class Vector2
{
private:
    T m_v[2];

public:
    // Deliberately empty default ctor.
    inline Vector2()
    {
    }
```

```cpp
    inline Vector2( T v0, T v1 )
    {
        m_v[0] = v0;
        m_v[1] = v1;
    }

    inline Vector2( T v[] )
    {
        m_v[0] = v[0];
        m_v[1] = v[1];
    }

//
// Access.
//
    T & x() { return m_v[0]; }
    T & y() { return m_v[1]; }
    T   x() const { return m_v[0]; }
    T   y() const { return m_v[1]; }
    T & operator[]( int Element );
    T operator[]( int Element ) const;

//
// Arithmetic.
//
    // Addition and subtraction.
    Vector2<T> operator+( const Vector2<T> & v ) const;
    Vector2<T> operator-( const Vector2<T> & v ) const;

    Vector2<T> & operator+=( const Vector2<T> & v );
    Vector2<T> & operator-=( const Vector2<T> & v );

    // Unary minus.
    const Vector2<T> operator-() const;

    // Scale by constant.
    friend Vector2<T> operator*(T s,const Vector2<T>&v);
    friend Vector2<T> operator*(const Vector2<T>&v,T s);
    Vector2<T> & operator*=( T s );

    // Dot product.
    T operator*( const Vector2<T> & v ) const

    // Division by constant
    Vector2<T> & operator/=( T Divisor );

    // Length.
    T Length() const;
    T LengthSquared() const;
```

```
    // Make unit length.
    Vector2<T> Normalised() const;
    void        Normalise();
    T Normalise( Vector2<T> * const pvUnit ) const;

    // Comparison.
    bool operator==( const Vector2<T> & v ) const;
};

}
```

The `Vector3<T>` and `Vector4<T>` classes are similar – but not quite identical.
The vector or cross-product is defined only for 3D vectors, for example.

Not surprisingly, the `Matrix22<T>`, `Matrix33<T>` and `Matrix44<T>` classes
are written using similar principles. However, we need to be a little careful when
writing the matrix classes. In the back of our minds, we wish to be able to write
a snippet of code like this:

```
typedef Vector3<float> Vector3f;
typedef Matrix33<float> Matrix33f;
Vector3f MVMul3(Matrix33f const& m,Vector3f const&v)
{
    return m*v;
}
```

In other words, multiply a vector by a matrix. Now, where would that multiply
operator reside? In the Vector3 class maybe? Well, there is a feeling that a
matrix is a slightly higher-level object than a vector, so simply in terms of basic
design that seems wrong. In the matrix class, then? Well, maybe, but remember
our principle about avoiding illogical dependencies and keeping classes simple.
If our matrix class deals only with matrices, then that's a simple, clean object
design. So let's apply the logic of said principle and put the multiplication into a
separate linear algebra component (see Figure 5.9).

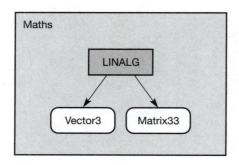

Figure 5.9
Avoiding the binding of
matrices and vectors by
creating a linear algebra
subcomponent.

While we're thinking about this, what else would go into the linear algebra component? Anything that could turn a vector into a matrix or a matrix into a vector. For example, getting a row or column of a matrix, or creating a skew matrix from a vector (don't worry if that means zip to you, since it will be explained later). In code:

```cpp
// File: MATHS_LinearAlgebra.hpp
#include "MATHS_Vector3.hpp"
#include "MATHS_Matrix33.hpp"

namespace MATHS
{
/*
 * Note: operators need to be in the MATHS namespace.
 */
inline
Vector3f operator*(Matrix33f const &A,Vector3f const &x)
{
    return Vector3f( A(0,0)*x[0] + … );
}

//----------------------------------------------------------

namespace LINALG
{

//----------------------------------------------------------

inline Vector3f MultiplyTranspose( Matrix33f const & A,
                                   Vector3f const & x )
{
    return Vector3f( A(0,0)*x[0] + … );
}

//----------------------------------------------------------

inline Vector3f GetColumn(Matrix33f const & A, int iCol)
{
    assert( (iCol >= 0) && (iCol <= 2) );

    return Vector3f( A(0,iCol),A(1,iCol), A(2,iCol) );
}

//----------------------------------------------------------
```

```
inline Matrix33f CreateSkewMatrix( Vector3f const & x )
{
    return Matrix33f( 0.0f, -x[2],  x[1],
                      x[2],  0.0f, -x[0],
                     -x[1],  x[0],  0.0f );
}

} // end of namespace LINALG

} // end of namespace MATHS
```

This is an unusual way of structuring code, but it is quite liberating and extremely powerful.

Quaternions are naturally four-dimensional vectors, but they have an arithmetic unique to themselves. In addition, there are operations to convert between quaternions and matrices, to transform vectors by the rotation that a unit quaternion represents, and so on. As you should have guessed, these belong in the linear algebra subcomponent of the maths component.

Next up: random numbers. Now there's a lot of maths out there detailing how to write random-number generators (RNGs) with specific properties, but that's beyond the scope of this book. The RNG I've used consistently in games is based on the C standard library generator and it's been just fine. Architecturally, it's important that you don't simply use the rand() and srand() functions: not that there's anything wrong *per se* with these calls, but because they may be implemented differently from library to library or platform to platform. In some circumstances, that may make no difference. But when it does …

There are two classes of random numbers needed by games: a plausibly random sequence that is the same every time through the game or level so that events are repeatable (and remember, repeatable means easily testable); and a sequence that is plausibly random and doesn't (necessarily) repeat every time through. This motivates us to have at least two random-number generators in the game, and you can't have that with the standard library calls. Time to build some classes:

```
// File: MATHS_Random.hpp
namespace MATHS
{

class RandomGenerator
{
public:
    RandomGenerator() : m_iSeed( 0 ) { ; }
    RandomGenerator( float fSeed ) { SetSeed( fSeed ); }
    RandomGenerator( int iSeed ) : m_iSeed( iSeed ) {}
    ~RandomGenerator() {}
```

```cpp
    void  SetSeed( float fSeed );
    void  SetSeed( int iSeed );
    float OneToZero();
    float MinusOneToOne();
    float Ranged( float fMin, float fMax );
    int      Ranged( int iMin, int iMax );

    static RandomGenerator Default;
private:
    int m_iSeed;
};

inline
void RandomGenerator::SetSeed( int iSeed )
{
    m_iSeed = iSeed;
}

//----------------------------------------------------------

inline
void RandomGenerator::SetSeed( float fSeed )
{
    m_iSeed = *( (int *)&fSeed );
}

//----------------------------------------------------------

inline
float RandomGenerator::OneToZero()
{
    m_iSeed = 1664525L * m_iSeed + 1013904223L;

    int iSixteenSixteen =
      (((m_iSeed >> 10)^(m_iSeed << 10))& 0x7fff) << 1;
    float fResult =
        (((float)(iSixteenSixteen & 0xffff))/65536.0f);

    fResult += (float)( iSixteenSixteen >> 16 );

    return fResult;
}

//----------------------------------------------------------
```

```
inline
float RandomGenerator::MinusOneToOne()
{
    return (float) ( (OneToZero() - 0.5f) * 2 );
}


//----------------------------------------------------

inline
float RandomGenerator::Ranged( float fMin, float fMax )
{
    return( fMin + ((fMax - fMin) * OneToZero()) );
}


//----------------------------------------------------

inline
int RandomGenerator::Ranged( int iMin, int iMax )
{
    return( int(Ranged(float(iMin),float(iMax))));
}


}
```

We can now replace `rand()` completely by the following function:

```
namespace MATHS
{


template<class T>
T Random( T tMin, T tMax )
{
    float fMin = float(tMin);
    float tMax = float(tMax);
    return RandomGenerator::Default.Ranged(fMin,fMax);
}


}
```

All this brings us neatly on to transcendental functions. They're called transcendentals because they transcend ordinary algebraic functions. They're more familiar to you as `sin()`, `cos()`, `tan()`, their inverses, and the related `exp()`, `log()`, `log10()` and hyperbolic functions. Now, your game will probably need the trig functions more than the others, but they're all useful in their place.

Bearing in mind that all these functions take a single argument and return a single value, there isn't really a problem with having a procedural interface:

```cpp
// File: MATHS_TranscendentalFunctions.hpp
#include <cmath>

namespace MATHS
{

template<class T>
inline T Sin( T x )
{
    return( (T)::sinf(float(x));
}

// and so on...
}
```

Implementing our own transcendentals lets us control how the functions are evaluated. For example, the trig functions can be implemented by table look-up (though the days when that was a requirement are fast receding).

Now it's time to consider the intermediate-level maths components. Interestingly, they are generalisations of low-level components, adding the ability to change size dynamically to those classes. This is accompanied by a growth in the computational cost of using these classes.

The `MATHS::Vector` class is a general-purpose mathematical vector. It is resizable like an array class, but it supports all the arithmetical and mathematical operations of the low-level vector classes (except the cross-product).

```cpp
// File: MATHS_Vector.hpp
namespace MATHS
{

template<class T>
class Vector
{
public:
    // Lifecycle.
    Vector( int Size );
    Vector( const Vector<T> & rVector );
    ~Vector();
```

```
    // Access.
    int GetSize() const { return m_iSize; }
    void SetSize( int iNewSize );

    // Operators.
    Vector<T> & operator=( const Vector<T> & rVector );
    T           operator[]( int n ) const;
    T &         operator[]( int n );

    Vector<T> & operator+=( const Vector<T> & rVector );
    Vector<T> & operator-=( const Vector<T> & rVector );
    Vector<T> & operator*=( T s );
    friend T operator*(const Vector<T>&v1,
                        const Vector<T> &v2);
    friend Vector<T> operator+( const Vector<T> & v1,
                                const Vector<T> & v2 );
    friend Vector<T> operator-(const Vector<T> & v1,
                               const Vector<T> & v2);
    friend Vector<T> operator*(T s,const Vector<T> & v);
    friend Vector<T> operator*(const Vector<T>& v, T s);
    friend bool operator==( const Vector<T> & v1,
                            const Vector<T> & v2 );
    const Vector<T> operator-();

    // Other processing.
    T  Length() const { return Sqrt( LengthSquared() ); }
    T  LengthSquared() const { return((*this)*(*this)); }
    void     Normalise();
    Vector<T> Normalised() const;
    void     Fill( T tValue );

private:
    int      m_iSize;
    int      m_iAllocatedSize;
    T    *  m_Data;

};

}
```

Structurally, there's very little new here. However, its relation, the arbitrarily sized matrix, is quite a bit more complicated than its low-level cousins. The complexity comes about because simple matrix operations can cause quite a number of dynamic memory operations. Consider, for example, the `Transpose()` method. This turns an $n \times m$ matrix into an $m \times n$ matrix (see Figure 5.10).

Figure 5.10
Transposing a matrix
changes its shape.

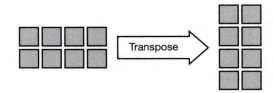

Unless the matrix is square – $n \times n$ – there's going to be quite a bit of shuffling around of data in memory to effect that transposition. In order to make this a bit easier, we create an auxiliary class called a `Buffer`, which is private to the matrix. Buffers (and hence matrices) can be constructed from either a new block of dynamic memory or a preallocated static memory block. The latter allows us on certain target platforms to point the matrix at areas of fast (uncached) memory, and in general it can avoid the multiple calls to dynamic allocations and deletions that can occur during seemingly innocent matrix operations.

```
// File: MATHS_Matrix.hpp
namespace MATHS
{

template<class T>
class Matrix
{
public:
    // Error codes
    enum Error
    {
        ERR_NONE,
        ERR_OUT_OF_MEMORY,
        ERR_SINGULAR
    };

    // Lifecycle.
    Matrix();


Matrix( int iRows, int iCols );
    Matrix( const Matrix<T> & m );
    Matrix( int iRows, int iCols, void * pBuffer );
        // Construct a matrix from a static buffer.
        // Note that the buffer can be single or
        // multi-dimensional, ie float aBuffer[n*m]
        // or float aBuffer[n][m] will work equally
        // well.
```

```
~Matrix();

// Management.
bool Resize( int iRows, int iCols,
                bool bRetainData=true );
int  GetSizeBytes() const;

// Operations.
void      Transpose();
Matrix<T> Transposed() const;
int       Rank() const;
int       Rows() const;
int       Columns() const;
int       Capacity() const;
Matrix<T> GetSubMatrix( int iStartCol,
                        int iStartRow,
                        int iRows,
                        int iCols ) const;
bool   IsSquare() const;

// Unary/class operators.
Matrix<T> & operator-();
T     operator()( int iRow, int iCol ) const;
T &   operator()( int iRow, int iCol );
Matrix<T> & operator=( const Matrix<T> & m );
Matrix<T> & operator+=( const Matrix<T> & m );
Matrix<T> & operator-=( const Matrix<T> & m );
Matrix<T> & operator*=( T s );

Matrix<T> operator+( const Matrix<T> & m ) const;
Matrix<T> operator-( const Matrix<T> & m ) const;

// Binary operators.
friend Matrix<T> operator*( const Matrix & m1,
                            const Matrix & m2 );
friend Matrix<T> operator*(T s,const Matrix<T>&m1);
friend Matrix<T> operator*(const Matrix<T>&m1,T s);

// In-place operations.
static void InPlaceTranspose( Matrix<T> & rTrans,
                              const Matrix<T> & m );
static void InPlaceMultiply( Matrix<T> & rProduct,
                             const Matrix<T> & m1,
                             const Matrix<T> & m2 );
```

```
private:
    class Buffer
    {
    private:
        T *      m_pData;
        int      m_iStride;
        bool     m_bStatic;
    public:
        Buffer(int iRows, int iColumns);
        Buffer(int iRows, int iColumns, void *pBuffer);
        ~Buffer();

        T   GetAt( int iRow, int iCol ) const;
        T & GetReference( int iRow, int iCol );
        void SetAt( int iRow, int iCol, T tValue );

inline T * GetDataPtr() const;
    inline bool IsStatic() const;
};

    int        m_iRowCount;
    int        m_iColCount;
    Buffer<T> * m_pBuffer;
};

}
```

As with their low-level cousins, the matrix and vector classes are kept logically and physically separate by locating functions that would ordinarily bind them in the linear algebra subcomponent. For example, here's the function that gets the *n*th column of a matrix:

```
// File: MATHS_LinearAlgebra.hpp
//...
#include "MATHS_Matrix.hpp"
#include "MATHS_Vector.hpp"
//...

namespace MATHS
{

template<class T>
Vector<T> GetColumn( Matrix<T> const & m );

// etc.
}
```

What's that you say? A C-style (free) function? Isn't that not at all object-oriented? Worry not. Remember that a class member function is really a C function that gets a hidden 'this' pointer. Besides, consider what one objective of encapsulation is – to protect client code from internal changes to a class. A possible way of measuring encapsulation loss, therefore, is to consider how many files need to be recompiled as the result of the addition or removal of a method. If we added `GetColumn()` as a member function, then all the client files that included MATHS_Matrix.hpp would rebuild. By adding it as a free function in another file, we have preserved encapsulation.

Finally, it's time to look at the high-level services offered by the maths component. The first – and most straightforward – class to consider is the complex number class. Now, it's going to be pretty unusual to find complex numbers in game code. However, when we write tools that perform intricate offline graphical calculations, it is not beyond the bounds of possibility that complex solutions to equations may arise, so a complex number class is useful to have ready to hand.

In this circumstance, the STL version,

```
template<class T> std::complex<T>
```

will suffice, because although it's pretty top-heavy it's only really used in code that is not time-critical.

The next – and altogether more important – class (actually set of classes) is the interpolators. In non-technical terms, an interpolator is a mathematical function (here, restricted to a single real parameter) that returns a real value based on a simple relationship over an interval. For example, a constant interpolator returns the same value (said constant) whatever the argument (see Figure 5.11a). A linear interpolator returns a value based on a linear scale (see Figure 5.11b).

We start off with a base class that describes the generic behaviour:

```
// File: MATHS_Interpolator.hpp
namespace MATHS
{
```

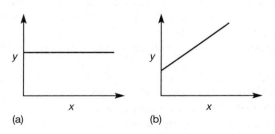

(a) (b)

Figure 5.11
Constant and linear interpolants.

```
template<class T>
class Interpolator
{
public:
    virtual T Interpolate( T x ) = 0;
};


}
```

And we extend the behaviour in the expected fashion:

```
// File: MATHS_InterpolatorConstant.hpp
#include "MATHS_Interpolator.h"

namespace MATHS
{

template<class T>
class InterpolatorConstant : public Interpolator<T>
{
private:
    T m_C;

public:
    InterpolatorConstant( T c )
    : m_C(c)
    {
    }

    T Interpolate( T x )
    {
        return m_C;
    }
};


}
```

This defines a series of classes, each using a higher-degree polynomial to compute the return value, none of which is particularly powerful on its own.
However, consider the graph shown in Figure 5.12. A relationship like this
might exist in a driving game's vehicle model between engine rpm and the
available torque.

Of course, this is a greatly simplified model, but it has most of the characteristics of the real thing. The range of the rpm parameter will be something
between zero and 10 000. Now, we could encode this graph as a look-up table. If
there's one 32-bit float per entry, that's nearly 40KB for the table, which is quite a

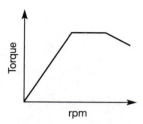

Figure 5.12
Piecewise relationship
between engine rpm and
available torque.

lot considering how simple the relationship looks. It's what's known as a 'piecewise relationship', the first piece being increasingly linear, the second constant, and the third decreasingly linear. So let's design a piecewise interpolator object. After many hours in my laboratory, the results are as shown in Figure 5.13.

The piecewise interpolator contains a series of (non-overlapping) ranges, each of which has its own interpolator (which can itself be piecewise). The code looks like this:

```cpp
// File: MATHS_InterpolatorPiecewise.hpp
#include "MATHS_Interpolator.hpp"
#include "MATHS_Array.hpp"

namespace MATHS
{

template<class T>
class InterpolatorPiecewise : public Interpolator<T>
{
private:
    struct Range
    {
        T tMin;
        T tMax;
        Interpolator<T> * pInterp;
    };
    array<Range> m_Ranges;
```

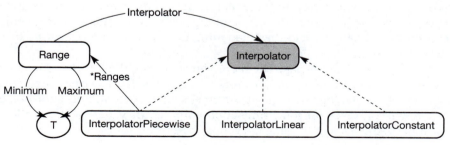

Figure 5.13
Object diagram for the
interpolator component.

```
public:
    T Interpolate( T x )
    {
        // Find interval containing x.
        for( int j = 0; j < m_Ranges.size(); ++j )
        {
            Range & r = m_Ranges[j];
            if ( x >= r.tMin && x < r.tMax )
            {
                return(r.pInterp->Interpolate(x));
            }
        }

        // Return 0 for illustration - you should add an
        // "otherwise return this" value.
        return( T(0) );
    }

    void AddInterval(T tMin,T tMax,Interpolator *pInt);
    //...
};
```

```
}
```

Integrators: who needs 'em? Well, there are uses for these fairly high-power classes as we'll see later, but I should digress a little and explain what they actually are for those readers who don't know.

Suppose there's a projectile with position (vector) **x** and velocity vector **v**. Then, after a time interval t the new position is given by

$$\mathbf{x}(t) = \mathbf{x} + t^*\mathbf{v}$$

However, this works only if **v** is constant during the time interval. If **v** varies, then the calculated position will be wrong. To get better approximations to the new position, we can split t into successively smaller slices of time, calculate the position at the end of each of these subintervals, and accumulate the resulting change. And that process is the job of an integrator. Since games are frequently concerned with objects, velocities and positions, you might appreciate why they have their uses.

Integration is not cheap. The more you subdivide the interval, the more work gets done, though you get more accurate results. For basic projectile motion, objects falling under gravity or other simple cases, an integrator would be overkill. However, for some simulation purposes, they are essential. So let's focus our OO skills on designing integrator classes.

The first thing to realise is that there are many ways to perform the integration. Each method comes with an associated error term and stability. A stable integrator has the property that the error term stays small no matter how big the interval *t* is. As you can imagine, very stable integrators are gratuitously expensive in CPU cycles. However, it's possible to write a moderately stable integrator (which will work nicely for small time intervals) that is reasonably accurate. So we're looking at a family of integrator classes based on an abstract base class.

However, there's a twist. Integration is something that is done to an object, so consider the following method declaration:

```
void Integrate( /*???*/ & aClient );
```

Exactly what type do we pass in? The integrator needs to be able to get at client data, so we should think about providing an abstract mix-in property class with an abstract interface that allows just that. As a first step on this path, consider the following class:

```
// File: MATHS_VectorFunction.hpp
#include "MATHS_Vector.hpp"

namespace MATHS
{

typedef Vector<float> VectorNf;

class VectorFunction
{
public:
    virtual void GetArgument( VectorNf & v ) = 0;
    virtual void GetValue( VectorNf & v ) = 0;
    virtual void SetArgument( VectorNf const &v ) = 0;
    virtual int GetDimension() const = 0;
};

}
```

This class abstractly represents a vector equation

$$\mathbf{y} = \mathbf{f}(\mathbf{x})$$

where **f** is a function that takes a vector **x** as an argument and returns a vector **y**.

With the aid of this class, we can create a subclass that confers the property of being integrable:

```cpp
// File: MATHS_Integrator.hpp
#include "MATHS_VectorFunction.hpp"

namespace MATHS
{

class IsIntegrable : public VectorFunction
{
public:
    IsIntegrable () : VectorFunction() { ; }

    void GetStateVector( VectorNf & vLhs );
    void GetDerivativeVector( VectorNf & vLhs );
    void SetStateVector( VectorNf & vResult );
};

inline
void IsIntegrable::GetStateVector( VectorNf & vLhs )
{
    GetArgumentVector( vLhs );
}

//------------------------------------------------------

inline
void IsIntegrable::GetDerivativeVector( VectorNf & vRhs )
{
    GetFunctionVector( vRhs );
}

//------------------------------------------------------

inline
void IsIntegrable::SetStateVector( VectorNf & rResult )
{
    SetArgumentVector( rResultVector );
}


}
```

Now we can write our abstract integrator class:

```
class Integrator
{
public:
    // Lifecycle.
    Integrator();
    virtual ~Integrator() { ; }

    // Access methods.
    int    GetNumberOfUnknowns() const;
    void   SetStepGranularity( float Step );
    float  GetStepGranularity() const;
    float  GetIntegrationTime() const;

    virtual void SetNumberOfUnknowns( int n );

    // The integrator.
    virtual bool Integrate(IsIntegrable*,float h);
    virtual bool Step(IsIntegrable*, float h ) = 0;

protected:
    bool singleStep( IsIntegrable * pClient, float h );

    VectorNf m_ResultVector;
    VectorNf m_InputVector;
    VectorNf m_RhsVector;

private:
    // Maximum step size for one iteration. If h is
    // greater than this value then several iterations
    // will be performed as required.
    float m_StepGranularity;

    int       m_iNumberOfUnknowns;
    VectorNf m_InitialVector;

    // Current time within the integrator (from 0 to
    // step size) within Integrate().
    // If there is an early bail-out (Step returns
    // false), this will contain the time prior to the
    // exit step.
    float m_CurrentTime;
};

}
```

Figure 5.14
Object diagram for the
integrator component.

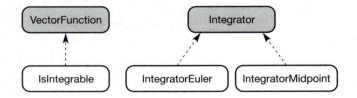

All of the hard work is done in the subclass implementation of the virtual function `Step( IsIntegrable * pClient, float h )`. All of the data that the integrator needs are extracted via the `IsIntegrable` interface so there is no need to violate encapsulation at any level. The only slight concern we might have is the protected status of the Input, Result and Rhs vectors within the integrator base class. In-line set and get accessors can quell your fears. The overall structure is summed up in Figure 5.14.

The `IntegratorEuler` and `IntegratorMidpoint` subclasses express two simple ways of performing the integration (the details of which are unimportant here). Other methods exist, but an object that has a reference to an integrator need not care about exactly what mathematics are going on inside the `Step()` method.

5.4.5 Text and language processing

Most games process text in some way. Although it is bulky and slow to turn into a useful internal format, it is very handy early on in the product lifecycle to be able to read text files with an eye to reading their binary equivalents later on in development. With this in mind, we define an abstract stream class whose subclasses can be either ASCII streams or binary stream readers – a client who has a pointer to a stream neither knows nor cares (see Figure 5.15).

The interface class will look something like this:

```
// File: STRM_ReadStream.hpp
namespace STRM
{
```

Figure 5.15
Object diagram showing
the stream component.

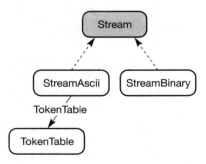

```cpp
class Position;

class ReadStream
{
public:
    /*
     * Constants/typedefs/enums.
     */
        enum
        {
            INVALID_TOKEN = -1
        };

    /*
     * Lifecycle.
     */
        ReadStream();
        virtual ~ReadStream();

    /*
     * Polymorphism.
     */
        virtual bool Open( const char * pFilePath ) = 0;
        virtual void Close() = 0;
        virtual int ReadToken() = 0;
        virtual int ReadByte() = 0;
        virtual int ReadShort() = 0;
        virtual int ReadInt() = 0;
        virtual float ReadFloat() = 0;
        virtual int ReadString( char * pBuffer,
                                int iBufferSize ) = 0;
        virtual bool EndOfStream() const = 0;
        virtual int GetLength() const = 0;
        virtual void Reset() = 0;
        virtual Position GetPosition() const = 0;
        virtual void SetPosition(const Position &aPos)=0;

    /*
     * API.
     */

protected:
    /*
     * Helpers.
     */
```

```
private:
    /*
     * Data.
     */
}; // end class


}
```

No big surprises there. The subclass that reads ASCII text requires a simple token-matching table with some way to recognise delimiters. The assumption is that we are not considering text data that consist of complex grammar – if we were, we'd be throwing some more heavyweight classes around or using code generated by yacc/lex or antlr. The `TokenTable` class encapsulates the translation functionality, mapping a string object to an integer token value – an ideal job for a hash table:

```
typedef CONT::hash_table<int,CONT::string> tTokenMap;
```

One of the big shocks for new developers is the complexities and subtleties of writing software that needs foreign language support. The problems are, in reality, not difficult to solve, but they will cause difficulties if you attempt to retro-fit them into an existing game structure. The good news is that by and large, linguistic support is not difficult to add. A string table class is just about all that's required, mapping an integer to a text string (see Figure 5.16).

Figure 5.16
The constituents of a
string table.

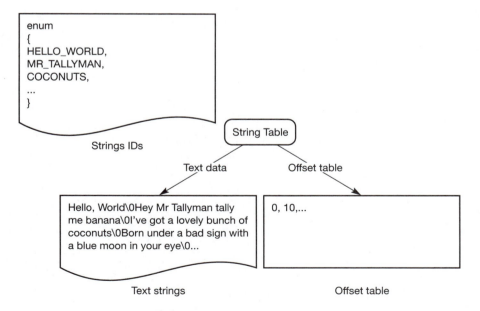

```
enum
{
HELLO_WORLD,
MR_TALLYMAN,
COCONUTS,
...
}
```

Strings IDs

String Table

Text data   Offset table

Hello, World\0Hey Mr Tallyman tally
me banana\0I've got a lovely bunch of
coconuts\0Born under a bad sign with
a blue moon in your eye\0...

0, 10,...

Text strings   Offset table

Some magical external tool exports three files: a C++ header file that contains string enumerations with helpful names, a binary data file containing the text data itself, and a mapping table that maps the enums to the strings. Simple, eh? Well yes, but those enumerations could cause a problem. After all, every time you add or remove a string, the enums will change. Which means a new header file. Which means that everything that includes that header file needs recompiling. That could hurt, especially if – as in some of the products I've consulted on – the string table is global.

Remember that principle about keeping it local? Well, let's try to follow it. In this case, suppose that our game supports an extensive menu system. All the text entries in the menus will have string table entries. If we have a single string table, we recompile every file associated with every page, even though most pages don't change. So it really makes sense to have a single string table per page. Keep it local, people.

5.4.6 Graphics

To describe how to write a complete rendering system is beyond the scope of this book – here, we're interested primarily in architecture. A rendering package is going to be quite a bit larger than the very low-level systems we've seen so far. To keep it all manageable, we'll break the rendering systems into the components shown in Table 5.2.

This is not a flat hierarchy of components. We apply the same principles to the subcomponents of the rendering system as we have discussed; this allows us to easily replace subcomponents with new versions with little or no impact on their parent components. The structure is shown in Figure 5.17.

The hierarchy breaks down into three levels – high, intermediate and low. The dependencies between the levels operate only downwards and – most importantly – there are no cyclic dependencies. Without these two properties, maintenance would become much harder, and the replacement and upgrade of the individual subcomponents would become messy. Notice that as we move from small towards large components, the focus shifts from reusability to maintainability.

Another valuable property of this hierarchy is that the high and intermediate levels are completely generic systems that make no reference to the hardware they are running on; in general, the high and intermediate levels (if you like, the 'interface' components) know little or nothing about their low-

Table 5.2

Component	Function
SCENE	Top-level scene management
MODEL	Connects visuals and hierarchies
REND	Defines a renderer and renderable elements
PRIM	Describes how to draw primitives

Figure 5.17
Component architecture
for the rendering
package.

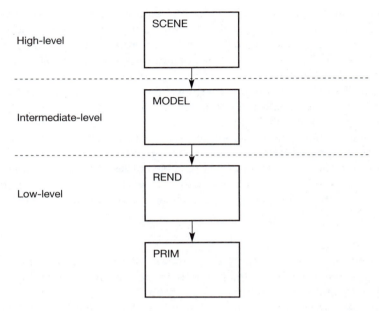

level ('implementation') component. This minimises the amount of rewriting required when porting to other systems and keeps low-level graphics code out of your top-level game code. We'll discuss cross-platform development in more detail in Chapter 6.

Let's now look more closely at these components to see how they function.

SCENE

The SCENE component is comprised of the classes shown in Figure 5.18.

The `Matrix44` and `Vector3` classes are borrowed from the MATHS component; this is fine, because the SCENE component is a higher-level component than these classes and the classes are self-contained (after all, our objective is to reuse classes that we have written, not rewrite them for every component).

MODEL

We've already looked at the MODEL component, so refer back to the earlier section in this chapter to refresh your memory if you need to. Deep in the bowels of this component lies the `Visual` class hierarchy – we've seen the base class and the `VisualPlex` class so far. By writing further subclasses of `Visual` (not to forget the parallel `VisualInstance` hierarchy), we can implement the really powerful graphical systems that create quality and performance in video games. As an example, let's implement a model with level of detail, as shown in Figure 5.19.

Note that each level has its own visual, which can itself be a level-of-detail visual.

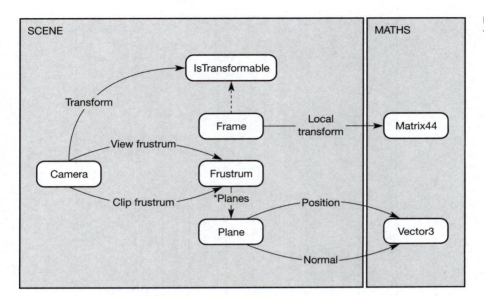

Figure 5.18
The SCENE component.

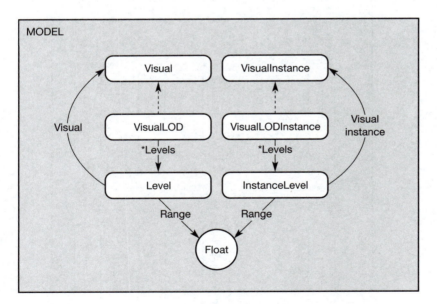

Figure 5.19
The MODEL component.

REND

The REND component defines a simple renderable entity and is basically the home of the `Renderer` class that we all know and love. Figure 5.20 shows the major participating classes in the system.

Figure 5.20
The REND component.

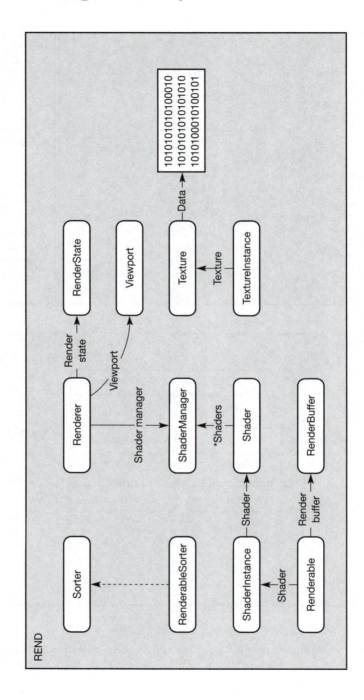

Figure 5.20
The REND component.

We see more evidence of our guiding principles in action, in particular the use of instancing in the `Texture` and `Shader` classes. The key class in the component is clearly `Renderable`. Think 'mesh' when you see this class and you'll get the general idea (of course, we have abstracted the concept of renderability to allow any type of graphical representation). Instances of these objects point at a `Shader`, an object that 'knows' how to create the primitives involved in drawing these sorts of objects, and a `RenderBuffer`, which is effectively a stream for lower-level primitive data. The top-level `Renderer` class manages all the `Shaders` used in the scene and provides the interface for submitting `Renderable` data into the component and down into the lower-level systems. This then begs the question: how do we get data from the MODEL component into the REND component? Surely we have to write this sort of thing:

```
namespace MODEL
{

class VisualInstance : public REND::Renderable
{
//...
};


}
```

which is a definite no-no because it would be reversing the flow of dependency, as shown in Figure 5.21. Note the creation of a cycle in the graph, a sure sign that our engineering is amiss.

To get around this, we invoke the trick we discussed when looking at avoiding illogical dependencies: we introduce a third component, which we call VISUAL, and move all the bindings into there (see Figure 5.22).

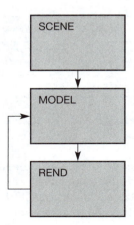

Figure 5.21
A cyclic dependency in the rendering package.

Figure 5.22
Removal of a cyclic
dependency by creating a
third component.

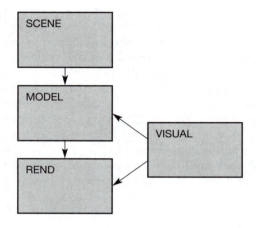

Figure 5.23
The VISUAL component
bridges MODEL and
REND.

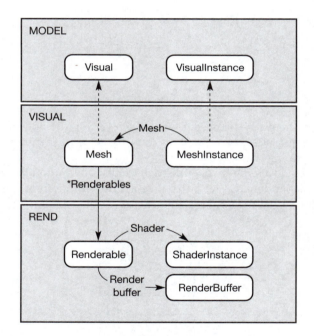

The VISUAL component is shown in Figure 5.23.

5.4.7 PRIM

The PRIM component is where the data pumped through SCENE, MODEL, REND and VISUAL end up, ready to be sent from the render buffers to whatever rendering hardware is available. This makes PRIM a data bottleneck, and we really want code residing in this component to fly. This means that virtual functions are banned unless there is a viable case that using them will increase, or at the very least not decrease, performance. Just to knock another nail in the virtual coffin, since virtual functions place an invisible vtable pointer inside our classes, we cannot map classes directly to memory without yet another indirection, making things even slower:

```
class Primitive
{
public:
    // No no no!
    virtual void Upload( void * pRenderData );
private:
    // Now why are my frame rates so poor?
    struct PrimData * m_pData;
};
```

This problem becomes quite acute when we remember that PRIM needs to be implemented over several platforms. We'd like to do the polymorphic thing, but we shouldn't, so what are the alternatives?

- *Use template-based static polymorphism*: this would work fine were it not for the fact that hardware can be radically different from platform to platform – each class would need to be specialised for its target, the template therefore becoming irrelevant.
- *Use a directory hierarchy* that supports each target platform and include only the relevant files in the project build system.

Figure 5.24 shows how this can be achieved.

The directory PRIM contains the generic files common to all platforms. The other directories contain platform-specific files implementing primitives on target hardware. Figure 5.25 shows this partitioned component.

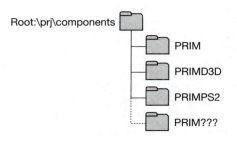

Figure 5.24
Directory layout for the PRIM components.

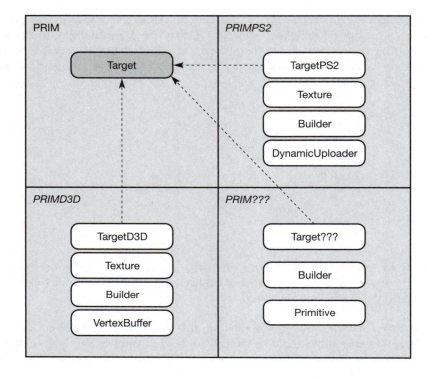

Notice that there are three different types of class here:

1 PRIM::Target is a true polymorphic class. It represents a destination for primitive data to be drawn to (the display, or another texture perhaps). We justify the virtual function overhead because there are typically few calls to set up targets, and the set-up cost is usually much higher than the call overhead. Subclasses exist in all the platform-dependent parts.

2 The PRIM::Texture classes exist only in the platform-dependent parts of the component, but they must exist in each part.

3 The classes PRIM::VertexBuffer and PRIM::DynamicUploader are hardware-specific classes and are therefore encapsulated by the particular implementation.

Because of this, we should be a bit careful with our file-naming conventions. We adopt the rule that files are given a component/package prefix dictated by the directory they live in and a postfix only if required to distinguish subclasses. So, the hpp files for the above classes should have the paths:

```
Root:\prj\components\PRIM\PRIM_Target.hpp
Root:\prj\components\PRIMD3D\PRIMD3D_TargetD3D.hpp
Root:\prj\components\PRIMPS2\PRIMPS2_TargetPS2.hpp
Root:\prj\components\PRIMD3D\PRIMD3D_Texture.hpp
Root:\prj\components\PRIMPS2\PRIMPS2_Texture.hpp
Root:\prj\components\PRIMD3D\PRIMD3D_VertexBuffer.hpp
Root:\prj\components\PRIMPS2\PRIMPS2_DynamicUploader.hpp
```

The `Builder` class is the class that submits the primitive data to the hardware in the correct format. Since each of the builders is platform-dependent, they act as factories creating and processing the hardware-specific data types. This architecture allows near-optimal tuning of the components on a per-platform basis. And they said C++ was slow.

5.4.8 Collision detection

What we're talking about here is the low-level collision detection that answers the question 'Are two models intersecting?' If you've written collision detection libraries, then you'll know that it is a very hierarchical affair, because to answer the question accurately is really quite time-consuming and you want to avoid doing the more cycle-hungry operations if a simpler one could say 'no'.

There are many ways to perform the detection, and – as stated before – this is not the place to examine the particulars of how they work. Here, we'll implement the hierarchical test architecture for two models only. Writing a component for the higher-level tests that operate on many objects is left as an exercise for the reader.

Remember that in the MODEL component we defined a hierarchy of frames? Wouldn't it be nice, even powerful, if we could use that hierarchy in our collision system (because after all most objects we wish to collide will be hierarchical)?

The answer is: 'No, it would not be even slightly nice to do that'. Yet a frightening number of projects do it; and if your game does as well, it's time to stop it. The collision component should be utterly independent of the graphical component. Why? Because the data they share are superficially similar. Collision calculations are very expensive when performed on a per-primitive basis, so a model used for collision should contain considerably less detail than the visible polygon data. You may be tempted to use the lowest level-of-detail model as a collision model, but (in general) you shouldn't: you need different auxiliary data for collision models and you don't want to bloat your models with data that could belong elsewhere. Keep the visual model and the collision model separate physically and logically, and make the selection and generation of collision models a function of your asset-extraction process, and you'll be just fine.

Which motivates us to declare the architecture of the collision component, shown in Figure 5.26. The most important class in the collision component is the `Unit`, a staggeringly dull name by all accounts. A `Unit` defines an abstract geometrical entity that we can provide a collision test for; subclasses of `Unit` implement particular collision primitives.

Figure 5.26
The COLL component.

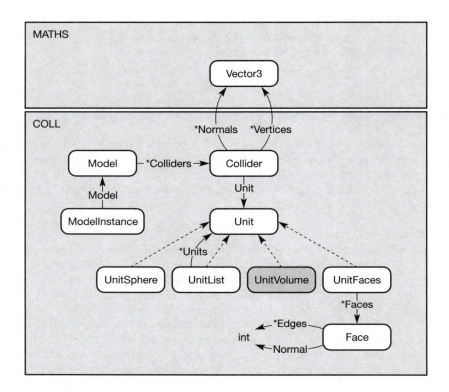

Figure 5.26
The COLL component.

This is not an easily maintained system. If there are *n* unit subclasses, then adding a new type of unit means writing O(*n*) tests for colliding the old types with the new. Unfortunately, there are no neat solutions to this problem, and C++'s lack of polymorphism based on both the type of `this` and the dynamic type of an argument means only more verbose drudgery:

```
bool TestSphereSphere(…);
bool TestBoxBox(…);
bool TestCylinderCylinder(…);
bool TestSphereBox(…);
bool TestSphereCylinder(…);
bool TestBoxCylinder(…);
```

In theory, we could use `dynamic_cast` to tell us – given a `Unit` – what flavour it was and so select an appropriate test. However, we've banned the use of `dynamic_cast` because of the requirement for everything to have vtables and be RTTI-enabled, but we can achieve the same effect by adding our own simple RTTI to the `Unit` classes:

```
// File: COLL_Unit.hpp
namespace COLL
{

class Unit
{
public:
    Unit( int iRtti );

    int GetRtti() const { return m_iRtti; }

private:
    int m_iRtti;
};

}

// File: COLL_UnitSphere.hpp
#include "COLL_Unit.hpp"

namespace COLL
{

class UnitSphere : public Unit
{
public:
    UnitSphere();

    static int ClassRtti() { return s_iRtti; }
private:
    static int c_iRtti;
};

}

// File: COLL_UnitSphere.cpp
#include "COLL_UnitSphere.hpp"

using namespace COLL;

int UnitSphere::c_iRtti = int(&c_iRtti);

UnitSphere::UnitSphere()
: Unit( c_iRtti )
{
}
```

Crude, but effective.

5.4.9 Resource management

As useful as `fopen()` and its family of buffered IO function calls are, most games cannot survive on these alone. On consoles, the loading of single files via the standard C library interface is far too slow, and there are particularly stringent limitations in the ISO 9668 filing system: 8.3 file names and maximum of 32 files or directories per directory. Modern games involve many thousands of files, so clearly this won't work at all. Even on a PC-type platform, the calls to `fopen()` *et al.* are blocking, and although they are fast when operating from hard disk, the penalty of opening many files and filling buffers starts to degrade performance – and whilst it's doing that, the game is frozen.

Loading many files of widely varying sizes can often be a very quick and tasty recipe for memory fragmentation, especially if RAM is at a premium (when is it not?). Since the C standard library gives us no control over how much memory it allocates and when, we really do need a way of bypassing this system entirely.

So, at the very core of the resource management component, we need a system that can:

- load files with virtually no overhead;
- load files in bulk with reduced overhead;
- load files asynchronously while the game code runs obliviously;
- manage memory efficiently.

These tasks are accomplished by the BNDL (BuNDLe) and FSVR (File SerVeR) components of our resource management package. See Figure 5.27 for an overview of the resource management package.

Incidentally, if you have a weak stomach for contrived acronyms, you might like to skip to the start of the next paragraph. My resource system is called DEMIGOD: the Demand Initiated Game Object Database, which I contract to DMGD.

Figure 5.27
The resource management system components.

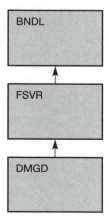

A bundle is just another term for one of those data file formats that the games industry revels in: WADs, PAKs, POD. The general structure of the BDL file is shown in Figure 5.28.

There's a header that contains information about the contents of the data section, followed by the files themselves as contiguous binary. The file data may be compressed using some suitable tool, and there can be optional padding inserted between the files. More about that padding shortly.

The file server loads files from bundles. It needs to support the following four ways that load requests could occur in a game:

- *Foreground load*: the file server reads data from the bundle and returns when they're all resident.
- *Background load*: the file server returns immediately after the read request is issued and the data are loaded asynchronously. When the entire file has been loaded, a call-back-like mechanism is invoked to allow the caller to use the newly loaded data.
- *Burst load*: like a background load, only it acts on all the files in a bundle that resides inside the outer bundle. The call-back-like mechanism is invoked as soon as individual files within the bundle are loaded (see Figure 5.29).
- *Virtual bundle*: a file that is itself a bundle is background-loaded and becomes memory-resident to allow extremely fast loading of the contained files.

(Note: a foreground load can be implemented easily as a background load wrapped with a wait-until-completed test.)

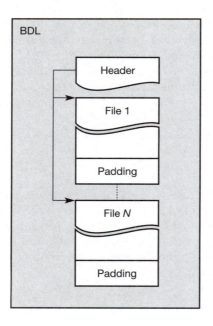

Figure 5.28
Internal structure of a bundle.

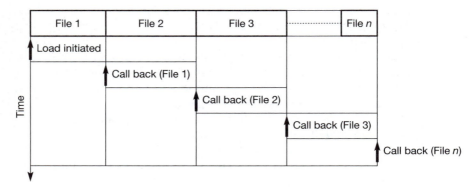

When loading is taking place, speed is a real issue. No user wants to sit watching a loading bar for minutes on end, and console software requirements often stipulate the sort of times that loading should take. PC and Apple programmers may be forgiven for forgetting that having a hard disk in their machine is a luxury. However, consoles – the most numerous game platform on the planet – are still reading data from CD-ROM or DVD-ROM. Transfer rates are not quick, so it is of utmost importance that the data on the storage medium are arranged optimally, or as near as possible. What this arrangement is depends on the game you're writing, but it stands to reason that logically close data should be physically close on the media. Since CDs and DVDs organise and read their data on a track-wise basis, it stands to reason that contiguously required files should be in contiguous sectors on the medium, hence (i) those padding bytes in the bundles, which align the next file to sector boundaries, and (ii) the burst load mechanism, which gets files from media into memory and usable as fast as is possible.

The file server component is shown in Figure 5.30.

The system maintains a queue of load requests that is serviced every game loop. A load request in the file server has an API as follows:

```
void BackgroundLoad( const char * pszPath,
                     const char * pszFile,
                     Loader       * pLoader,
                     Resource     * pResource );
```

The `Resource` class is the base for a type of resource to be loaded. When the load completes, this will hold the data that have been read. Each resource has a unique identifier – denoted here as an ID. For performance reasons, this really wants to be an integer, but it's a real pain when in development you're presented with 'Hey Jules, I get a load error on resource ID 2172'. It's better to typedef this to something like

```
typedef CONT::string tID;
```

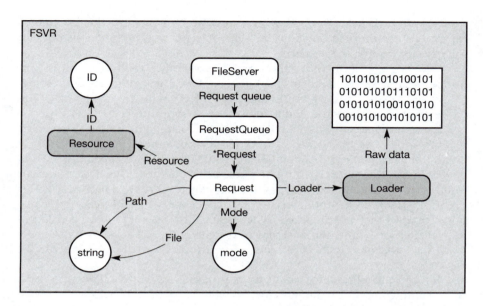

Figure 5.30
The FSVR component.

which will magically transmute the sentence above into 'Hey Jules, I get a load error on walther_ppk.mod'. Later in development, when it's all nice and stable, changing the typedef to make `tID` an integer and adjusting the toolset accordingly brings about a performance increase for relatively little effort.

The abstract `Loader` class has a public interface that looks like this:

```
class Loader
{
public:
    virtual void OnLoadComplete( Resource * pRes ) = 0;

    void LoadForeground( FileServer * pServer,
                         const char * pszFileName,
                         Resource   * pResource );

    void LoadBackground( FileServer * pServer,
                         const char * pszFileName,
                         Resource   * pResource );
    char * GetRawData();
    int    GetRawDataSize();
    void   SetRawData( char * pRaw, int iSizeBytes );
};
```

When a load request completes, the `Loader` subclass that is stored in the request has its `OnLoadComplete()` method invoked. This is the call-back-like mechanism mentioned above, but by having a class rather than a function pointer we can carry state information about on a per-object basis. The loader also has an interface for loading the resource.

Once we have a file in memory, the data are raw – we have to turn them into something useful, a process I call *instantiation*. Then we typically do something with them. Then we (optionally) get rid of them. We can think of the lifecycle of a resource as the simple state machine shown in Figure 5.31.

A resource starts off in a bundle. When the load request comes in, it starts loading and is in the *Loading* state. When loading completes, the resource is either in its raw data form or compressed; if the latter, it gets decompressed and is now in the *Raw* state. Then the resource is instantiated. This need not occur immediately – some resource types can stay raw until they're needed. (At this point, the data can be optionally put into a `Locked` state; they cannot be disposed of until they are unlocked.) The resource is then `Active` and considered usable; after some time, the asset may be disposed of.

This state management is handled within the DMGD component (see Figure 5.32).

Now, loading a resource can be a time-consuming process. If we get several loads completing on the same frame, a whole series of call-backs will be initiated and we could find a drop in performance. One strategy to avoid this is to make the file server aware of how quickly the game is running and scale the number of call-backs it initiates in a frame by that:

```
const int MAX_CALLBACKS_60FPS = 8;

void FileServer::Update( Time aDeltaT )
{
    //...
    int iNumCallbacks =
        (MAX_CALLBACKS_60FPS * Time(1.0f/60.0f))/aDeltaT;

    if ( iNumCallbacks > MAX_CALLBACKS_60FPS)
    {
        iNumCallbacks = MAX_CALLBACKS_60FPS;
    }
}
```

Figure 5.31
State diagram showing the lifecycle of a resource.

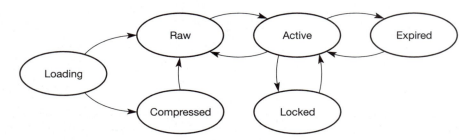

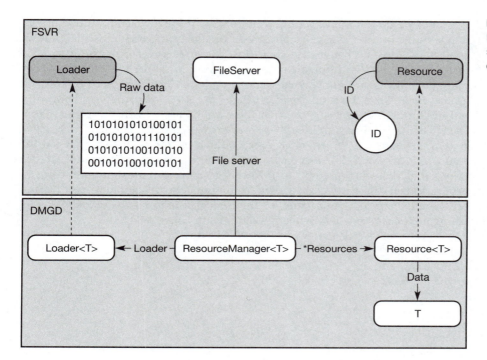

Figure 5.32
DEMIGOD and the file server component diagrams.

The `ResourceManager` class drives the show. It is a templated class: you create a resource manager for each type of asset you want to load, and an associated loader for that type derived from the file server's `Loader` class. The manager supports the following basic operations:

- *Load resource*: clearly, you can't do anything without loading the data!
- *Get resource*: acquires a pointer to a loaded resource, performing reference counting. This operation forces instantiation of the resource if it has not already been done.
- *Free resource*: decreases a resource's reference count. Even if this hits zero, the resource won't be deleted – it is marked as expired.
- *Purge resource*: the resource is forcibly removed from the manager, freeing all allocated resources irrespective of reference counting or any other status.
- *Lock resource*: prevents a resource from being freed.
- *Unlock resource*: guess.

Now we delve a little deeper into the resource management issue. There are a number of problems to solve; some are pretty obvious, but the others are a bit subtler. First, let's deal with the obvious one. Most games have considerably more assets than available RAM, and although they won't all be in memory simultaneously, we may have to deal with the situation that we run out of the space we reserved for that type of asset.

So, if we do run out of room, what do we do? Well, we could throw up our hands in horror and assert or halt or quit or something else antisocial, but we can actually do a bit better than that. How about we look for an asset that is no longer being used and purge that, thus making room for the new guy? Nice plan! But how do we know what's not being used? Well, we can look to see if any resources have the state *Expired*. If they have, then we can purge them without hesitation. But let's suppose that there are no assets with this status. What then? One possibility is to keep a least recently used (LRU) counter. Each active resource's counter is incremented every game loop and reset to zero when the resource is accessed. The asset with the highest LRU count is a candidate for removal. This technique will work nicely in some circumstances but not in others. In fact, the particular strategy for finding a purge candidate will depend on the mechanics of your game, so the best plan is to let the user create and configure the strategy. This scheme is outlined in Figure 5.33.

The abstract purge strategy could look like this:

```
// File: DMGD_PurgeStrategy.hpp
namespace FSVR
{
     class Resource;
}

namespace DMGD
{

class PurgeStrategy
{
public:
     virtual int Evaluate( FSVR::Resource * aResources,
                           int iNumResources ) = 0;
}
```

Figure 5.33
Purge strategies for the
DMGD cache.

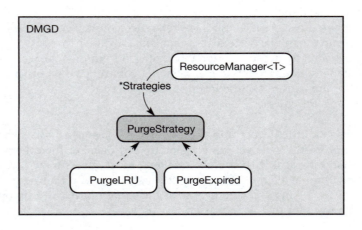

The `Evaluate()` virtual function returns the index of a resource that can be purged, or –1 if none fulfils the criteria. Add to the resource manager the following method:

```
void AddPurgeStrategy( PurgeStrategy * pStrategy );
```

and allow the resource manager to process the strategies in the order they are added (you could add a priority parameter, but that would overcomplicate the system):

```
FSVR::Resource * pRsrcs     = &m_Resources[0];
int              iRsrcCount = m_Resources.size();
for( int j = 0; j < m_PurgeStrategies.size(); ++j )
{
    PurgeStrategy * pPS = m_PurgeStrategies[j];
    int iPurge = pPS->Evaluate(pRsrcs,iRsrcCount);
    if (iPurge >= 0)
    {
        PurgeResource(i);
        break;
    }
}
```

OK, so we've decided that we want to get rid of a resource. What do we do? Something like

```
void Resource<T>::Purge()
{
delete m_pData;
}
```

looks fine, but this might cause you a couple of really nasty problems. Consider the case that T is a model that has graphical data – textures or vertex buffers, maybe – in video memory. Now, most rendering systems today use multiple buffering to keep graphical updates tear-free and smooth (see Figure 5.34).

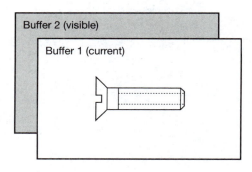

Figure 5.34
Graphics being shown in the visible buffer cannot be deleted until (at least) the end of the display frame.

The act of deleting may well purge the video memory associated with a resource that is currently in the visible buffer, possibly resulting in a business-class ticket to Crashington when the buffers are switched. Moral: some data cannot be deleted immediately; you need to schedule their deletion at a point in time when it's safe to do so.

To achieve this, we add a garbage-disposal system to the resource manager (see Figure 5.35).

When an item is to be purged, its data are removed from the resource manager and placed in an entry in the garbage list. An integer is used to count the number of frames that elapse; when this hits a specified value, the asset can be deleted and the entry is removed from the list.

This is when the second really nasty problem hits. The purge operation can often be expensive, and if a number of resources are purged at the same time, then the frame rate can take a spike in the wrong direction. To get around this, we allow the user to specify the maximum number of purges that can take place per game loop. Note that because this is a parameterised class (i.e. the type T) we can set this maximum value on a per-class basis, so if one of your objects is particularly time-consuming to dispose of, then you can process fewer of them every cycle:

```
template<class T>
void GarbageDisposal<T>::Update( Time )
{
    int iPurgeCount = 0;
```

Figure 5.35
Object diagram for the DMGD garbage-disposal system.

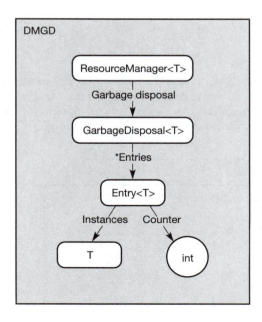

```
iterator itKak = m_Garbage.begin();
iterator itEnd = m_Garbage.end();
while( itKak != itEnd )
{
    iterator itNxt = itKak; ++itNxt;

    Entry & anEntry = *itKak;

    if ( anEntry.m_iCounter > 0 )
    {
        --anEntry.m_iCounter;
    }
    else
    {
        delete anEntry.m_pInstance;
        m_Garbage.erase( itKak );

        ++iPurgeCount;
        if ( iPurgeCount == m_iMaxPurgesPerFrame )
        {
            break;
        }
    }

    itKak = itNxt;
}
}
```

The last problem we're going to look at in this section is one mentioned a few times here and elsewhere, in somewhat hushed tones: *fragmentation*. Refer back to the state diagram in Figure 5.31 and consider the dynamic memory operations that can take place when a compressed resource is loaded:

1   The load operation itself creates a buffer and fills it with data from storage (one new, no deletes).
2   The decompressor reads the header from this buffer and allocates a new buffer to send the uncompressed information to (two news, no deletes).
3   Having decompressed the data, the original compressed buffer can now be deleted (two news, one delete).
4   The raw data are instantiated. Any number of dynamic memory operations can occur, depending on how complex the parameter class T is. It's safe to say that at least one T is allocated ($\geq$ three news, one delete).
5   Having instantiated the raw data, they can now be deleted. The object is now loaded and ready to use ($\geq$ three news, two deletes).

I make that at least five dynamic memory operations per object. That is just begging to fragment main RAM, and maybe even video RAM or sound RAM too. One feels that we can do better, and we can, but it's a bit fiddly. The trick is to do a single new once per object in a buffer sufficiently large. See Figure 5.36 to get an idea of how this works.

The compressed data are loaded at an offset from the start of the buffer. This offset is calculated by the compressor, which must calculate it so that no overwrite of compressed data occurs before they are used. A trial-and-error method is usually employed, as the operation is relatively quick and offline. The algorithm is illustrated by the following pseudo-code:

```
offset = data_size - compressed_size
while Decompress( compressed_data, offset )==ERR_OVERLAP
    offset += DELTA
end while
```

The value DELTA can be either a fixed constant or a heuristically determined value. The end result is a buffer of size offset + compressed_size, large enough to decompress the packed data without overwriting unused data. Note that this works with any linear compression scheme, for example RLE or LZ.

At the cost of some extra RAM, we've eliminated two news and one delete. Now, let's get rid of some more. This bit is harder because it depends on designing the classes within the resource manager in a particular way: their instantiation must cause no extra dynamic memory operations. Consider the following simplified class:

```
class Mesh
{
private:
    Vector3 * m_avVertices;
    int     * m_aiTriangles;
    int       m_iNumVertices;
    int       m_iNumTriangles;
public:
    Mesh( int iNumVertices, int iNumTriangles );
};
```

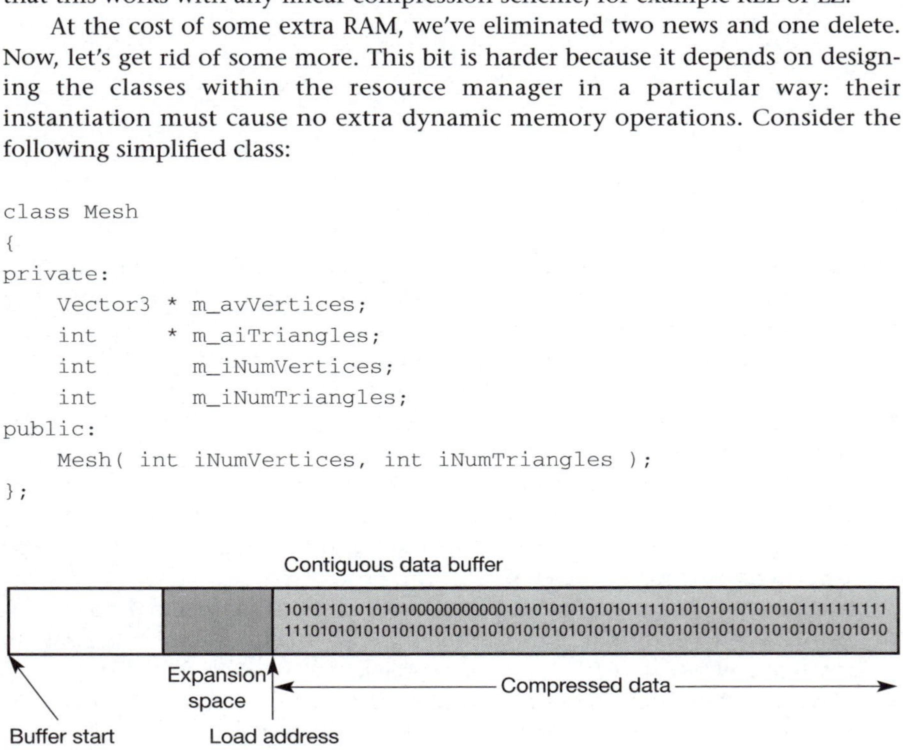

Figure 5.36
Decompressing data on top of themselves.

Contiguous data buffer

1010110101010100000000000101010101010101111010101010101010101111111111
1110101010101010101010101010101010101010101010101010101010101010101010

Expansion space   ←——————— Compressed data ——————→

Buffer start   Load address

We could write the constructor as follows:

```
Mesh::Mesh( int iNumVertices, int iNumTriangles )
: m_avVertices( new Vector3 [ iNumVertices ] )
, m_aiTriangles( new int [ iNumTriangles ] )
, m_iNumVertices( iNumVertices )
, m_iNumTriangles( iNumTriangles )
{
}
```

This causes two dynamic memory operations – no use for our resource system. Consider the memory layout shown in Figure 5.37, however.

By allocating the mesh and the vertex and triangle buffers in contiguous memory, instantiation becomes a matter of lashing up the pointers; no dynamic allocations are required:

```
Mesh::Mesh( int iNumVertices, int iNumTriangles )
: m_avVertices( 0 )
, m_aiTriangles( 0 )
, m_iNumVertices( iNumVertices )
, m_iNumTriangles( iNumTriangles )
{
    m_avVertices = (Vector3 *)(this+1);
    m_aiTriangles = (int *)(m_avVertices+iNumVertices);
}
```

Of course, the memory has already been allocated (it's the loading/decompression buffer), so we need to use an in-place method to perform the construction:

```
void Mesh::NewInPlace(int iNumVertices,int iNumTriangles)
{
    m_iNumVertices = iNumVertices;
    m_iNumTriangles = iNumTriangles;
    m_avVertices = (Vector3 *)(this+1);
    m_aiTriangles = (int *)(m_avVertices+iNumVertices);
}
```

(Alternatively, we can use the C++ 'placement new operator'.)

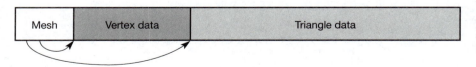

Figure 5.37
Keeping data contiguous helps to alleviate fragmentation.

Congratulations! We've reduced the dynamic memory operations down to just one `new`, at the cost of some extra RAM and some restrictions on the layout of the participant class.

Now let's tie up some of the loose ends I've dangled in this section. Figure 5.38 shows how a game might manage texture resources using components we've been discussing.

In code, this is something like this:

```
// File: TextureLoader.hpp
#include <DMGD\DMGD_Loader.hpp>

namespace REND { class Texture; }

class TextureLoader : public DMGD::Loader<REND::Texture>
{
public:
    TextureLoader();

    REND::Texture *Instantiate(char *pData,int iSize);
    void            OnLoadComplete( DMGD::Resource * );
};


// File: ResourceManager.hpp
#include <DMGD\DMGD_ResourceManager.hpp>
#include <REND\REND_Texture.hpp>
```

Figure 5.38
The application's resource management system implements concrete versions of the DMGD abstract classes.

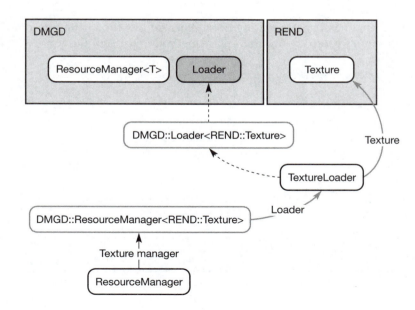

```
class ResourceManager
{
public:
     /* Blah */
private:
     DMGD::ResourceManager<REND::Texture> m_TextureMgr;
};


// File: TextureLoader.cpp
#include "TextureLoader.hpp"
#include <REND\REND_TextureLoader.hpp>
#include <REND\REND_Texture.hpp>


/*virtual*/
REND::Texture *
TextureLoader::Instantiate( char * pRaw, int iRawSize )
{
    REND::TextureLoader aLoader;
    REND::Texture *     pTexture = 0;

    // Note: all textures assumed to be in TGA format.
    aLoader.ParseTGA( pRaw, pTexture );

    return( pTexture );
}


/*virtual*/
void TextureLoader::OnLoadComplete(FSVR::Resource *pRes)
{
    // Make the texture immediately available.
    REND::Texture * pTexture =
            Instantiate( GetRawData(), GetRawDataSize() );
    DMGD::Resource<Texture> * pTextureResource =
            static_cast<DMGD::Resource<Texture> *>(pRes);
    pTextureResource->SetData( pTexture );
}
```

5.4.10 Newtonian physics

Having a background in astrophysics, physics is a topic close to my heart, and I am not alone: there is a small but dedicated community of game developers who have an interest in raising the profile of physics in video games, heralding it as a technology whose time has come.

True, there is a general movement towards realism in games. As consoles evolve and graphics become higher-resolution, use more realistic lighting models and support higher-detail models, any elements that behave in unnatural ways tend to stand out. For a truly immersive experience (the physics proponents argue), objects in games need to behave more like objects in the real world: stacking, sliding, rolling, colliding, even bending, cracking and smashing.

To get these sorts of behaviours into the game, you need physics. Let's be quite clear what we mean by 'physics', though. Almost all games have physics of some description: objects move – they have positions and velocities if not accelerations; objects collide and bounce off each other or explode. This suggests that game physics is nothing more than the updating of positions and velocities over time. But clearly this isn't what the hardcore mean, so let's try the following definition:

> *Physics in the context of games is a set of rules that consistently and equivalently control the motion of objects within the game.*

By 'consistently', I mean that the rules are applied every game loop (or more frequently). There are no special cases for controlling the motion – we don't, for example, stop at some point and switch to (say) animation.

By 'equivalently', I mean that the rules are applied to all the objects in the set. If the objects are required to have differing behaviour, they do so by altering their response to the rules via internal parameters.

Note that we're not just thinking of the motion of vehicles in a driving game or the balls in a pool game. We could also consider using cellular automata to generate game data. But whatever we find ourselves using, we're going to realise one thing: we're very much at the mercy of the rules we choose because they generate behaviour; they are not behaviour in themselves. For better or worse, the behaviours we get as a result of running our rules may be the ones we want and/or never expected. There can be a lot of work in mitigating the unwanted emergent behaviour; that is the cost of the physics. The benefit is that when we get the behaviour right for one object, we get it right for all objects that follow the same rules.

Now to get to the point: Newtonian physics. This is a set of rules that controls the motion of game objects by applying forces to them. It's a simple enough principle, but there's a snag: physics is really quite hard. Even in a simple world of inflexible boxes and planes, physics can be really tough. For example, stacking a number of boxes on top of each other in real time could be enough to grind some computers to a halt; and even then, it's hard to make stable to the extent that it behaves just like a real stack of boxes. And if rigid cubes are hard to get working, what does that say about more complex systems such as soft, jointed humans?

The long and the short of it is that if you want to use Newtonian physics in a game, then you've got to have a darn good reason for doing so. For example, if you're writing an adventure or platform game, you may be tempted to make a puzzle out of platforms, weights and ropes that are physically simulated. Once it's set up, it just works. Well, that's the benefit; the cost is that it's very much harder to control and constrain than a puzzle based on a state machine and animations. The designer of the puzzle must have a good understanding of the mechanics of the problem, and in more complex situations they must have a deep understanding of how to change the physical properties of the objects in a system to be able to achieve a desired result. This is specialist knowledge, and it's not a simple task. Think about making a big nasty Boss spider walk, applying a sequence of forces and torques at the joints in the legs to get it perambulating over an undulating terrain. It's decidedly not easy.

Introducing physics into a game must start at the art and design level. Masses and mass distributions must be set within the editing environment where the game is constructed. The first problem that a designer may encounter is 'physics creep'. Suppose that one wishes to limit the number of objects that are physically simulated. Those objects had better not be able to interact with non-simulated objects, as the result may be decidedly unrealistic. But we were using physics to *add* realism! So, inevitably, it's hard to avoid more and more of your simulation space using Newtonian physics as a means of updating itself. Keeping control can be tough.

Something else to watch out for when planning a game with physics on board is units. Most game art is created to an arbitrary scale – as long as all objects are the right size relative to each other, everything will work out just fine. And it's true that Newtonian physics is oblivious to what the units are – it still works.[3] However, physics programmers may well feel more comfortable with SI units (metres, kilograms, seconds) than other systems, so artwork should be prepared with this in mind. It seems pointless to swallow CPU cycles and create extra confusion during the game converting between unit systems when some forethought would save you the trouble. Of course, a clever C++ programmer might like to write a units class that did all the conversions for you transparently. It's a fun exercise, but that doesn't make it clever. Choose game world units at the start of development and stick to them.

If physics is hard for the designer, then it's pretty hellish for the programmer. Again, specialist knowledge may be required – not just physics, but maths well beyond high-school level, maybe even beyond graduate level. Even with that knowledge, the systems can be hard and time-consuming to stabilise to the extent that they can be used in a commercial game. Attempts – such as Dreamworks' 1998 *Jurassic Park: Trespasser* – have not really succeeded either technically or commercially.

However, if you've read all that and have decided that you really want to use Newtonian physics in your game, then here is a component that will get you started. If you really want to use high-power physics, you would do well to consider a middle-ware solution – two currently popular systems are *Mathengine* and *Havok*. They may allow you to sidestep many months of mental pain.

---

3   A technical note. Only in the SI unit system does Newton's law $F=ma$ hold true. In other systems, it is generally $F=kma$, where k is a constant.

Right, let's get down to designing a physics system. Since Newtonian physics is about updating positions and directions (we want things to spin, don't we?), let's start by embedding those into a class called a `ReferenceFrame`. This is a term you meet a lot in physics – it's precisely what is meant here, so why not? Figure 5.39 shows the reference frame $\{(\pmb{x},\pmb{y},\pmb{z}),(\pmb{X'},\pmb{Y'},\pmb{Z'})\}$ – the first numbers denote position with respect to some other reference frame $\{(0,0,0),(\pmb{X},\pmb{Y},\pmb{Z})\}$, and the second set are vectors representing orientation.

A mention needs to be made of coordinate systems here. We have deliberately chosen to keep our rendering systems and our simulations systems separate, and there is a danger that whoever writes the graphics code may not have the same notions as the person writing the physics code about which way the z-axis goes or how angles are measured. Many hours of hair-pulling debugging can result, because physics code is full of vector cross-products that have ambiguities in their results (there are two vectors 180 degrees apart that satisfy orthogonality with the arguments). Although it is quite feasible to write a generic coordinate transformation component, for performance reasons it is better to avoid doing so. Programmers need to agree on the conventions of axial directions and senses of rotation about very early on in development.

Remember way back when we were looking at the MATHS component, we met this thing called an `Integrator`? No? Well, better rewind and review. An integrator is used to update a dynamic system over time, taking into account the variable rates of change of the internal variables over time. If we want to update our physical object over time, then we want one of those, which means inheriting the `IsIntegrable` property class. Such is the power of component design, we're now building a huge amount of abstract power into a class and turning it into concrete functionality.

Newtonian physics is nothing without forces, and something generally has to apply those forces. At this point in the design, we have only an abstract object – we don't know if it's soft (in which case, forces will deform it) or rigid (forces will only move it). So we defer explicit mention of forces until later in the hierarchy, because the force interface will be determined by the type of body (a virtual function isn't really sufficiently flexible, since it has a fixed signature). However, we can introduce forces implicitly via controllers, a physical object having a number of these pushing them around:

Figure 5.39

A reference frame is described by a position and three orthogonal unit vectors.

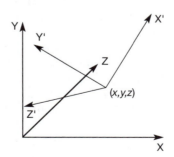

```
// File: PHYS_Controller.hpp
namespace PHYS
{

class Object;

class Controller
{
public:
    virtual bool ComputeForcesAndTorques(Object *) = 0;
};


}
```

Your subclass of `Controller` either will know what type of `Object` is being supplied or will be able to work it out via your own typing mechanism. The `ComputeForcesAndTorques()` method should return `true` always, unless something catastrophic happens, in which case returning `false` allows the `Object` update to be terminated.

Figure 5.40 summarises the design so far.

Notice the use of multiple inheritance in `PHYS::Object`. Worry not: it will be nigh invisible by the time we get to classes that really do things. Also observe that all `Objects` have mass, a fundamental property of Newtonian mechanics.

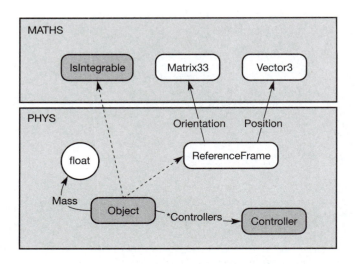

Figure 5.40
Bindings between the physics and maths components.

Here's the `Object` interface:

```
class Object
: public ReferenceFrame
, public ::MATHS::IsIntegrable
{
public:
    /*
     * Typedefs, constants and enumerations.
     */

    /*
     * Lifecycle.
     */
        Object();
        Object( float fMass );
        ~Object();

    /*
     * Polymorphic methods.
     */
        virtual void Update( MATHS::Integrator * pInt,
                             float fDeltaT ) = 0;
            // Update state of object wrt time.

        virtual void SetMass( float fMass );
            // Sets the mass of an object.

        virtual void SetInfiniteMass();
            // Makes an object immovable.
    /*
     * Unique methods
     */
        float GetMass() const;

        void AddController(Controller * pController);
        void RemoveController(Controller * pController);
            // Controller interface
};
```

In the `Update()` method, we pass in an arbitrary integrator to calculate the new state. Some objects in the game may require very accurate and stable integrators (for the technically minded, Runge–Kutta high-order, or even an implicit integrator such as backwards Euler); some may require simple ones (such as forwards Euler or Guassians). This choice of interface allows us to share a few integrators between many objects, as opposed to having either an integrator per object or one integrator for all objects (a yukky singleton integrator).

From the `Object` base class, we can now start building concrete classes. There are two families of these – the *body* classes that are solids, and the rest. A *Body* is just an *Object* with mass properties and some underlying geometrical attributes. We're going to make two concrete subclasses of `Object`: a *rigid body* (a subclass of `Body`) and a *rope*.

First, let's design the `Body` class. We need to get some geometrical data in. Remember that we are dealing with the update side of game objects here; we can make no mention of or use no instances or references to anything visual. The data we require are in the form of a 3×3 matrix called the inertia tensor, which describes how the mass is distributed in the body. For simple geometric shapes, there are formulae for the elements in this matrix. So, if you're writing a pool game, life is easy. For less than simple shapes (and that means most game objects), things are not so simple. There are three choices for computing the matrix in this circumstance:

- Offline computation of the inertia tensor by direct surface integration over the polygonal elements in the object's model. This is extremely accurate, but some careful thought must be given to how density varies over the model.
- Approximate the object using a series of simple volumes whose inertia tensors can be evaluated easily. This is illustrated in Figure 5.41, where we use three boxes to model a car. To compute the inertia tensor for the entire object, you can use the parallel axis theorem.
- Represent the model as a set of point masses and use the definition of the inertia tensor to compute the elements directly (see Figure 5.42).

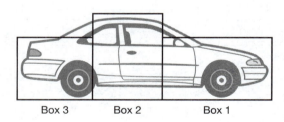

Box 3   Box 2   Box 1

Figure 5.41
A car modelled as a series of boxes (whose inertia tensors are simple to represent).

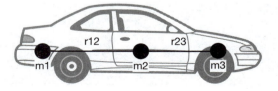

Figure 5.42
The car modelled as point masses.

As I said earlier, if you use physics in games it quickly gets pretty technical. Of the three methods, the third is the most flexible and as a big bonus, the point mass model can be updated easily in real time. So let's create a point mass model for the component (see Figure 5.43).

The point masses have positions and masses of course. When you add a point to the set, the mass is accumulated, along with adjusting the centre of mass. After you've added all your points, you can then obtain the inertia tensor. The interface to this class is interesting:

```
typedef int PointMassHandle;

void BeginEdit();
// Call this before adding, removing or modifying points.
// Must be paired with EndEdit().

void EndEdit();
// Ends edit operations on the set and forces a refresh
// of the internal state. Must be paired with BeginEdit()
// and no Add/Remove/Modify operations are allowed
// afterwards.

PointMassHandle AddPointMass();
// Adds a point mass to the set and returns a handle to
// it.
```

Figure 5.43
The point mass in the physics component.

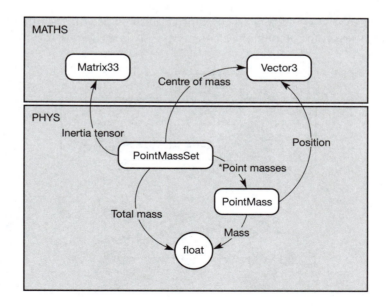

```
void RemovePointMass( PointMassHandle & hPoint );
// Removes an instance of a point mass from the set. The
// handle is invalid after this call.

void Clear();
// Remove all point masses from the set. Must be called
// within BeginEdit()/EndEdit(). All handles will be
// invalid after this call.

void SetPointMass( PointMassHandle &hPoint, float m );
// Sets the mass of a point. Only call within
// BeginEdit/EndEdit().

void SetPointPosition( PointMassHandle const & hPoint,
                       MATHS::Vector3 const & vPos );
// Sets the position of a point in local coordinates.
// Only call within BeginEdit/EndEdit().

MATHS::Vector3 const & GetCentreOfMass() const;
// Gets centre of mass for the set.

Tensor33 GetInertiaTensor() const;
// Gets inertia tensor for the set.

float GetTotalMass() const;
// Gets the total mass of the object.
```

Notice that we add point masses one at a time. Until all the point masses have been added to the set, the internal state is incomplete, so asking for the inertia tensor will not produce a valid result. Once we have added all our points, adding more would also invalidate the internal state, so we need a way to be able to control when it is legal to add points and when it is legal to query state. That's what the `BeginEdit()/EndEdit()` interface is for, and it's a paradigm I use quite frequently.

Notice also the use of a handle type for the point masses. As far as the user is concerned, it's an integer. Internally, it has a specific meaning that is totally opaque to the outside world. Since there is no class hierarchy here, there is no loss of type information so a handle is fine, and it frees the user from the burden of having to manage point mass memory. Now if we'd returned a pointer to a point mass, a user might feel that they were obliged to delete it.

So we can now supply the inertia tensor to our body. What else would we like to be able to do with it? Well, one important thing is to somehow prevent it from doing undesirable things, such as falling through surfaces (we may want a ball to roll over an undulating terrain, for example). Or we may want it to follow some other object. We do this by means of *constraints*, and we allow a body to have an arbitrary number of them. Constraints are similar to controllers, but they evaluate external forces rather than the controller's internal forces. This is summarised in Figure 5.44.

Finally, we get to the `RigidBody`. There are three 3D vectors that describe the linear properties of the body's motion:

- Position **x** from the ReferenceFrame base class.
- Velocity **v**.
- Acceleration = **F**/*m* by Newton's second law.

where **F** is the total force acting on the body. There is one 3D vector describing the rotational velocity:

- Angular velocity **ω**.

The orientation is stored in the `ReferenceFrame` base class, just like the position, but in my implementation I use a unit quaternion **q** to represent this. Quaternions are nearly as stable numerically as matrices (there's less redundancy

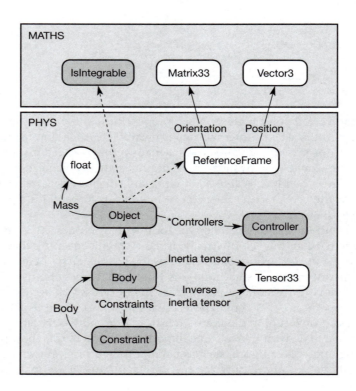

Figure 5.44
The physics component
with controllers
and constraints.

because there are fewer elements, but it's a small difference), and the smaller size means fewer FLOPs. There's also an auxiliary vector quantity – the angular momentum – which is used to simplify the calculations, and a matrix that is the inverse inertia tensor in world space (it is stored in local space elsewhere).

With all these variables defined, we can express the update of the rigid body's state over an infinitesimally small time Δt as follows:

$$\begin{bmatrix} \mathbf{v} \\ \mathbf{x} \\ \mathbf{L} \\ \mathbf{q} \end{bmatrix}(t + \Delta t) = \begin{bmatrix} \mathbf{v} \\ \mathbf{x} \\ \mathbf{L} \\ \mathbf{q} \end{bmatrix}(t) + \Delta t. \begin{bmatrix} \mathbf{F}/m \\ \mathbf{v} \\ \mathbf{T} \\ \mathbf{q}^* \end{bmatrix}$$

Here, $\mathbf{T}$ is the total torque acting on the body, and the quaternion $\mathbf{q}^*$ is the skewed value obtained via

$$\mathbf{q}^* = \tfrac{1}{2}\boldsymbol{\omega}\mathbf{q}$$

The $[\mathbf{v}\ \mathbf{x}\ \mathbf{L}\ \mathbf{q}]^T$ vector is called the *state vector*. For larger time intervals, we need to integrate the state over time to account for the fact that forces and torques change in that interval. However, we have built integrability into our `Object` class, so to make this all work is a case of implementing the required virtual functions, computing the forces and torques (via controllers and constraints) and gluing the pieces together.

The rigid body object diagram is shown in Figure 5.45, and the entire class declaration is presented for clarity:

```
// File: PHYS_RigidBody.hpp
#include "PHYS_Body.hpp"

namespace PHYS
{

class RigidBody : public Body
{
public:
    /*
     * Typedefs, constants and enumerations.
     */

    /*
     * Lifecycle.
     */

    RigidBody();
    ~RigidBody();
```

Figure 5.45
Adding the rigid
body class to the
physics component.

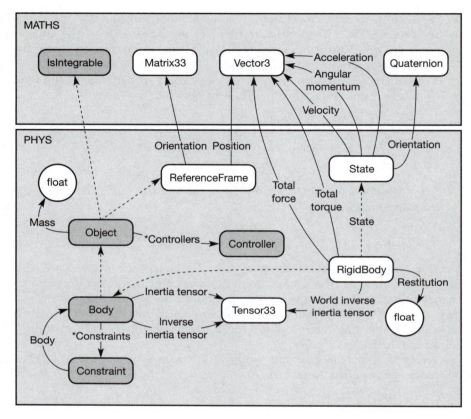

Figure 5.45
Adding the rigid body class to the physics component.

```
/*
 * Polymorphic methods.
 */
void Update( MATHS::Integrator * pIntegrator,
             float h );
    // From Object.

void GetArgumentVector( MATHS::Vector & rLhs );
void GetFunctionVector( MATHS::Vector & rRhs );
int  GetDimension() const;
void SetArgumentVector( MATHS::Vector & rArgs );
    // Instances of IsIntegrable methods.

void ApplyForce( const MATHS::Vector3& vForce,
                 const MATHS::Vector3& vPos,
                 const ReferenceFrame* pFrame );
void ApplyTorque(const MATHS::Vector3& vTorque);
```

```
        void ApplyCentralForce(const MATHS::Vector3& F);
            // Force API from Body class.

    /*
     * Unique methods
     */
    void  SetVelocity( const MATHS::Vector3 & v );
    const MATHS::Vector3 & GetVelocity() const;

     MATHS::Vector3
            PointVelocity(const MATHS::Vector3& r ) const;
    MATHS::Vector3
            PointAccel( const MATHS::Vector3 & r ) const;

     const MATHS::Vector3 & GetAcceleration() const;

    const MATHS::Vector3 & GetAngularVelocity() const;
    void SetAngularVelocity( const MATHS::Vector3 & w );

    void SetAngularMomentum( const MATHS::Vector3 & L );
    const MATHS::Vector3 & GetAngularMomentum() const;

    float GetRestitution() const;
    void SetRestitution( float r );

    void BeginSimulation();
    void EndSimulation();
            // Simulation control.

    float GetKineticEnergy() const;
            // Energy API.

    Tensor33 const &
            GetWorldInverseInertiaTensor() const;
            // Mass properties.

private:
    /*
     * Helpers
     */
       void resolveForces();
       void vectorToState( MATHS::Vector & rVector );
       void stateToVector( MATHS::Vector & rVector ) const;
       void preIntegrationUpdate();
       void postIntegrationUpdate();
```

```
/*
 * Hinderers
 */
    RigidBody( RigidBody const & );
    RigidBody & operator=( RigidBody const & );

/*
 * Data
 */
    MATHS::Vector3  m_vVelocity;
    MATHS::Vector3  m_vAcceleration;
    MATHS::Vector3  m_vSumForces;
        // Linear quantities.

    MATHS::Quaternion m_qOrientation;
    MATHS::Vector3      m_vAngularVelocity;
    MATHS::Vector3      m_vAngularMomentum;
    MATHS::Vector3      m_vSumTorques;
        // Angular quantities.


    Tensor33 m_mWorldInverseInertiaTensor;
        // Inverse inertia tensor in the world system.

  float m_fRestitution;
        // Coefficient of restitution for collisions.

  ForceAccumulator * m_pForceAccumulator;
        // Stores force-related data.
};

}
```

Notice that although we chose to represent the state as a discrete object in Figure 5.45, the position is actually stored in the ReferenceFrame base class, so we can't gather together all the quantities in one contiguous block. When we come to integrate, we therefore need to pack the state into one contiguous vector, and when we're done integrating we unpack it back into the state variables again. This is not optimal behaviour, because instead of using memcpy() to copy the state into and out of the integrator, we need to add and extract discrete values. We can get around this by duplicating the position within the rigid body – so long as we make sure to synchronise it every time the object moves or an integration takes place:

```
// File: PHYS_RigidBody.hpp
namespace PHYS
{

class RigidBody
{
public:
    // As before.

private:
    struct State
    {
        MATHS::Vector3 vVelocity;
        MATHS::Vector3 vPosition;
        MATHS::Vector3 vAngularMomentum;
        MATHS::Quaternion qOrientation;
    };

    State m_CurrentState;
};

}
```

Ropes are considerably simpler objects than rigid bodies. A rope is made out of a number of stiff springs, linked together and fixed at one or both ends. They are considered to be geometrically uninteresting, so there's none of the nasty tensor stuff going on, and although they have mass, it's not as important a parameter as for a body. Figure 5.46 shows us the ropes (groan).

There are vertices at the ends of each spring – they have a notional mass equal to the mass of the rope divided by the number of vertices. It's easy to allow them to have variable mass though. Each spring has a spring constant, K_s, and damping value, K_d, (usually quite high), and the springs pull the vertices around with a force F given by

$$F = - K_s \cdot x + K_d \cdot v$$

where x is the length of the spring minus the rest length and v is the velocity of the vertex along the spring axis.

This has been quite a difficult section. That's because physics *is* pretty difficult. We've not covered the really hard stuff here – soft bodies, hierarchically linked bodies, and such like. If you feel motivated to put physics in your game, there are many excellent resources to show you how to do the maths required to get up and flying. Now that you know how to architect the C++ code, nothing can stop you except the laws of physics themselves (and in games at least, you can actually change them, Mr Scott).

Figure 5.46
Adding ropes to the
physics component.

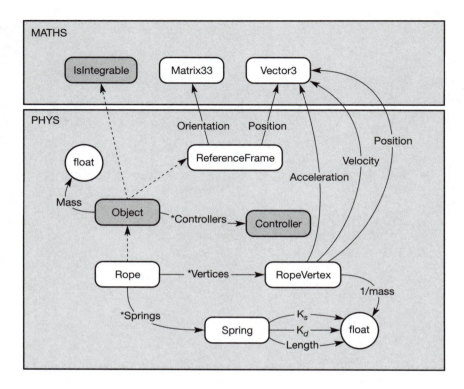

5.4.11 Network gaming

There's a lot of fun to be had playing games with friends or colleagues in the office. Programming games to run over a network is not particularly difficult, but there are some really fiddly issues that will almost certainly bite you at some point when you are writing your distributed game code. However, this section doesn't deal with those! For an excellent treatment of networking, see Singhal and Zyda (1999). Our mantra is this: the components allow you to reuse functionality and structure over several projects – what is important is the architecture, not the details. So our goal here is to come up with an architecture for (small-scale) network games that mentions no particular transport mechanism or protocol but provides a framework for building the games that lends networkability as almost a transparent option.

There is a lot of jargon in networking, so we'd better start by defining some terms. These may be defined differently to how you understand them – if so, I apologise. But even if you don't like them, you'll know what I'm talking about, which is the real issue:

- *Host*: an object that is responsible for coordinating one or more instances of a specific game on a single machine.
- *Session*: an instance of a specific game controlled by a host.

- *Data model*: a class that stores the entire state of a session. Remember how we wanted to keep the simulation and visual sides of the game separate? The data model is the simulation part.
- *Player*: a human (or maybe an AI entity) that generates control information.
- *Server*: a class that handles the update of a game session. Everyone who runs a session on a machine has a server – it is not a reference to the machine the game runs on.
- *Client*: a class that handles the input from a player.
- *Master*: a server whose data model is the definitive version of the game.
- *Slave*: a server whose data model needs periodic synchronisation with the master server's.

These are our basic terms. Now, what is networking really about? At its heart, it is a messaging problem. Data on one machine need to be sent to another, so package them up into a message and (somehow) transport them to the destination. Since the ability to transmit and receive messages is fundamental, we start our analysis with an abstract class called a `Conduit`:

```cpp
// File: NET_Conduit.hpp
namespace NET
{

/*
 * Forward declarations.
 */

class Message;

/*
 * Class declarations.
 */

class Conduit
{
public:
    /*
     * Constants/typedefs/enums.
     */

    /*
     * Lifecycle.
     */
        Conduit( Conduit * pParent, int iRtti );
        virtual ~Conduit();
```

```
        /*
         * Polymorphism.
         */
            virtual bool Transmit( Message * ) = 0;
                    // Sends a message. Returns true if the
                    // send succeeds (though this is      no
                    // guarantee that the message arrives).

            virtual bool HandleMessage( Message * ) = 0;
                // Called when a message is received.
                // Must return true if the message is
                // recognised and acted upon.

        /*
         * API.
         */
            Conduit *        GetParent();
            const Conduit * GetParent() const;
                    // Get the parent conduit.
                    // NULL (0) is a legal value.

            int GetRtti() const;
                // Obtain the type of the class instance.
protected:
    /*
     * Helpers.
     */

private:
    /*
     * Data.
     */
        Conduit * m_pParent;
                // Pointer to the parent conduit.
                // If 0 (NULL), there is no parent.
        int m_iRtti;
                // Type information.
}; // end class

}
```

Note that we can create a simple hierarchy of Conduit instances. In reality, the topology of the instance hierarchy will be mostly fixed and always simple, as we shall see shortly.

We now create a concrete class that generically sends and receives messages. This will be used as the base class for all game classes that require network messaging support. We call this class a `Transceiver`. Each transceiver in a game has a unique ID that is allocated at run time.

This allows us to determine uniquely where a message needs to go: not just the machine, but also the session or even the transceiver within the session that the message is targeted at. I'll assume (without loss of generality) that the machine identifier is an Internet protocol (IP) address (four bytes). The `Address` class is written as follows:

```cpp
// File: NET_Address.hpp
namespace NET
{

class Address
{
public:
    typedef unsigned char IpAddress[4];
    static const int NULL_ID;

    Address();
        // Empty address: message goes nowhere.
    Address( const IpAddress & Ip );
        // Addresses a machine only.
    Address( const IpAddress & Ip, int iSession );
        // Addresses a session on a machine.
    Address( const IpAddress & Ip,
            int iSession,
            int iTransceiver );
        // Addresses a transceiver on a session on
        // a particular machine.
    Address( int iSession );
        // Addresses a session on the local machine.
    Address( int iSession, int iTransceiver );
        // Addresses a particular transceiver on a
        // session on the local machine.
    Address( const char * pIpString,
            int iSession,
            int iTransceiver );
        // Convert a ABC.DEF.HGI.JKL TCP address
    Address( const Address & );
    ~Address();

    const IpAddress & GetIp() const;
    int               GetSessionId() const;
    int               GetTransceiverId() const;
        // Access to the components of the address.

    Address & operator=( const Address & );
```

```
private:
    IpAddress m_cIp;
        // TCP/IP address a.b.c.d defines which host
        // the address specifies.
    int m_iSession;
        // Identifies the session on the host.
    int m_iTransceiver;
        // Identifies the transceiver on the session.
};

}
```

That plethora of constructs enables an address to specify any conduit we like, including those on the local machine. Since this is easy to recognise – the IP address field is NULL_ID – we don't need to bother sending anything over the network, and the transmission becomes a simple function call.

Figures 5.47 and 5.48 show the story so far – the classes and the implicit instance hierarchy.

Now let's add in servers, clients and the rest. Client and Server are sub-classes of Transceiver, not Conduit, which makes them optional parts of the system. If you want to create a class Peer from Transceiver, thereby changing your network topology, you are free to do so. Figure 5.49 takes us on a step further.

Rather than subclass Server into ServerSlave and ServerMaster, we've elected to allow the server to change behaviour dynamically. This is useful behaviour when the master server in a network game disappears because of a hardware failure or the player quitting: the remaining servers can then negotiate over who is to be the new master without lots of dynamic memory allocations and the associated rebuilding of internal state.

Figure 5.47
Object diagram for the
basic NET component.

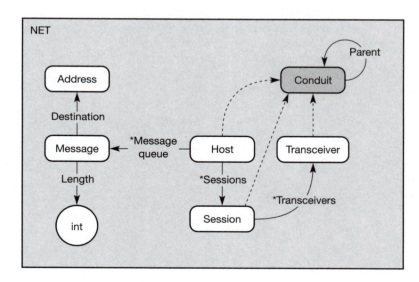

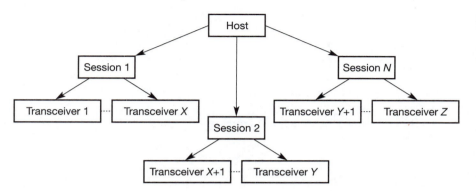

Figure 5.48
Hierarchy of hosts, sessions and transceivers.

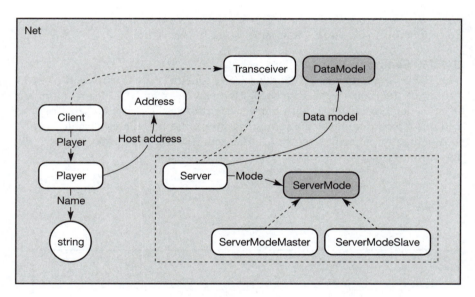

Figure 5.49
Adding clients and servers to the NET component.

```
class ServerMode
{
public:
     virtual bool HandleMsg(Server * s, Message * m) = 0;
     virtual void Update(Server * s, Time dt ) = 0;
};

class Server
{
public:
    void SetMode( ServerMode & aMode )
    {
        m_pMode = &aMode;
    }
```

```
        void Update( Time dt )
        {
            m_pMode->Update( this, dt );
        }

        bool HandleMsg( Message * pMsg )
        {
            m_pMode->HandleMsg(this,pMsg);
        }

private:
    ServerMode * m_pMode;
};
```

To couple this to an actual game, subclass again (see Figure 5.50).

5.4.12 Summary

This has been a long chapter. And yet we've touched only briefly on the technicalities of the topics we've discussed. That was the plan: the idea all along has been to demonstrate that, with a few straightforward OO design principles, we can create component architectures that minimise bloat, are reusable, flexible and light, and perform decently. To that end, this chapter has been a start. The rest is up to you.

Figure 5.50
Game implementations of abstract or overridable behaviours in the NET component.

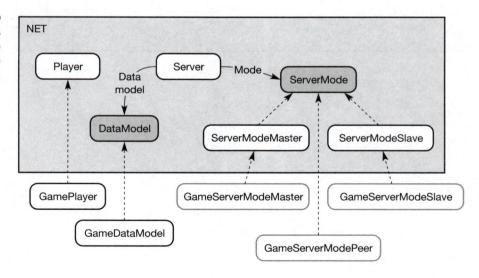

5.5 Summary

- Game engines allow teams to focus on game-play issues rather than technical issues.

- By their nature, they are tightly coupled and monolithic – anathema to software engineering principles.

- A component-based object model – a set of independent building blocks – allows much more freedom and extensibility than a game engine. What's more, the components (by virtue of their independent nature) are easier to use and reuse than traditional code.

- Localise simple auxiliary classes within a component to minimise external dependencies.

- Keep data and their visual representation logically and physically separate.

- Keep static and dynamic data separate.

- Avoid making unrelated systems interdependent.

- Try to avoid using threads in a game. They make debugging a nightmare, and you may lose the precise control over scheduling and timing that sequential methods give you.

- All high-level game systems can be written as components.

Cross-platform development

6

6.1 Introduction

If there is a single constraint that will either invalidate parts of or even entirely break your painstakingly nurtured object-oriented design, it is that your game will have to work on a variety of target hardware. And what a diversity of hardware! PCs – with a combinatorially huge and broadly unregulated set of constituent components, Macs, and, perhaps most importantly of all, the ever-expanding console market, including handhelds.

Starting from scratch (with nothing but some middleware, perhaps), a single platform's implementation will – on average – take about one and a half to two years to get on to the shop shelves. A lot can happen in that time! Platforms can come and go, and bottom-line hardware will double in speed. It would be inexcusable to spend another similar amount of time to produce a similar version of the game for another machine, which would look seriously out of date by the time the shrink-wrap cools. More to the point, it can be economic suicide.[1]

In other words, if we are to release the game for n platforms, then we've got to do it all pretty much in parallel. There are two ways we might go about this: either support n teams to write bespoke and largely (maybe even entirely) independent versions of the game, or support m teams (where $m \leq n$), with some amount of common code shared between platforms.

Clearly, having n development teams for n platforms is an expensive luxury that the majority of games developers cannot afford. Since all developers are inevitably slaves to the vagaries of the free market (albeit occasionally happy slaves), there is clearly a strong motivation to develop the skus (as they are called) in parallel.

6.1.1 Analyse this

First off, let's consider two parameters in the analysis of platforms: *capability* and *methodology*.

---

1   This doesn't apply to all genres of game. Those that can escape are the lucky ones, but usually they will generate a whole new set of challenges for developers.

Capability

This is a measure of what the hardware can do: number of instructions executed per second, number of colours displayed, number of simultaneous sounds, number of executables that can be run in parallel, etc.

Methodology

This is how the hardware goes about doing the things it's capable of. Factors contributing to this are things such as byte ordering (big or little Endian), bitmapped screen memory versus display list generation, and presence or absence of a hard disk.

In real life, these are not mutually exclusive concepts. How something is done can inevitably determine what it can do. For the purpose of this analysis, though, it remains useful to keep the distinction. We need to consider several possible circumstances for cross-platform development:

- Platforms A and B are broadly similar in capability and broadly similar in methodology.
- Platforms A and B are broadly similar in capability but radically different in methodology.
- Platforms A and B are quite different in capability but similar in methodology.
- Platforms A and B are so different in capability and methodology that the game cannot even potentially be the same on both systems.

6.1.2 Welcome to Fantasy Land

The case in which two target platforms are similar in both the what and the how is pretty rare. It's an appealing notion that we just need to select a different compiler, hit 'build', go for a coffee and return to find a game that looks and plays near as damn identically on platforms A and B. Let's just assume for the sake of discussion that this is the case. The challenges that we meet will form the minimal experience of writing multiplatform.

So we've changed the flag in the make file (or selected the build type on our favourite integrated development environment (IDE)) and initiated the compilation. What might take us by surprise? Well, experience overwhelmingly dictates that you are going to be very lucky to get through the build without a compilation error. Welcome back to the real world! Compilers that really ought to comply with the ANSI C++ standard don't. And even those that do still have a bewildering scope for behavioural difference, sometimes subtle, sometimes less so.

Depending on how conservatively you have written your code, you will get fewer compile-time errors the less you use templates (and STL in particular), recently added keywords and multiple inheritance. Indeed, the number of errors and warnings you can get is related directly to how far your C++ code is from a purely procedural interface. Disturbingly, though, even a totally procedural implementation will cause warnings and errors – perhaps lots of them. What will these errors and warnings be about? Here are some perennial issues.

Give us a sign
Signed and unsigned arithmetic or comparison. Yet another reason to ditch those unsigned variables wherever possible! Compiler writers just can't agree about how serious a problem mixing signed and unsigned is. You should be less accommodating.

Out of character
Is a character signed or unsigned by default? Is an enum signed or unsigned by default?

Fruity loops
I write my 'for' loops like this:

```
for( int j = 0; j < 10; ++j )
{
    /* Do some stuff */
}
```

For some compilers, the scope of j is inside the parentheses. For others, it's everywhere after the declaration of j. So if you do this

```
    int j = 7;
```

later on in that scope, on some machines it's an error but on others it's fine.

Static constants
Some compilers are happy with initialising static constant values at the point of declaration:

```
class Error
{
    static const int PROBLEM = 10;
};
```

Others aren't, and they don't like being argued with.

STL
Ah, if only the 'standard' in the expansion of STL was so. Surprisingly, there is a remarkable variation in STL implementations over a multiplicity of platforms. Although the ANSI standard describes quite categorically how the participant classes should behave, some compilers – most notably Microsoft's – don't follow that standard. And even among those that do, there is still a wide variation in implementation (though there is nothing wrong with that *per se*), which means that the performance you get on one platform may not happen on another.[2]

---

2   There is a version of STL called STLPort that is currently free and works on a number of different targets.

And so on. Point being that there are a lot of nitpicky issues to deal with. Now, if this wasn't enough, in order to deal with these pesky messages you will have to deal with the various ways that development systems let you control these warnings and errors. There is no standard for writing this: some compilers use command-line switches, some use IDE settings, some use #pragma directives, and none will agree what a warning level means.

Now don't go jumping to the conclusion that this means you should abandon all the powerful stuff we've discussed so far when faced with a parallel development scenario. Quite the reverse – as we'll see, object orientation, advanced C++ features and component methodologies are all going to help you to develop across multiple platforms. What it does suggest is that you need to understand your tools quite a bit more deeply, and that more experienced teams are going to fare better when going cross-platform. Teams with less experience are therefore probably better suited to the expensive one-team-per-sku model. Conversely, if your company hires less experienced developers (because they were cheap, yes?), then you're better off spending the money you saved (and then some) on those *n* teams. Free lunch, anyone?

So the first technique for solving these niggling compiler issues is to not write the offending code in the first place and to put into practice coding standards that make sure nobody else does. Usually, though, you'll find out that something isn't liked after you've written it. And so up and down the land you'll meet code that looks like this:

```
#    if defined( TARGET_PLATFORM_1 )
     /* Do something nice */
#    else
     /* Do the same thing slightly differently */
#    endif
```

This is by far the most common method of multiplatform development: isolate the variable bits of code into platform-specific blocks. And it's fine, so long as a couple of common-sense conditions are met:

- you don't target too many platforms;
- the blocks of code encompassed by the preprocessor statements are 'small'.

It's easy for this technique to produce code that is hard to understand and maintain. Too many target platforms will result in lots of preprocessor statements that aren't conducive to tracing control flow. As for the size of isolated blocks, an important maxim to bear in mind is the principle of smallest effect, which says that if you have a block of code like this:

```
void MyClass::Method()
{
    // Statement block 1
    {
    }

    // Statement block 2 - the bad apple
    {
    }

    //…

    // Statement block N
    {
    }
}
```

then it's better to isolate it like this:

```
void MyClass::Method()
{
    // Statement block 1
    {
    }

#    if defined( TARGET_PLATFORM_1 )
    // Statement block 2 for target 1
    {
    }
#    else
    // Statement block 2 for other targets
    {
    }
#    endif

    //…

    // Statement block N
    {
    }
}
```

than like this:

```
#if defined( TARGET_PLATFORM_1 )
void MyClass::Method()
{
    // Platform 1 code
}
#else
void MyClass::Method()
{
    // Other platform code
}
#endif
```

Not only is the former easier to understand, but it also avoids the unnecessary duplication of nearly identical code. In general, prefer isolating lines to isolating a function, isolating a function to isolating several functions, and isolating several functions to isolating classes.

If you find yourself isolating large blocks of code, then that suggests that the one file you're working with defines non-negligible amounts of platform-specific code. If so, that code could be cut and pasted into a platform-specific file that helps to isolate the behavioural variations in toolsets.

This can end up generating a whole bunch of problems. Multiplatform build systems – especially ones that involve the use of manually edited make files – need to be able to select the appropriate files for a particular build, and they can do that either manually (someone – poor soul – is responsible for maintaining the lists of files and tools and rules) or automatically (someone – poor soul – writes tools that use batch-processing utilities such as *sed* or *awk* to generate and update the make files and auxiliary systems).

Some IDEs make the process easier by allowing custom toolsets to compile and link for a number of different target types. Usually, someone – poor soul – will have to write the tools necessary to bind the compiler, linker and other programs to the IDE, so the route isn't clear-cut this way either.

All of which amounts to the following: though you may get away with it depending on what system you're writing for, it's best not to tempt fate as it has a habit of having bigger weapons than you. Avoid writing the offending code in the first place.

Now wouldn't it be nice if there was a tool, a kind of über-compiler, that didn't actually generate any code but could be configured to understand the idiosyncrasies of all your target platforms and would warn you of any problem areas before they started giving you headaches? Well, such tools exist, with programs such as Gimpel Software's PC-Lint (www.gimpel.com). Though requiring a bit of effort to set up and maintain, these utilities can not only spot platform-specific incompatibilities but also find language-related bugs that no other compiler can spot, thus saving you a considerable amount of debugging time.

So, in short, language issues can generate a lot of minor, but annoying, problems when developing for multiple platforms. If you know the toolset, avoid writing potentially problematic code and isolate the minimal amount of that source, then you will maximise maintainability and clarity. Coding standards can help to avoid the pitfalls, and there are tools out there that – with some amount of effort – can help to catch the awkward variations in grammar and behaviour before they bite.

6.1.3 Same capability, different methodology

It's hard to be general in this case, as there are many different ways of doing a particular task. But clearly the worst-case scenario is that we will have to write code (and generate data) that works identically (or near as dammit) on radically different hardware architectures. The word 'identically' should be suggesting that getting n teams to write the skus isn't going to be a viable option. Let's assume that team A writes its AI code using a combination of fuzzy logic and the usual state-based heuristics. Team B writes it using a series of neural nets with a different heuristic system. If AI is a big part of the game then how easy will it be to ensure similar behaviour between skus? Not particularly.

So, we assume that a certain amount of code sharing will be going on. The question is: 'How much code can be shared?' The flippant answer is: 'As much as possible but no more'. It's better to be this vague, otherwise you will find yourself trying to justify exactly what 25% of your code means – one-quarter of your files? Classes? Packages? Lines of code? Lines of code that aren't comments? Trust me, don't go there.

Consider the similarities and differences between two current platforms – PC and Macintosh. At the time of writing, the average PC runs at about 2 GHz and although Macs haven't got quite such big numbers in front of their specifications, they're at least of equivalent power. Both platforms' 3D capabilities are similar – they share similar hardware after all. Both platforms have lots of memory – at least 128 MB comes as standard. They also have big hard disks.

What's different? Byte ordering for one thing. Little Endian on PC, big on Mac. This gives you a couple of choices when considering how to load data into the game.

Same data, different code

Use the same data on your PC game and your Mac game. If you do that, there's no need to keep two versions of your data lying around and potentially unsynchronised. However, one version of your software – which one depends on what is your lead platform, the one you generate your data on – is going to have to do some byte twiddling, and this has repercussions for your serialisation code. Supposing you have a component like this:

```
struct MyClassData
{
    int   x;
    short a;
    char  c;
};

class MyClass
{
public:
    MyClass( MyClassData * pData );

private:
    MyClassData m_Data;
};

class MyClassLoader
{
public:
    MyClass * Load( FILE * pFile );
};
```

Then your loading implementation might look like this on a single-platform project:

```
MyClass * MyClassLoader::Load( FILE * pFile )
{
    MyClassData aData;

    fread( &aData, sizeof( MyClassData ), 1, pFile );

    return( new MyClass( &aData ) );
}
```

while on a multiple-sku project you're going to need to write something like this:

```
MyClass * MyClassLoader::Load( FILE * pFile )
{
    MyClassData aData;

    aData.x = readInt( pFile );
    aData.a = readShort( pFile );
    aData.c = readChar( pFile );

    return( new MyClass( &aData ) );
}
```

The read functions will vary – on the native platform they'll just read the size of the entity, but on the non-native platform they'll need to swap bytes for data sizes over one byte. That means reading every data element individually. Is there a problem there? Well maybe, maybe not. If your real-world structure is big (and they usually get that way), then your loading could be slowed down big time.

Same code, different data

Realising that the byte swapping during load is unnecessary, we can – as hinted above – add an option to our toolset that generates either big- or little-Endian data. Pushing data manipulation from run-time game code to offline tools code is always a good thing (and is perhaps a good example of where optimising early on can sometimes benefit the product).

A couple of caveats here:

- Don't mix up the file formats. I've seen the wrong data type imported by accident, much to the bafflement of developers. Keep the files penned in an appropriate directory hierarchy, and make sure there's a byte in the file header that uniquely determines which platform that file is to be loaded on.
- If you need to support several platforms and the data generation is expensive – I've seen systems that do a lot of static analysis and can take up to two or three hours per level – then having a single save format might well be preferable not only for programmers but also for designers and artists (who want to see the results of their changes as quickly as possible after making them).

Intermediate file formats

If we are prepared to sacrifice some disk space and some simplicity, then we can make our lives a whole lot easier by creating a series of intermediate file formats. These are files that are exported directly by a piece of asset-generation software in a format acceptable to the host machine. They can be processed further by additional tools to generate data files targeted at any platform. In Figure 6.1, we can see this in action.

The tool APP2IFF – a notional one, since it is probably written as a plug-in to an existing asset-creation package or as a function of a bespoke application – extracts the asset data from the host application and writes out the intermediate file format. In Figure 6.1, the IFF is a text file, and this is no accident. The only real cost of storing like this will be disk space, but we gain human readability. This is very important. The tool APP2IFF may have bugs in it, and if we exported directly to a binary format they would be hard to find. With a text file, they can be spotted with considerably greater ease.

A further set of tools reads the IFF and converts them into the platform-specific binary files. These are labelled as IFF2P1 and IFF2P2 in Figure 6.1. Again, if we spot errors (crashes or data not corresponding to the source graphics), we can inspect the IFF visually to see if there's anything odd in there.

Figure 6.1
Flow of data from
asset-creation software
to the game.

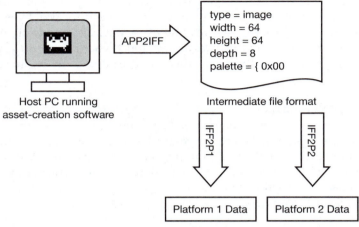

Figure 6.1
Flow of data from
asset-creation software
to the game.

Host PC running
asset-creation software

Intermediate file format

Platform-dependent data files

Another benefit of the IFF is that humans can write them as well as read them. Programmers needn't get their hands dirty with asset-generation packages. For example, if a cube or other simple graphic is needed in the game, then the programmer can just knock up a quick text file in the intermediate model format. Indeed, this concept can be extended because the IFFs clearly don't care what generates them – any application can be coerced to spit them out, and we don't have to change the rest of our toolsets to accommodate this.

What else does the IFF do for us? Well, the whole asset-generation process is much easier to automate and runs quickly and smoothly. Most asset-generation packages are big programs with a significant start-up time, and they are often awkward or even impossible to automate from the host machine. Using IFF, the platform-specific data generation is performed via command-line-driven tools that are quick to load and execute. We'll revisit this later when we discuss tools and assets in more detail.

Another benefit of IFF is that data can be stored in an optimally accurate format. For example, coordinates can be represented by double-precision numbers in both the IFF and the associated toolset, even if the representation on the target platforms is single-precision floats or even fixed-point integers. There is no need for the toolset to have a small footprint or to be fast to execute, because the host machines will have buckets of RAM and the files will be processed offline. In this way, the IFF can actually contain more information than was exported from the asset-generation software. For example, MIP-maps using complex filtering can be generated when textures are exported.

So, what might we create IFFs for? Here are some suggestions:

● models
● palettes

- textures (in a generic bitmap format)
- materials
- animations
- collision hulls.

In short, just about any external resource that will be loaded in binary by the game. (Of course, text files such as behaviour scripts don't need to be IFF'd, as they are already text.)

Finally, here's a sample of an IFF file for a 3D model to illustrate the points made in this section:

```
Hierarchy "WOMAN"
{
    Frames
    [
        Frame "Scene_Root_0"
        {
            Transformation Matrix44 (0.01 0 …)
            Children [1 41 44 47 50 51 52]
        }
        Frame "Root_1"
        {
            Transformation Matrix44 (-1.04 …)
            Children [2 39]
        }
        ...
    ]
    RootNodes [0]
}
MaterialList "WOMAN"
[
    Material "WOMAN_MESH_MESH0_MATERIAL0"
    {
        Texture "WOMAN_KITE 01"
        DiffuseColour (1 1 1 1)
        AmbientColour (1 1 1 1)
        SpecularColour (1 1 1 1)
        SpecularPower 0
        EmmissiveColour (0 0 0 1)
    }
    Material "WOMAN_MESH_MESH1_MATERIAL0"
    {
        Texture "WOMAN_BUGGY WOMAN"
        DiffuseColour (1 1 1 1)
```

```
            AmbientColour (1 1 1 1)
            SpecularColour (1 1 1 1)
            SpecularPower 0
            EmmissiveColour (0 0 0 1)
        }
        ...
    ]
VisualList "WOMAN"
[
    VLMesh "MESH0" "FRAME37"
    {
        Vertices
        [
                (
                [(3.16834 -0.447012 -0.187323)]
                [(-0.475341 0.0444252 -0.878679)]
                [(1 1 1 1)]
                [(0.701362 0.00476497)]
                )
                (
                [(3.10494 0.0622288 -0.127278)]
                [(-0.157954 0.134406 -0.978256)]
                [(1 1 1 1)]
                [(0.366187 0.0437355)]
                )
            ...
        ]
        Primitives
        [
            TriList ("WOMAN_MESH0_MATERIAL0" [0 1 2])
            TriList ("WOMAN_MESH0_MATERIAL0" [0 3 1])
            TriList ("WOMAN_MESH0_MATERIAL0" [4 1 5])
            ...
        ]
    }
    VLEnvelope "MESH1" "FRAME40"
    {
        BlendFrames
        [
            ("Abdomen_2" (-0.775194 7…)
            ("Right_hip_28" (-0.775194…)
            ("Right_elbow_16" (-0.775194…)

            ...
```

```
        ]
        Vertices
        [
            ...
        ]
        Primitives
        [
            TriStrip ("WOMAN_MESH1_MATERIAL0" [0 1...])
            TriStrip ("WOMAN_MESH1_MATERIAL0" [3 3...])
            TriStrip ("WOMAN_MESH1_MATERIAL0" [4 6...])
            ...
        ]
    }
    VLMesh "MESH2" "FRAME43"
    {
        Vertices
        [
            ...
        ]
        Primitives
        [
            TriList ("WOMAN_MESH3_MATERIAL0" [0 1 2])
            TriList ("WOMAN_MESH3_MATERIAL0" [0 3 1])
            TriList ("WOMAN_MESH3_MATERIAL0" [4 5 6])
        ]
    }
    ...
]
```

What else might be different between platforms? Data types can vary in sign and bit-size for one.

Those platform-specific integral types

Almost every cross-platform development system has a file that looks a bit like this:

```
// File: TARGET_Types.hpp
#if !defined( TARGET_TYPES_INCLUDED )
#define TARGET_TYPES_INCLUDED

#if TARGET == TARGET1
typedef char int8;
typedef unsigned char uint8;
typedef short int16;
typedef unsigned short uint16;
```

```
typedef int int32;
typedef unsigned int uint32;
typedef long long int64;
typedef unsigned long long uint64;
typedef float float32;
typedef double float64;
#elif TARGET == TARGET2
//etc
#endif

#endif
```

As a definition of atomic data types this is fine, but it prompts a short discussion on exactly how useful these types are.[3]

There's no question that at the lowest level, all hardware is controlled by writing bits into registers. So at that level you really do need these data types with guaranteed bit lengths. Nevertheless (and a product I have consulted on was a fine example of this), one sees a lot of stuff like this function prototype:

```
uint32 MODULE_SomeFunction( uint32 XPos, int8 aChar );
```

Notice that for this function to be declared, we've had to pull in the types header file. And for what? Clearly, the function body cannot write its arguments directly to hardware (unless the stack has been memory-mapped to the registers). And why 32 bits for the first argument? And why force an unsigned data type?[4] In most circumstances

```
int MODULE_SomeFunction( int iXCoord, int iCharacter );
```

is just fine.

For the sake of discussion – but mainly because it will be relevant later on in this chapter – we'll assume that the code to perform some specific task cannot be the same on the platforms we need to support. How do we write the *minimal* amount of platform-dependent code to fulfil that task?

First – and fairly obviously – since C++ uses a header file for declaration and a source file for definition, we have the following permutations of files that can vary.

---

3 The author understands that the ANSI committee is considering adding sized types to the next revision of the C++ standard.
4 A colleague and I recently had the 'unsigned' argument. I couldn't persuade him that most uses of unsigned were unnecessary. At least, not until he changed a loop like this – `for( unsigned j = 0; j < 100; ++j )` – into `for( unsigned j = 99; j >= 0; --j )`. When I found the bug (an infinite loop), the teasing commenced. It hasn't stopped yet.

Same header file, same source file

Let us make the bold assertion that writing platform-dependent code where there is only a single header and source file is, in general, not such a good idea. In the cases where there are only a few isolated differences, then it's possible to get away with this sort of stuff:

```
// File: COMPONENT_MyClass.cpp
#include "COMPONENT_MyClass.hpp"

using namespace COMPONENT;

MyClass::MyClass()
{
#if TARGET == TARGET_1
{
    // Platform 1 initialisation.
}
#elif TARGET == TARGET_2
{
    // Platform 2 initialisation.
}
#elif TARGET == TARGET_3
{
    // Platform 3 initialisation.
}
#else
#    error "Invalid TARGET"
#endif
}
```

This class does nothing but still looks sort of complicated. Put some code in there and it's safe to say that it doesn't get any prettier. In the long term, this sort of multi-platform technique isn't very sustainable. Consider, for example, the use of version control with this file where different programmers write the various implementations for each platform. For those databases that don't allow multiple checkouts, development can be blocked while one programmer edits the file. If multiple checkouts are allowed, then there will be a lot of merging going on, with a lot of scope for conflicts and errors. These merge errors can take hours of painstaking reconstruction to resolve, and you wouldn't want to do that, would you?

Even worse, look at the shenanigans going on in the header file:

```
// File: COMPONENT_MyClass.hpp
#if !defined( COMPONENT_MYCLASS_INCLUDED )
#define COMPONENT_MYCLASS_INCLUDED
```

```
#if TARGET == TARGET1
#    if !defined( TARGET1_TYPES_INCLUDED )
#        include <TARGET1_Types.hpp>
#    endif
#elif TARGET == TARGET_2
#    if !defined( TARGET2_TYPES_INCLUDED )
#        include <TARGET2_Types.hpp>
#    endif
#elif TARGET == TARGET_3
#    if !defined( TARGET3_TYPES_INCLUDED )
#        include <TARGET3_Types.hpp>
#    endif
#else
#    error "Invalid TARGET"
#endif

namespace COMPONENT
{

class MyClass
{
public:
    MyClass();

    int GetData1() const;
#    if TARGET == TARGET1
    int GetData2() const;
#    endif
#    if TARGET == TARGET_2 || TARGET == TARGET_3
    char const * GetName();
#    endif
private:
    // Common data.
    int m_iData1;

    // Platform-specific data.
#    if TARGET == TARGET_1
    int m_iData2;
#    elif TARGET == TARGET_2
    char * m_szName;
    // Uh-oh: I might need delete[] ing on destruction.
    // Wanna bet that you forget with all these defines?
#    elif TARGET == TARGET_3
    int m_iData2;
```

```
        char m_szName[ 32 ];
        // Uh-oh. You might accidentally try to delete me if
        // you get confused about which platform you're on.
#    else
#        error "Invalid TARGET"
#    endif
};


} // end of namespace COMPONENT


#endif // included
```

It's easy to see that this could become a real maintenance nightmare and a fertile source of bugs. Though the class might be simple enough when first written, we can only expect it to grow over the course of a product (or products). In other words, beware of relying on the preprocessor to do your platform-specific code selection.

Same header, different source file
So, let's assume that (i) we've got rid of most or all of the preprocessor selection of platform-specific code and (ii) we have a build system that can select a different source file for building the component:

```
// Target1/COMPONENT_MyClass.cpp
// for TARGET_1
#include "COMPONENT_MyClass.hpp"
#include <TARGET1_Types.hpp>
using namespace COMPONENT;


MyClass::MyClass()
{
    // Target 1 specific init
}



// Target2/COMPONENT_MyClass.cpp
// for TARGET_2
#include "COMPONENT_MyClass.hpp"
#include <TARGET2_Types.hpp>
using namespace COMPONENT;


MyClass::MyClass()
{
    // Target 2 specific init
}
```

These files live – by necessity, since they are called the same – in a separate directory in the project (one subdirectory for each platform). If we structure our code like this, the header file is almost entirely 'clean' – in other words, generic. When we create an object instance, we are oblivious to the actual type of the object created:

```
#include "COMPONENT_MyClass.hpp"

COMPONENT::MyClass * pObject = new COMPONENT::MyClass;
```

This is fine, and a considerable improvement over the preprocessor method. However, it is of limited use because it assumes identical data members in the class on all versions of the code. It's rare to see a multiplatform class that uses identical data in its various implementations.

Different header, different source file

More often than not, you will be faced with writing a class whose implementation, data members and helpers are different on each target platform. Even though this sounds like they are all different classes, one thing remains the same (or, more accurately, *should* stay the same): the class should fulfil exactly the same objective on all respective platforms. Now this should ring some bells. What do we call a class that describes a behaviour without specifying how we achieve it? An *interface*.

Technically speaking, an interface is a class with no data members and entirely pure virtual member functions (see the discussion in Chapter 4 to refresh your memory). So, now we have a source structure like that shown in Figure 6.2.

This has now physically separated what are logically separate objects. We're well on our way to writing cross-platform object-oriented code. But before we get carried away with this elegance and power, we should remember that we

Figure 6.2
Cross-platform
class hierarchy.

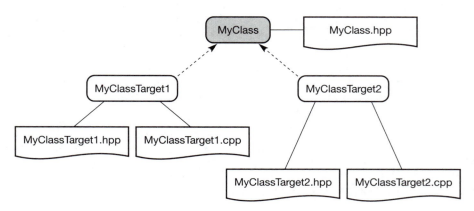

would like to write as little of this sort of code as is necessary. There are two reasons for this: first, writing lots of small classes like this is going to be fiddly – lots of files and directories kicking around; second, there is a small performance penalty inherent because of the virtual functions in those platform-dependent concrete subclasses. If the granularity of the class functionality is too small (as discussed in previous chapters), then this structure will start to become as much of a maintenance bottleneck as we were hoping to avoid and the game could start to run slowly to boot.

So let's keep the objects that we write using this paradigm larger than small, if that's not too meaningless an expression. What sort of objects are we talking about?

Renderers

Renderers are not easy to write minimal amounts of platform-specific code for relative to the amount of generic code. In fact, graphics systems are about as specialised as they come, because they tend to rely on idiosyncratic hardware to perform optimally, and hardware varies hugely from platform to platform. This tends to limit the amount of generic code that can exist in a rendering system, and it is usually limited to support classes (such as maths types for the higher-level systems).

For this reason, the sort of cross-platform structure we see in a rendering system looks like that shown in Figure 6.3 (grossly simplified for brevity).

Notice in particular that the primitive types have not been subclassed from a generic primitive type. This is because they are generally small objects and the

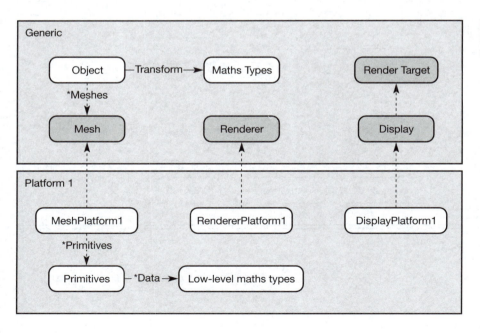

Figure 6.3
Bare-bones framework minimalist renderer.

penalty of a virtual method call would be prohibitive for objects with a lot of primitives (we can safely assume that is almost all of the graphical data we shall be required to handle nowadays), and also because it may not even work, because the low-level objects may need to map to hardware requirements (ah, so that's where these platform-specific data types are used). Ditto for the low-level maths classes.

Sound system

There was a distinct absence of structure evident in the graphics system because of wide variability in platform methodology. Audio systems are easier to genericise than renderers. At the topmost level, the sorts of things you do with sounds are:

- load and unload a sound or set of sounds;
- play a sound;
- set sound parameters (position, volume, frequency, filtering, etc.);
- stop playing a sound.

This doesn't just suggest an interface to a sound system; it actually hints at a generic management layer that performs all the logical operations on sounds (see Figure 6.4).

Figure 6.4
Audio system overview.

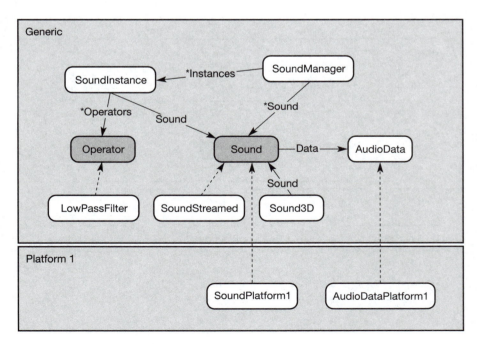

As it stands, this looks really great: we need implement only two classes for each new platform, the sound and audio data (which is really just a data holder and has no deep functionality). However, there is a complication, which manifests itself in the relationship between the sound and the audio data. If the sound manager class is generic, then it can't know specifically about any subclass of sound or audio data. What this means in practice is that manager classes need to implement a factory interface for creating the subclasses, and that we probably need to make some of the sound manager functionality polymorphic (see Figure 6.5).

Notice that we could have made the `CreateSound()` method pure virtual (and hence made `SoundManager` an abstract class). Instead, we've chosen to allow the base class to return an object instance. The object has the required interface but might do nothing other than print messages.

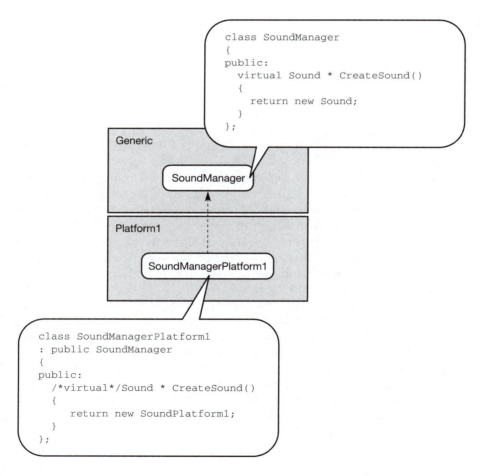

Figure 6.5
The sound manager as a factory.

```
namespace SOUND
{

class Sound
{
public:
    Sound();
    virtual ~Sound();

    virtual void Play()
    {
        printf("Playing sound 0x%.8X\n",this);
    }

    virtual void Stop()
    {
        printf( "Stopping sound 0x%.8X\n",this);
    }
};

}
```

This 'null object' class allows us to test the base class without getting bogged down in details of the platform specifics and is a useful technique in many contexts.

Renderers and audio systems represent near-extremes in the balance of platform-specific to generic code in a system. Certainly, it is hard to imagine a system (as opposed to a single piece of software) that is 100% platform-dependent, and renderers are about as near to that as they come. On the other hand, it is common for some systems to work perfectly well as completely generic components (though they may well depend on systems that are – transparently – not generic). For example, consider a package for performing basic Newtonian physics. It might look a bit like Figure 6.6.

This illustrates the power of the paradigm: generic systems can be written without a care in the world about the nature of the systems they depend on. The linear algebra services a physics system might exploit (for example, hardware-assisted matrix and vector operations) can be implemented efficiently on the target platform. However, we would be disingenuous to suggest that this structure is optimally efficient. In most cases, some performance or memory sacrifice will be overwriting bespoke, handcrafted, platform-specific software. In the vast majority of cases, careful design of the systems will yield at least acceptable, and more often better results, and in some cases, because we have control and flexibility over the structure and the way data are processed, we can actually design

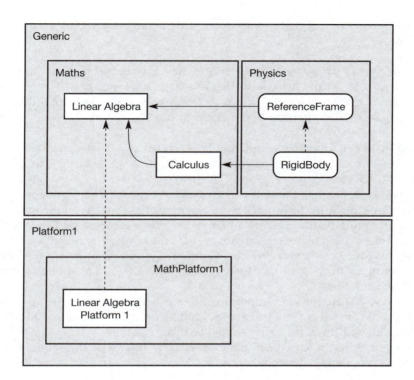

Figure 6.6
Class hierarchies on
the major and
minor platforms.

superoptimal components. Furthermore, by writing the generic services first, we have a working system early on that can be used to get the first phases of a product under way, maybe even complete should they prove to be good enough.

6.1.4 Platforms of different capability

In some respects, if the platforms differ in capability by a significant margin then the fact that their methodologies may be different is neither here nor there. A PC with 512 MB of RAM, a 2-GHz CPU, a 60-GB hard disk and an nVidia GeForce4 video adapter is going to seriously outperform a Sony PlayStation. If your brief is to produce a title for both platforms, then there are going to be some tough decisions to make.

First and foremost, can the game be the same on both platforms? This isn't just a technical question: it's as much – if not more – a matter of design. While it is beyond the scope of this book to discuss the complexities of designing game mechanics, we are extremely interested in what the consequences will be for how we design our systems.

So, first off: one of the platforms will have features that the other doesn't, and by this merit will become the dominant target. We'll call this the Major Platform and the other the Minor Platform. If the difference in capabilities between the Major Platform and the Minor Platform is – for some appropriate metric – suitably big, then something must change. Generally speaking, we can vary:

- *the types of things*: the Minor Platform may not be able to support the diversity of objects and behaviours that the Major Platform does;
- *the amount of things*: the Minor Platform may not support the number of object instances that the Major Platform can.

I also make the following distinction between the two platforms: the platform on which development will take place first is called the Leading Platform. The other I'll call the Trailing Platform. This reflects the fact that although we wish to develop in parallel, rarely is it the case that the skus evolve independently. Sometimes this is for technical reasons: perhaps the team has more experience on the Leading Platform; maybe there is an existing code base to work from. Other times, there may be pragmatic justifications: maybe there just aren't the staff, maybe there aren't any development systems available. One way or another, more likely than not, there'll be a Leading Platform and one (or more) Trailing Platforms.

These distinctions are important: they will shape the architecture of the game, and for that reason, if there are choices of who is Major and Minor and who Leads and Trails, then they should be made carefully.

So why are these definitions so crucial? Well, two of the foundations of good object-oriented design are thus:

- If the behaviour of a class needs to vary, then the class should be polymorphic; otherwise, the change in class properties should come about through varying the instance data.
- Subclassing an object should always change or add behaviour, never remove it.

So, consider an abstract class that should be implemented on the targets and that the Major Target is also the Leading Target. Then the two class hierarchies could look like this:

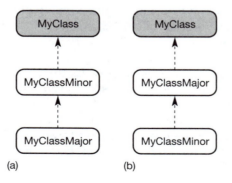

(a)   (b)

In case (a), we are taking the class as written on the Minor Platform, which will have restricted features – less complex behaviours and/or fewer instances – and expanding on it on the Major Platform. Now, if we are following the principles above (and we should be), then in this circumstance we can say that the only justification for `MyClassMajor` existing is if it has different or additional behaviour. If it is simply in terms of the particular values that the class instances use, then it should be a data issue and no subclassing is necessary.

The situation is quite different in case (b). Here, the Major Platform component is being subclassed on the Minor Platform. Oops! That doesn't sound quite right. According to our design principles, we should never be thinking of removing behaviour when subclassing, which leaves us only the option of altering data.

In other words, if the Major Platform is also the Leading Platform, then the only variability in component behaviour should come about through differing data.

Ouch! This can affect the entire balance of programming/design/art resource allocation, because different data could mean one or more of:

- tweaked constants in source files;
- different art resources (fewer or more polygons, textures of different bit-depth);
- changes to the scripting or behaviours of entities within the game.

Clearly, we are not looking at arbitrary choices here, and, ideally, we would like to choose the Minor Platform to be the Leading Platform.

Alternatively, we might choose to arrange the classes differently:

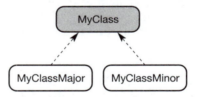

If we are to implement this efficiently, then we want to have as much common code in the base class as possible (after all, that is the whole point of the exercise). This will be feasible and practical only if there is only a small difference between the Major and Minor implementations, which in turn will be dictated by the difference in capability of the two sets of hardware.

At some point, such will be the difference in platform capability that some behaviours will not be feasible on the Minor Platform. At this point, it is clear that code sharing via inheritance is probably not going to happen: the Minor Platform may in fact require an entirely different design.

It would be madness to try to share an architecture for products that shared nothing in common. This doesn't lock the door on reusability altogether but – at this point – it looks very much like the products share only superficial similarity, and in terms of the data they manipulate and the way they manipulate they are entirely different.

The reader may ask why I am stating the obvious! If the games are radically different, why try to share an architecture? Well, I'm just being even-handed. There's no point in using the wrong tool for the job, but it happens all too frequently and can cost dearly. This is a common *Antipattern* called the 'Golden Hammer' (see Brown *et al.*, 1998). Basically, it can be paraphrased thus:

I have a hammer and everything else is a nail.

In other words, people who take a lot of time and trouble to acquire a skill (be it juggling or cross-platform development techniques) become attached to that skill and can favour it over and above the bigger picture (or the obvious referred to above).

Less flippantly, it is occasionally the case that the games simply have to be similar on both platforms, in which case the lowest common denominator comes into effect for better (but often for worse): the Minor Platform becomes the Leading Platform, so the title risks suffering painfully against the competition on the Major Platform. The choice to make this call is often outside the influence of the development team, but if the software architecture won't fit the business model, then that's useful information for someone to dwell on.

OK, enough patronisation (for now, anyway). We'll assume from now on that the architectures are not so radically different as to require independent development.

6.1.5 Cross-platform component architecture

Let's look in detail at the high-level architecture we can use to guide our multi-machine development. Since we've already discussed some of the concepts at length, we've essentially invoked our brainstorming process, so we start from the most obvious of places: the platform.

The platform component

What – in software terms – is a platform? It represents an abstraction of a variety of hardware-specific services that our games will use to do their bidding with. Ergo, all platforms will share some services (if they don't, then there's little hope for code sharing at this level). Some platforms will offer services that others don't (though it may be a legitimate choice to provide software emulation of that service on the other platforms, making it effectively a shared resource). Each platform will be unique, so the subclasses will typically be final – not subclassed themselves. So we expect to see a flat class hierarchy, like this:

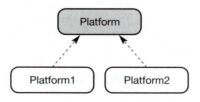

The other thing about the platform class is that you need only one of them; indeed, it could be an error to create more than one. It is therefore a logical singleton. (Recall the discussion of the singleton pattern in Chapter 4.)

The implementation of the platform base class is straightforward enough: it is an interface class for a factory (see Chapter 4) that returns pointers or references to platform-specific objects:

```
// File: PLATFORM_Platform.hpp
#ifndef PLATFORM_PLATFORM_INCLUDED
#define PLATFORM_PLATFORM_INCLUDED

namespace REND
{
    class Renderer;
}

namespace SOUND
{
    class SoundManager;
}

// More service types here.

namespace PLATFORM
{

class Platform
{
public:
    Platform();
    virtual ~Platform() { /*…*/ }

    virtual REND::Renderer *CreateRenderer() = 0;
    virtual SOUND::SoundManager *CreateSoundManager()=0;
    // One for each service type.
private:
};


}

#endif
```

Some readers may worry about the binding implied above: the platform package is now dependent on every service that the applications will require. Isn't this totally against the component methodology? Well, yes it is, so what might we do about it?

What we want to do is move the abstract concept of renderers and sound managers into the PLATFORM namespace without bogging down said namespace with any specifics about hardware or implementation. In other words, we'd like the sort of structure illustrated in component terms here and in classes in Figure 6.7:

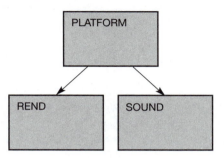

which decouples the packages. The Renderer and SoundManager types within the PLATFORM package are Strawman classes (again, see Chapter 4) that define no behaviour, only pass type information, e.g.

```cpp
// File: PLATFORM_Renderer.hpp
#ifndef PLATFORM_RENDERER_INCLUDED
#define PLATFORM_RENDERER_INCLUDED

namespace PLATFORM
{

class Renderer
{
public:
    Renderer();
    virtual ~Renderer();
};
```

Figure 6.7
Object diagram for platform-independent renderer and sound manager.

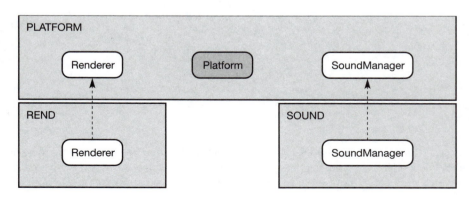

```
} // end of PLATFORM namespace

#endif
```

The Renderer within the REND package defines the generic renderer behaviour. Though in principle we could have placed that generic behaviour within the PLATFORM component, that would probably result in contamination of the PLATFORM name space with generic renderer specifics, which it really has no business in knowing. This way keeps it sparkling clean.

Cast your mind back to Figure 6.3, the outline of a cross-platform renderer. Notice that there is no provision for rendering to off-screen buffers (for example, to draw shadows or a rear-view mirror in a vehicle-based game). This is because we may not be able to assume that all targets have sufficient video RAM (VRAM) to allow this. It's often better – and easier – in the long run to not define a piece of non-generic functionality in a generic system than to provide it and disable it in a platform-specific system. It is always possible to create a new component associated with the renderer that provides the functionality in the middle-level functionality band.

Now, we have to make the abstract into the concrete. For each platform type we need to support, we define a namespace that implements the Platform class and defines the specific services (see Figure 6.8).

In the PLATFORM1 package, we define and implement our Platform class something like this:

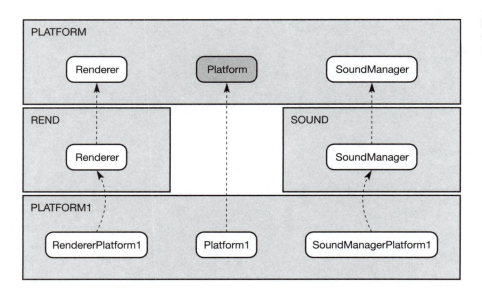

Figure 6.8
Cross-platform infrastructure.

```
// File: PLATFORM1_Platform1.hpp
#ifndef PLATFORM1_PLATFORM_INCLUDED
#define PLATFORM1_PLATFORM_INCLUDED

#ifndef PLATFORM_PLATFORM_INCLUDED
#include <PLATFORM\PLATFORM_Platform.h>
#endif

namespace PLATFORM1
{

class Platform1 : public PLATFORM::Platform
{
public:
    Platform1();
    ~Platform1();

    Renderer * CreateRenderer();
    // etc.
};

}

#endif

//--------------------------------------------------------

// File: PLATFORM1_Platform.cpp
#include "PLATFORM1_Platform.hpp"
#include "PLATFORM1_Renderer.hpp"

using namespace PLATFORM1;

Platform1::Platform1()
{
}

Platform1::~Platform1()
{
}

/*virtual*/
PLATFORM::Renderer * Platform1::CreateRenderer()
{
    return( new PLATFORM1::Renderer );
}
```

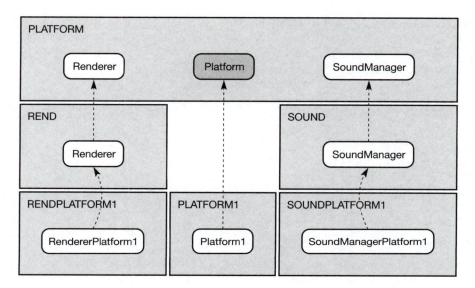

Figure 6.9
Cross-platform
infrastructure with
partitioned name
spaces.

Notice that the PLATFORM1 namespace looks a bit 'flat'. We've lost the component structure we'd introduced to keep independent functionality neatly partitioned. To remedy this, we can subclass the service namespaces just as we did for PLATFORM (see Figure 6.9).

The application component

So, by using the PLATFORM package we can define a factory for creating platform-specific classes and components. The intention is to use these in an application, so the next element in our model is to define an abstract application class. Platform-specific subclasses of the application class will create an appropriate Platform subclass and use that to create the required service components for the game, thus:

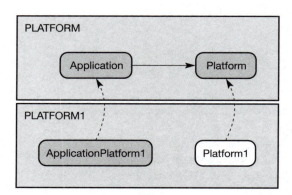

Which translates to C++ like this:

```cpp
// File: PLATFORM_Application.hpp
#ifndef PLATFORM_APPLICATION_INCLUDED
#define PLATFORM_APPLICATION_INCLUDED

namespace PLATFORM
{
class Platform;

class Application
{
public:
    Application( Platform * pPlatform )
    : m_pPlatform( pPlatform )
    {
    }

    virtual ~Application()
    {
        delete m_pPlatform;
    }

    // Main loop code for the application.
    virtual void Run() = 0;

    Platform * GetPlatform()
    {
        return( m_pPlatform );
    }
private:
    Platform * m_pPlatform;
};

} // end of namespace PLATFORM

#endif

//---------------------------------------------------------

// File: PLATFORM1_ApplicationPlatform1.hpp
#ifndef PLATFORM1_APPLICATION_INCLUDED
#define PLATFORM1_APPLICATION_INCLUDED
```

```
#ifndef PLATFORM_APPLICATION_INCLUDED
#include <PLATFORM\PLATFORM_Application.hpp>
#endif

namespace PLATFORM1
{

class ApplicationPlatform1 : public PLATFORM::Application
{
public:
    ApplicationPlatform1();
    ~ApplicationPlatform1();

    // Still abstract because of Run().
private:
};

} // end of namespace PLATFORM1

#endif

//-------------------------------------------------------

// File: PLATFORM1_ApplicationPlatform1.cpp
#include "PLATFORM1_ApplicationPlatform1.hpp"
#include "PLATFORM1_Platform1.hpp"

using namespace PLATFORM1;

ApplicationPlatform1::ApplicationPlatform1()
: PLATFORM::Application( new Platform1 )
{
}
```

can now be used as a base from which to derive a game class:

```
// File: GamePlatform1.hpp
#ifndef GAME_PLATFORM1_INCLUDED
#define GAME_PLATFORM1_INCLUDED

#ifndef PLATFORM1_APPLICATIONPLATFORM1_INCLUDED
#include <PLATFORM1\PLATFORM1_ApplicationPlatform1.hpp>
#endif
```

```cpp
namespace RENDPLATFORM1
{
    class Renderer;
}

class GamePlatform1
: public PLATFORM1::ApplicationPlatform1
{
public:
    GamePlatform1();
    ~GamePlatform1();

    // Accessors for the services required by the game.
    RENDPLATFORM1::Renderer * GetRenderer();

private:
    RENDPLATFORM1::Renderer * m_pRenderer;
};

#endif

//------------------------------------------------------

// File: GamePlatform1.cpp
#include "GamePlatform1.hpp"
#include <RENDPLATFORM1\RENDPLATFORM1_Renderer.hpp>

GamePlatform1::GamePlatform1()
: PLATFORM1::ApplicationPlatform1()
, m_pRenderer( 0 )
{
    // Note: DON'T try to set up the services here -
    // virtual functions don't work in a constructor.
}

GamePlatform1::~GamePlatform1()
{
    delete m_pRenderer;
}

REND::Renderer * GamePlatform1::GetRenderer()
{
    if ( m_pRenderer == 0 )
    {
```

```
        // These casts are safe because we know what
        // platform we've created the object for.
        PLATFORM1::Platform1 * pPlatform =
            (PLATFORM1::Platform1 *)GetPlatform();

        m_pRenderer = (RENDPLATFORM1::Renderer*)
            pPlatform->CreateRenderer();
    }

    return( m_pRenderer );
}


/*virtual*/
void GamePlatform1::Run()
{
    /* Initialisation… */
    bool bGameOver = false;

    /* Main loop for the game… */
    while( !bGameOver )
    {
        /* … */
    }

    /* Termination… */
}
```

Hmmm, now that we can see it in the flesh, that Run method seems to be a bit of a code-sharing obstacle. Suppose that we had identical main loops on our *n* target platforms – which we can achieve using (say) the State Manager system described in Chapter 4 – then we'd write the same loop code *n* times. Let's avoid that by writing a game loop class with which we can initialise our application:

```
// File: PLATFORM_GameLoop.hpp
#ifndef PLATFORM_GAMELOOP_INCLUDED
#define PLATFORM_GAMELOOP_INCLUDED

namespace PLATFORM
{

class GameLoop
{
public:
    GameLoop();
    virtual ~GameLoop();
```

```
        virtual void Initialise() = 0;
        virtual void Run() = 0;
        virtual void Terminate() = 0;

private:
};

} // end of namespace PLATFORM

#endif
```

The amended application looks like this:

```
namespace PLATFORM
{

class GameLoop;

class Application
{
public:
    Application( Platform *pPlatform,
                 GameLoop *pGameLoop );

    // etc.
private:
    GameLoop * m_pGameLoop;
};

}

//...

Application::
Application( Platform * pPlatform, GameLoop * pGameLoop )
: m_pPlatform( pPlatform )
, m_pGameLoop( pGameLoop )
{
}

void Application::Run()
{
    m_pGameLoop->Initialise();
    m_pGameLoop->Run();
    m_pGameLoop->Terminate();
}
```

The only thing left to do now is to choose what sort of application we want to create. Though we could do this using a preprocessor macro, let's try to avoid using one of those altogether, as the use of it as either a command-line option or a global include file will invite physical dependencies where none is needed. Instead, let's use a separate file defining `main()` for each build platform:

```cpp
// File: mainPlatform1.cpp
#include <GamePlatform1.hpp>
#include <MyGameLoop.hpp>

void main()
{
    MyGameLoop aLoop;
    GamePlatform1 * pGame;
    pGame = new GamePlatform1( &aLoop );

    pGame->Run();
}


//-------------------------------------------------------

// File: mainPlatform2.cpp
#include <GamePlatform2.hpp>
#include <MyGameLoop.hpp>

int main( int argc, char * argv[] )
{
    MyGameLoop aLoop;

    GamePlatform2 * pGame =
        new GamePlatform2( argc, argv, &aLoop );

    pGame->Run();

    return( pGame->GetExitCode() );
}
```

6.2 Summary

- Cross-platform development is not easy. There are many ways to screw up, and if you do it can be costly. Object orientation provides natural ways to organise the development of code on multiple target platforms in parallel. By separating and subclassing the variant behaviours, we can – with care – create a generic set of components to be used in all the skus without compromising performance or structure, in some cases irrespective of the differences between the various hardware architectures. In the cases where we cannot do this, object-oriented analysis still gives us metrics that we can use to organise our code and data in ways that are beneficial to the development process.

- The differences in toolsets between platforms can make life pretty awkward for the developer. Use tools such as PC-Lint to analyse code more thoroughly than compilers to find the trouble spots.

- Use intermediate file formats to simplify, segregate and clarify the import and export of data.

- As well as the capability and methodology of hardware, the distinction between major and minor platforms can have an impact on the game architectures. Identify these and plan the architecture accordingly.

- Components work well in multiplatform systems. By introducing platform components, we can abstract away the differences in underlying hardware and still use generic components in the majority of the game.

Game objects   **7**

In this chapter, we'll examine the design and implementation of the central participants in a game's architecture, the game object or GOB. Getting the correct logical and physical structure here is particularly critical, since the game's functioning will depend intimately on the operation and cooperation of these class instances, and we will find that the project's compile and link times also depend critically on how your object classes are written.

We'll look at three strategies for implementing game objects and analyse the pros and cons of writing them that way. We'll then go on to discuss management of the objects, in particular memory-allocation strategies and some other common implementation issues that you'll meet along the way.

7.1 Open your GOB

The term 'game object' is both accurate and misleading. After all, every class in your game will have an instance that is an object. And while we're at it, doesn't every application – never mind game – contain objects? Flippancy aside, there's an important issue here: every non-trivial application has an object hierarchy. What sort of hierarchies might we see?

7.1.1 Collapsed hierarchy
The collapsed hierarchy is shown below. There is no inheritance in this whatsoever. It's a throwback to those bad old C programming days, and you're pretty unlikely to see it in a medium to large modern C++ project.

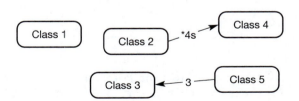

Notice that there are only 'has a' relationships between classes. This makes reuse at least awkward and more likely than not near impossible. Nevertheless, there are benefits to be gained from this structural organisation. First, remember that inheritance is a strong binding between classes: physically, you have to include the header file of the base class in the derived class's header file. With no inheritance, there are fewer compile-time dependencies: things are going to compile and link just about as quickly as they can.

Second, one of the classes in the hierarchy will be the 'ApplicationObject', the class around which almost all behaviour pivots. Since these are all identical in size and basic functionality, the creation and deletion of these objects can be made arbitrarily efficient by *pool allocation*. At run time, allocate a block of these, slap them into a free list and allocate as required. When the pool dries up, allocate another bunch, add those to the free list, and so on. This kind of allocation strategy is extremely fast compared with the usual new/malloc combination and also helps to reduce fragmentation within the memory manager (which can lead to increasingly long allocation times when the application has been running for some time).

So that's the good news. Now, why might we choose not to adopt a collapsed hierarchy? Well, for one thing, we may have made allocation efficient and reduced fragmentation, but this is at the cost of storage overhead. Each of our objects needs to support the functionality of any entity in the system. That means its data fields and member functions are comprised of the union of all the subclasses it needs to support functionality for.

That means a lot of wasted space: many of the subclass objects will require only a small subset of the data and functionality in the object. If there are lots of objects in the system, then that's potentially a lot of RAM that you know you will be grovelling for as you near master. Do you really want to do that? Even more importantly, you have created a software engineering bottleneck here: the object grows in complexity, functionality depends on state, and state is sometimes far from obvious. One piece of legacy code I inherited on a project (admittedly written – badly – in C) a while back had this sort of thing going on:

```
struct OBJECT
{
    //...
    int var1;
    int var2;
    //...
};
```

Because the object has to be different things at different points in time, having named fields means that your object grows in size exponentially fast. So, the author put these var1 ... var*n* fields in and used them differently depending on context. With hilarious consequences.

In a team environment where there is only one object class, there will be a big demand from your colleagues to edit and modify that class. Over the course of time, they'll add more and more var fields, or find novel and bug-ridden ways to use the existing ones. Welcome to development hell.

Having a monolithic, do-everything class is exactly what object orientation tries to avoid. Yes, a well-written C++ project will have quite a few more files kicking around than a C project of equivalent scope might have had, but the ease of maintenance gained by the divide-and-conquer methodology is not to be sniffed at.

So, in summary, the collapsed hierarchy has little to recommend it to the twenty-first-century developer.

7.1.2 Shallow hierarchy

The temptation for inexperienced developers (or, for that matter, some so-called experienced ones) is to use this wonderful thing called inheritance to scatter some basic properties (such as the ability to have a name, or to be serialised).

The defining pattern for the shallow hierarchy is, for most, if not all, of the objects in your system to inherit from one single base class, as here:

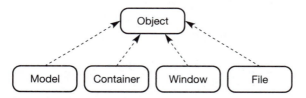

If your object hierarchy looks a bit like this, then you're in good company: Microsoft's MFC is one system that looks quite similar. But don't let that put you off.

The act of factoring common functionality into a base class is commendable and certainly correct in principle. Which is really damning with faint praise, because although the shallow hierarchy has certain traits that look like object orientation, it exhibits the hallmarks of a flawed design or a serious lack of design.

Why, for example, do a file and a container share a common base class? The fact that they can be serialised does not, in itself, justify the cost of inheriting from the purportedly common class. And what does it mean to serialise a window? In other words, are there classes in the system that have functionality that it doesn't even make sense for them to have?

Let's assume the base object confers useful functionality or passes type information meaningful to some higher-level system. There is no pressing need to slap all those bits of functionality into the space of one class if they can happily sit in separate classes and be inherited where needed.

The shallow hierarchy is definitely an improvement on the collapsed hierarchy; at least we have a bunch of smaller classes that are more easily maintained and reasonably defined. Its flaw is that base class, which has become the place to dump functionality that looks even slightly useful to its client classes.

Those of you who have worked on projects with this sort of structure will also be familiar with the terrifying announcement towards the end of development that someone has changed ('fixed') a problem with the base class, and you just know that invoking a build is going to take the best part of the morning away.

7.1.3 Vertical hierarchy

This structure is usually the result of realising that the collapsed hierarchy is unusable and that the shallow hierarchy gives little gain and a moderate deal of pain. The general idea is to start from an abstract description of the object and incrementally add properties in a series of subclasses. Figure 7.1 shows an abstract vertical hierarchy. We start with a near-dataless base class and add properties 1, 2, 3 and 4 in a series of subclasses.

As a concrete example, I'll use a design I was playing with for a space game a while ago. First, here's the base class, which as you can see is not atomic in itself; it depends on a reference-counting property class:

```
// Object.hpp
#include "IsReferenceCounted.hpp"

class Object : public IsReferenceCounted
{
public:
    Object();
    virtual ~Object();
```

Figure 7.1
Abstract vertical
hierarchy.

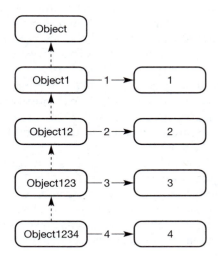

```
    virtual void Draw( Renderer * pRenderer ) = 0;
    virtual void Update( float fDeltaT ) = 0;
private:
};
```

Reference counting is an integral part of almost all non-trivial game systems. It is tempting to make this a common base class for all application classes, but that really ought to be resisted without further thought. Here's a first take on a reference counting class:

```
class IsReferenceCounted
{
public:
    IsReferenceCounted()
    : m_iCount(0)
    {
    }

    virtual ~IsReferenceCounted()
    {
    }

    void AddRef()
    {
        ++m_iCount;
    }

    void Release()
    {
        --m_iCount;
        if ( m_iCount == 0 )
        {
            delete this;
        }
    }

private:
    int m_iCount;
};
```

This is fine, so long as:

- the object was allocated via new;
- you want to delete only unreferenced objects.

In other words, it's not so fine. Suppose we allocated the object from a pool? Suppose we want a garbage collector to dispose of unreferenced objects to avoid other objects referencing a deleted object? We can fix the problem quite easily by abstracting the behaviour when the object becomes unreferenced:

```
class IsReferenceCounted
{
public:
    // As before.

    virtual void OnUnreferenced()
    {
        delete this;
    }

    void Release()
    {
        --m_iCount;
        if ( m_iCount == 0 )
        {
            OnUnreferenced();
        }
    }
private:
    // As before.
};
```

There are no data in the object base class, only a few pure virtual functions. The first instantiable class was called a proxy object: it served as an invisible supervisor object that watched what other (concrete) objects were doing or coordinated system activity:

```
class ObjectProxy : public Object
{
public:
    void Update( float fDeltaT );
    void Draw( Renderer * ) {}
};
```

The next level was called a null object. This was a proxy object that had a location in space and an orientation. For example, it could be used as a proximity test, running some game function when another object came within its target radius:

```
class ObjectNull : public ObjectProxy
{
public:
    ObjectNull();

    void SetPosition( const Vector3 & );
    void SetRotation( const Matrix33 & );

private:
    Vector3  m_vPosition;
    Matrix33 m_mRotation;
};
```

At the next level, there was the actor object. This added the properties of render-ability and collidability:

```
class ObjectActor : public ObjectNull
{
public:
    ObjectActor();

    void SetModel( Model * );
    void SetCollisionModel( CollisionModel * );

    void Draw( Renderer * pRenderer )
    {
        pRenderer->DrawModel( m_pModel );
    }

    virtual void OnCollision( ObjectActor * pThat )
    {
    }

private:
    Model * m_pModel;
    CollisionModel * m_pCollisionModel;
};
```

From then on, we had the concrete object subclasses such as asteroids and the various types of player and NPC vehicles, as shown in Figure 7.2.

I was quite fond of this hierarchy, and it certainly has some merit. Of the schemes we've looked at so far, it certainly packages functionality into small discrete classes that are well defined and easier to maintain than either a huge monolithic system or a shallow one. However, it is by no means perfect. We

Figure 7.2
A near-vertical
object hierarchy.

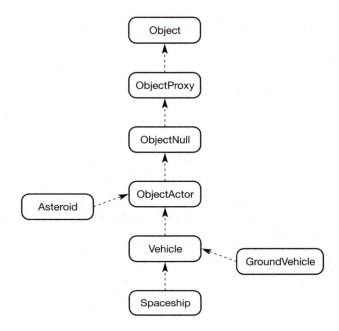

have failed to counteract the 'touch the base class and you rebuild everything' characteristic. Indeed, you could argue that it has got worse, since you can now touch one of several classes and most of the game rebuilds. However, the idea was to provide an incremental family of classes, with the change between any two neighbouring classes in the tree being small and simple enough to avoid having to continually maintain the lower parts of the graph.

Clearly, the vertical hierarchy goes some way towards providing a logical and maintainable game object inheritance pattern. Ideally, we would like to compromise between the shallow and mostly pointless tree and the vertical and highly dependent tree.

7.1.4 Mix-in inheritance

In an earlier chapter, we discussed the touchy topic of multiple inheritance (MI). The conclusion was that though there are undoubtedly complex issues that arise through the arbitrary application of MI, it is a useful and powerful programming paradigm if used carefully.

Now we wish to use MI to help us to design our object hierarchies. We'll be using a technique called *mix-in*. This makes objects easier to engineer, and allows us to place functionality only where needed. The idea is to decompose the functionality of an object into several behaviours that can be mixed together to yield the intended result (hence the name). This technique is illustrated in Figure 7.3.

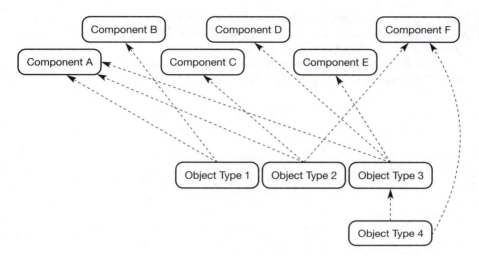

Figure 7.3
Using multiple
inheritance to define
game object properties.

In this scheme, all the derived object types inherit from Component A. Other object types include only the functionality that they require. This means that objects are less likely to include functionality that they do not need – a characteristic of vertical inheritance. And simply through the power of combinatorics, a huge number of class variations are possible through even a small set of base components.

All this power comes with some responsibility. Not only do individual components have to be designed carefully, but they must also be designed with some regard to the capabilities of all the other base components. The ideal situation is where the bases are orthogonal to each other – no classes should contain the same data or methods. The situations we want to avoid at all costs look like this:

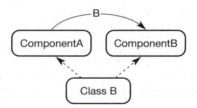

Class B will logically and physically contain two copies of Component A – one directly, the other through the contained data of Class A. C++ will get confused (as will you) as to which one you really want to access. Now, there is a solution: make the base class virtual:

```
class B : public class A, public virtual ComponentA
{
};
```

but although this works, it is the thin end of a wedge that will end up with your code underperforming and hard to understand and maintain. Avoid, avoid, avoid!

However, one need not resort to multiple inheritance to get the same sort of effect. We could use replace 'is a's with 'has a's, as shown here:

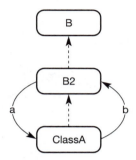

In C++ code, it looks like this:

```
class A : public ComponentA
{
public:
private:
    ComponentB  m_B;
};
```

Since ownership is a less strong relationship than inheritance, this can be considered to be a more flexible design, but there are hidden pitfalls that can seriously dilute that flexibility. Consider a function – class member or free function – that takes a ComponentB as an argument:

```
void Foo( const ComponentB & aB );
```

Given an instance of a ClassA, using the multiple inheritance mix-in method (the MIMIM?), then we are quite happy about the following:

```
ClassA anA;
Foo( anA );
```

However, if we replace the 'is a' with a 'has a', then we cannot call Foo without having an accessor:

```
const ComponentB & ClassA::GetB() const;
```

This is a mild weakening of encapsulation, and certainly

```
ClassA anA;
Foo( anA.GetB() );
```

isn't as elegant or expressive (though, arguably, it is clearer). But that isn't the
end of the story. The problem arises when ComponentB has virtual functions
that subclasses must implement. Clearly, the implementation is straightforward
in the multiple-inheritance model:

```
class ComponentA
{
public:
    virtual void Bar() = 0;
};

class ClassA : public ComponentA, public ComponentB
{
public:
    void Bar() { /*…*/ }
};
```

Notice that Bar() has access to all of the ClassA interface and data: it can implement a synergistic behaviour, which is just the sort of thing we would like to do.
Hold that thought.
   Now, consider replacing the 'is a' with a 'has a'. To get the same functionality, we need to write a ClassB2 that overrides Bar(), say:

```
class B2 : public B
{
public:
    void Bar() { /*…*/ }
};
```

and then put that into the owner class:

```
class ClassA : public ComponentA
{
public:
    const B & GetB() const;
private:
    B2 m_b;
};
```

Phew! That's a bit harder to get going, but was it worth it? Perhaps not, as
B2::Bar() cannot see anything in ClassA, so that 'top-level' or 'whole greater
than sum of parts' behaviour is lacking. No problem, you say; define:

```
class B2 : public B
{
public:
    B2( ClassA * pA ) : m_pA( pA ) {}

    void Bar()
    {
        m_pA->DoSomething();
    }
private:
    ClassA * m_pA;
};
```

In pictures, it looks like this:

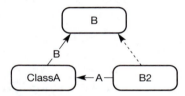

This relationship is not a great one: first of all, it is cyclic – ClassA depends on B2, and B2 depends on ClassA (since it can call methods of ClassA). In other words, in order to get rid of a coupling, we have introduced an even stronger one. Class B2 is not reusable in any other context because of its binding to ClassA.

Further, what happens if we want to inherit from ClassA and modify the behaviour acquired from B? We're in a bit of trouble. What we really need is:

```
class ClassA : public ComponentA
{
public:
    ClassA( B * pB );
private:
    B * m_pB;
};
```

OK, let's call it a day here. While it's safe to say that you can eventually accomplish everything done using MI with single inheritance and ownership, the keyword is 'eventually', and the couplings and design compromises that result along the way certainly don't help.

In short, multiple inheritance can help us to achieve clean implementations that reflect a logical design. Ownership and inheritance are not quite the same animals, and we should think carefully before opting for either one.

So, back to our game objects, and since we've been talking theoretically for a bit, let's illustrate our discussion with a real object hierarchy from a game. The design brief required that all objects in the game have the following attributes:

- They should be dynamic entities: reference counting is required.
- They should be spatially sortable.
- They should be controllable by a script.
- They should be able to collide with each other.

These are broadly orthogonal; the only question mark we may have is whether spatial sortability is tantamount to a subset of collidability, so we need to be careful to maintain independence of symbol names, stored data and interface.

Assuming we're happy with those definitions, we can define classes within four packages to implement these properties:

Common package

```
class comm_IsReferenceCounted;
```

This implements reference counting as described earlier.

Partition package

```
class part_Object;
```

This class is an entry in the spatial partitioning system. Internally to the package, these are objects that can be stored in a dynamic octree, as shown here:

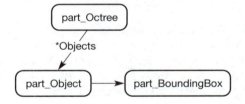

Scripting package

```
class script_IsScriptable;
```

Confers scriptability to an object. Acts as a target for messages from the scripting system.

Collision package

```
class coll_Collider;
```

Confers collidability on an object. Internally to the package, a collision manager maintains a collection of colliders, which themselves have a tree of oriented bounding boxes terminating in primitive lists. Colliders have a polymorphic interface to handle collision events:

```
class coll_Collider
{
public:
    virtual void OnCollision(coll_Collider & that) = 0;
};
```

as shown here:

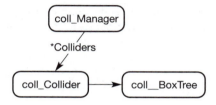

Putting these classes together gives us our base game object, shown here:

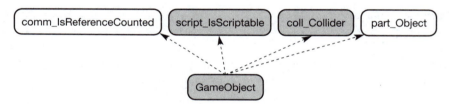

The GameObject is still an abstract class. Concrete objects – real in-game types – are still to be derived from it. However, by not putting all the required behaviour into a single object, we can reuse the property classes in other places where appropriate. For example, the game's NPC types also need scripting control and reference counting. However, NPCs cannot collide and be sorted spatially (though their in-game representations, called Avatars, can), so making an NPC a GameObject would not be correct. Refer to the figure below:

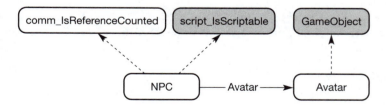

An analysis of dependencies for the mix-in system for creating game objects is both good and bad news. In certain respects, the inheritance tree resembles that for the shallow hierarchy, which is good. However, because the classes that you inherit from cannot be forward-declared – they must be included – there is still potential to deliver parent dependencies to all classes that include the game object's header file.

It is also still possible to build vertical inheritance graphs from a mix-in game object. Indeed, because a game often has a number of similar graphical objects with a variety of behaviours, the tendency for this to happen is strong, even with the best will in the world. To counteract it, it is worth remembering that just because superficially two classes seem to be so similar that it is natural to inherit one from the other, that doesn't necessarily justify doing so, from either a philosophical or a software engineering standpoint.

For example, consider a game where you require a bullet class to represent gunfire. Is a `Bullet` a `GameObject`? It certainly has a position, and the `GameObject` has a position. It certainly is collidable, otherwise it wouldn't be much of a bullet. It can be drawn, and we can certainly draw `GameObject`s. There seems to be a good case for a bullet being a `GameObject`. Yet – looking at the `GameObject` outlined above – scriptability is not really required for bullets: they just travel in straight lines until they hit something. Also, they are small enough not to need extent; they can be approximated with a line segment for collisional purposes. In other words, a bullet would be carrying around a fair amount of pointless baggage. If we have a lot of them – add a few machine guns to the design doc – then that could amount to a significant waste of precious storage on a console with limited RAM. So the correct decision may be not to inherit `Bullet` from `GameObject` (which is exactly the choice we eventually made during the development of this game).

7.2 Game object management

However you choose to structure your object hierarchies, you will still need a way of allocating them. Of course, the assumption is that we need to do a bit more than just:

```
GameObject * pObject = new GameObject;
```

First of all, we'll probably need quite a few of these game objects. The common-or-garden `new` probably calls `malloc`, which is not the quickest standard library function off the blocks. You don't want to be calling `new` too many times in every game loop (or `delete` for that matter).

7.2.1 Creation and destruction

Previously, we discussed the `ObjectFactory` pattern. Sounds like just the thing we need? Could be, but we should make some adjustments first of all. First, recall that rather than using an enumerated type that binds the physical types generated by the factory, we chose to use a class registration method that maps a string type[1] to a private free function that allocates an object of the required class. Previously, we had just written this function as:

```
// Thing.cpp
namespace
{
    Thing * createThing()
    {
        return new Thing;
    }
}
```

Because this is private to the object component, we are free to allocate the object as we choose, though we need to be a little careful here, because we need to be sure that no one is going to assume that we have called new when we've actually allocated the object statically.

We can avoid this problem by overriding operators new and delete. Now, remember that there are two ways you can do this: globally and on a per-class basis. In this circumstance, we mean the latter. In fact, we shall almost always mean the latter, and it is worthwhile digressing to investigate why.

Overloading global operator new and delete means plumbing in a completely new memory manager that all classes and functions will use. The reality of doing this is not just writing a couple of functions and pointing them at some memory. It really can be a bit of an ordeal. You have to be sure that your memory manager is initialised before the C++ run-time system makes any allocations or starts constructing objects at global scope but after the application heap is created (and you have to point your manager at the heap). And when your game exits, you need to make sure that you release that memory as the very last thing that happens before returning to the calling context. Now, this all usually means modifying start-up and shutdown code, and in short it is not a trivial process.

OK, so it's tricky, but is it worth doing? I've worked on projects that use incredibly sophisticated memory managers. Developers are concerned about the speed of allocation and freeing, the potential waste of memory blocks and the fragmentation of RAM, resulting in degraded performance over time. All of the memory managers have improved one of these parameters at the cost

---

1 We don't need to use a string as the 'key' type: we could use any type of unique identifier, for example the integer run-time type identifier also discussed in Chapter 4.

of another. There isn't such a thing as a fast, non-space-wasting, non-fragmenting global memory manager.

Indeed, the whole fragmentation issue is quite a bit more opaque than many assume. Fragmentation can occur when many small allocations are interspersed with medium and large allocations followed by freeing of blocks in a non-optimal order (the optimal sequence being the exact reverse of the allocation order). The consequence is that the global allocator contains a large number of small blocks that, when a medium or large allocation occurs, have to be skipped or merged, leading to increasing delays when free store is requested.

So, the longer an application runs, the more fragmented memory gets, yes? Well, not necessarily. The important parameter is the *pattern* of allocations and frees. And with many types of games with a completely deterministic set of resource requirements, it is entirely possible to avoid `new`s and `delete`s altogether; by allocating all the required memory at game initialisation, no requests for dynamic memory need be serviced, so fragmentation is not an issue.

Well that's the good news. The bad news is that you're pretty lucky if you're working on this sort of game, and with architectural complexity on the increase it's getting less and less likely that you will be. So, we're really going to have to assume that, in general, you are going to have to call `new` and `delete` an arbitrary number of times at indiscriminate points in the application's life.

So, we're going to be bitten by fragmentation, right? Again, not necessarily, but it may depend on who you ask, or rather on how they estimate how fragmented memory actually is. These estimates are based on modelling 'typical' application behaviour and use a variety of statistical methods involving random numbers to ensure that they emulate 'real' programs in their memory usage pattern.

Remarkably, for any given allocation strategy, the various metrics can indicate vastly different levels of fragmentation. This has led to an unnecessarily widespread level of alarm regarding the potential amount of fragmentation to be expected using the memory managers shipped as default with the commonly used development environments such as GNU C Compiler (GCC).

In fact, a study by Johnstone and Wilson (1998) showed that using a different and more realistic way of measuring the fragmentation of free store revealed that 'standard' implementations of malloc and free could perform exceptionally well, showing less than 1% fragmentation on large, memory-hungry applications. Nevertheless, there were other applications that, with the same allocation and freeing strategies, fragmented up to 50%!

From this, we must conclude that it is very difficult to write a good, all-purpose global storage allocator. We may actually get away with not writing one at all, and it will depend critically on the pattern of resource requests, our application's unique heap memory fingerprint as to how fragmented memory may become. In other words, writing a global memory manager really ought to be one of the last things you do for a game, because only then do you know how it will actually be allocating and releasing store. That said, there are a few things you can do to help it along its way that will reduce the possibility of fragmenting memory.

Pool allocation

Using pool allocators is one way of reducing fragmentation and speeding up allocation. This scheme allocates a fixed number of identical small to medium-sized objects and then hands them out, one by one, as required. If more allocations come in than there are objects in the pool, then the allocator returns NULL. This is an example of a local allocation strategy because the pool deals with only one sort of object.[2]

Now, this strategy would really not do very well for – say – a word processor. If I said, 'No more than 1000 pages in the page pool', then *War and Peace* would never have been written (assuming Tolstoy used a word processor). But for a game – or, at least, certain types of game – this limit is not only feasible, it may actually be desirable.

Why? Because most games are, by nature, *limited* systems. They don't expect (say) scenery blocks to appear from nowhere. If the designers and artists placed 223 in the level, then 223 is what you'd get.

Furthermore, all console games have absolutely fixed memory limits. There is no virtual memory to dip into when system RAM becomes short. Development systems have to enforce this limit somehow. As part of the design and plan phase, we'd expect to have some physical map of the use of memory. If we allocate 100 KB for scenery blocks in the map, and each block is, for the sake of argument, 1 KB in size, then that means we have a limit of 100 scenery objects. Rather than just silently take the creation of the 101st scenery block on the chin (and bearing in mind that development kits give you the false sense of security of increased RAM allowance), we really ought to yell that we've exceeded our limit. We then get the opportunity either to increase the limit or to tell the designers and artists to reduce the scenery block count.

In other words, this local memory allocation strategy can be perfect: zero fragmentation, near-zero overhead for `new` and `delete`.

Implementation

The pool allocator uses a fixed-size array-based stack as a very fast free list. We deliberately avoid using the `std::stack` class because of performance issues, though we make ours broadly interface-compliant with the STL class (note we use a convention of placing `_ff` after our container names to designate a faster, fixed-size data structure):

```
template<class T>
class stack_ff
{
public:
    stack_ff( int iMaxSize );
    ~stack_ff();
```

---

2   It is possible, though not great OO design, to create a pool of objects that can be cast to different, hopefully related, types after allocation. The objects must be identical in size, or at least bounded above by the size of the object in the pool.

```
    void push( T anItem );
    void pop();
    T & top();
    const T & top() const;
    void clear();
private:
    T * m_Data;
    int m_iTop;
    int m_iMaxSize;
};
```

With all the methods in-lined, this stack structure is extremely quick to push and pop, which forms the basis of our allocation and freeing operation. Our pool is then implemented thus:

```
template<class T>
class mem_Pool
{
public:
    mem_Pool( int iNumItems );
    ~mem_Pool();

    T * Allocate();
    void Free( T * pItem );
    void FreeAll();
private:
    stack_ff<T *> m_FreeItems;
    T * m_Items;
    int m_iNumItems;
};


template<class T>
mem_Pool<T>::mem_Pool( int iNumItems )
: m_FreeItems( iNumItems )
, m_Items( new T [ iNumItems ] )
, m_iNumItems( iNumItems )
{
    FreeAll();
}


template<class T>
mem_Pool<T>::~ mem_Pool ()
{
    delete [] m_Items;
}
```

```
template<class T>
T * mem_Pool<T>::Allocate()
{
    T * pItem = m_FreeItems.top();
    m_FreeItems.pop();
    return( pItem );
}


template<class T>
void mem_Pool<T>::Free( T * pItem )
{
    // Some security checks required here, to
    // prevent multiple frees, frees of invalid data
    // and so on.
    m_FreeItems.push( pItem );
}
template<class T>
void mem_Pool<T>::FreeAll()
{
    m_FreeItems.clear();
    for( int i = 0; i < m_iNumItems; ++i )
    {
        m_FreeItems.push( &m_Items[i] );
    }
}
```

Notice that the pool class allocates an array of objects dynamically. This means that any class that requires pooling must provide a default constructor. Notice also that simply allocating from the pool returns an object that may have been used previously and so contains 'garbage': no constructor will have been called. This motivates the use of the placement form of operator new: this calls a constructor on an existing memory block:

```
class Duck
{
public:
    enum Gender { DUCK, DRAKE };
    enum Breed { MALLARD, POCHARD, RUDDY, TUFTED };

    Duck( Breed eBreed, Gender eGender );

    // etc.
};
```

```
namespace
{
    mem_Pool<Duck> s_DuckPool( 100 );
}


Duck * pDuck = s_DuckPool.Allocate();

// Call placement new on our raw data.
new (pDuck) Duck( MALLARD, DRAKE );
```

Some *ad hoc* tests on my PIII 500 laptop indicate the pool class to be about ten times faster than `malloc()`. The class is extremely simple and robust, and does not demand the sort of person-power resources that a global allocator does. Furthermore, plumbing it in to your code is as simple as adding operator new and delete for each class to be pool allocated:[3]

```
// Thing.hpp
class Thing
{
public:
    void * operator new( size_t n );
    void operator delete( void * p );
};


// Thing.cpp
namespace
{
    const int MAX_THINGS = 100;

    mem_Pool<Thing> s_Pool( MAX_THINGS );
}


void * Thing::operator new ( size_t  )
{
    return( s_Pool.Allocate() );
}


void Thing::operator delete( void * p )
{
    s_Pool.Free( reinterpret_cast<Thing *>(p) );
}
```

---

3 You may also wish to add a static `Initialise()` function to the class to call `pool<T>::FreeAll()` at certain points within the code.

A really dull application for pools

In the course of development, you'll write some really fun code and you'll write some really bland stuff. Annoyingly, a lot of how your game performs may well be dictated by how well the dull stuff runs.

There isn't much duller stuff than linked lists. Yet, if you need a data structure where you can add and remove items in constant time, you'd be hard-pushed to find a better container class. The temptation to use STL's `std::list` class is overwhelming, but a cursory investigation of any of the common implementations will yield the slightly disturbing realisation that a fair number of calls to operators `new` and `delete` take place during `add` and `remove` operations. Now, for some purposes that may not matter – if you do only one or two per game loop, big deal. But if you're adding and removing lots of things from lists on a regular basis, then `new` and `delete` are going to hurt.

So why are `new` and `delete` being called? If you require objects to be in several lists at once, then the link fields need to be independent of the object in a node class. And it's the allocation and freeing of these nodes that can cause the invocation of dynamic memory routines.

The thought occurs: why not write an allocator for nodes that uses our pools, and plug it into the STL list class? After all, they provide that nice little second template argument:

```
template<class T,class A = allocator<T> >
class list { /*…*/ };
```

Brilliant! Except for the fact that it really doesn't work very well. It depends too critically on which particular version of STL you are using, so although your solution may possibly be made to work for one version of one vendor's library, it is quite unportable across versions and platforms.

For this reason, it's usually best to write your own high-performance container classes for those situations (and there will be many in a typical game) where STL will just not cut the mustard. But we digress.

Asymmetric heap allocation

Imagine an infinite amount of RAM to play with. You could allocate and allocate and allocate, and not once would you need to free. Which is great, because it's really the freeing that catalyses the fragmentation process.

Now, it'll be quite a while before PCs and consoles have an infinite quantity of free store. However, the only constraint you need be concerned with is not an infinite amount but just all that your game requires. In fact, we can be a bit more specific than that, because if the game is level-based, and we know ahead of time exactly how much we need for a level, then we can pre-allocate it at the start of the level, allocate when required, and the only free we will ever need is the release of everything at the end of the level.

This technique generalises to any object or family of objects whose exact maximum storage requirements are known ahead of time. The allocator – called an *asymmetric heap* because it supports only allocation of blocks, not freeing bar the ability to free everything – is an even simpler class to implement than the pool allocator:

```cpp
// mem_AsymmetricHeap.hpp
class mem_AsymmetricHeap
{
    // This constructor creates a heap of the
    // requested size using new.
    mem_AsymmetricHeap( int iHeapBytes );

    // Constructs a heap using a pre-allocated block
    // of memory.
    mem_AsymmetricHeap( char * pMem, int iHeapBytes );

    ~mem_AsymmetricHeap();

    // The required allocate and free methods.
    void * Allocate( int iSizeBytes );
    void FreeAll();

    // Various stats.
    int GetBytesAllocated() const;
    int GetBytesFree() const;

private:
    // Pointer to the managed block.
    char * m_pData;

    // Precomputed end of the heap.
    char * m_pEndOfData;

    // Where we get the next allocation from.
    char * m_pNextAllocation;

    // Size of the heap.
    int m_iHeapBytes;

    // Should the memory be freed on destruction?
    bool m_bDeleteOnDestruct
};
```

```
// mem_AsymmetricHeap.cpp
#include "mem_AsymmetricHeap.hpp"

mem_AsymmetricHeap::mem_AsymmetricHeap( int iHeapBytes )
: m_pData( new char [ iHeapBytes ] )
, m_pEndOfData( m_pData + iHeapBytes )
, m_pNextAllocation( m_pData )
, m_iHeapBytes( iHeapBytes )
, m_bDeleteOnDestruct( true )
{
}

mem_AsymmetricHeap::
mem_AsymmetricHeap( char * pMem, int iBytes )
: m_pData( pMem )
, m_pEndOfData( pMem + iBytes )
, m_pNextAllocation( pMem )
, m_iHeapBytes( iBytes )
, m_bDeleteOnDestruct( false )
{
}

mem_AsymmetricHeap::~mem_AsymmetricHeap()
{
    if ( m_bDeleteOnDestruct )
    {
        delete [] m_pData;
    }
}

void * mem_AsymmetricHeap::Allocate( int iSize )
{
    void * pMem = 0;
    // Ensure we have enough space left.
    if ( m_pNextAllocation + iSize < m_pEndOfData )
    {
        pMem = m_pNextAllocation;
        m_pNextAllocation += iSize;
    }
    return( pMem );
}

void mem_AsymmetricHeap::FreeAll()
{
    // You can't get much faster than this!
    m_pNextAllocation = m_pData;
}
```

The remaining methods, along with the required bullet-proofing, and other bells and whistles such as alignment, are left as exercises for the reader.

Control your assets

Having said all I have about fragmentation, you may be forgiven for thinking that I'm a bit blasé about it. You'd be wrong. In some applications, there comes a time when fragmentation doesn't just slow things down, it actually brings down the whole house of cards. Witness this error message from a recent project:

```
Memory allocation failure
Requested size: 62480
Free memory: 223106
```

Fragmentation has left memory in such a state that there is more than enough RAM free; it's just formed of itty bitty blocks of memory that are no use on their own.

Time to panic? Not quite yet. The first step is to get rid of anything in memory that is no longer needed until there is enough RAM. The scary bit comes when you realise that the error message appeared after we'd done that.

Time to panic now? No, we'll take a deep breath and hold on a moment longer. The next step to take here is for some sort of block merging to be performed. To be able to perform this efficiently, internally your memory allocator ideally needs to support *relocatable blocks*. Now, to be able to do this, the access to the things that can be relocated needs to be controlled carefully, because simply caching a pointer could lead you to accessing hyperspace if the object is moved. Using some kind of *handle* will solve this problem – we will discuss handles shortly.

This motivates us to control our game resources carefully in databases. Within these databases, we can shuffle and shunt around the memory-hogging resources at will without adversely affecting the remainder of the game.

We'll look at the asset management issue in some detail in a later chapter.

Strings

If there is one class above all that is going to fragment your memory, then it is probably going to be the string. In fact, you don't even need to have a class to do it; just use a combination of char *'s, functions such as strdup() and free(), and you are almost just as likely to suffer.

What is it about strings that hammers allocators? Well, for starters, they are usually small and they are all different sizes. If you're malloc()'ing and free()'ing lots of one- and two-byte strings, then you are going to tax the heap manager beyond breaking point eventually.

But there is a further – related – problem. Consider the programmer who writes a string class because they hate having to use ugly functions such as strcmp(), strdup() and strcpy(), and having to chase down all those string pointer leaks. So they write a string class, and this allows such semantic neatness as:

```
String a = "hello";
String b = a;
```

Now there are (at least) two schools of thought as to what that innocent-looking = should do. One says that the request is to copy a string, so let's do just that. Schematically:

```
strcpy( b.m_pCharPtr, a.m_pCharPtr );
```

However, the second school says that this is wasteful. If b never changes, why not just sneakily cache the pointer?

```
b.m_pCharPtr = a.m_pCharPtr;
```

But what happens if b changes? Well, we then need to copy a into b and update b. This scheme – called copy-on-write (COW) – is implemented by many string classes up and down the land. It opens up the can of worms (which is what COW really stands for) inside Pandora's box, because the string class suddenly becomes a complex, reference-counting and rather top-heavy affair, rather than the high-performance little beast we hoped for.

So if we're to avoid COW, we are then forced into using strings that forcibly allocate on creation/copy/assignment, and free on destruction, including passing out of scope. In other words, strings can generate a substantial number of hits to the memory management system(s), slowing performance and leading to fragmentation. Given that C++ has a licence to create temporary objects whenever it feels like it, the tendency of programmers who know how strings behave is to forgo using a string class and stick with the combination of static arrays and the C standard library interface. Unfortunately, this does reject some of the power that can be derived from a string class. For example, consider a hash table that maps names to objects:

```
template<class Key,class Type>
class hash_table
{
    // Your implementation here.
};

namespace
{
    hash_table<char *,GameObject *> s_ObjectMap;
}
```

The problem with this is that if the hash table uses `operator==` to compare keys, then you will compare *pointers* to strings, not the strings themselves. One possibility is to create a string proxy class that turns a pointer into a comparable object – a 'lite' or 'diet' string, if you will:

```
class string_proxy
{
public:
    string_proxy()
    : m_pString(0)
    {
    }

    string_proxy( const char * pString )
    : m_pString( pString )
    {
    }

    bool operator==( const string_proxy & that ) const
    {
        return(!strcmp( m_pString, that.m_pString ));
    }

private:
    const char * m_pString;
};

namespace
{
hash_table<string_proxy,GameObject *> s_ObjectMap;
}
```

This works reasonably well, but beware of those string pointers! Consider the following code:

```
namespace
{
    string_proxy s_strText;
}

void foo( const char * pText )
{
    char cBuffer[256];
```

```
        strcpy( cBuffer, pText );
        s_strText = string_proxy( cBuffer );
}

void bar()
{
        int x;

        // Some stuff involving x.
}

void main()
{

        foo( "hello" );
        bar();
        if (s_strText == string_proxy( "hello" ) )
        {
                printf( "yes!\n" );
        }
        else
        {
                printf( "no!\n" );
        }
}
```

This will – at least some of the time – print 'no!' and other times may print 'yes!' or perhaps just crash. Why? Because cBuffer is allocated on the stack, and the call to bar() can overwrite the region where the text was, and the string proxy is pointing to. Boy, did I have fun with those bugs!

We are left with the distinct impression that a string class is still the least bad of several evils. How might we go about creating one that doesn't fragment, isn't slower than a snail on tranquillisers and doesn't leave us with dangling pointers?

One way – a poor way – is to create strings with fixed-size buffers of the maximum expected string length:

```
class string
{
public:
    // A string interface here.
private:
    enum { MAX_CAPACITY = 256; }
    char m_cBuffer[ MAX_CAPACITY ];
};
```

The trouble with this is that it is very wasteful: if most strings are shortish – say 16–32 characters long – then we are carrying around a lot of dead storage space. It might not sound much, but you could well be scrabbling around for that space at the end of the project.

Our preferred solution is to use a series of pool allocators for strings. Starting with a minimum string buffer length (say 16), we allocate a pool for 16-character-length strings, another for 32-character strings, and so on up to a maximum string length. By allowing the user to control how many strings of each length can be allocated, we can bound the amount of memory we allocate to strings, and we can customise the sizes according to the game's string usage pattern.

Strings then allocate their buffers from the pools. As they grow, they allocate from the pool of the smallest suitable size that can contain the new length. Since the strings use pool allocators, no fragmentation of string memory occurs, and the allocation and free processes are very fast. And there are no pointer issues to fret over. Job done.

The moral of the tale is this: prefer local object allocation strategies to global ones. In the end, our game should be a collection of loosely coupled components. This degree of independence means that if we solve the memory allocation issues within the components, then we get the global level pretty much for free. Hurrah!

But – and there's always a but – some people insist that this isn't the whole story. And they have a point. They say that there *are* reasons why you may take the step of writing a global allocator early on. It's just that those reasons have nothing to do with performance or fragmentation. In fact, given that your allocation strategies will depend critically on your pattern of usage, you will need some sort of mechanism to instrument the existing allocator so that you can find out what those patterns are. Calls to new and delete should be logged, allowing you to trace leaks and multiple deletions and also to build up a picture of how your game uses heap memory.

These are fine motivations. However, they should be evaluated in the context of the priorities of the project, and they may do more harm than good. Consider the following code skeleton:

```
// Memory.hpp
#if defined( DEBUG )
#define MEM_LogNew( Class )\
    new( __FILE__,__LINE__) Class

// Provide a new 'new' that logs the line and file the
// memory was allocated in.
void *
operator new(size_t size, const char * pFile, int iLine);
#else
#define MEM_LogNew( Class )\
    new Class
#endif
```

Every time you need to create a new object and keep a record of its creation (and presumably deletion), you need to include memory.hpp. That creates one of those dependency things that is going to hamper reusability. If a colleague feels like using one of your components but has already written a different memory management system, then they're going to have to modify the code. Chances are, they won't take the code, or they'll sulk if they do.

In general, anything that causes universal (or near-universal) inclusion of header files can seriously weaken the reuse potential of your systems, and changes to those universal files will cause rebuilds left, right and centre. Of course, we have heard this argument before.

There's no reason why we can't apply this same global technique at the package local level, though. If each package keeps track of its own memory, then we get the global tracking without the binding. Interestingly, though, at the local level memory management can often be so simple that the problem can simply dissolve away.

7.2.2 Referencing

So we're writing (say) an air combat game, though the genre is largely unimportant for this discussion. We create a type of object called a missile, of which there are two varieties: one that just flies in a path dictated by an axial thrust and gravity, and another that homes in on a specific target that the player or NPC has selected. It's the latter object we're interested in. Here's a sketch of the code sections we're interested in:

```
class Missile : public GameObject
{
public:
    // yada yada.
};


class HomingMissile : public Missile
{
public:
    HomingMissile( /*stuff*/, GameObject * pTarget );

    /*virtual*/ void Update( float dt );

    // bada bing.
private:
    GameObject * m_pTarget;
};
```

When the homing missile is created, we provide a target object that it should head towards. When we update the missile, it does some sums to work out trajectories and then adjusts itself accordingly:

```
void HomingMissile::Update( float dt )
{
    MATHS::lin_Vector3 vTargetPos =
                        m_pTarget->GetPosition();

// Some maths, depending on how clever you are.
}
```

But we're not concerned about the maths and physics at this moment. The problem we need to address is this: suppose another missile blows up our target, which is deleted (and potentially new objects such as explosions and debris put in their place)? But hold on, our homing missile still has a pointer to a now non-existent object, so next time it is updated we can be sure that something undesirable will happen.

How do we solve this? It's part of the general problem of how we reference objects safely. One common method is to prevent the application from holding pointers to allocated game objects at all. Instead, all object transactions use object handles, which cannot be deleted. We then have some kind of object management interface that accepts handles and returns the relevant data:

```
class ObjectManager
{
public:
    ObjectHandle CreateObject( const char * pType );
    void FreeObject( ObjectHandle hObject );

    MATHS::lin_Vector3 GetPosition( ObjectHandle hObj );

private:
    ObjectFactory * m_pFactory;
};
```

So what is an `ObjectHandle` exactly? In short, it's anything you want it to be. It's called an *opaque type* because as far as the outside world – the client code – is concerned, it cannot see what the type does. Only the `ObjectManager` knows what to do with handles – how to create them, validate them and dereference them.

As an oversimplified example, consider using a 32-bit integer as the handle type:

```
typedef int ObjectHandle;
```

Within the object manager, we have a table of pointers to objects that the integer indexes into:

```
// ObjectManager.cpp
namespace
{
    const int MAX_OBJECTS = 200;

    GameObject * s_Objects[ MAX_OBJECTS ];
    int s_iNextFreeObject = 0;
}
```

Now whilst that's not the whole story, suffice to say that many games use a system such as this, so there is a lot to recommend it. Unfortunately, it's not a system that I favour. The main objection is that handles collapse type information. We went to such pains to design an elegant object hierarchy, and now we've reduced everything to either a lowest-common-denominator interface or a hugely bloated monolithic one, because you need to be able to do anything with a handle that you could do with a GameObject *or any of its subclasses*.

Handles do have their uses, however, and we'll discuss those later. To solve our immediate problem, though, we can invoke the flexible reference-counting mechanism we discussed in the previous section. Recall that we used a base class to implement reference counting, which had a virtual function OnUnreferenced() and that was called when the reference count hits zero. This mechanism can be piggybacked to do exactly what we require:

```
// GameObject.hpp
#include "comm_IsReferenceCounted.hpp"

class GameObject : public comm_IsReferenceCounted
{
};

// Scenery.hpp
#include "GameObject.hpp"

class Scenery : public GameObject
{
    /*virtual*/
    void OnUnreferenced();
};

// Scenery.cpp
#include "Scenery.hpp"
#include "mem_Pool.hpp"
```

```
namespace
{
    int MAX_SCENERY = 111;

    mem_Pool<Scenery> s_SceneryPool( MAX_SCENERY );

    // Creator called by ObjectFactory.
    GameObject * createScenery()
    {
        return( s_SceneryPool.Allocate() );
    }
}

/*virtual*/
void Scenery::OnUnreferenced()
{
    ~Scenery();
    s_SceneryPool.Free( this );
}
```

The only thing we have to watch out for is always to call `Release()` on pointers to `GameObject`s rather than `delete`. Protecting the destructor could enforce this somewhat, but protected status is too easy to remove via inheritance to be watertight, and making the destructor private would cause compiler errors since we could never destroy the `GameObject` class from a subclass.

There's another little gotcha waiting to bite us when we allocate game objects from a pool. Previously, we encountered problems because we held on to a pointer to an object that was deleted. The pointer becomes invalid; considerably more likely than not, it will address data inside a new object or point at fragile memory manager data. Dereferencing it would be a disaster. However, when we allocate objects from a pool, it is now extremely likely – indeed, given long enough, 100% certain – that our cached pointer will point to the start of a new object that is actually in use. Ouch! This is a subtle and annoying bug.

To get around this one, we need to create a smart pointer class. Also, whenever we create an object, we need to give it a unique identifier. The simplest way is to use a 32-bit integer:

```
// GameObject.hpp
class GameObject
{
public:
    GameObject();

    int GetId() const { return m_iUniqueId; }
```

```
        // blah.
private:
    int m_iUniqueId;
};

// GameObject.cpp
#include "GameObject.hpp"

namespace
{
    int s_iIdGenerator = 0;
}

GameObject::GameObject()
: // …
, m_iUniqueId( s_iIdGenerator++ )
{
}
```

Our smart pointer class obtains the unique identifier when it is created. It can then tell if the referred object is valid by comparing its cached identifier with the actual ID of the object (which is safe because being in a pool, the data are never deleted as such during game execution):

```
// ObjectPointer.hpp
class ObjectPointer
{
public:
    ObjectPointer();
    ObjectPointer( GameObject * pObject );

    GameObject * operator*();
    // Const versions of this, too.

private:
    GameObject * m_pObject;
    int m_iObjectId;
};

// ObjectPointer.cpp
#include "ObjectPointer.hpp"
#include "GameObject.hpp"
```

```
ObjectPointer::ObjectPointer()
: m_pObject( 0 )
, m_iObjectId( -1 )
{
}


ObjectPointer::ObjectPointer( GameObject * pObject )
: m_pObject( pObject )
, m_iObjectId( pObject->GetId() )
{
}


GameObject * ObjectPointer::operator*()
{
    GameObject * pObject = 0;

    if ( m_iObjectId == m_pObject->GetId() )
    {
        // The object is valid.
        pObject = m_pObject;
    }

    return( pObject );
}
```

It should be stressed that this technique works only for pool objects, because of the call to `GameObject::GetId()` within `operator*()`. If the object has been heap-allocated and subsequently deleted, and we make that call, then it's Game Over before the game's over. So how can we make it work for an arbitrarily allocated object? Well, the Achilles' heel is that pointer, so perhaps if we ditch that, we can use the ID value itself to refer to an object. Since the ID is a continuously increasing integer, it won't work as an index, and in fact even if it were, using an index just gives us the same problem all over again. So how about a scheme that looks up a table of existing objects, compares IDs and returns a pointer to the referred object if it was found?

That works, but it is painfully slow if you do a modest amount of referencing and have a large (say, more than 100) set of objects. Even putting the objects into a map or hash table keyed on the ID field would still make this a costly operation.

Clearly, we need to be a bit cleverer if we want to have an efficient referencing system for heap-allocated objects. We'll appeal to our good friend, the reference count, to help us. Only this time, we are not reference counting the object itself so much as the reference object that looks at it:

```
template<class T>
class sys_Reference
{
public:
    sys_Reference();
    sys_Reference( T * pInstance );
    ~sys_Reference();

    T *   GetInstance();
    const T * GetInstance() const;
        // Returns the ref'd object or 0 if deleted.

    void AddRef();
    void DecRef();
    int  GetRefCount() const;
        // The usual reference counting interface.

    void Invalidate();
        // Call this when the instance is deleted.

private:
    T * m_pInstance;
    int m_iRefCount;
};

template<class T>
sys_Reference<T>::sys_Reference()
: m_pInstance(0)
, m_iRefCount(0)
{
}

template<class T>
sys_Reference<T>::sys_Reference( T * pInstance )
: m_pInstance( pInstance )
, m_iRefCount(0)
{
}

template<class T>
sys_Reference<T>::~sys_Reference()
{
    m_pInstance = 0;
}
```

```
template<class T>
const T * sys_Reference<T>::GetInstance() const
{
    return( m_pInstance );
}

template<class T>
T * sys_Reference<T>::GetInstance()
{
    return( m_pInstance );
}

template<class T>
void sys_Reference<T>::AddRef()
{
    ++m_iRefCount;
}

template<class T>
void sys_Reference<T>::DecRef()
{
    --m_iRefCount;
}

template<class T>
int sys_Reference<T>::GetRefCount() const
{
    return( m_iRefCount );
}

template<class T>
void sys_Reference<T>::Invalidate()
{
    m_pInstance = 0;
}
```

In itself, the reference class solves the problem only partially. Creating more than one reference to an instance will really mess up the reference counter and we're back in Crashville. So now we reintroduce our handles, only this time they point at a reference, not at an object:

```
template<class T>
class sys_Handle
{
```

```
public:
    sys_Handle();
    sys_Handle( sys_Reference<T> * pStub );
    ~sys_Handle();

    void Release();
    // Relinquish use of the controlled object. All
    // dereference operations will return NULL after
    // this call. This is called automatically on
    // destruction.
    T * operator*();
    T * operator->();

    sys_Handle<T>& operator=(const sys_Handle<T> &that);
    bool operator==( const sys_Handle<T> & that ) const;

private:
    sys_Reference<T> * m_pReferenceStub;
};
```

Now anyone can hold a handle to an object and there can be any number of object handles. The handle points at the reference stub, which is the actual thing that points at the object. Dereferencing is therefore a double indirection. Starting to sound expensive? Well, possibly, but bearing in mind that only a handful of dereferences will happen every game loop, and there isn't too much pain involved, certainly not compared with the table-lookup-per-indirection method we saw previously.

The reference stub is created by the object itself – we'll see that in a minute – and will hang around even after the object itself is deleted. It will free itself only when its reference count becomes zero: no other entities reference the object. If the object is deleted, the object will invalidate the reference in its destructor. When an object (e.g. our missile) has finished referencing its target, it calls `Release()` on the handle. The reference stub will return NULL on indirection, and the handle will continue to return NULL on `operator*()` even after the stub is deleted.

The down side of all this is that we must now be vigilant and remember to `Release()` when we're done with object handles. A thorough dose of assertions and in-game integrity checks can help to sort this out. A picture paints a thousand words, so have a look at Figure 7.4.

Here's the implementation:

```
template<class T>
inline sys_Handle<T>::sys_Handle()
: m_pReferenceStub( 0 )
{
}
```

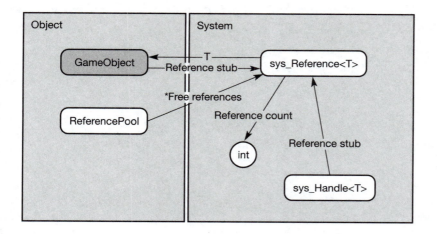

Figure 7.4
Referencing system for
heap-allocated objects.

```
template<class T>
inline
sys_Handle<T>::sys_Handle( sys_Reference<T> * pStub )
: m_pReferenceStub( pStub )
{
    pStub->AddRef();
}

template<class T>
inline void sys_Handle<T>::Release()
{
    if ( m_pReferenceStub != 0 )
    {
        m_pReferenceStub->DecRef();
        if ( (m_pReferenceStub->GetInstance() == 0) &&
             (m_pReferenceStub->GetRefCount() == 0) )
        {
            // All references to the object (via the
            // stub) have Release()d. We can now kill
            // the stub.
            T::FreeReference( m_pReferenceStub );
        }

        m_pReferenceStub = 0;
    }
}

template<class T>
inline sys_Handle<T>::~sys_Handle()
{
    Release();
}
```

```cpp
template<class T>
inline T * sys_Handle<T>::operator*()
{
    T * pObject = 0;

    if ( m_pReferenceStub != 0 )
    {
        pObject = m_pReferenceStub->GetInstance();
    }

    return( pObject );
}

template<class T>
inline T * sys_Handle<T>::operator->()
{
    T * pObject = 0;

    if ( m_pReferenceStub != 0 )
    {
        pObject = m_pReferenceStub->GetInstance();
    }

    return( pObject );
}


template<class T>
inline sys_Handle<T> &
sys_Handle<T>::operator= ( const sys_Handle<T> & that )
{
    if ( this != &that )
    {
        m_pReferenceStub = that.m_pReferenceStub;
        if ( m_pReferenceStub != 0 )
        {
            if ( m_pReferenceStub->GetInstance() != 0 )
            {
                m_pReferenceStub->AddRef();
            }
        }
    }

    return( *this );
}
```

Notice that individual objects (the T class in the template) create the handles (potentially by allocating a reference stub from a pool and initialising it using its 'this' pointer), and a static member function `T::FreeReference()` is used to free the object reference.

You may also see that we have a slightly worrying relationship between objects and references – they are mutually dependent. However, the T link between the reference and the referenced type (in our case, a `GameObject`) is very nearly a name-only one, in that all that the reference cares about is a pointer to a `GameObject`, not what that class can do. I say 'very nearly' because in order to release a reference, the `GameObject` class is forced to implement the `FreeReference()` function. However, since the reference class does not need the referenced class's header file, this binding is light enough to allow us the luxury of the co-dependency.

As we've said, creating a reference becomes the task of the object you wish to refer to. There must be only one reference stub per object instance, so we bury the whole reference and handle creation within the `GameObject` component:

```
// GameObject.hpp
#include <system\sys_Handle.hpp>

typedef sys_Handle<class GameObject> ObjectHandle;
typedef sys_Reference<class GameObject> ObjectReference;

class GameObject
{
public:
    GameObject();
    ~GameObject();
    // stuff…

    ObjectHandle CreateReference();
    static void FreeReference( ObjectReference * pRef );

    static void Initialise();
    // Call this to set up or clear object referencing.

private:
    ObjectReference * m_pReferenceStub;
};

// GameObject.cpp
#include "GameObject.hpp"
```

```cpp
namespace
{
const int MAX_OBJECTS = 1000;
mem_Pool<ObjectReference> s_ReferencePool( MAX_OBJECTS );
}

GameObject::GameObject()
: /*initialisers*/
, m_pReferenceStub(0)
{
    m_pReferenceStub = s_ReferencePool.Allocate();
    new (m_pReferenceStub) ObjectReference( this );
}

GameObject::~GameObject()
{
    // Do NOT delete the object reference stub!
    m_pReferenceStub->Invalidate();
    m_pReferenceStub = 0;
}

ObjectHandle GameObject::CreateReference()
{
    // A bit of C++ jiggery-pokery here. The line that
    // returns a handle will silently generate a
    // temporary handle. When the temp is deleted at the
    // end of this function call, Release() will be
    // called and our reference count will drop! Hence
    // we need an extra AddRef().
    m_pReferenceStub->AddRef();

    return( ObjectHandle( m_pReferenceStub ) );
}

/*static*/
void GameObject::FreeReference( ObjectReference * pRef )
{
    s_ReferencePool.Free( pRef );
}

/*static*/
void GameObject::Initialise()
{
    s_ReferencePool.FreeAll();
}
```

There is a lesser – though no less pernicious – version of the referencing problem that occurs when we prematurely delete an object that is not actually referenced but may be needed later on within the same game loop. For example, consider a collision between a plane and a (non-homing) missile:

```
// Somewhere deep in the collision system.
GameObject * pObject1 = //…;
GameObject2 *pObject2 = //…;

coll_Info aCollInfo;
if ( Collided( pObject1, pObject2, &aCollInfo ) )
{
    pObject1->OnCollision( pObject2, &aCollInfo );
    pObject2->OnCollision( pObject1, &aCollInfo );
}

// Plane.cpp
void Plane::
OnCollision( Missile *pMissile, coll_Info * pInfo )
{
    doDamage( pMissile->GetDamageLevel() );
    Explosion * pExplosion =
        new Explosion( pMissile->GetPosition() );

    delete pMissile;
    // Oops! This might cause some problems.
}
```

The deletion of the missile before calling its collision handler was a fifty/fifty chance (it just so happened that object number one was the plane). Thankfully, the solution to this referencing problem is a little simpler than the more general case. The simplest way to implement this is to flag the object to be removed as garbage so that some other system (a 'garbage collector') can get rid of it when it is safe to do so. In fact, the reference/handle system described above is also a garbage-collection system. In that case, the flag is that no active handles to the object are left. In this case, we can physically embed a Boolean into the object to signal that it is or is not a valid instance:[4]

4　This is preferable to some systems that use 'kill lists': the object is removed from the active list and put on a 'death row' list. We prefer the flag version because it acts at the object level, whereas the list method operates at the object management level and therefore comes with a higher – and potentially circular – dependency.

```
class GameObject
{
public:
    bool IsValid() const { return m_bValid; }
    void Invalidate() { m_bValid = false; }
private:
    bool m_bValid;
};
```

Ordinarily, when we would have deleted the object, we now invalidate it:

```
void Plane::OnCollision( Missile   * pMissile,
                         coll_Info * pInfo )
{
    doDamage( pMissile->GetDamageLevel() );
    Explosion * pExplosion =
            new Explosion( pMissile->GetPosition() );
    pMissile->Invalidate(); // Sorted, guv'n'r.
}
```

We should be careful not to involve invalid objects in any further processing:

```
void Game::Update( float dt )
{
    for( GameObject * pObject = FirstObject();
        pObject != 0;
        pObject = NextObject() );
    {
        if ( pObject->IsValid() )
        {
            pObject->Update( dt );
        }
    }
}
```

So, when is a safe time to physically remove the invalid objects? At the end of a game loop is as good a choice as you will get:

```
void Game::Update( float dt )
{
    GameObject * pObject;
    for( pObject = FirstObject();
        pObject != 0;
        pObject = NextObject() );
```

```
    {
        if ( pObject->IsValid() )
        {
            pObject->Update( dt );
        }
    }

    // More stuff to update.

    // Remove invalid objects.
    for( pObject = FirstObject();
        pObject != 0;
        pObject = NextObject() );
    {
        if ( !pObject->IsValid() )
        {
            RemoveObject( pObject );
            delete pObject;
        }
    }
}
```

Referencing failures account for some of the most common, insidious and brain-hurting bugs that you'll meet during game development. It is therefore simple fear of pain that should motivate you to put robust object-referencing systems in place. Ninety per cent of the code above is reusable since it depends on two templated classes with no bindings to object definitions other than the soft requirement that a static `FreeReference()` function is provided within the controlled class. Write it once, use it for ever. Hell, you'd be mad *not* to use it, wouldn't you?

7.2.3 Persistent damage

The more memory we have to store data, the more detailed information about object state we can pack in. In the olden days (five or ten years ago, that is), most objects were either alive or dead: if you were writing a shooting game, then a single bit would suffice for determining the status of a game object.

Nowadays, we need to do much better: walls can have myriad bullet holes, bottles can be shot to pieces, vehicle bodies can be dented to varying degrees. Strangely, because we have more storage, we pack in more detail, so we can store fewer objects. For example, if we were to set a game in even a small town, we could not reasonably keep all the buildings, people and objects in RAM at the same time – they'd typically be created on demand. A particular instance of an object might disappear at one point in the game, only to reappear later. If we'd damaged it – say it was a wall we'd shot our name into with bullets – we might expect to see that as we'd left it. Hence, the need for damage to be persistent.

This sort of functionality can be added to our game objects easily with no loss of generality but still with the sort of control we need to keep resource requirements finite. We certainly don't want to allow any object to be damaged arbitrarily, as that will demand an increasingly large amount of storage. What we want is a system that allows objects to say how they can be damaged and to keep records of actual damage.

So, let's start by describing an abstract atom of damage – let's call it a `DamageTag`:

```cpp
class DamageTag
{
public:
    enum { MAX_TAG_NAME = 32 };

    DamageTag( char const * pszUniqueName );
    virtual ~DamageTag();

    virtual void Apply( GameObject * const pObject ) = 0;

    char const * GetName() const;

private:
    char m_szName[ MAX_TAG_NAME ];
};
```

Giving a damage tag class a unique name is important, as we'll see soon. For example, fire damage tags could be given the name 'scorch'.

To actually show the damage, we use the `Apply()` method, passing a pointer to the object to be modified in. We could construct the tag passing the pointer in and caching it internally:

```cpp
class DamageTag
{
public:
    // As before, except -
    DamageTag( char const * pszUniqueName,
               GameObject * pObject );

    // When I call this I trust that I'm acting on the
    // correct object. Hmmm...
    virtual void Apply() = 0;

private:
    char m_szName[ MAX_TAG_NAME ];
    GameObject * m_pObject;
};
```

However, this means that a damage tag can never be reused with another object: we'd have to delete it and `new` another one, unless we also add a `SetObject()` method. That's adding complexity where none is required, so for that minor reason we prefer the ever so slightly less strongly coupled version.

To confer the ability to be damaged on an object, we'll create a property class, which we'll call `IsDamageable`. This can be (multiply) inherited by the objects in the game that can sustain damage (alternatively, you could just add virtual functions to the object base class, but if you keep that habit up, you could end up with a monolithic base class – just what we'd like to avoid!).

Let's make another assumption – there is a function that gets called when an object collides with another object. Since collision detection and response is a whole other discussion, we'll go light on the details of that, except to say that the base object supports a polymorphic interface:

```
virtual void GameObject::OnHit( GameObject * pThat );
```

We'll also assume that we have three object flavours:

- scenery objects (walls, floors, ceilings)
- furniture objects (tables, vases)
- bullets (projectile weapons).

We're interested primarily in collisions between scenery objects and bullets and between furniture and bullets (since bullets tend to do quite a lot more damage in collisions than the other two).

To handle the specific collisions, we'll use a double-dispatching system to allow us to write virtual functions:

```
virtual void Scenery::OnHit( Bullet * pBullet );
virtual void Furniture::OnHit( Bullet * pBullet );
```

This gets called when an object of dynamic type (furniture or scenery) gets hit by an object of static type (bullet) (remember that the argument type is resolved at compile time, whilst the type of `this` is determined at run time).

Now, here are the game design rules for when bullets collide with things:

- When a bullet hits scenery, it leaves a bullet hole.
- When a bullet hits furniture, it shatters it.
- When a bullet hits a bullet, nothing happens (though we may be impressed).

OK, so much for the wordy stuff. How about the cody stuff? First off, let's look at that damage-conferring property class:

```
class IsDamageable
{
public:
    IsDamageable();
```

```
            virtual ~IsDamageable();

            virtual DamageTag * CreateDamageTag() = 0;

            void SetDamageTag( DamageTag * pTag );
            DamageTag * GetDamageTag();
    private:
            DamageTag * m_pTag;
    };
```

The method `CreateDamageTag()` simply allocates a damage tag and returns a pointer to it. Notice that we can override this behaviour on a per-class level, so let's use this to apply the damage rules as required. We create new subclasses of `DamageTag` to create bullet hole damage and shattering damage. The former can be achieved by blending a texture or textures on the object's visual, as illustrated in Figure 7.5.

The latter can be implemented by selecting either a different mesh or a set of submeshes in the object's visual (see Figure 7.6).

Figure 7.5
Adding bullet holes:
the hole is stored as a
texture with transparency
and is blended into
the background in
an additional
rendering pass.

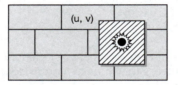

Figure 7.6
Visual hierarchy used to
create damaged
furniture. The model is
exported with a number
of meshes. The
_Damaged tag is
appended to the names
of the meshes that
represent the damaged
object. Note that this can
be extended to show
various degrees of
damage by a simple
change to the naming
convention.

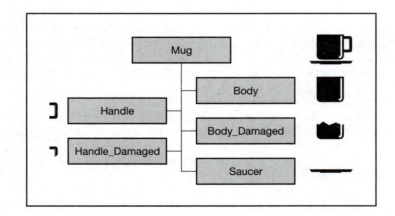

Note that an object can support several types of damage (it has a list of tags rather than a single tag). That's a powerful system, but coder beware! Its power is also its weakness. Applying a bullet hole to a shattered object will need careful attention to avoid visual incongruities. For now, we'll consider only objects that sustain a single type of damage. The point here isn't so much to show you how to implement object damage, since that will depend largely on details I cannot know here. Rather, the message is that the damage is implemented in entirely different ways, and the damage system should – at the game object level – neither know nor care about these mechanics. Note also that we can easily generalise from damage to any persistent property of the game object. That is an exercise left to the reader. For now, let's stick with destruction.

So, let's create two different types of damage tag: one for bullet holes and one for shattering. First, let's look at the bullet hole class. This is quite an interesting problem, because in most games with shooting, bullets can be sprayed around with abandon, and we don't want to write a system that gobbles resources or CPU/GPU bandwidth.

```cpp
#ifndef OBJECT_DAMAGETAG_INCLUDED
#include "DamageTag.hpp"
#endif

#ifndef STD_VECTOR_INCLUDED
#include <vector>
#define STD_VECTOR_INCLUDED
#endif

class Texture;

class DamageTagBulletHole : public DamageTag
{
public:
    DamageTagBulletHole();

    // Adds a mark at the given texture coords with
    // the specified size.
    void AddMark( float u, float v, float fSize );

    // Removes all marks stored in the tag.
    void Clear();

    // Magic accessor that returns us a texture pointer.
    Texture * GetBulletHoleTexture();

    void Apply( GameObject * const pObject );
```

```
    Texture * GetBulletHoleTexture();

    void Apply( GameObject * const pObject );

    static char const CLASS_NAME[];
private:
    struct Mark
    {
        float u;
        float v;
        float fSize;
    };

    std::vector<Mark> m_Marks;
};
```

We choose to use one tag to hold all the bullet marks for an object as opposed to creating a new tag for each mark. This is – probably – a bit more memory-efficient, considering how std::vector is usually implemented.

```
char const DamageTagBulletHole::CLASS_NAME[] =
                                      "bullet_hole";

DamageTagBulletHole::DamageTagBulletHole()
: DamageTag( CLASS_NAME )
{
}

void DamageTagBulletHole::AddMark( float u, float v,
                                   float fSize )
{
    Mark aMark;

    aMark.u = u;
    aMark.v = v;
    aMark.fSize = fSize;

    m_Marks.push_back( aMark );
}

/*virtual*/
void DamageTagBulletHole::Apply( GameObject * pObject )
{
    for( int j = 0; j < m_Marks.size(); ++j )
```

```
    {
        Mark const & aMark = m_Marks[j];
        float u = aMark.u;
        float v = aMark.v;
        float s = aMark.fSize;

        pObject->AddDecal( u, v, s, s,
                    GetBulletHoleTexture() );
    }
}
```

When a piece of scenery gets hit by a bullet, we add a bullet hole:

```
/*virtual*/
DamageTag * Scenery::CreateDamageTag()
{
    return( new DamageTagBulletHole );
}


/*virtual*/
void Scenery::OnHit( Bullet * pBullet )
{
    // Kill the bullet, add particles, make noise
    GenericBulletStuff( pBullet );

    // Does a bullet hole tag exist?
    DamageTagBulletHole * pTag;
    pTag = (DamageTagBulletHole*)GetDamageTag();

    if ( pTag == 0 )
    {
        // If not, create one.
        pTag = (DamageTagBulletHole *)CreateDamageTag();

        SetDamageTag( pTag );
    }

    // Work out hole texture coords and size from bullet
    // position and add the mark.
    float u,v, fSize;
    Texture * pTexture = pTag->GetBulletHoleTexture();
    GetBulletHoleTextureData( pBullet, &u, &v, &fSize );

    // Note that we don't want to add all the existing
```

```
            // bullet holes multiple times by calling Apply, or
            // incur the overhead of removing them all then re-
            // adding them, so we just add the new
            // bullet hole to the object and adjust the book-
            // keeping.
            pTag->AddMark( u, v, fSize );
            AddDecal( u, v, fSize, fSize, pTexture );

            // In real life, we'd probably cap the number of
            // bullet holes that an object can have, removing the
            // oldest hole when adding a new one if we're full
            // up. We might also allow bullet holes to
            // "evaporate" over time.
        }
```

OK, so much for bullet holes. What about the shattering cup? Well, we need some way to track the state of the object, so we'll add a simple hit counter. If it's zero, no damage; if it's one, the object is damaged; two or more and the object is destroyed. The counter gets incremented every time the object is hit:

```
class DamageTagShatter
{
public:
    DamageTagShatter();

    void Clear();
    int GetHitCount() const;
    void IncrementHitCount();

    void Apply( GameObject * const pObject );

private:
    int m_iHitCount;
};

//--------------------------------------------------------

namespace
{

void useDamagedMesh( Model * pModel, Mesh * pMesh )
{
    // A string object might be better here.
    char szDamagedName[ 256 ];
```

```
    // Copy the base name of the mesh and tack on
    // "_damaged".
    char * pszMeshName = pMesh->GetName();
    char * pszBase     = szDamagedName;
    while( *pszMeshName != '_' )
    {
        *pszBase++ = *pszMeshName++;
    }
    *pszBase = '\0';
    strcat( pszBase, "_damaged" );

    Mesh * pMesh = pModel->FindMesh( szDamagedName );
    pModel->HideMesh( pMesh );
    pModel->ShowMesh( pDamagedMesh );
}


}


DamageTagShatter::DamageTagShatter()
: DamageTag( CLASS_NAME )
, m_iHitCount( 0 )
{
}


/*virtual*/
void DamageTagShatter::Apply( GameObject * pObject )
{
    if ( m_iHitCount == 1 )
    {
        // Object has been hit once: show damaged visual.
        Model * pModel = pObject->GetModel();
        for( int j = 0; j < pModel->GetNumMeshes(); ++j )
        {
            Mesh * pMesh = pModel->GetMesh(j);
            if
            (
                pMesh->InUse()
                &&
                pMesh->GetName().Contains( "_undamaged" )
            )
            {
                useDamagedMesh( pModel, pMesh );
            }
```

```
        }
    }
    else if ( m_iHitcount > 1 )
    {
        // Object has been destroyed and can be removed.
        pModel->HideAllMeshes();
    }
}
```

Within our shattering furniture object, we can implement the required functions like this:

```
/*virtual*/
void Furniture::CreateDamageTag()
{
    return( new DamageTagShatter );
}


/*virtual*/
void Furniture::OnHit( Bullet * pBullet )
{
    // Kill the bullet, add particles, make some noise
    GenericBulletStuff( pBullet );

    DamageTagShatter * pTag;
    pTag = (DamageTagShatter*)GetDamageTag();
    if ( pTag == 0 )
    {
        pTag = (DamageTagShatter*)CreateDamageTag();
        SetDamageTag( pTag );
    }

    pTag->IncrementHitCount();
    pTag->Apply( this );
    if ( pTag->GetHitCount() > 1 )
    {
        // Destroy me...
    }
}
```

So, now we can record damage to objects in the form of tags. There's one more part of this system that we need to implement, and that's the part that keeps track of the damage applied to objects. The best place to put this functionality is in an object factory – the centralised place for the creation and destruction of all game objects.

Let us distinguish between two operations that the factory can perform:

```
class ObjectFactory
{
public:
    //… stuff

    void DeleteObject( GameObject * pObject );
    void DestroyObject( GameObject * pObject );
};
```

In this context, 'delete' means that an object instance simply gets removed from storage – it still exists out there, but at the moment it can have no influence upon the game, visually, aurally or functionally. It may well do later.

On the other hand, 'destroy' means to erase an object instance permanently from the world, for example blowing up a particular car. The object can have no further impact on the course of events (other than through its non-presence, that is).

Now that we've clarified that, it is clear that when we call `DeleteObject()`, we shall need to keep track of any damage tags pertaining to that object because it could conceivably appear later on. On the other hand, `DestroyObject()` can happily get rid of the damage tag because the object is no longer needed. Implementing this would be straightforward, were it not for the fact that *not all game object subclasses support damage.*

Still, no problem: let's allow the persistent damage system to grow a little bit (it's starting to form its own little package now, and it will benefit from being put in a name space DMG). We'll create a registry of all the damage tags that are created, which is updated when we call `IsDamageable::SetDamageTag()`. This will associate damage tags with objects through a unique object ID, which can be parameterised (i.e. a template class). This allows us to decouple the registry from any particular implementation of a game object ID. As long as the ID class supports `operator==` (e.g. a string – but not a raw char* – or an integer), then this class will function dandily:

```
#ifndef CONTAINER_HASHTABLE_INCLUDED
#include <CONTAINER\CONTAINER_HashTable.hpp>
#endif

namespace DMG
{

class DamageTag;

template<class IdType>
```

```
class Registry
{
public:
    Registry();
    ~Registry();

    void AddEntry( const IdType &anId, DamageTag * pTag )
    {
        // If I weren't so damn lazy, I'd check for
        // uniqueness before adding.
        m_Entries.insert( anId, pTag );
    }

    void RemoveEntry( const IdType & anId )
    {
        m_Entries.remove( anId );
    }

    DamageTag * FindEntry( const IdType & anId ) const
    {
        DamageTag * pTag = 0;

        CONT::hash_table<IdType,
                         DamageTag*>::iterator itTag;
        itTag = m_Entries.find( anID );
        if ( itTag != m_Entries.end() )
        {
            pTag = itTag->Data();
        }

        return( pTag );
    }

    void Clear()
    {
        m_Entries.clear();
    }

private:
    // An associative map of damage tags keyed by
    // the ID type for fast lookup.
    CONT::hash_table<IdType,DamageTag *> m_Entries;
};

}
```

We can then add this to the object factory:

```
#ifndef DMG_REGISTRY_INCLUDED
#include <DMG\DMG_Registry.hpp>
#endif

#ifndef OBJECTID_INCLUDED
#include <ObjectId.hpp>
#endif

class ObjectFactory
{
public:
    // As required.

    void RegisterDamageTag( const ObjectID& anID,
                            DamageTag* pTag );

private:
    DMG::Registry<ObjectID> m_DamageRegistry;
};
```

Now, we put the last parts in place: when we create an object, we check to see whether an object with the unique ID has a damage tag. If it has, then we apply the tag:

```
GameObject *
ObjectFactory::CreateObject( char const * pszType,
                             ObjectID anID )
{
    GameObject * pObject = 0;
    if ( !strcmpi( pszType, "scenery" ) )
    {
        pObject = new Scenery( anID );
    }
    else if ( !strcmpi( pszType, "furniture" ) )
    {
        pObject = new Furniture( anID );
    }

    if ( pObject != 0 )
    {
        // Note that because we use ID's here, not object
        // pointers, it doesn't matter if the game object
```

```
                // supports damage or not. We still get a valid
                // return from the search because if it doesn't
                // support damage it will never get in there.
                DamageTag * pTag =
                          m_DamageRegistry.FindEntry( anID );
                if ( pTag != 0 )
                {
                    pTag->Apply( pObject );
                }
        }
}
```

Here are the corresponding DeleteObject() and DestroyObject() functions:

```
void ObjectFactory::DeleteObject( GameObject * pObject )
{
    delete pObject;
}

void ObjectFactory::DestroyObject( GameObject * pObject )
{
    DamageTag * pTag =
        m_DamageRegistry.FindEntry(pObject->GetId());
    if ( pTag != 0 )
    {
        m_DamageRegistry.RemoveEntry( pObject->GetId() );
        delete pTag;
    }
    delete pObject;
}
```

And finally, here's the glue that makes it all work:

```
void ObjectFactory::
RegisterDamageTag( ObjectID const& anID,
                   DMG::DamageTag * pTag )
{
    // Assert( entry does not already exist );
    m_DamageRegistry.AddEntry( anID, pTag );
}
```

The modified version of the object subclass 'hit' functions looks like this:

```
/*virtual*/
void Furniture::OnHit( Bullet * pBullet )
{
    // Kill the bullet, add particles, make noise
    GenericBulletStuff( pBullet );

    DamageTagShatter * pTag;
    pTag = (DamageTagShatter*)GetDamageTag();
    if ( pTag == 0 )
    {
        pTag = (DamageTagShatter*)CreateDamageTag();
        SetDamageTag( pTag );

        ObjectFactory & anOF = ObjectFactory::Instance();
        anOF.RegisterDamageTag( GetId(), pTag );
    }

    pTag->IncrementHitCount();
    pTag->Apply( this );
    if ( pTag->GetHitCount() > 1 )
    {
        // Destroy me...
    }
}
```

Epilogue

The above fulfils the design criteria to implement persistent damage, but there are some engineering question marks we can raise about it. Consider the level of an object. If object A either has an object B or is an object B, then B is considered to be at a lower level than A. In other words, objects of type B shouldn't be aware of the existence of A's either via ownership or inheritance (see Figure 7.7).

Looking now at our object system, we see this structure: the object factory is at a higher level than the objects it creates – the object really doesn't need to know how it was brought into the world and who owns it. Yet – for a variety of reasons – game objects need to call factory methods (to register damage, to destroy other objects, etc.).

So should we be concerned? And if we are concerned, should we do something about it? 'Yes' and 'Probably not' are the respective answers.

We should always try to preserve the precedence of objects if we can. Failing to do so can result in spaghetti systems that limit reuse and are harder to understand, use, debug and maintain. However, if the result of preserving precedence is a loss of efficiency and an increase in system complexity, it may not always be a smart move to change things.

Figure 7.7
Model hierarchy including
damageable elements.

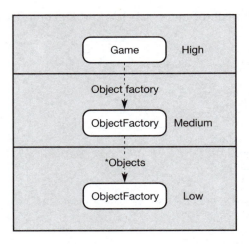

Consider how we might fix the requirement for objects to register damage with the factory. Let's put a flag into the game object that says 'I've been damaged'. The object management system can then scan through all the objects on every update looking for objects that have been damaged. If it has, then it registers the tag (the flag needs to be cleared once it has been read otherwise it will have its tag registered multiple times).

Notice how – by embedding a flag at the base level – we've immediately coupled the property of damageability to objects that cannot be damaged. OK, so let's put the flag into the IsDamageable class and have the object management system keep separate lists of damageable and non-damageable objects. Well, you can sort of see where this is going. In this sort of situation, TINSTAAFL (there is no such thing as a free lunch).

The bottom-line question is this: is the level coupling between objects and their factory acceptable? Considering that it takes place at the application (game) level, which will, in general, yield less reusability than at the library (component) level, the answer is a resounding 'Probably'.

Moral: don't seek perfect engineering solutions everywhere. Try to keep any coupling and unpleasantness at as high a level as possible. In fact, make every effort to move dependency out of base classes into derived classes. But remember that complex functionality is the result of interaction between systems. If at some level there was no coupling between systems/packages/components/classes, then there would be no behaviour, ergo no game, so what are we doing here?

7.3 Summary

- Game objects: you'll have lots of them, so they need to be carefully designed, implemented and managed.

- Memory management will be an issue with your game objects. Allocate from fixed object pools where possible. Otherwise avoid the use of generic memory management strategies because fragmentation depends on the unique pattern of allocations and frees that your application executes.

- That said, some objects perennially cause more problems than others – strings, for example.

- Objects referencing other objects can be tricky – especially in games with many entities that support network play (and all the issues that latency brings). Failure to do it properly can create all sorts of nasty bugs. So do it properly!

- It's nigh impossible to write real-life systems that are architecturally perfect. This should in no way prevent you from trying to do so.

Design-driven control 8

Many games companies choose to employ a team of professional game designers to specify the content of their multimillion-pound development ventures, even those that don't nominate parts of the team – artists or programmers – to have the controlling influence on how the game behaves when it is running. We'll assume, therefore, that there are a bunch of guys and gals referred to as 'designers' who have some degree of control regarding game content.

Game designers often have the responsibility of implementing high-level behaviour through a data-driven scripting interface. To be used effectively, scripting requires the implementer to have both design skills and the analytic mindset of a programmer, and this can be a problem if the designer has not come from that sort of a background. Much of modern game content development involves the use of a scripting system, be it explicit through text entry or implicit through some high-level GUI that writes the scripts for you. The trouble with the latter system is that development of GUIs is time-consuming, and it can work only when the lower-level (text) scripting system is in place (otherwise, what would it be writing?). In other words, designers are usually coerced into using the text interface with the carrot of the GUI to come later.

The introduction of a scripting language can be a bit traumatic. I don't intend to be patronising here: designers are often uncomfortable with abstract programmer concepts, and if the syntax and semantics of the language are not easily accessible, then the result can be frustration and inevitably a substandard product. (Come to that, many *programmers* will struggle with a poorly thought-out scripting language.)

Worse, the introduction of a new bespoke scripting system every time a game is in development will almost certainly be unpopular. The learning of new paradigms (along with their idiosyncrasies) will again cause some annoyance and adversely affect productivity and quality.

There is, therefore, a powerful argument for designing and implementing a single, flexible scripting system that will work with a number of products. This gives the design/programming team time to learn how to use the system. Meanwhile, the team writing the scripting system can be involved in documentation and training, if these are not too dirty words.

How to write a powerful, fast and flexible scripting system for game development would require a book in itself. However, it is worth outlining the broad architecture and some relevant technologies that you might meet along the way.

First – and perhaps most important of all – is understanding the motivation for having a scripting language. They can often be written for well-intentioned but ultimately bogus reasons, and we would hope to be using the right tool for the right job.

8.1 Decoupling behaviour from game code

Often, the ability to implement game functionality independent of the code base is a motivating factor. Rebuilding a project may take a significant time – perhaps five to ten minutes for a small to medium-sized project near completion. It would be frustrating to have to endure that every time changes were made in a high-level system. Since a script is simply data loaded into the game, no rebuilds are required on change, and at most a restart would be in order (for well-written systems, even that would not be required).

Ah, if only it were that simple! Consider a multimodule scripting system that allows the designer to access in-game C++ classes in a controlled way, create and test variables and write functions to encapsulate the functionality. If script A requires to access a function defined in script B, then clearly a sophisticated compile-and-link system is in order, because if the function in script B does not exist and there is no attempt to validate the call (or indeed the number and type of parameters or the return value if any), then errant behaviour, and/or a crash, and/or data corruption will be the inevitable consequence.

In other words, a robust and sensible script system will necessarily have a build process analogous to that of C++: an optional compilation stage, provided that you have a very fast ASCII interpreter in the game, and a linking stage where references to external functions and data are resolved. Clearly, we would like to automate the process of regenerating program data whenever a script changes: if script B is altered, then it may affect other scripts that access it, and it will certainly need to be recompiled and linked.

Now, we may consider using an interpreted language rather than a compiled one, if we are prepared to sacrifice both space and time (CPU) penalties. Matching tokens in an ASCII stream can get quite expensive for a modest to large lexicon, and if there are many script-controlled elements in the system, these costs can accumulate. More worryingly, an interpreted system cannot spot an error until it encounters it. If there is no resolution of identifiers when the game is built, then an error in an infrequently executed script branch could go undetected, resulting in an embarrassing and/or expensive bug.

We may also need to rebuild scripts if the in-game script interfaces change (though this depends intimately on how the internal engine functions). With this view of scripting, the distinction between a script and a C++ component starts to become quite blurred. With this motivation alone, the need for a modular scripting system is difficult to justify; you might as well give designers a C++ development system, a library of object and function calls they can make and let them get on with it. Clearly, this is not a very designer-friendly way to go about development.

8.2 Simplifying the creation and management of high-level behaviour

What we want is to make our jobs easier by spreading the load – getting as far away as is sensible from the sort of model where a designer sits with a programmer and tells them what they want, and they tweak code and numbers until they get it. If designers are to work relatively independently from programmers, then the language itself must be accessible to non-programmer types. All of the powerful and difficult constructs that programmers deal with on a day-to-day basis need to be totally encapsulated within the language. For example, pointers: nowhere should there be even the merest whiff that if you ask for something in a script, then you need to delete it later. The language should be simple and intuitive.

The most familiar language to most people who have had exposure to computers is probably some flavour of BASIC. These days, Microsoft's Visual Basic can be used to automate all the common Office packages; it even has access to the most powerful graphics capabilities through the DirectX COM mechanism. Basing a scripting system on the syntax of such a BASIC is a good start, particularly because so many resources for learning how to use these languages exist already: instant documentation!

However, having a dialect of BASIC talk to the game code is not enough in itself, because the language is usually limited in its ability to talk to and extend high-level game systems. For example, most BASICs have no concept of event management.

8.2.1 A functional paradigm

In other words, the language defines a way of doing things over and above the ability to set variables and call functions. For example, the ability for the script-controlled C++ object to respond to in-game events, or the definition of state and transition management for the controlled game objects.

This goes hand in hand with an execution model. C++ runs in a linear fashion. A script, however, is associated with a C++ object or objects; it must coexist with other scripted objects and scripts, so execution must be 'time-sliced'. So, with scripting running on a per-scriptable-game-object, per-n-frames basis, the method of instruction execution is anything but linear. Exactly how and when the scripting system runs defines the extra power that the language gives us over writing functionality in C++.

Now, we're starting to get to the nub of the scripting issue, but we have to be a little careful. If we seek a common scripting language for several games that have radically different architectures, we could easily shoot ourselves in the foot by having to rewrite a lot of C++ in the script execution systems to talk to the game code and vice versa. And we certainly shouldn't consider compromising the game architecture just because of the way our scripting language works.

How do we resolve this? By writing a scripting language that is powerful and fast enough to write intermediate-level systems as well as the high-level systems. The C++ side of the scripting system is relegated to being a fast, compact execution kernel that defines the framework that the higher levels are built on (see Figure 8.1).

This layered approach has some appealing benefits. The system should be highly portable across target platforms, since only the kernel – and only parts of it at that – are likely to be hardware-specific. It also allows both programmers and technically oriented designers control over game functionality, and it goes some way towards creating a system that can be rewritten without having to rebuild any C++ at all.

An interesting question to ask is what functional paradigm should we use? Here are three possibilities, outlined for brevity. (There are obviously many other paradigms, but we'll restrict our discussion to these because they highlight most of the key issues.)

Linear control

In this scheme, scripts are executed in a linear fashion, with the usual conditional tests, loops and the like to control the flow of control. There is a distinction between commands that are executable immediately (atomic) and those that require some amount of time to complete (re-entrant). For example:

```
wait 10                        // Re-entrant

this.set_position 0, 0, 0   // Atomic
this.set_velocity 0, 0, 1   // Atomic

wait_until( this.z >= 10 )   // Re-entrant
```

Figure 8.1
Architecture for a
scripting system.

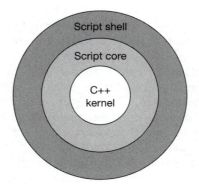

Allowing re-entrancy means that the scripts can be time-sliced to any granularity providing that some concept of elapsed time can be accounted for in the scripts.

Event-driven

We start with a precise object-oriented definition of an event: an event is an object that has an associated condition and an action. The condition is an object that evaluates to either true or false. If the result is the former, then the action is performed:

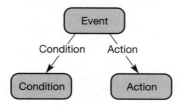

The scripting system supplies a number of built-in conditions, such as 'is created' and 'is destroyed', which can be applied to those in-game objects that require event-driven behaviour, and also allows the author the ability to write their own conditions via a custom event class (e.g. 'if door is unlocked', or 'if energy < 10', or 'if variable1 equals variable2') whose associated actions drive the game logic.

```
event create
    this.energy = 1000
end_event

event destroy
    message "bang!"
end_event

event time > 30
    message "It's getting late…"
end_event

event custom MyCondition( this.x )
    message "Orangutan!"
    this.energy = 1000
end_event

function boolean MyCondition( real x )
    return x > 10
end_function
```

Prioritised task execution

A task is defined as a command that executes until completion. All tasks are, by their nature, re-entrant, though in practice some need be executed only once. For example, consider an aircraft flying at some arbitrary point in space. The task

```
fly_to_waypoint 27
```

will continue to execute until the waypoint (number 27) is reached. Since this is a re-entrant call, the actual code will not block. Consider now a list of tasks:

```
task1
task2
...
taskN
```

Within the task execution system, there is the concept of a current task, and this is executed once per frame (re-entrantly). We apply the following algorithm typically once every second or so but with controllable granularity:

```
algorithm evaluate_tasks
current_task = task1
    while( current_task != end_of_tasks )
        if (current_task is viable)
            execute current_task
        else
            current_task = next_task( current_task )
        endif
    endwhile
endalgorithm
```

A task is considered viable if it is not complete (e.g. the aircraft is not already at waypoint 27) and it refers to a valid object or state (e.g. if the task is 'attack Red Baron' and the Red Baron is dead, then the task is invalid). The fact that we start with task1 at the top upon every re-evaluation is significant. Given two tasks in a list:

```
Task M
Task M+1
```

Task M will always be executed before M+1, assuming both tasks are viable. Hence, the order of the tasks defines a set of decreasing priority. Implementing conditional tasks makes this system quite powerful:

```
Task List 1
    Task 1.1
    ...
    Task 1.M
        If ( <conditional expression> )
            Task List 2
                Task 2.1
                ...
                Task 2.N
            EndTaskList
        (EndIf)
        ...
    Task 1.N
EndTaskList
```

So which of these three schemes is preferable? From a purely functional stand-point, there is actually not very much to choose between them. Almost any high-level behaviour can be implemented using these paradigms, though with varying levels of complexity. Some constructs will be easier using one system than with another. In particular, when using a purely linear execution model, the number of IF/THEN/ELSE statements required to implement an event or task-like mechanism would result in hard-to-read (ergo hard-to-debug) scripts. Events can also get a bit complex, particularly if an event spawns other events, and in this case the complexity is implicit since the designers can't see how spaghettified things are just by inspecting the script.

Which leaves us with the task evaluation system. Let's look at that in a little more detail.

8.2.2 Task-based control
We'll start with a mix-in property class that confers taskability on anything that inherits it. The object needs to keep an execution context (what it's currently doing), and a reference to a prioritised list of tasks (see Figure 8.2).

Subclasses of the abstract task_Task implement the various task types. They support the interface:

```
class task_Task
{
public:
    enum Status
    {
        INVALID = 0,    // Task cannot be performed
        COMPLETE,       // Task has run to completion
        RUNNING,        // Work in progress
        VIABLE,         // Ready to run if required
    };
```

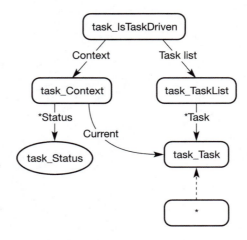

```
task_Task();
task_Task( float fGranularity );
virtual ~task_Task();

// Can the task be done?
virtual Status Evaluate() const = 0;

// Performs the task's duty.
virtual Status Execute() = 0;

// Get how long the task should run before re-
// evaluation.
float GetGranularity() const;

private:
    float m_fGranularity;
};
```

The `task_Task::Status` type records the status of the tasks in the list. The context keeps track of the status of all the tasks in the associated task list. This allows us to share task lists between several objects (a task may be complete for one object but running for another).

The `task_IsTaskDriven` property class implements the fundamental task algorithm in its update method:

```
// task_IsTaskDriven.hpp
class task_TaskList;
class task_Context;
```

```
class task_IsTaskDriven
{
public:
    task_IsTaskDriven();

    void Update( float dt );
    void SetTaskList( task_TaskList * pTaskList );

private:
    float m_fTaskTimer;
    task_Context * m_pContext;
    task_TaskList * m_pTaskList;
};

// task_IsTaskDriven.cpp
#include "task_IsTaskDriven.hpp"
#include "task_Context.hpp"
#include "task_TaskList.hpp"
#include "task_Task.hpp"

namespace
{
// Finds the index of a task in a task list.
int taskIndex( task_TaskList *pList, task_Task *pTask );
}

//...

void task_IsTaskDriven::Update( float dt )
{
    bool bEvaluateTasks = false;
    task_Task * pTask = m_pContext->GetCurrentTask();
    if ( pTask == 0 )
    {
    // Nothing to do?
        bEvaluateTasks = true;
    }
    else
    {
    // Have we run longer than granularity? If so,
    // look to see if higher-priority tasks are pending.
        m_fTaskTimer -= dt;
        if ( m_fTaskTimer <= 0.0f )
        {
```

```
            bEvaluateTasks = true;
        }
        else
        {
        // Run an iteration of this task.
            task_Task::Status eStatus =
                                pTask->Execute();
            switch( eStatus )
            {
            case task_Task::COMPLETE:
                {
                    int iTask =
                        taskIndex(m_pContext,pTask);
                    m_pContext->SetTaskComplete(iTask);
                    bEvaluateTasks = true;
                    break;
                }

            case task_Task::INVALID:
                bEvaluateTasks = true;
                break;

            case task_Task::RUNNING:
            case task_Task::VIABLE:
                break;

            default:
                    // ???
                    break;
            }
        }
    }

    if ( bEvaluateTasks )
    {
        m_pContext->SetCurrentTask(0);
        for( int iTask = 0;
            iTask < m_pTaskList->GetNumberOfTasks();
            ++iTask )
        {
            if ( !m_pContext->TaskAvailable(iTask) )
            {
                // Task has previously completed.
              continue;
            }
```

```
            task_Task * pTask = m_pTask->GetTask(iTask);
            task_Task::Status eStatus =
                          pTask->Evaluate();
            if ( pStatus == task_Task::VIABLE )
            {
                m_pContext->SetCurrentTask(pTask);
                m_fTaskTimer = pTask->GetGranularity();
                break;
            }
        }
    }
}
```

Cunningly, we can implement tasks such as IFs as compound tasks – tasks that contains subtasks. We use a context within this task to record the status of the subtasks. If and when all the subtasks are complete, we can return the status of the compound task as complete:

```
// task_CompoundTask.hpp
#include "task_Task.hpp"

class task_CompoundTask : public task_Task
{
public:
    task_CompoundTask(); // and other constructors.

    Status Evaluate();
    Status Execute();

    void AddSubtasks( task_TaskList * pSubTask );

private:
    task_TaskList * m_pSubTasks;
    task_Context  * m_pContext;
};


// task_IfTask.hpp
#include "task_CompoundTask.hpp"

class task_IfTask : public task_CompoundTask
{
public:
    Status Execute();
    Status Evaluate();
};
```

The tasking system is powerful, but it has a monolithic feel to it: the only things in task lists are tasks, and it does not readily support linear execution without some modification. Consequently, it doesn't quite match up with the component layering we are looking for (refer back to Figure 8.1). It is also a tad counterintuitive in that it looks like a sequence of linear commands but isn't really. So first up against the wall is task execution. (That's not to say that this paradigm is of no use in games – at least three commercially successful titles that I know of have employed such a system. However, we are looking for something more specific here.)

That leaves us with linear execution and event management.[1] Interestingly, the two paradigms are not mutually exclusive; in fact, a closer analysis reveals that the event-driven system requires some amount of linear execution to evaluate conditions and execute actions (though actions are considered atomic). We can therefore infer that the event system is a higher-level entity than the linear system, and we seem to be heading towards adapting Figure 8.1 to be more like that shown in Figure 8.3. Note that the choice of event management as the top layer is to some extent arbitrary; other systems might do just as well or perhaps even better. We're supporting events both at the script level to allow flexibility and directly at the C++ kernel level for efficiency.

Let's now look at the design and C++ implementation for an event management system in some detail.

Figure 8.3

Layers within the scripting system. Note that the C++ kernel can interact with both the intermediate (linear) and high (event) level layers.

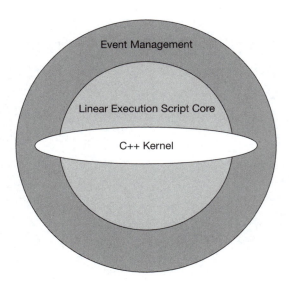

_____

1   We're ignoring hybrid methods here. There's nothing to stop us mixing events and tasks, other than the desire to keep things simple, but not so simple that we can't fulfil our design goals: a principle I refer to as 'Occam's Styptic Pencil'.

8.3 Event management details

First, we need to elaborate a bit on the actions and conditions shown in Figure 8.4. Recall that we want to have hard-coded event types and also custom event types so that we can have the following permutations:

- hard-coded (C++) condition, C++ action;
- C++ condition, script-defined action;
- script-defined condition, C++ action;
- script-defined condition, script-defined action.

In other words, conditions and actions both refer to abstract entities: commands that are articulated using C++, and commands that are articulated using scripts. We'll call these *articulations*.

Now, since multiple objects could share the same event definitions, it is probably worth our while reference counting the articulations and allowing the conditions and actions to be subclasses of things that have articulations, which we call *clauses*. Since several events may share the same clause, we also reference count the clause class. Figure 8.4 shows the relevant participating classes.

So, every event has zero or one condition clause and one action clause, both of which can be articulated in either code or script. Just what we want. Now, let's look a little bit more at the event class itself.

One feature that will definitely add power is to distinguish between one-shot events and repeatable events. The former executes its action once at most, while the latter runs the action at most *n* times, re-evaluating its condition periodically. Invoking the maxim that we subclass only when the behaviour

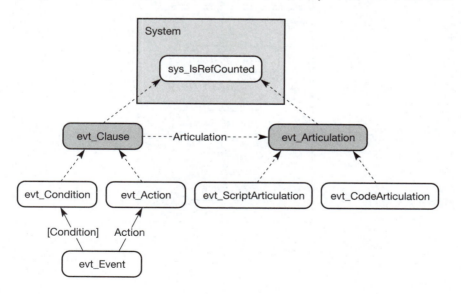

Figure 8.4
Event system part 1.

changes, not when some parameter changes, we can generalise this to a single event class, as shown here:

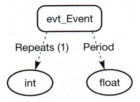

So far, so good. Now, how do we add event management to an in-game object? We'll assume there's a `GameObject` class already, and we're again going to use the multiple-inheritance component mix-in technique analogous to the task-based system we discussed above. Once per game loop, each object must look to see if there are events ready to evaluate. If there are, then their conditions are executed, and if they return true the actions are executed. The repeat count is then decremented, and if it hits zero then the event is not needed any more and can be freed. We'll create a property class IsEventDriven to encapsulate this behaviour (Figure 8.5).

Figure 8.5
Object diagram for the event management component EVT.

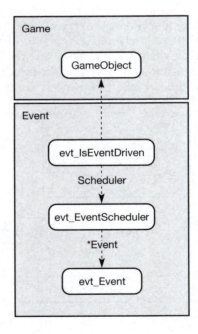

The property class should look like this:

```cpp
// evt_IsEventDriven.hpp

class evt_Event;
class evt_EventScheduler;

class evt_IsEventDriven
{
public:
    evt_IsEventDriven();
    virtual ~evt_IsEventDriven();

    void Initialise();
        // MUST be called before using events for reasons
        // that will become apparent later.

    void Update( float dt );
        // Brings the object up to date.

    void AddEvent( evt_Event * pEvent );
    void RemoveEvent( evt_Event * pEvent );
    void RemoveAllEvents();
        // Event control.
private:
    evt_EventScheduler * m_pScheduler;
};


// evt_IsEventDriven.cpp
#include "evt_IsEventDriven.hpp"
#include <cassert>

// The scheduler is an internal class, whose details need
// not concern the user.
class evt_EventScheduler
{
public:
    void Update( float dt );
    void AddEvent( evt_Event * pEvent );
    void RemoveEvent( evt_Event * pEvent );
    void RemoveAllEvents();
    // …
};
```

```
evt_IsEventDriven::evt_IsEventDriven()
: m_pScheduler(0)
{
    // Some of the classes which inherit from this
    // might not require event-driven behaviour.
    // Having a pointer to the scheduler in the
    // event class body keeps the size small if we
    // never use events and insulates the user from
    // the implementation details.
}

evt_IsEventDriven::~evt_IsEventDriven()
{
    delete m_pScheduler;
}

void evt_IsEventDriven::Initialise()
{
    assert( !m_pScheduler && "Called twice?" );

    m_pScheduler = new evt_EventScheduler;
}

void evt_IsEventDriven::Update( float dt )
{
    if ( m_pScheduler )
    {
        m_pScheduler->Update( dt );
    }
}

void evt_IsEventDriven::AddEvent( evt_Event * pEvent )
{
    assert( m_pScheduler && "Initialise() not called" );

    m_pScheduler->AddEvent( pEvent );
}

// other methods similar.
```

Before we leave events, it's worth looking at one big optimisation that we can make. The typical execution cycle for the scheduler will be to traverse its collection of events, looking to see if any are pending. If we create many events that are based on time (say at $t = 10$ seconds, go 'bang!'), then if the time is t there's no point looking at time events with times greater than *t*. This motivates the scheduler to maintain a sorted list (or more likely a heap, a collection class that uses a binary tree to maintain a sort order) of events separate from the other events (we'll call them state events) and bail out of updating timed events without having to traverse the entire list. Luckily, we hid the definition of the scheduler in the cpp file, so we need only modify the `evt_IsEventDriven` interface to add events of timed and state flavours, and subclass `evt_Event` appropriately, as shown here:

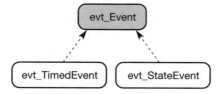

The interface to the event management system may then contain prototypes like this:

```
void evt_IsEventDriven::AddTimedEvent(evt_TimedEvent *);
void evt_IsEventDriven::AddStateEvent(evt_StateEvent *);
```

A purist might actually argue that there is a loss of encapsulation here. The fact that timed events are handled differently from state events is an implementation detail of the scheduler class, which is an internal class. Why should the interface of the property class distinguish them? The purist would probably get around this as follows: to the event management package, add a factory component that creates events:

```
struct evt_Factory
{
    evt_Event * CreateTimedEvent( float fTime,
                                  evt_Action * pAction,
                                  int iRepeats,
                                  float fPeriod );
    evt_Event * CreateStateEvent( evt_Condition * pCond,
                                  evt_Action * pAction,
                                  int iRepeats,
                                  float fPeriod );
};
```

Aside from holding pointers to the base event, the users never need tinker with the events after they are created. This means that the definition of timed and state event classes become private to the property component, and we can add methods:

```
class evt_Event
{
public:
    virtual void Schedule(evt_Scheduler *pScheduler)=0;
};


// evt_IsEventDriven.cpp
#include "evt_IsEventDriven.hpp"
#include "evt_Event.hpp"

class evt_TimedEvent : public evt_Event
{
public:
    void Schedule( evt_Scheduler * pScheduler )
    {
        pScheduler->AddTimedEvent( this );
    }
};

class evt_StateEvent : public evt_Event
{
public:
    void Schedule( evt_Scheduler * pScheduler )
    {
        pScheduler->AddStateEvent( this );
    }
};

class evt_Scheduler
{
public:
    void AddTimedEvent( evt_TimedEvent * pEvent );
    void AddStateEvent( evt_StateEvent * pEvent );
};
```

so we get to keep our encapsulation-preserving interface:

```
// evt_IsEventDriven.hpp
class evt_EventScheduler;

class evt_IsEventDriven
{
public:
    void AddEvent( evt_Event * pEvent );
```

```
private:
    evt_EventScheduler * m_pScheduler;
};

// evt_IsEventDriven.cpp
void evt_IsEventDriven::AddEvent( evt_Event * pEvent )
{
    pEvent->Schedule( m_pScheduler );
}
```

8.4 Language issues

If I had a penny for every time I'd seen a scripting system with a core loop looking like:

```
const char cToken[ MAX_TOKEN_NAME ];

while( aStream.ReadToken( cToken ) )
{
    if ( !strcmp( cToken, "set_position" ) )
    {
        float x, y, z;
        aStream.ReadFloat( &x );
        aStream.ReadFloat( &y );
        aStream.ReadFloat( &z );
        SetPosition( x, y, z );
    }
    else if ( !strcmp( cToken, "message" ) )
    {
        // ...
    }
    // ...
    else
    {
        Warning( "Unknown command '%s', cToken );
    }
}
```

then I'd have enough for a cappuccino and a skinny breakfast muffin at my
favourite multinational coffee bar. Leaving aside the horrors of case-sensitive
comparisons and the hideous inefficiency of a large number of per-object-
per-game-loop string comparisons, the main problem with this sort of scripting
is the lack of grammar.

For example, the above `set_position` command can fall flat on its face if presented with

```
set_position 10 15 + 2*sin( t * 6.28 ) 1.0E-2
```

for a multitude of reasons. There are two alternatives for handling grammar:

● an escalating series of special-case bodges in the scripting system;
● use of a grammar-definition language to generate the script toolset.

The latter is, in theory, more appealing than the former. In practice, programmers have to wrestle with tools such as lex and yacc or flex and bison, or – more recently – antlr (all these are available, free of charge, over the Internet). Often, it looks as if the cure is worse than the disease, as specifying, modifying and debugging a complete grammar can be a sizeable task.

The tools mentioned above can generate code for any platform, within limits defined mainly by the core systems that they insert into the project code base. For example, antlr uses STL, therefore your target platform would need to support that to use it at run time. They may make assumptions about things such as IO as well, for example reading from streams (cin) rather than stdio (stdin). So you will inevitably have to ask yourself: 'Is it really worth it?'

Suggested answer: 'Yes'. Remember that the goal is to write a script language that can support high- and intermediate-level behaviour. Programmers are going to get quite frustrated with a grammar-light language if they need to implement moderately sophisticated behaviour with it. Even designers will get annoyed with lack of reasonable semantic and grammatical power. One project I knew of had a bespoke scripting language that allowed IF statements but not an ELSE clause, much to the chagrin of the scriptwriters.

If the game would be served better by writing a GUI to implement drag-and-drop scripting, then much ugliness and syntactic limitation can be hidden, providing that no one will be required to debug the script that the GUI generates. Chance would be a fine thing! If the designers don't understand the scripting language (they do everything with point and click, so why should they?), then it will fall to programmers to do the debugging. Recall that another goal of writing a scripting system is to spread the load between disciplines, and it is clear that a GUI can have the opposite effect to that intended. There is also a question mark over how flexible a WIMP-based scripting environment really can be, and it is going to be difficult to write a generic GUI to wrap a scripting system. Writing a bespoke – per-project – GUI makes more sense in theory, but in practice it can be time-consuming. It depends on the complexity of the toolset to determine feasibility, as well as on having an existing library of tool-building components that can speed up the process of developing game-editing systems.

8.5 Summary

- Games that are data-driven need no or minimal recompilation between data changes, speeding up the development cycle, but if overused they can obfuscate the way the application works, slowing down development.

- Game designers need to be able to control the game in a legible, high-level fashion without having to worry about nasty technical issues. Data-driven systems are ideal for this.

- Scripting systems are, to a large extent, functionally equivalent. Though many execution paradigms exist, you can usually achieve the same results independent of the implemented methodology. Therefore, simplicity and clarity are paramount.

- Make the effort to create a familiar grammar for your scripting system, and don't waste time writing fancy graphical drag-and-drop interfaces.

Iterative development techniques

9

9.1 Introduction

In this chapter, we discuss two important questions in development and provide a single answer for both. They turn out to be fundamental not only to the logical structure of the code-development process but also to the production methodology. Here are the questions:

- What order should tasks be performed in?
- When is the game finished?

9.1.1 Prioritising tasks

The worst thing in the world as far as development is concerned is to be writing system-critical code towards the end of a project. Yet this is such a common occurrence you would think someone would have spotted it and put a stop to it. Not only will (and does) it induce huge amounts of stress in the team, but it is absolutely guaranteed to introduce all sorts of problems in other systems that were previously considered stable.

Ideally, we would like to pick an order in which to perform tasks that does not lead to this horror. Ideally, we would like to be able to know in advance which tasks and systems we need to work on first and which can wait a while. If we cannot attain this ideal state – and I would be foolhardy to suggest we can – we can certainly do better than writing critical-path code during alpha or beta phases in a project.

9.1.2 How long is a piece of virtual string?

Although a game is a finite piece of software, it is rather tricky to describe criteria for completion. It is almost universally true that the functionality and features of games that we see on store shelves are only some percentage of the development team's ambitions. More will have been designed than implemented, and not all that was implemented will have been used. Given, then, that games rarely reach the all-done mark, how are we to decide whether a game is releasable? What metrics are available to inform us how much is actually done and dusted?

Consider also a problem of scheduling subtasks. Say a programmer (let's call her Jo) has said it'll take ten days to write the 'exploding trap' object, and that she's four days into this time. Is her task 40% complete? It's very hard to tell, especially since we cannot see the trap exploding till maybe day nine or ten. But let's be optimistic and suggest that Jo works hard and gets the job done in eight days. Usually there is a profit of plus two days marked up, the task is marked as complete, and everything looks hunky dory for the project.

Later on, it turns out that the trap needs to be modified since (say) it needs to be able to trap larger objects. It's another four days of work for our Jo, and now we have a deficit of minus two days, and suddenly the project starts to look like it's slipping.

The point is this: most objects in a game rarely get written just once. We'll revisit them over the course of a project to fix bugs, add and remove features, optimise and maybe even rewrite them entirely. This isn't a pathological behaviour: almost all significant software systems grow and evolve over the course of time. How naive then does the 'four days in, 40% complete' metric look? Pretty damn naive, to put it politely. What we really need is a system that allows time and space for evolution without driving projects into schedule loss and the resulting state of semi-panic that characterises most development processes.

9.2 Incremental delivery

9.2.1 Milestones around my neck

Almost all software development (outside of research, which by its nature it open-ended) is driven by some kind of milestone system. Let me state unequivocally now that this is a good thing, and that the days of anarchic commercial software development should be buried and remain so. Nevertheless, just by virtue of it being a good thing does not mean that it doesn't come with its own particular set of pros and cons. In particular, if we accept (for all the pro reasons) that milestone-driven development is the way to go, then we must also pay attention to the con side, which will inevitably frustrate our attempts to make the process work with the efficiency we require for delivery on time and within budget.

One of the most difficult cons that games developers have to deal with is the different way that milestones and the associated schedules are interpreted by production teams and management. As most of those who have worked with non-trivial software products (or, in fact, any large project that requires multiple bespoke interacting component parts spanning a variety of disciplines) have come to realise, schedules represent a team's best guess at how the product will evolve over time.

On the other hand, management – perhaps unused to the way that schedules are produced, perhaps because it requires correlation of studio funding with progress – often read the document completely differently. They see the document almost as a contract between themselves and developers, promising certain things at certain times.

This disparity between seeing a schedule as a framework for project evolution to facilitate tracking, and as a binding agreement to deliver particular features at particular times, causes much angst for both developers and managers. The former often have to work ridiculous hours under pressure to get promised features out. The latter have responsibility for financial balances that depend on the features being in place.

9.2.2 Internal and external milestones

We can see that there are some basic premises about milestones that need to be addressed:

- Teams that do not work to milestones that mark important features becoming available in the game will not be able to deliver on time.
- Teams that are held to unrealistic milestones will not be able to deliver on time, irrespective of how financially important or lucrative that may be.
- Managers need to know how long the team thinks development will be and what the important markers are along the way. Without this, there can be no business plan and therefore no project.

Clearly, the sort of milestones that managers need to be aware of are cruder or at a lower granularity than the milestones that developers need to pace the evolution of the product. We can therefore distinguish between *external* milestones, which are broad-brush descriptions of high-level features with granularity of weeks (maybe even months), and *internal* milestones, which are medium- and fine-level features scheduled in weeks and days.

Managers therefore never need to know the internal mechanisms that generate the software. To adopt a programming metaphor, the team can be viewed as a black-box type of object with the producer as its interface. There are two types of question (public methods, to extend the analogy) that a manager can ask of a producer:

- Give me the latest version of the game.
- Give me the latest (high-level) schedule.

This is an unrealistically simple example of interaction between production and management. The latter will want to know issues of team dynamics, why things are running late (as they inevitably seem to) and a whole host of other project-related information. However, it draws a fuzzy – but distinguishable – line in the sand between the scheduling of features and accountability for their development.

9.2.3 The breaking-wheel of progress

There is one other important sense in which management and development perceive milestones differently. It is based on the concept of visibility and is, without doubt, the biggest millstone (half-pun intended) around developers' necks this side of Alpha Centauri.

Almost ubiquitously in the industry, management refuse to regard features that they cannot see (or perhaps hear) within a short time of picking up the game as importantly as those obviously visible (or audible) ones. For those of us that work on AI, physics, memory managers, scripting systems, maths, optimisation, bug fixing and all those other vital areas of a game's innards that are not open to visual inspection, this is particularly galling. To spend weeks and months working on hidden functionality only to have the team's work dismissed as inadequate because there was no new eye candy is an all too common occurrence.

The education of managers in the realities of development is a slow ongoing and painful process. Meanwhile, we developers have to work with what we are given, therefore it remains important to – somehow – build ongoing visible/audible progress into the development of the project.

There is an intimate relationship between the concept of visibility and that of completeness. Many tasks may not become tangibly present until they are complete. Saying that something is 40% complete, even if that was a rigorously obtained metric, might still amount to 0% visible. So, we'll only be able to address the issue of progress fully when we deal later with determining completeness for a task.

9.2.4 Always stay a step ahead

Despite our best – though sometimes a little less – efforts, we will slip. We will deliver a feature late or perhaps not even at all, and if the management is in a particularly fussy mood, then there may be much pounding of fists and red faces. Worse than showing no visible progress would be to show retrograde progress – fewer features apparent than a previous milestone. Nevertheless, it is a common and required ability for projects to arbitrarily disable and re-enable particular functionality within the code base. With the advent of version control systems, we are now able to store a complete history of source code and data, so in theory it is always possible to roll back to a previous version of the game that had the feature enabled.

Just because it's possible, does that make it desirable? In this case, yes. Indeed, I would argue that working versions of the game should be built frequently – if not daily, then at least weekly – and archived in some sensible fashion. When management asks production for the latest version of the game (one of their two allowed questions from the previous section), then the producer will return not the current (working) build but the one previous to that.

Why not the current working build? Because it is important to show progress, and development must ensure that to the best of their ability the game has improved visibly from one iteration to the next. If it becomes necessary –

and it usually does – to spend time maintaining, upgrading, optimising or rewriting parts of the code base, then releasing the next-but-one working version gives another release with visible improvements before we hit the calm spot with no apparent progress.

From one point of view, this is a sneaky manoeuvre. It's no more sneaky than (say) insuring your house against flood.[1] Publishers and managers always want to see the latest version, and a development team itching to impress may well be tempted to show them it. Resist this urge! Remember: development should be opaque to management inspection other than through the supplied interface. Anything else is just development suicide.

9.3 Iterated delivery

So we've decided that rather than work specifically to release code at external milestones, we'll supply work-in-progress builds at these times. Internally, we'll be working to our own schedule. How should we organise this schedule?

I'll start by assuming that there is a reasonably comprehensive design document for the game (but believe me, you'd be surprised at the number of times there isn't). This document should describe, in brief, what the game is about – characters (if any), storyline (if any), situations and rules. Step one to producing an internal schedule is to produce the object-oriented design diagram for the game. We are not interested here in the diagram specifying interrelationships between the objects; the end goal is simply to produce a big list of all classes that map directly to concepts in the game. Auxiliary classes such as containers and mathematical objects need not apply – we are looking only for classes that map to game-level concepts.

Once we have produced this list, it needs to be given back to the design team, as step two is really its call. It needs to classify all the objects in the list (I'll use the terms 'objects' and 'features' interchangeably in this section) into the following three groups:

- core
- required
- desired.

Core features form the basis for the game. Without them, there is only a basic executable shell consisting of (some of) start-up code, rendering, memory management, sound, controller support, scripting support, resource management, etc. Should any of these non-game systems require engineering, then they should be added to the core group, which will otherwise contain the most fun-

---

1 As I write this section, areas of Britain have been submerged as rain falls near continually and rivers burst their banks. Property owners will bless their house insurance.

damental objects. For definiteness, consider a soccer game; the most fundamental objects are:

- player (and subclasses)
- stats (determining player abilities)
- ball
- pitch (and zones on the pitch)
- goal.

An executable that consists of working versions of these objects (coupled to the non-game classes) is generally not of playable, let alone releasable, quality.

Required features expand the core functionality into what makes this game playable and unique. Often, these features are more abstract than core features. They will embody concepts such as NPC behaviour, scoring systems and rules. Also, they will pay some homage to the particular genre the game will fit into, because rival products will dictate that we implement features in order to compete effectively. To continue the soccer example, we might place the following features in this group:

- AI for player subclasses
- referee (either a visible or invisible one that enforces rules)
- crowd (with context-dependent sounds and graphics)
- knockout, league and cup competitions.

A game consisting of core and required features will be playable and releasable. Nevertheless, it should be considered the minimal amount of content that will be releasable, and it still requires work if the game is to be near the top of the genre.

Desired features provide the polish for the game. This will include such things as visual and audio effects, hidden features and levels, and cheats. Features in this group will not alter game play in significant ways, though they will enhance the breadth and depth of the playing experience and (as with required features) the competition may dictate their inclusion.

Depending on the type of game, they may be game-related objects. For example, in the soccer game, having assistant referees would be a desired feature, as the game will function just fine without them.

The end result is a list of features that is effectively sorted in terms of importance to the product. It is tempting to say that the optimal order of tasks is then to start at the top – the most important core tasks – and work our way down. We carry on completing tasks until we run out of time.

Well it's close, but there's no cigar for that method. There are fundamental problems in organising work this way. There is little evidence of anything that resembles continual progress. In the pathological case, the game is in bits for the entire development cycle until just before the end, when the bits are pulled together and – hopefully – fit. This is guaranteed to have producers and management biting their knuckles with stress. Furthermore, the most likely outcome is that components do not work together or have unforeseen side effects that may involve radical redesign very late on in the project.

Clearly, it is correct to do the most important tasks first and the superficial tasks last (time allowing). But if we wish to show continual improvement of the product, then we shall need to be a little smarter. So we will progress to the third phase of the iterated delivery method (the actual 'iterated' part). We'll start again with the list of features, which, because an object-oriented design process has generated them, map directly to classes.

Consider just one of these classes. How does it start off its life? Usually something like this:

```cpp
// File Player.hpp
class Player
{
public:
    Player();
    ~Player();

private:
};

// File Player.cpp
#include "Player.hpp"

Player::Player()
{
}

Player::~Player()
{
}
```

Over the course of the product development, much will be added and much will also be removed, but generally the object evolves. This evolution can occur in one of two ways. First, it can start with zero functionality and end up fully implemented. This is possible, but not very common. More realistically, the object is rewritten either fully or partially to have more complex, or more robust, or more efficient behaviour over the duration.

So far, so obvious. But consider the formalisation of the principle that objects evolve: instead of evolving the feature from zero functionality at the start to full functionality at the end, consider writing versions of the full object functionality. We define the following four versions of the feature:

1. The *null* version: this is the initial version of the object interface with no implementation (empty functions). Note that this is a complete project that can be compiled and linked and that will run, albeit not doing anything useful.
2. The *base* version: this has a working interface and shows placeholder functionality. Some of the required properties may be empty or have minimal implementation. For example, a shadow may be represented by a single grey sprite, and a human character may be represented by a stick person or a set of flat-shaded boxes. The intent is that the object shows the most basic behaviour required by the design without proceeding to full implementation, and therefore integration problems at the object level will show up sooner rather than later.
3. The *nominal* version: this iteration of the feature represents a commercially viable object that has fully implemented and tested behaviour and is visually acceptable. For example, the shadow may now be implemented as a series of textured alpha-blended polygons.
4. The *optimal* version: this is the ultimate singing and dancing version, visually state of the art, and then some. To continue the shadow example, we may be computing shadow volumes or using projective texture methods.

We'll refer to the particular phase that an object is in at any point in the project as the *level* of the class: a level 1 object has a null implementation, whereas a level 4 object is optimal.

Some points to note: first of all, some objects will not fit naturally into this scheme. Some may be so simple that they go straight from null to optimal. Conversely, some may be so complex that they require more than four iterations. Neither of these scenarios presents a problem for us, since we aren't really counting iterations *per se*. We're effectively tracking implementation quality. In the case of an apparently simple object, we can test it effectively only in the context of any associated object at whatever level it's at. In other words, systems and subsystems have a level, which we can define slightly informally as:

$$L(\text{subsystem}) = \min_j L(\text{object}_j)$$

$$L(\text{system}) = \min_i L(\text{subsystem}_i)$$

with L() denoting the level of an object, system or subsystem. Applying this idea to the application as a whole,

$$L(\text{application}) = \min_k L(\text{system}_k)$$

or, in simple terms, the application's level is the smallest of its constituent object levels.

Now we need to put together the ideas of level and priority to get some useful definitions, which form the basis of iterated delivery.

An application is defined as *of release quality* if, and only if, its required features are at the nominal level.

An application is referred to as *complete* if, and only if, its desired features are at the optimal level.

From these definitions, we see that there is a sliding scale that starts from a barely releasable product all the way up to implementing and polishing every feature that the design specifies. The product just gets better and better, and – provided that the tasks have been undertaken in a sensible order – can be released at any time after it becomes of release quality.

The second point to note is that object-oriented development is perfectly suited to a level-based scheme (and, conversely, procedural development does not adapt as easily). For example, consider our shadow code. An object that has a shadow may declare:

```
class Shadow;

class AnObject
{
public:
    // Interface...
private:
    Shadow * m_pShadow;
};
```

Each level of the shadow object can be implemented in a separate subclass:

```
// File Shadow.hpp
class Shadow
{
public:
    // Interface only: null implementation
    virtual void Compute( SCENE::Frame * pScene ) = 0;
    virtual void Render( REND::Target * pTarget ) = 0;
};

// File ShadowBasic.hpp
class ShadowBasic : public Shadow
{
public:
    // Base implementation.
    virtual void Compute( SCENE::Frame * pScene );
    virtual void Render( REND::Target * pTarget );
```

```
private:
    Sprite * m_pSprite;
};

// File ShadowPolygonal.hpp
class ShadowPolygonal : public Shadow
{
public:
    // Nominal implementation.
    virtual void Compute( SCENE::Frame * pScene );
    virtual void Render( REND::Target * pTarget );

private:
    Polygon * m_pPolygons;
};

// File ShadowProjected.hpp
class ShadowProjected : public Shadow
{
public:
    // Optimal version.
    virtual void Compute( SCENE::Frame * pScene ) = 0;
    virtual void Render( REND::Target * pTarget ) = 0;

private:
    Texture * m_pProjectedTexture;
};
```

Within our `AnObject` class, polymorphism allows us to control which available implementation of shadows we use:

```
m_pShadow = new ShadowProjected();
```

We can even use a so-called factory pattern to create our shadow objects:

```
// AnObject.cpp
#define SHADOW_LEVEL level_NOMINAL
// …
m_pShadow = Shadow::CreateShadow( SHADOW_LEVEL );

// Shadow.cpp
/*static*/
Shadow * Shadow::CreateShadow( int iLevel )
{
```

```
Shadow * pShadow = 0;

switch( iLevel )
{
    case level_BASE:
        pShadow = new ShadowBasic();
        break;

    case level_NOMINAL:
        pShadow = new ShadowPolygonal();
        break;

    case level_OPTIMAL:
        pShadow = new ShadowOptimal();
        break;
}

return( pShadow );
}
```

9.3.1 Waste not, want not

Does this mean that we have to write similar code three times? Yes it does, but all the process has done is highlight the fact that (by and large) this is what we do anyway. It just so happens that when we do things piecemeal in an *ad hoc* order, we're less aware of the partial and complete rewrites during development. By developing in the above fashion, we are, to some extent, duplicating work, but that duplication does not go to waste. First, we will acquire a degree of experience when writing our basic implementations that will be useful when we write the more complex ones. If we're clever (and we are), then we will write a number of support functions, systems and objects that will make implementation of the nominal and optimal versions considerably simpler.

Furthermore, by writing an object in a suitably object-oriented fashion, we may end up with a reusable component. Once we've written a basic shadow, then it can be used as a base implementation in any game that requires shadows. That means we can get instant functionality at the logical and visual level. It is the author's experience that it is harder to transpose nominal implementations and more difficult still to move optimal code in this fashion; the idea is to get placeholder functionality in as quickly as possible.

9.3.2 Ordering using priorities and levels

Returning to the two classification schemes, we can see that there is at least one sensible order in which to perform tasks that fulfils our goals: we would like to perform the important – core – tasks first, primarily because we shall be writing some of the major systems and subsystems that later layers will depend on.

Then, we would perform the required tasks, then the desired ones.[2] While this is a laudable attempt at doing the things that matter first, we can do much better by integrating the object's level.

So, our next attempt at task ordering will be this:

- Starting with the core tasks, then proceeding to the required tasks, then the desired tasks, create the null implementation of each object. Once this has been done (most projects can get to this state in a week or two), the project should build and run without doing very much.
- Now go back to the core tasks and start writing the nominal implementations, carrying on through the required tasks. At this point, the code is – by our definition – releasable. We can then carry on getting the desired features to their nominal status.
- Finally, we repeat the sweep from core to desired until we either run out of tasks or are stopped in our tracks by external factors.

This – breadth-first – approach is much better than a single sweep from core to required to desired with no reference to level. It is a universe better than the 'let's do the cool bits first' approach. It shows near-continuous growth throughout the development cycle, and it makes sure that we focus our attention early on in the places where it is most required. We have a handle on how complete our product is, and it is now considerably simpler to create meaningful internal and external milestones. However, it has a problemette that arises in its day-to-day implementation:

- In a nutshell, it is not clear that it is more advantageous to undertake base-level desired features than nominal-level core features, or to write nominal-level desired features in preference to optimal-level core features. There are a number of factors that will determine whether it is or not.
- Although progress is continuous, it isn't smooth.

Consider a project with 12 features to implement (labelled F1 to F12). Assuming for the moment just a single programmer, we may order tasks as shown in Table 9.1 (the numbers representing the ordinal number of the task).

Tasks are undertaken in priority order. When we've finished the pass at the current level, we start at the top again at the next level. This is fine. Indeed, it's better than most hit-and-miss attempts, but it does suffer from the disadvantage that after the base level, no new functionality appears – the existing stuff just improves. While this is OK from a purely theoretical standpoint, it does make it

---

2 Typically, it would be nice if game development followed this scheme because at least it makes some commercial sense. The usual approach, however, is to attempt all the optimal-level desired tasks first in order to make an impression and then somehow backstitch a game into the demo.

Features	Level	Null	Base	Nominal	Optimal
Core	F1	1	13	25	37
	F2	2	14	26	38
	F3	3	15	27	39
	F4	4	16	28	40
Required	F5	5	17	29	41
	F6	6	18	30	42
	F7	7	19	31	43
	F8	8	20	32	44
Desired	F9	9	21	33	45
	F10	10	22	34	46
	F11	11	23	35	47
	F12	12	24	36	48

Table 9.1 Naive programmer scheduling.

Features	Level	Null	Base	Nominal	Optimal
Core	F1	1	13	22	37
	F2	2	14	23	38
	F3	3	15	24	39
	F4	4	16	25	40
Required	F5	5	17	26	41
	F6	6	18	27	42
	F7	7	19	28	43
	F8	8	20	29	44
Desired	F9	9	21	32	45
	F10	10	30	33	46
	F11	11	31	34	47
	F12	12	35	36	48

Table 9.2 A better ordering of tasks.

difficult to impress. Since we always want to be able to keep one step ahead of the demands put on development, it remains prudent to tweak the order a little. Consider the ordering in Table 9.2. Here, we've deferred implementing the lower-priority tasks F10, F11 and F12 at the base level until around the second half of the project. This places a greater emphasis on getting the most important games systems to a releasable state. It also means we can spoil ourselves a little and get to work on one or two of the flash bits early on, and from week to week we can see our game both grow and improve.

So much for one-programmer teams: they are the exception, not the rule. The concept extends readily to multiprogrammer teams, and Table 9.3 shows an

Table 9.3 Naive ordering for two programmers A and B.

Features	Level	Null	Base	Nominal	Optimal
Core	F1	1A	7A	11B	19A
	F2	1B	7B	12A	19B
	F3	2A	8A	12B	20A
	F4	2B	8B	13A	20B
Required	F5	3A	9A	13B	21A
	F6	3B	9B	14A	21B
	F7	4A	10A	14B	22A
	F8	4B	10B	15A	22B
Desired	F9	5A	11A	16B	23A
	F10	5B	15B	17A	23B
	F11	6A	16A	17B	24A
	F12	6B	18A	18B	24B

ordering of tasks based on two programmers based on the previous ordering. Notice, however, that there is a slight problem with the allocations. Looking at task F1, programmer A implements the null- and base-level functionality of the feature; however, it just so happens that programmer B ends up doing the nominal level and A is finally scheduled to implement the optimal level.

Now it really depends on your point of view as to whether this is a problem. One school of thought suggests that it is bad policy to put all your eggs in one basket. If there is only one programmer who can do a set of tasks, then what happens when they get ill or they leave? Without someone else who knows the system, there is a significant loss of momentum while programmer C is brought in to fill A's shoes and learn their ways.

The other school of thought is that a Jack of all trades is a master of none. Programmers who work on many systems spend a lot of time getting into a paradigm, only to spend a short while doing it and then starting another one. It's scarily easy to forget even the stuff that seems obvious when you don't actively use it for a while, and if the code has been implemented sloppily or the paradigm is complex and/or undocumented, there is again a loss of momentum whenever the programmer changes task. Although the changes are probably smaller, it can happen several times over the course of the project, and the damage is cumulative.

On the other hand, it is reasonable – indeed, vital – to recognise and effectively utilise the basic skill sets of your team. If you have a renderer specialist on board, then it seems a bit of a waste having them write AI if there are graphics tasks to be done.

There is no simple answer to this dilemma, The author suggests that communication is vital: all programmers should know about what other programmers are doing via code reviews; code should be clear and documented informatively (either via meaningful commenting or actual paper or electronic

Features	Level	Null	Base	Nominal	Optimal
Core	F1	1A	7A	12A	19A
	F2	1B	7B	11B	19B
	F3	2A	8A	13A	20A
	F4	2B	8B	12B	20B
Required	F5	3A	9A	14A	21A
	F6	3B	9B	13B	21B
	F7	4A	10A	15A	22A
	F8	4B	10B	14B	22B
Desired	F9	5A	11A	16A	23A
	F10	5B	15B	16B	23B
	F11	6A	17A	18A	24A
	F12	6B	17B	18B	24B

Table 9.4 Schedule for two programmers accounting for skills.

documentation); and systems should be engineered to be as self-contained and maintainable as is humanly possible.

Assuming that we wish to keep the same programmer with (basically) the same task types, Table 9.4 shows the improved two-programmer itinerary.

9.3.3 Scheduling with an iterated delivery system

The iterated delivery system shifts the focus of production from 'When will it be finished?' to 'When will it be good enough?' Since there is no meaningful definition of 'finished', but we have provided a definition of 'good enough', we have established a metric by which to measure the progress of our project. Consequently, iterated delivery solves a number of difficulties that arise in the scheduling of work.

The major mistake of developers when estimating schedule times is that they perform a top-down analysis of the problem, breaking the large, complex tasks into smaller, more manageable ones, and then estimating the times for those. The task time is then the sum of the subtask times, with some amount of contingency added. Usually, no account is taken of learning curve, code revision or assembly of components. Is it any wonder, then, that tasks almost ubiquitously overrun?

I am not suggesting that top-down analyses are wrong – it is nigh impossible to schedule without them – but they miss out important information that is an integral part of the software development process. Iterated delivery puts that information back in. The developers still do a top-town analysis, they still estimate subtask times and add them up to get task times, and risk-analysis/buffering[3] contingency times still need to be accounted for. The important difference is this:

---

3 Buffering adds on a fixed proportion of schedule time to allow for illness, holidays, meetings and other unforeseeable but likely eventualities.

> The time scheduled for a task is the sum of the times for the null, base, nominal and optimal levels.

I'm hoping that you didn't recoil too much from that assertion. What it sounds like on a naive level is that you are taking a task time, multiplying it by four – once for each level – and then delivering within the allotted time, which has been grossly exaggerated, thus earning some kudos for finishing early. If you think that I'm suggesting that, then let me reassure you that I am not. The statement is to be read as follows: account in the schedule for the fact that you rewrite significant portions of code when you understand more about the problem. Schedule the less important tasks so that rewriting them, if at all, occurs after the important ones.

Thus, iterated delivery becomes its own risk-management and contingency system. The harder, more time-consuming (and therefore riskier) tasks are deferred to times when they cannot hurt the project if they do not come in on time (assuming that they are, at least, at nominal level towards the alpha date). We simply go with the nominal version if the optimal version is slipping and we must ship tomorrow. Or else we are granted more time to complete the task because it would make a visible improvement (though one ought to ask why it had such a low priority if this was so).

9.4 Summary

- Iteration is an intrinsic property of software development. Most non-trivial tasks get written, scrapped, rewritten, improved, refactored, reorganized and optimized in the course of their lifecycles.

- Given this, we should make it work for us – or at least acknowledge and account for its existence.

- Iterated delivery – formalising the notions of task ordering and completion – allows us to schedule and allocate tasks in priority order.

- Iterated delivery fits well with a component-based object-oriented programming paradigm.

Game development roles   **10**

Modern game development isn't a single discipline: it is a synergy of disciplines. The final product is at least the sum of its constituent design, art, programming, audio and video components. This can result in large teams – more than, say, ten members – and, consequently, production and communication become as important as any technical problem.

With time tight and budgets all too finite, it is important for a team to maximise the use of its personnel to get as much as possible achieved before the shrink-wrap cools. Though production issues vary from product to product and from team to team, the major problems that teams will encounter are (for the best and worst reasons) pretty much the same from game to game and (surprisingly) even across companies, irrespective of their size. In this chapter, we will examine the structure of teams, the roles of individual members and how to squeeze the most from your colleagues without wringing them dry.

10.1 The cultural divides

First, let's talk about the culture of development. This is how the teams within the team interrelate on a day-to-day basis. In almost all the teams I have worked in, there is an unspoken divide between artists and programmers. The artists are often perceived by the programmers as technically naive and unrealistic, while the programmers are seen as controlling and uncreative. Usually, this subliminal culture difference is taken with good humour. Even so, when the pressure is on, people are less inclined to be so forgiving and tension can increase within the team.

And what of the unspoken relationship (or even the spoken one) betwixt programmers and designers? Game designers are often less technically fluent than artists: they work in the realm of ideas, where anything is possible. Being brought down to earth by programmer's realism (often mistaken for, or sometimes identified correctly as, pessimism) often disappoints. Again, petty tensions can result.

You don't need to be Sigmund Freud to realise that tension within a team can cripple development at a time when it most needs to be cruising. And it's probably a cliché that communication is what is required to bridge these gaps.

However, it's true that communication is a big part of avoiding disputes and misunderstandings in the first place. Wise people say:

> Communication is not the problem: we are communicating all the time, consciously or otherwise. What is important is to communicate what really matters.

In other words, if the team sits in silence all day and never talks, its members are communicating via the mechanism of non-communication. Psychologists call this 'indirect aggression', and it represents the worst excess of inter- or intra-disciplinary failure.

Almost as bad, a team that spends more time talking about details than doing anything about them is still working almost as ineffectively as the sulkers. It is getting the relevant information across to those who need it that is the essence of good communication.

OK, so we agree that effective communication is important. To be able to communicate, we need to understand the languages that our colleagues use (and they ours), since it is unlikely we will all be able to share a common inter-disciplinary language.

10.2 The programming team

I'm going to step out on a limb here. Some designers and artists are not going to like what I am going to suggest. Many programmers will also not like it! I would only ask that they all bear with me while I try to justify myself. Anyway, here's the contentiousness in all its glory:

- Programming is the pivotal discipline in the development cycle.
- Programming is a production process.

Let's deal with these points separately.

Everything that happens in a video game takes place because a programmer wrote a series of instructions that caused it to occur. If a model explodes, then it is because code is executing to make it so. If a piece of music plays, then it's because the music-playing code tells it to. If a script written by a designer moves an object, then it is the programmer's script-execution code running that moves the object.

Nothing can happen in a game without a programmer making it do so.

This is not a boast; it is a simple statement of fact. While designers may well construct game scenarios whose whole is greater than the sum of its parts, it is because the programming team's code allows them to do so.

For this reason, I shall dwell in somewhat more detail on programming team issues than the other disciplines.

Before we programmers get carried away with being the pivotal discipline, as we've discussed in previous chapters, programming is not *per se* a form of creative expression or a lifestyle choice. The function of a programming team is to take a design specification document and, to the best of their abilities, make it happen. Maybe more, but certainly little less. It is categorically *not* the programmer's job to dictate content unless the reasons are shortage of time or technical infeasibility.

These are the maxims of game programming. They define the boundaries of how the programming team should influence content (and should dictate how other team members, production and management should interact with the programming team). As far as programmers are concerned, their role is this: to convert the game-play design into a technical design and implement this accordingly.

We should note that although I trot out glib phrases such as 'a programmer's role', there is, in fact, quite a bit of variation within the various strands of software development: they do their jobs in slightly different ways and produce different types of code. I'm not just meaning style here. There is real qualitative and structural difference between the specialisations within the team, and it's interesting to take a look at these.

10.2.1 Programming roles

Within the team, there will be variations in personality, experience, skill sets and temperament. What is often (to my continuing amazement) overlooked by managers is that not all programmers are alike, and even those that are alike in some respects are completely different in others. When building a programming team, you may be in the lucky position of being able to pick and choose suitable personnel for the project in question. In other cases, you may have to make do with the resources at your disposal. In either case, it stands to reason that, when recruiting new staff or team members, identifying the skills you need – or the ability to translate certain skills into other, similar ones – is critical. Looked at in another way, recruiting individuals just because of their availability could lead to an unbalanced team, and it becomes a matter of great skill and judgement to decide whether it is better – in terms of productivity and team dynamics – to employ that person than not to and be a team member down.

The roles outlined in the next sections are not necessarily mutually exclusive: some programmers can wear multiple hats. However, it is generally the case that individuals excel in one role and then go from competent to adequate to risky in others. There is a pernicious trend within the business for programmers to be funnelled into specialising themselves – once they have proved competence at a task, they are more likely to be offered that task (or similar) in the future, to the point that they will have spent years doing little else. In the long term, this is bad for the individual, ergo detrimental to the company's interest, so it is very important that role specialisation is monitored from project to project.

The technology programmer

Writing libraries – components, packages, systems, layers and beyond – is not a simple business. There are many factors to weigh up, as too general a system could result in degraded performance, too complex a system will discourage reuse, too simple a system and others might not bother reusing it, and too specific a system will only be usable by a select few.

Mix into this equation the requirements that a well-designed class library should be robust with respect to user requirements, should be implemented efficiently in both logical and physical aspects, and may need to work on a number of target platforms whose core architecture varies widely, and it should be obvious that it takes a great deal of experience and skill in order to be a technology programmer.

The tools programmer

Most of the development houses I have visited have had a tools programmer. They've probably spent a lot of time using Microsoft's MFC and writing plug-ins for a variety of third-party products such as Adobe Photoshop and Softimage. They typically write very little game code, though they are often recruited into the team towards the end of projects to mop up small to moderate tasks that are outstanding. Because of their PC-centric development exposure, they are of limited use in hardware-specific projects or systems. This is not to demean the role of the tools programmer. Indeed, I am tempted to argue that they are central to the entire development process.

The architect

Modern game application code can be as complex as the most sophisticated of multipass rendering pipelines. If we choose to use specialised technology programmers to write the graphics systems (etc.), then by the same principle it makes sense to have architecture specialists to design, write and maintain the high-level game code. Most of the principles discussed elsewhere in this book pertain as much to engineering a game system as to engineering a rendering library.

The architect is the individual who can answer the 'Where does this class fit in?' sort of question that arises during development. Often, the crowbarring of classes into arbitrary locations in a game can cause sustained – if not irreconcilable – problems with maintenance, dependencies and even the inability to fulfil design requirements. Having an architect on the team can get projects rolling very quickly and promote good practice within the rest of the team.

Architects are, as a rule, stronger with C++ classes than with CPU instruction pipelines. Though inevitably all software systems have to pay some homage to the underlying hardware design, the architect will deal with the high- and intermediate-level abstractions that form the big picture of how the game functions.

Expect to see sweeping class hierarchies, much use of templates to foster genericity and copious amounts of abstraction. On the flip side, beware of systems that are overengineered: sprawling and hard to maintain because complex functionality is distributed over many systems and low performance due to no awareness of CPU instruction caching or underlying hardware architecture.

The low-level programmer

At the other end of the spectrum, the low-level programmer deals with assembly language modules, and low-level and intermediate-level classes. Do not expect elegant patterns and abstractions – their code is built to be light and optimally quick. Expect to see classes thinly, even barely, wrapping hardware-bashing code.

However, what it lacks in academic structure, it more than compensates for in utility. The code is quick, minimal and – the other side of the blade – quite hard to understand. Low-level programmers can be hard to come by, so it becomes important to make sure that at least one other team member understands what the metal-head is doing.

The game-play programmer

Somewhere between the big-picture architect and the 'dot the i's and cross the t's' atomic scale of the low-level programmer lies the game-play programmer. Their responsibility is to sequence the high- and intermediate-level constructs together to turn a set of disparate and – if well engineered – independent software systems into a playable game.

More than other types of programmer, the game-play programmer may well find themselves on the critical path of the project. This is because as well as writing their own code, they are writing a lot of glue code between the high-level abstract systems, their own game classes and the intermediate/lower-level library systems. The code they write is subject to the vagaries of both, and it can be tricky to write and make robust.

Expect to see pragmatic coding: the use, and occasionally abuse, of the top-level abstractions with only a slight regard for either physical and logical design criteria or low-level hardware niceties. Game-play code will probably not be elegant. Neither should it be – it should be enough to get the job done.

The physics programmer

For certain types of game, there is the requirement to have a realistic physical simulation of an object's behaviour. The most common example of this requirement is for driving games, which require quite sophisticated physical models. For this sort of task, a physics programmer is – pardon the pun – wheeled in.

There are two levels to physics programming. The first is the development of a solid Newtonian physics library[1] to perform a general simulation. This can range in complexity from a single rigid body with applied forces to soft and/or

---

1   I have yet to encounter a game that makes use of relativistic or quantum effects in its physics.

jointed bodies with contact solvers. The latter is a task that is so specialised and time-consuming that, should a game require it, a significant amount of resources will need to be directed at it. In particular, getting these systems robust and numerically stable takes a great deal of mathematical skill, so the physics programmer really becomes a technology programmer too.

The second level of physics programming is to use the physics library to simulate a system. Though the skill sets are related, a high-level physics programmer can probably function with the basic $F=ma$, though invariably more specific knowledge is required: equations describing such forces as aerodynamic drag, static and dynamic friction, or a damped spring.

The AI programmer

AI is the big lie of the games business. Though some games really do use systems that learn, adapt to volatile environments and react to player input (etc.), in terms of the end results they are usually indistinguishable from, or perhaps even inferior to, traditional game AI. Bearing in mind that they may well have cost a considerable amount of development time (equals money!), they'd have to be pretty special to justify themselves.

Learning to fake AI is as much of an art as real AI and lends itself to specialisation. An AI programmer will be very busy from the moment the systems that support pseudo-intelligent entities are at the basic level until the very last character is typed in.

The mop-up programmer

Games programming may have a superficially glamorous veneer, but the reality is that it's a 9-to-6 job (6 am, occasionally!), and there are some tasks that can be as tedious as they are necessary to a finished product. For example, implementing foreign-language support, user-interface definitions and adjustments, and the finding and fixing of those truly evil and evasive bugs. If the team consists of programmers committed to large chunks of specialised work, then a lot of these tasks may well fall between the cracks.

That's where the mop-up programmer comes in. To make a soccer analogy, they are the sweeper of the team, ensuring that the small things that need doing are done. Small they may be, but a few small tasks soon add up to one big one, so the mopper-upper does the team a big favour in time. They also help to create a more cohesive, polished game, which has a positive effect on morale (doubly so because those unpleasant tasks have been removed from the schedule).

Mop-up programmer code is restricted to quite small sections of code. Like game-play code, it's utilitarian rather than elegant. On occasion, to fix a nasty bug, unpleasant hacks may be required because the mop-up programmer doesn't have the time to learn the fine print of how the offending systems work independently and together. This is fine towards the back end of a project. On no account, though, should it be happening in the first phase of development!

The special-effects programmer

The special-effects programmer is another late-phase team member. They have much in common with the low-level programmers, though they add a fair degree of artistic skill to the mix. They're usually highly skilled at combining multipass rendering techniques with additive and subtractive transparency and some physical modelling to make realistic-looking water, rocket trails, glares and flares, steam, fire, explosions, etc. In terms of their knowledge base, they'll be comfortable with the maths of 3D transformations, as well as having an intimate understanding of the underlying hardware. Oh, and a smattering of physics comes in handy too.

An effects programmer needs to come in late for two reasons. First, cosmetic enhancements do not belong in the early stages of development. Second, the systems from which they will hang their effects need to be in place before they come on board, and since the effects themselves may need some horsepower behind them, it is better to wait until most of the game is written to best balance the CPU requirements.

10.2.2 Recruitment

Recruitment of new talent is not an easy business. For a start, there may be many more seats to fill than bottoms to fill them, and not all of those bottoms will be what you are looking for. Often, the choice is between a programmer or no programmer, not (say) a physics programmer or an AI programmer. Many studios may simply grab what they can when they have the opportunity: 'If you know what a byte is, you're in'.

Such desperate measures may hurt in the medium to long term: a team filled with inappropriate specialist skills, or simply missing key skills, will struggle to deliver on time. On the other hand, there are all too many 'experienced' developers who have spent a great deal of time acquiring poor habits that may turn out to have a similarly detrimental impact on development.

It is, therefore, vital that teams are built with some thought for the technical and social roles that are required, given the current team make-up and the particular demands of the project in question.

10.2.3 Programming production phases

Now that we've identified the programming team roles, let's look in a little more detail at the phases of the project and how the specialisations affect them. Figure 10.1 shows a Gantt-esque chart that breaks the project timeline into phases, from design, planning and prototyping (DPP) to release.

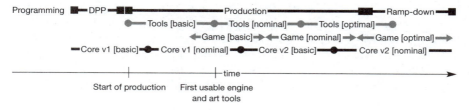

Figure 10.1

Timeline for programming development phases.

We've restricted the role breakdown to three basic teams: tools, game and core. This is the most natural (and probably the most common) subdivision.

Core technology

Notice first of all that there is a core technology team, which is composed (not too surprisingly) of those technology programmers we discussed earlier. Writing core technology is a never-ending task that starts on new iterations as soon as the previous one finishes. The code is almost certainly going to be shared (reused), either vertically or horizontally (see Chapter 3), and possibly across target platforms, so there really is a need for top-notch software engineering skills in this team.

As we are all aware, game and graphic technology tend to advance on timescales shorter than the duration of the average project (say a generous 18 months). Consequently, there will always be a need to have a core technology team – or, at the very least, a *core* core technology team – to keep up the technological quality from product to product.

Notice that the core technology team has had a bit of a head start on the other teams. How else would it be able to write tools and prototypes? This early (pre-project) phase is a critical time in the lifecycle of a project or projects. Many patterns will be set in place by the time that the basic revision of the core technology comes online. These patterns will be absorbed quickly into the fledgling project(s) and may be quite hard to shift should they prove inefficient in the future. Ergo, it's important to get it broadly right quite quickly.

To précis: writing core technology is tricky and time-consuming, and a lot rides on it. Specialist skills are required that are above and beyond many competent game programmers' repertoires.

The tools team

The next team to start writing code will be the tools team. Quite categorically, it should be stated that until the tool requirements are well understood and mostly implemented, no game code should be written. Note that by 'game code', I mean software devoted to game play or glue systems. The tool designs will motivate the creation of components, packages and systems that will function equally well (indeed, identically) be they linked into the game or the editing, conversion and extraction utilities necessary to make the beast walk and talk.

The most important part of the tool team's task is highlighted by the word 'understood' in the last paragraph. The tool facilities required may be exceedingly complex (on our current project, the tools form the bulk of the programming schedule and require a significantly greater amount of technology than will exist in the game). It would be unrealistic, nay commercially suicidal, to write no game code until after the tools were finished, and it is still risking it to wait until they're even at the basic level before starting to write the actual game. However, given that the toolset can potentially be large and complex, it is not only worthwhile but also positively necessary to throw some significant proportion of the programming resources at it in the early parts of the project.

Tools are important. I don't want to understate this point, so I'll say it again, only bolder:

> The quality of your toolset will greatly determine your ability to deliver high-quality entertainment software on budget and on time.

Tools are important, and the usability of tools is even more important. Remember, it's likely that non-technical types such as designers and artists – your customers, if you will – will be using your tools. If they've been cobbled together in a hurry, then your clients will be frustrated, they'll end up pestering you, and consequently you won't be able to get your work done because of this firefighting.

The game team

These guys and gals are the last of the programmers to enter the fray, and by the time that they do, they should be utterly clear as to what they are doing. The time for R&D is long gone. Any tools they may require to be able to create and build game code and data will be written, working and maybe in the second revision. There should be preliminary art and design material ready to construct and develop the game to the nominal level, and progress to that stage should be straightforward.

10.3 The art team

At the broadest level of description, the role of the art team in games development is to provide appropriate, high-quality visual and animated material for the product.

10.3.1 Art roles

Pre-production

The initial phase of development will involve a deal of fast and loose exploration of the game you're trying to create. Some key members of the programming team may be investigating technologies or putting together prototyping demonstrations. The artwork demands of these mini-projects should be light: they exist to demonstrate the validity of concepts. Whilst all this is going on, what should the art team be doing? Well, ideally, nothing. In fact, there really shouldn't be an art team as such. A well-organised studio will schedule its art teams to be, at most, ramping down on existing projects while the new projects are in their pre-pubescent state. As with the programmers, a couple of key personnel are all that should be required. These artists' duties are to provide a little artwork for the programmers and, more to the point, to provide a look and feel for the game. In fact, they should provide several looks and feels, and the more varied the better. Later, one will be selected to be *the* look and feel. It will be easier to pick that one if the pros and cons of several can be weighed up.

So what sort of artists will we find in this early stage of a product's development?

Concept artist – 2D

Though there is still a big market for 2D games, mainly on the smaller consoles (witness Nintendo's Gameboy Advance), console development is dominated by 3D titles. Nevertheless, this by no means diminishes the work of the pencil-and-paper 2D artist. Early sketches will start to create those looks and feels and will serve as guides for others in the pre-production phase as well as when production is properly under way.

Concept artist – 3D

Using material that the 2D concepters are producing, it is helpful to produce 3D models to give a more in-game feel. As with the programmers writing temporary prototyping code, these models may well be throw-away material. No matter, much may well be learned along the way.

Production

Assuming that day zero is when production proper gets under way, what art resources are required at this time? We can say pretty safely that the programmers will not have produced any tools or any working game code. Much of the structural work is yet to occur, and products will be severely hampered, perhaps even fatally so, by having a full art team brought on line on day zero.[2]

There are two reasons for this. First, the team members will either be bored by having nothing to do or they will start to build models and create textures without reference to any parameters or restrictions that will be imposed by whatever game systems the programming team eventually create. This almost certainly leads to wasted work by somebody. Second, a large team is expensive. If a large art team spends (say) three months spinning in neutral, then that can cost a project dearly, and that is only compounded if there is work that needs redoing after that time.

> Art production must not start simultaneously with programming production. It should commence significantly into development, perhaps one-third to halfway through.

---

2   We are talking here about in-game art; non-game art, such as FMV sequences, is less prone to the code/graphics dependency and can be scheduled more liberally.

We illustrate this point in Figure 10.2 for a single project. The DPP phase lasts quite a bit longer for the art team than for the programming team. Remember, though, that the team size is small for this particular part of development. The programming team will spend two to three months in DPP. At the end of this time, there will be a full set of programmers. Art will still be minimal, with the studio artists still busy in production and ramp-down on other projects. Programmer art is perfectly acceptable at this juncture.

When the team gets to the 'First usable engine and art tool' part of the timeline, then the art requirements for the project should be understood thoroughly. This set of prerequisites will include:

- a list of all the models that have to be built for the game;
- a list of all the animations that need to be done;
- rules for material creation;
- rules for model building:
    - restrictions on size and colour depth of textures;
    - restrictions on polygon counts for model types;
    - special naming conventions for components.

From thereon in, the production phase of art should be a case of dividing up the lists of things to do among the team, and the individuals going down those tasks, ticking them off as they are done. Art production is a scalable process, unlike programming production. If time is running short, then it is a sensible approach to enlist more artists – recruited, freelance or borrowed from other teams (providing, of course, that those teams are not inconvenienced).

Here's an interesting question: can the iterative techniques that we've discussed for programming work for art too? Superficially, at least, the answer is yes. Versioning is possible with any creative process. Pragmatically, the answer is yes too. We expect to be using nasty programmer graphics early on in the evolution of our game. Gradually, we'll replace these with incrementally improved models, textures and animations.

There is another interesting possibility of exploiting incremental techniques with artwork that has no direct analogue for programming. Almost all game systems employ level-of-detail (LOD) systems for their visuals. Often, this is implemented as a series of increasingly complex models with associated range

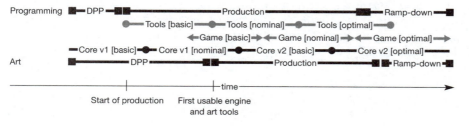

Figure 10.2
Timeline showing art and programming development phases.

values. As the camera gets closer to the object that uses the visual, the more detailed versions are swapped in (and swapped out as the camera moves away).

It's fairly likely that the lower-detail levels will require less work than the high-detail levels. This is the key to a degree of iteration in artwork: the basic version corresponds to the low-detail level(s). The nominal version will be the intermediate-detail levels, and the optimal versions can correspond to the high-detail levels. Obviously, this scheme doesn't work for those projects that use progressive meshes with continuous levels of detail.

In order to analyse the art timeline further, we need to understand the roles that members of the visual content team will adopt. So, let's have a look at some of the skill specialisations we'll see in production artists.

2D artist

It's vital to have a skilled 2D artist in your art team. They really ought to be a whizz with Adobe Photoshop, a multi-industry standard tool. They may even be totally useless at making 3D models, but no matter. The quality and richness of textures in the game will inevitably determine the degree of visual impact that the title has. If the 2D artist does nothing except generate gorgeous textures, then they will have served their team well.

However, not all textures are destined to appear mapped on to 3D geometry. Much work will be required for user-interface design, look and feel. Since this is a complex area – there are often requirements imposed by publishers about user-interface layout and design – it is obviously important to have an artist on board who has an awareness of GUI design issues.

3D modeller

Simply having a bunch of textures is not going to get you very far. Those textures have to be sliced and diced then wrapped around geometry. Our 3D modeller is there to create that geometry.

Animator

It is a fundamental characteristic of our vision and cognitive systems that we quickly tire of things that just sit there and that we demand things that change over time to capture our interest. The skill of making a model – or models – move is therefore as vital to development as creating the objects in the first place. Skill sets for these tasks are obviously not the same, though they are often overlapped into the role of modeller/animator. Nevertheless, it makes sense to separate the tasks, as it will allow us later to consider a production-line process for generating art content.

Human modeller/animator

Human beings have specialised cerebral hardware, the sole purpose of which is to recognise and interpret the appearance and actions of other human beings (in particular, faces). This means that we are extraordinarily sensitive to errors or inconsistencies in something that is meant to look like or move like another person but falls a bit short. For this reason, modellers and animators who create human figures have a much tougher time than those who create (say) cars or guns. There is a huge level of specialisation required, with an understanding of human anatomy and the mechanics of motion.

Technical artist

Occasionally, there are programmers who are dab hands at some aspect of game art. Most programmers can do some basic stuff, but programmer art stands out a mile (in all the wrong ways) and really ought not to end up in a final product.

Once in a while, though, there's a programmer who can produce adequate 3D models, textures and animations. Or there's an artist who has a good grasp of programming, programming issues and algorithms. This individual is a good candidate for the esteemed position of technical artist. If programmers and artists are to communicate effectively, then someone who can understand both sides of the argument is clearly quite an asset.

FMV/cut-scene artist

Most artists have to work within the constraints of a polygon, vertex, keyframe and texture budget. It takes great skill and experience to make the best use of the resources available – and that is the nub of great game art. However, a select few may be given *carte blanche* to create jaw-dropping artwork that exercises the capabilities of the art package (as opposed to the game's target platform) for FMV sequences in intros, outros and story-telling sequences. Again, this is a specialised skill: they'll be using modelling and animation facilities that are simply not practical to use in a game context and, consequently, are never used.

10.4 The design team

The game design team also has dependencies on programming. And, clearly, the programmers have a dependency on design, lest they have nothing to implement. Chickens and eggs! An iterative process – one of the major themes of this book – can solve this mutual interdependency. That process is the iterated delivery system, discussed earlier.

The programmers need to be implementing the core features of the game while the designers work on intermediate detail, and while the programming team is working on those, the designers are refining existing systems and working on the small details.

10.4.1 Design risk management

So far, so good. However, a moderate amount of game development experience will teach you that even with the best game designers in the universe, you get to points on projects where a really cracking concept on paper turns out to be technically infeasible or physically unplayable. This hiccup could well endanger development, because now programming and design are coupled and we're back to the bad old days. The scale of the damage caused by the failure will depend on several factors:

- *Is the feature that malfunctioned critical to the project?* If so, why wasn't it proto-typed before development started? Proof of concept for core game mechanics is extremely important, and projects could be in deep trouble if they wade in to development regardless of success being dependent on risky concepts.
- *Can the feature be replaced with another one?* Redundancy of ideas – having more than you actually need – could just save your bacon. Contingencies should be an automatic part of project planning. Experienced contract bridge players know this, since planning is a vital component of the card play. Having constructed an order of play, the declarer (as they are called) asks the question, 'What could possibly go wrong?' The answer to this could change the game plan entirely, with the declarer using other informa-tion – e.g. statistical knowledge – to mitigate risks that would otherwise lose them the game. As with cards, so with projects. When all looks rosy and the project is about to roll, take a step back and ask yourself: 'What could possi-bly go wrong?' A word or two of common-sense caution: if you can possibly avoid it, don't replace a small feature with a big feature, or use an unproto-typed feature in place of a prototyped one.
- *Can the feature be ditched?* Presumably this would be a low-priority feature, as ditching high-priority ones will almost certainly compromise the game. Nevertheless, it is a common experience for developers to feel, midway through a project, that it isn't the game they thought it would be. Taking a broader view, a designer may decide that less is more and remove the errant element. It may turn out to improve the product, which is now a little less cluttered and more fluid.
- *Can the feature be salvaged?* In some cases, the feature may not work exactly as the designer intended, but it can either be downgraded to a lower-priority element or form the basis for a new feature (either in terms of code or game play).

Clearly, risk is an important element in software development. One way of miti-gating risk is to do all the risky stuff at the start. If an important feature is to appear late on in the product, then the risk associated with that feature is expo-nentiated with time. But with a finite (and usually small) development team, and the amount of risky feature inclusion generally increasing as target plat-forms become faster and more capacious, one comes to the realisation that not everything can be done at once. In other words, it is just plain impossible to avoid growing risk.

The battle is not about eliminating risk but *minimising* it. That's what led us to iterative development. Now, we can take the model a little further, because if we break development into phases, then by treating each phase as an individual project, we can stack the risk for each phase towards the beginning.

To understand this, consider the (simplistic) flow of development shown in Figure 10.3.

Elliptical bubbles indicate which personnel are responsible for which part. Boxes denote stages of development. The interpretation of this diagram is broadly as follows: first we design the game, then we implement it, then we test it. If the test fails, it's passed back to the implementation phase, changes are made, then it's resubmitted.

Each of the stages is complete in its own right. For example, the output of the design team will be a manual (or, more probably, manuals) detailing all the mechanics and features that a player will encounter in the game. This then passes to the implementers, who type and click away for a year or two, producing executable and data, which are submitted to a test department for bug and guideline testing.

If we view Figure 10.3 as linear in time, then by the end of 'Test', we sink or swim depending on how good the design ideas were and how well they were implemented and represented. There is no concept of risk management in this scheme, and it is therefore extremely risky by definition.

Clearly, this is a naive way to develop a product, but it is surprisingly widespread. Can we do better? Yes! Using our old friend iteration. Let's alter the scope and make a small change to the flow to see how we can improve on it – check out Figure 10.4.

The first change is to apply the process over development phases instead of the entire project. The second is to allow redesign of systems that do not work. In the previous scenario, because no risk was associated with design, by the time we got to 'Test' it was too late to do anything. Here, we make sure that we catch

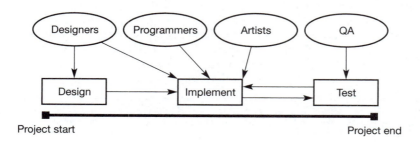

Figure 10.3
The ideal involvement of design, programming, art and QA in the development cycle.

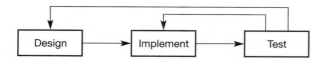

Figure 10.4
Iteration within a single development cycle.

problems as early on as we can and fix them before they strand us at the point of no return.

The timeline has been removed because the idea is to iterate over each project phase until it has been completed to the satisfaction of the team and perhaps an internal QA group, whose (highly technical) job it is to thrash and stretch the submitted software. Having your own technical test team might seem a bit of a luxury, but there are a number of issues with the traditional QA departments that are worth mentioning. First, QA teams in the games business are non-technical. It is a specific requirement that they know little or nothing of what goes into the game technology-wise. They are testing game play. Because of this, testing is a game of pin the tail on the donkey. Testers are trying to guess what to do to break code, or they may be randomly doing things. This is great for what it's worth, but you are as likely to miss problems as you are to spot them. If you are serious about risk management in production, then this is clearly a weak point within the development cycle. Second, though a related issue, products submitted to QA are usually required to have test and debugging information stripped out of them – they are testing final product. This is fair enough, but it means that when critical failures occur, it can be time-consuming and painstaking for programmers to recreate the game's internal state and hopefully the failure to determine the cause. Both of these issues can be remedied by having an internal test team that knows exactly which buttons to push to make life difficult for the game and that can accept code with internal diagnostics still present.

So now each of our project phases becomes a mini-project in its own right, as Figure 10.5 attempts to communicate.

Notice, now, how design has become embedded into development as a key element of the iterative and evolutionary creation of the game. By involving design in design issues in all the development phases, we can respond to problems sooner than if they produced their bible of the game and then twiddled their thumbs until the test had determined that it didn't work very well. The result:

● Better product quality because duff elements are knocked out as early as is feasible.
● Better risk management because problems are detected and can be solved early. In the unfortunate circumstance that things don't work out, the project can be cancelled significantly earlier than the linear development model.

Figure 10.5
Iteration over the three development phases.

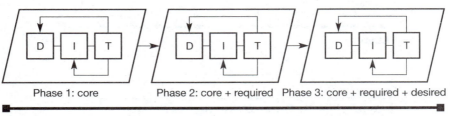

Phase 1: core   Phase 2: core + required   Phase 3: core + required + desired

Project start   Project end

- Less up-front workload for designers. We can dispense with the game bible documentation approach and start with broad overviews that grow with the game during the course of development.

One point worth noting is that a publisher's QA department cannot now realistically perform the 'Test' sections of each phase. This team usually deals only with games that are close to submission for mastering, and we want to have a lot of early testing. The most logical choice for performing these internal test procedures is the design team. After all, this team knows more than most how things ought to behave. And it's been freed from producing huge amounts of documentation. There are many reasons why this is a good thing. Perhaps the best is that it enables designers to design rather than to write. And it frees the rest of the team from the burden of reading and absorbing tens to hundreds of pages of often gratuitous fluff. Note that usually it is unrealistic to expect the team to have done so, and in general people prefer the combination of:

- a snappy, short (five to ten pages at most) overview document that gives the general idea about the game;
- a number of short documents that describe special areas in more detail.

Remember, I guarantee that whatever you plan initially, it will change. If you do a lot of work and find that it's a turkey, then you have risked much unnecessarily. Now why would you want to do that?

10.4.2 Design personnel
As we did for the programmers, now we do for the designers, examining briefly the spectrum of roles that the design team undertakes.

Game-play designer
This is what most people think of as a game designer. They have the big ideas: the core essence of the game – the context in which it takes place, the characters or systems that are involved and the rules that govern them.

Level builder
The level builder is the production unit of the design team. Games do not come cheap these days, and customers rightly expect their money's worth. There needs to be many hours of content in a title, so no matter how clever or addictive the game concept, there needs to be volume, and not just empty or repetitive volume at that. Someone needs to take the contexts, rules and scenarios created by the game-play designers and make them happen, expanding and stretching them in new, interesting and progressive ways. Cue the level builders.

Creative designer
The modern computer game is more than just a set of objects and rules: there are stories to tell, complete with characters who are (usually) at least as well

defined as a film star. These stories need writing and the characters need person-
alities, and this is a full-time job in itself.

Hence the role of creative designer. These are typically wordy people, more
likely to spend the duration of the project writing text in a popular office package than positioning objects in a level editor. Their role will be especially
important if there are external teams involved – for example, the use of voice
talent or companies specialising in FMV.

Technical designer

Designers who have had exposure to programming are fundamental to the
modern video game. Most development studios write their game engines to be
data-driven by either a bespoke or a standard scripting language. Much of the
game's content and high-level behaviour will be controlled by this language.
Clearly, without designers who understand programming – flow control, variables, functions, etc. (features common to most scripting languages) – not very
much is going to happen in your game world.

Again, there is the need for points of contact between the programming
team and the design team. And analogously to the technical artist discussed earlier, the technical designer is able to talk the language of both disciplines.

Internal test

As discussed earlier, if an iterative development philosophy is to be successful,
then testing needs to happen early on in the product lifecycle and continue
periodically. Since having a QA department to do that would be serious (and
expensive) overkill, it is logical for designers to take on this role. Their aim is to
find out as quickly as possible what is and isn't working: what needs redesign-
ing, reprogramming or remodelling. This isn't explicitly a bug hunt. We're more
concerned with systems that fundamentally don't work, not ones that crash or
perform slowly.

10.5 Putting it all together

The team is not just a collection of individuals. The whole is intended to be
greater than the sum of its constituent parts. If this is to be the result, then it is
of prime consideration to make the most of the interactions between the groups
and subgroups. With all these people trying to communicate effectively, some
kind of common language would obviously be of benefit. We're not talking
about (say) the low-level programmer being able to describe the technicalities of
branch delay slots and pipeline optimisation; rather, we are thinking of a way of
getting the broad picture of what the software is about, how the bits fit together,
what is and is not possible.

Object orientation is that language. OO is not just a programmer's tool; it is a way of being able to capture concepts pictorially that might otherwise remain abstract and intangible. Visual representations make things that are otherwise difficult to describe orally accessible almost immediately to anyone with knowledge of what the symbols mean. Indeed, it is hard to imagine how teams managed in the days of procedural breakdown, because all that they could do was enumerate features and behaviours.

Object orientation is the future of game development. It is a medium of communication. It is a visualisation system. It is a production tool. It allows us to create powerful and reusable systems that shorten development times and focus effort on innovation, not reinvention. Is there *anything* it can't do?

10.6 Summary

- The management headache with game development is the requirement to individually supervise the disciplines of programming, art, sound and music and to simultaneously effect the communications between them.

- Programming dictates the viability of the end product. A title should never be driven by art or design.

- Programming is a production process, not a creative one. Its input is a game-play design and its output is code.

- Within a programming team, there are specialisations that have their own idiosyncrasies.

- Tools are a vital and often neglected component of development. Poor or non-existent tools can bring the development cycle to its knees over the course of a project.

- Art is a production process. Its input is a requirement list – so many models, so many polygons, so many textures of such and such a size, etc.

- Design is the real creative discipline in game development. As such, it needs careful risk assessment. Iterative development fits well with a system that acknowledges the need for contingency.

- Technical designers and technical artists are very important personnel who effect the interfaces between the big three disciplines (programming, design and art).

Case study: Cordite

So far, we've looked at the building blocks called components or packages (somewhat interchangeably). The components define methodologies and abstract behaviours that we use and subvert via polymorphism when writing games. Now it's time to look at a case study of a real game, or as near as dammit, to see how this all hangs together.

The purpose of this chapter is not to bore you with all the details of how to design a game. It will illustrate that writing components is not just like writing an external library: the game is the union of internal and external components, as well as glue code (and, perhaps, middleware). These internal components can be promoted to external components as and when they prove to be of use in other games or component hierarchies.

11.1 Technical analysis

This game will be called Cordite. It is based on a real commercial game design (with name changes where appropriate to protect the innocent). I've simplified it, where required, for brevity's sake. The game is of the same genre as Sega's *Virtua Cop* or Namco's *Time Crisis*, and it uses a light gun as its principal controller (although the design specifies that the game should be playable with a standard console controller). The unit of Cordite's game play is a 'scene', where the player is presented with a number of enemies who shoot back at the player, dodge, dive, roll and generally attempt to avoid bullets. Other non-hostile targets give variation and bonuses. The backdrop to all the scenes is a nearly photo-realistic 3D environment. When a player completes a scene by shooting all – or most – of the targets, they are propelled through the world on a fixed path to the next scene. And so on, until either the player takes too many hits or the level ends.

To make things a bit more interesting, there are scenes where, depending on how well the player does or some other condition, the game branches to take the player through an alternative set of scenes, with the restriction that at some later scene, the various branches must merge.

The analysis that follows is for the implementation of the major game systems. The toolset required to produce the data for the game is a case study in itself. As usual, we shall focus on the big picture – the architecture – rather than the minutiae of implementation.

The first stage of analysis should be identification of the technically challenging areas, because these will be areas of maximum risk. What worries us most about the game design? The more alert lead programmer will have picked up on that term 'photo-realistic 3D', because what it implies is a lot of polygon data with high-resolution textures. We must assume that we are not going to fit the entire level into RAM and VRAM, and we really need to think about how we're going to cope with that.

11.1.1 Low-level file management

From the game description, we realise that in theory we don't need everything in RAM anyway. Only the current scene really matters, so as long as the data for that are in RAM, we're fine, depending on exactly how much of the world we can see at one time. This is the great and awful thing about game development: in areas such as this, the technology and the art and design become interlinked inextricably. A good game design here will result in a fast, fun-to-play yet challenging scene *that does not differ significantly in viewpoint from the previous scene yet is varied enough not to be repetitive*. In other words, as programmers, we should flag this as a constraint and let artists and designers worry about the implementation.

Time for more detail: this will flesh out the technological and design parameters that we are working with. Although the unit of game play is a scene, we stand back a little and say: 'But that's a sort of visual concept. We want to solve an abstract problem here'. So, we generalise the route through a complete level as a topological map or graph, with nodes representing scenes and edges representing the transitions between them. Figure 11.1 shows the sort of route we can expect, and we call this a *logical map* of the level.

At the node labelled 'Start', the first scene takes place. All the assets required to display that scene and to play it (models, textures, animations, sounds, light maps, scripts) must be loaded and instantiated immediately (there will also be assets required for the entire level that will be permanently resident). When that has happened, the bullet-fest can commence.

Much shooting later, consider what happens when the player finishes the first scene and progresses to the second. Some new scenery may come into view, and some existing scenery may disappear from view. Let's think about the latter category first.

Figure 11.1
A simple logical map
in Cordite.

Since we cannot hold every model and texture in RAM (I'll refer occasionally to memory generically rather than the verbose 'system RAM, or video RAM, or sound RAM, or CD buffer RAM, etc.'), we may be tempted to dispose of objects that disappear from view immediately so we have the maximum space left for new data. However, that would be rash. What about an object that gets obscured in one scene but remains visible in all other scenes in the level? If (a big 'if') we had enough RAM to hold on to that object, shouldn't we try? And, correspondingly, shouldn't we get rid of an object that we know we're never going to use again? Clearly, some look-ahead is required, to scan the objects later on in the level to see if they're reused. Luckily, our camera tracks fixed paths through a level. We can work out all the details of the objects that come and go offline in our extraction process, looking ahead until the actual end of the level, leaving all the easy work to the game.

So, with each node in the graph, we associate two sets of resources: one contains the new resources that will be needed for the scene; and the other contains those that are no longer required. Figure 11.2 shows this architecture (it assumes we have a simple GRAPH component to represent graphs).

Notice that although we are very much involved in the development of the game code, the MAP component contains nothing specific to Cordite. It becomes yet another component in our library of parts to use when developing titles. As long as we keep component-wise development as an objective, we will

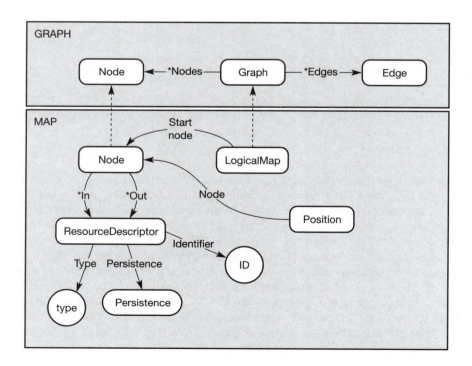

Figure 11.2
The logical MAP and
GRAPH components.

find that each game becomes a fertile source of recyclable material for future development, and because components are small and easily testable, they are not going to hurt schedules.

The `ResourceDescriptor` has some interesting fields. The type field is an enumeration that represents the flavour of asset we're describing:

```
enum Type
{
     RT_UNDEFINED,
     RT_MODEL,
     RT_COLLISION,
     RT_ANIMATION,
     RT_SOUND,
     RT_FONT,
     RT_TEXTURE,
     RT_SCRIPT,

     RT_NUM_TYPES
};
```

In applications where we need to support extra types, we can't easily extend the enum, but we can write (somewhat verbosely):

```
enum MyType
{
     MT_UNDEFINED = RT_UNDEFINED,
     MT_MODEL     = RT_MODEL,
     //...
     MT_SOMETHING = RT_NUM_TYPES,
     //...
     MT_NUM_TYPES
};
```

Enumerations lack power, and the code isn't elegant, but still they are often simpler than the alternative 'register your types in a database' kind of interface.

The other field – Persistence – is also an enumeration. It controls how the resource is handled by the Demigod purging system (see Chapter 5). It can have the values shown in Table 11.1.

These four values can be used by subclasses of Demigod's purge strategies to decide which resources to remove. The first test is to determine whether there are any resources ready for purging with the persistence RP_FLUSH. If there are, then remove the one with the highest LRU count. If not, then scan the resources with RP_HOLD persistence (again, looking at the LRU field).

Now consider the map shown in Figure 11.3. This represents a linear section of game play with no splits or joins.

Table 11.1

Value	Interpretation
RP_UNDEFINED	Something went wrong somewhere
RP_FLUSH	The resource can be purged when it is no longer needed
RP_HOLD	The resource is needed later on but can be purged if there is no space left elsewhere
RP_LOCK	The resource can never be purged

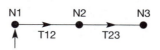

Figure 11.3
Node and transition
labelling in a logical map.

The current scene is described by node N1. Consider the state the game will be in when the scene is completed and the transition towards N2 begins. New objects will start appearing, and they must already have been loaded (and decompressed and instantiated). We are clearly in a difficult position if we start loading the N2 resources only when the T12 transition starts, as there's no guarantee that everything will be in RAM when we get to N2. So, it's not enough just to load the current map node's resources; we must also load the next one, too, long before the transition to the next node can occur (this places another small constraint on the design and art: a stage must last long enough to background-load everything necessary).

We're not finished yet; consider the map segment in Figure 11.4. When executing transition T12, we will have N1's and N2's resources in RAM, but as yet we don't know whether we will branch later on to either N3 or N4. As a result, we must background-load both N3's and N4's resources. Therefore, the final map-imposed limitation on art and design is that if we have splits in the map, then we need to hold the start of both branches at once. More complexities follow from this: when the branch has split, then at the node after the split, when we've selected the branch we're travelling along, we can eject anything we've loaded previously related to the other branch. And when branches merge, if we list the entire set of resources required at the joining node, then we can perform a purge of all unnecessary data.

11.1.2 Object streams

When executing a transition, objects appear and disappear. In order to keep the set of objects rendered per frame as small as possible, we can generate a stream

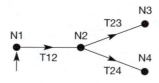

Figure 11.4
A logical map with a
branch.

of object creates and destroys that add and remove objects from the rendered set. This is called a *scenery object stream* (SOS), because it is used primarily for scenic (non-interactive) objects. Cue another component, shown in Figure 11.5.

A scenery stream consists of a series of time-stamped events. These events either create object instances in the game or delete them. The pure abstract class EventHandler defines an interface for the object creation and deletion:

```cpp
// File: SOS_EventHandler.hpp
namespace SOS
{

class EventCreate;
class EventDelete;

class EventHandler
{
public:
    virtual void OnCreate( EventCreate * ) = 0;
    virtual void OnDelete( EventDelete * ) = 0;
};

}
```

Figure 11.5
The scenery object streaming (SOS) component.

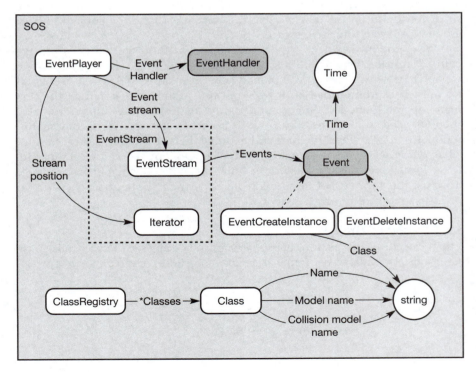

The concrete version of the `EventHandler` is created in the game itself – the mechanisms of object instantiation and destruction will be game-specific after all. Consequently, the SOS component is kept independent of any specific game system.

You may raise an eyebrow at the number of virtual functions in the SOS component, in particular those in the `Event` subclasses and the `EventHandler`. Worry not! Events are relatively uncommon occurrences (we're talking a few object creates and destroys per frame), and the call overhead will ultimately be dwarfed by that of creating or destroying an object instance (along with any collision or auxiliary data that the object needs).

The SOS component also defines a class registration service. A 'class' in this context describes all the data that are required to create an object instance – the name of the visual model, the name of any collision model, etc. When it comes to creating an object instance, the event will contain a class name: we look up the class in the class registry and can then start to create the parts required for the object.

11.1.3 Collision

Collision detection is much simpler than in many 3D games, because as it is described currently, the only collisions of consequence are of bullets with models. Since bullets can be represented by line segments, we only really need to test meshes against lines. On the other hand, there could be quite a number of meshes and a great number of bullets, so we can't afford to be slapdash about performing the required tests.

The really great news is that we already have a component – COLL – that can test lines against models. So, the only part we have to worry about is the high-level collision system and spatial partitioning.

First, let's look at the spatial partitioning. Now, there are many ways to go about dividing up the world, but since the game play is essentially two-dimensional, the initial thought might be generating a quadtree, as shown in Figure 11.6, cells being split whenever objects occupy them down to some fixed granularity. The par-

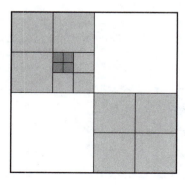

Figure 11.6
A quadtree used to partition the world.

tition test is now simply the process of finding intersections of a ray with an axis-aligned cell, with the quadtree ensuring that only occupied cells are tested.

Floors and ceilings really muck up this scheme, though. They force subdivision of the world to the maximum level everywhere, so we end up with a uniformly divided grid. We can either treat floors and ceilings as special cases or simply use a uniform cell grid. We choose the latter method, and consequently choose the component name GRID. Figure 11.7 shows the participating classes.

The grid contains instances of `GRID::Objects`. This class confers the property of having a rectangular extent, which is all that is really required here. The objects are added to the grid one at a time, which keeps track of the minimum and maximum coordinates of all objects, thus dynamically sizing itself. The grid is then divided into a fixed number of cells. Each cell keeps track of the objects that are wholly or partially inside its bounds (via a bitset class, which stores a 1 in the nth position if it contains the object with index n, and 0 if not). This is a fast and compact representation that can rapidly combine results from several cells by bitwise OR operations.

To increase speed further, the grid state can be cached at any point and quickly restored to the cached state. If we add all the static objects in the world to the grid and then cache that, we need only add the dynamic objects every frame, as it's faster to restore and re-add than it would be to adjust the cell contents when objects move.

When we've added objects to the grid, we can then perform various tests to see whether line segments, rectangles and circles intersect objects in the world.

Figure 11.7
The GRID component.

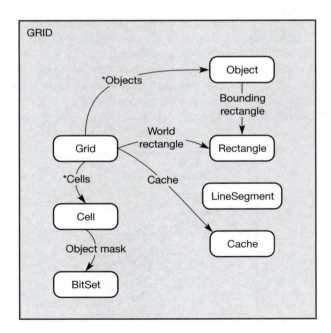

This functionality is used for object collision checks and also for graphical systems such as dynamic lighting. Let's look briefly at the collision system, which we name CNUT (CollisioN UTility, named after a king of England for no particular reason) (see Figure 11.8). I say 'briefly', because as you can see, there's not a lot to it.

Its function is primarily to act as a central place for resolving collisions. This can be performed by free functions:

```
int CNUT::ResolveCollisions( CNUT::Ray const &aRay,
                             CNUT::Collider  &aTest,
                             CNUT::Result    *pResults );
```

to test a ray against a model, for example.

11.1.4 Scripted behaviour

As ever, the ability to control the actions of game objects by external scripts is a vital requirement for ease of development. In a game such as this with simple mechanics, we elect to use a relatively simple event-driven system; we have already met this in Chapter 8 in the evt_IsEventDriven property class, so it's quite a simple job to adapt that component to our ends. We create an EVTSCR (EVenT SCRipt) component for this, shown in Figure 11.9.

As you can see, there's a fair degree of complexity in writing the scripting system, and we don't want to get too bogged down in the details here because the specifics of the execution model may vary somewhat from game to game. The script system borrows some functionality from the 'evt' package (in Cordite this was achieved through *protected* inheritance). Most of the complexity is encapsulated in the Executor class, whose responsibility is to decode lines of

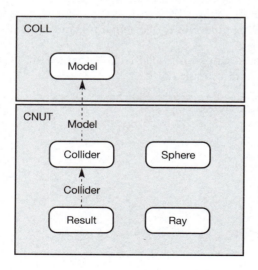

Figure 11.8
The CNUT component.

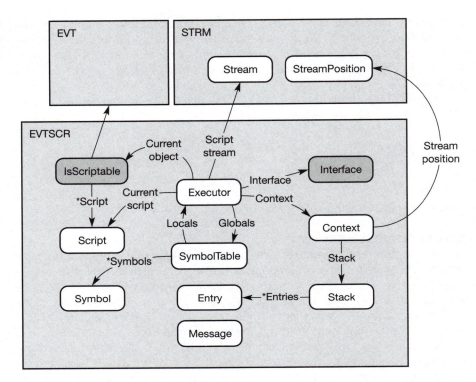

Figure 11.9
The scripted event
(EVTSCR) component.

scripts composed of tokens and parameters and then to execute them. The
result is the calling of one or more virtual functions to perform a script action in
the `Interface` class, which is just that – a completely abstract interface. This
means that the EVTSCR component can be coupled to either a game executable
or an editor executable simply by rewriting the interface class for the host application, thus allowing ourselves to see actual in-game behaviour in an external
editing environment.

The ability to be script-controlled is conferred by the `IsScriptable` property class. This is quite a simple object:

```
// File: EVTSCR_IsScriptable.hpp
#include <EVT\EVT_IsEventDriven.hpp>

namespace EVTSCR
{

class Message;

class IsScriptable : protected evt_IsEventDriven
{
```

```
public:
    /*
     * Constants/typedefs/enums.
     */



    /*
     * Lifecycle.
     */

    IsScriptable();
    virtual ~IsScriptable();

    /*
     * Polymorphism.
     */

    /*
     * API.
     */

    // Set script to be called on given event
    void SetEventScript(int nEvent, Script* pScript);

    // Call event script for given event
    void RunEventScript(int nEvent);

    // Script control.
    void EnableScript(bool bEnable);

    // handle message from scripting system
    virtual bool HandleMessage(Message* pMessage) = 0;

protected:
    /*
     * Helpers.
     */

private:
    /*
     * Data.
     */
```

```
        // The event scripts
        CONT::array<Script*>  m_EventScripts;

        // can an event script be run?
        bool              m_bCanRunEvent;

}; // end class


}
```

As you can see, the main job of a scriptable object is to respond to a `Message`, sent by the `Executor`. This is handled on a per-class basis by the pure virtual `HandleMessage()` method (surprise).

11.1.5 Objects

Cordite is quite light on its use of game objects – there aren't really that many classes required. The base class is a composition of the property classes we've talked about so far in this chapter (see Figure 11.10) plus a reference-counting helper class from a common component (which is, in truth, a bit ugly – reference counting is basically very simple, provided that you can override the 'delete on unreferenced' behaviour for certain subclasses. Sometimes it's OK to have a dumping ground name space for common code or code that doesn't fit anywhere else, as long as you're methodical about keeping it clean).

Notice that we use a prefix rather than a namespace for the base class. This is partly deliberate – since game code is not component code and we are using namespaces for components, it enhances clarity. It is also partly pragmatic, because if there are several classes called `Object` and there are a few indiscriminate `using namespace BLAH` statements, then code can become confusing for compilers, never mind humans.

Now we have a basic object, we can subclass it as we please. We discuss three subclasses of `CorditeObject` in this chapter: `Actor`, `Scenery` and `Avatar`, as depicted in Figure 11.11.

Figure 11.10
Cordite objects are created with the multiple inheritance mix-in method.

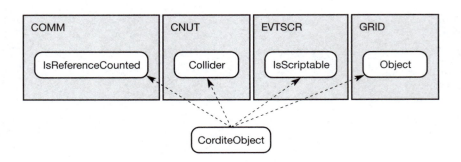

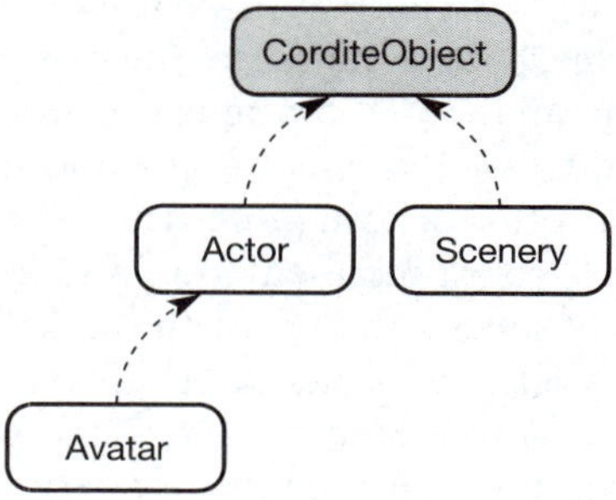

Figure 11.11
Some subclasses of a Cordite object.

An `Actor` is a visible, animatable object. There is a class database for actors (just like we described in the SOS component) that defines the properties of a number of actor types. The `Actor` class itself is abstract owing to a virtual member

```
virtual void Instantiate( const char * pszName,
                          ActorClass * pClass ) = 0;
```

which gives some flexibility in how – and, indeed, when – the actual object comes into existence.

An `Avatar` is the visual representation of a human character in the game. Both players and NPCs can be seen in-game, so we perform the usual trick of separating the data model from the visual representation, as shown in Figure 11.12.

Here, we have abstracted the property of 'having an avatar' into a class called an `Agent`, from which both human and NPC participants descend. The human player is not just an `Agent`; it's also something that uses a controller, so we multiply inherit from the `User` class in a controller component (which we discuss in the next section).

Finally, there is the `Scenery` class, which is the concrete type that will be created by the SOS component discussed earlier. This is just pretty graphics that have a minimum of interactivity (however, as we have seen in Chapter 7, we

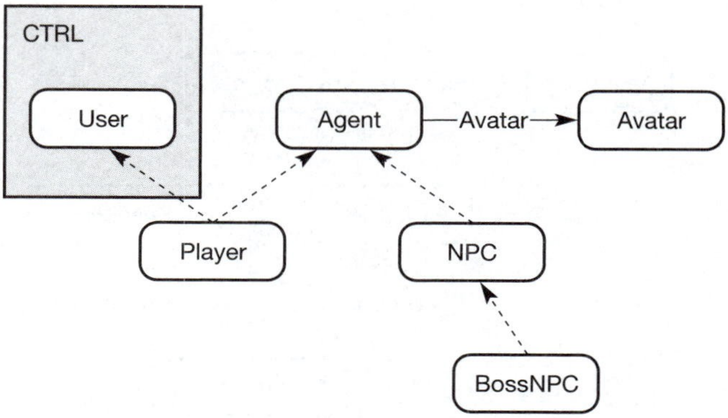

Figure 11.12
The Cordite player and non-player character classes.

can add persistent damage to scenery to make it more interesting and enhance game play by providing feedback about where the player is shooting).

The game object hierarchy for Cordite is therefore a small, shallow hierarchy, which, as we've discussed, is about as good as it gets. We have partially achieved this by using a soft subclassing mechanism: `ActorClass` allows us to create an object with any visual representation and animate it, as opposed to creating a huge number of subclasses, each with similar or even identical behaviours. A good question might be: 'When do I subclass and when do I create a new `ActorClass` database entry?' Since we have logically separated objects and their behaviours, we can make any object do anything. Clearly, if there is a family of objects whose role is to perform some particular behaviour, then subclassing is called for. However, if objects require flexible behaviour, then using an `ActorClass` database entry is the way to go.

'But what about bullets?' I hear you cry. Well, bullets are very light objects – they require no animation and none of the more complex services that a `CorditeObject` offers. So rather than derive from that, we create a new class, `Projectile`, which defines just the interface that the bullet requires.

Perhaps surprisingly, we differentiate between player bullets and NPC bullets. Not only do we render them differently (different colours), but player bullets are assumed to travel infinitely quickly, while NPC fire moves at a rate that allows the player to dodge incoming shots. As a result, we choose to subclass the projectiles. Figure 11.13 shows the bullet hierarchy together with its accompanying weapon class.

Figure 11.13
Bullets and weapons in Cordite.

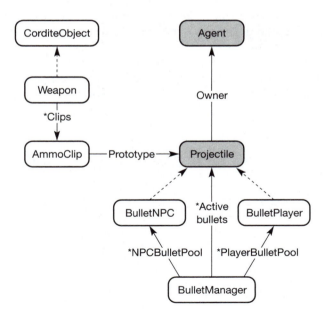

Since bullets are going to be allocated and freed frequently, we've added a manager class that creates and destroys bullets from fixed-size pools, which is fast and won't contribute to fragmentation of system RAM. Notice, though, that the AmmoClip class has a prototype pointer in it (ergo, it uses the GoF Prototype pattern). The Projectile contains an abstract Clone() method, which BulletNPC and BulletPlayer implement. This means that the bullet subclasses need to allocate from the manager, which is a sort of cart-before-horse relationship:

```
/*virtual*/
Projectile * BulletNPC::Clone()
{
      Projectile * pNew = BulletManager_AllocNPC();
      if ( pNew != 0 )
      {
            new (pNew) BulletNPC( *this );
      }

      return( pNew );
}
```

We use the placement version of operator new to construct an object in previously allocated memory. Although Figure 11.13 shows the BulletManager as an object, it is a natural singleton, and because we are hard-wiring it to generate a fixed number of types of bullet, its reuse potential is low. Consequently, little damage is incurred by writing it as a procedural interface.

11.1.6 Human control

As we mentioned right at the start, the game's primary controller is a light gun, but we need to be able to fit other controller types in too. So, we want to write a controller component, don't we? A generic and extendable control system would be particularly nice, because this is something we should be able to comfortably reuse in many games. We discussed some aspects of the design of this component in Chapter 4; here, we will flesh out more of the implementation architecture.

So, we start off with the basic concepts: a player (we call it a user) and a peripheral (hereafter known as a controller) in their hand(s). Obviously, a user 'has a' controller, and since there can be more than one controller (and player) in a game at once, we appoint a manager class to service all the controllers. Figure 11.14 shows the basic controller component.

We have abstracted more than just the controller type – we have separated that abstraction out to recognise ports – slots that controllers can be plugged into. This is useful, nay essential, because our game will have to recognise the situation when one controller is removed and another is added. Instead of subclassing the controller type, we create a fixed controller class whose port has a Mode object subclass that describes the physical peripheral in the slot. If that

Figure 11.14
The CTRL controller
component.

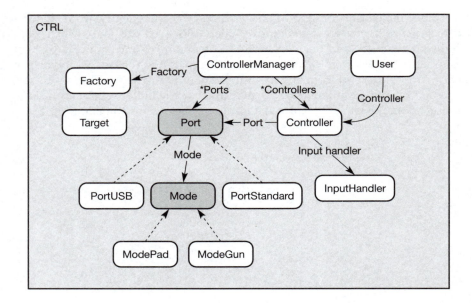

peripheral is swapped for another, then the user still has the same controller; it's just the lower-level encapsulated instances that change, making the operation totally transparent to the player.

All the hardware-specific operations happen within the Mode subclasses, so you might wonder how we get the controller data from within that encapsulated system back into the game. That's where the InputHandler, User and Target classes come in. The Mode has a pure virtual function that looks like this:

```
virtual void DispatchState( User         * pUser,
                            Target        * pTarget,
                            InputHandler  * pHandler ) =0;
```

The InputHandler has the following interface:

```
// File: CTRL_InputHandler.hpp
namespace CTRL
{

class GunData;
class PadData;

class InputHandler
{
```

```
public:
    virtual void HandleGun( const GunData & aGunData,
                            Target        * pTarget,
                            User          * pUser );
    virtual void HandlePad( const PadData & aPadData,
                            Target        * pTarget,
                            User          * pUser );
};


}
```

In short, there's a Handle method for every supported controller type. In the base class, the implementations of these methods do nothing, so for an application that does not support a particular controller, the compiler and linker are happy and the executable is oblivious.

Subclasses of `InputHandler` in the application code receive notification of the controller state via these methods. For example, with the gun controller:

```
void ModeGun::DispatchState( User          * pUser,
                             Target        * pTarget,
                             InputHandler * pHandler )
{
    pHandler->HandleGun( m_MyState, pTarget, pUser );
}
```

where the member variable `m_MyState` holds the current and previous gun states. The Handle methods with the application's `InputHandler` subclass can then decide on what action to take based on the controller data (or changes therein), the `User` (i.e. who sent the input, essential for handling situations such as split-screen views) and the `Target`. The latter class describes the object that the results of the changed peripheral data – if any – should be sent to. In Cordite, this is usually a cursor, which tracks the gun position on screen. The cursor object just needs to inherit from the (Strawman) `Target` class:

```
class Cursor : public CTRL::Target
{
//...
};
```

Within the game code, the `InputHandler` classes know that their target is a cursor, and the pointer to the `Target` can be safely upcast to a `Cursor`:

```
void MyHandler::HandleGun( const GunData & aGunData,
                           Target        * pTarget,
                           User          * pUser )
```

```
{
    Cursor * pCursor = static_cast<Cursor *>(pTarget);
    //...
}
```

11.1.7 Particles

Particle systems form the basis of most in-game effects. I've seen many attempts to write a generic particle system; they've all performed poorly. I've also seen many bespoke particle systems written; they've performed well but they're so nearly identical, both logically and physically, to other bespoke particle effects that one can't help but feel that you could write them generically.

There are many ways of approaching a generic particle system. One can write a *physical simulator* that determines particle behaviour in terms of entities being acted on by *force fields*. This makes it difficult to get the particle behaviours just right. So, instead, we simply make specific particle behaviour a property of the object.

The naive interpretation of this would be:

```
class Particle
{
public:
    virtual void Update( Time aDeltaT ) = 0;
    virtual void Render( Renderer * ) = 0;
};
```

but this would result in a very poorly performing system (for medium to large numbers of particles, anyway) because of the per-particle virtual function call overheads relative to the amount of work being done in the update and render methods (clearly, particles must be fast to process). Also, notice that it is hard-wired to one specific renderer. This is not very reusable.

Clearly, we need the benefits of polymorphism while minimising the overhead. We would like to be able to parameterise our system so that behaviours can be built out of simple elements and it is independent of any specific rendering system. We achieve this through the use of templates. Figure 11.15 shows the particle system component.

Let's focus on the emitter side first of all. We have created a number of very small (but perfectly formed) property classes that confer a well-defined simple behaviour on a particle. Here, we've shown four properties: lifespan, speed, direction and spin. We create a specific emitter by mixing the base `Emitter` class with the appropriate property classes:

```
namespace PRTCL
{
```

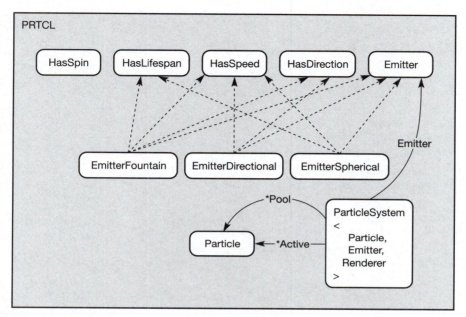

Figure 11.15
The PRTCL particle
system component.

```
class HasLifespan
{
public:
    HasLifespan();
    HasLifespan( float fMin, float fMax );

    float GetLifespan() const;
    void SetLifeRange( float fMin, float fMax );

private:
    float m_fMinLife;
    float m_fMaxLife;
};


//-------------------------------------------------------

class HasSpeed
{
public:
    HasSpeed();
    HasSpeed( float fMin, float fMax );

    float GetSpeed() const;
    void SetSpeedRange( float fMin, float fMax );
```

```
private:
    float m_fMinSpeed;
    float m_fMaxSpeed;
};

//----------------------------------------------------------

class HasSpin
{
public:
    HasSpin();
    HasSpin( float fMin, float fMax );

    float GetSpin() const;
    void SetSpinRange( float fMin, float fMax );

private:
    float m_fMinSpin;
    float m_fMaxSpin;
};

//----------------------------------------------------------

class HasDirection
{
public:
    HasDirection();
    HasDirection( const MATHS::Vector3 & vDir,
                  float fPerturbation=0.0f );

    void SetDirection( const MATHS::Vector3 & vDir );
        // Set the direction vector.

    void SetPerturbation( float fPerturbation );
        // Sets the amount of randomness in the direction.

    MATHS::Vector3 GetVelocityVector( float fSpeed ) const;

private:
    MATHS::Vector3 m_vDirection;
    float          m_fPerturbation;
};

/**********************************************************/
```

```
class Emitter
{
public:
      /*
       * Constants/typedefs/enums.
       */

      /*
       * Lifecycle.
       */
       Emitter( const MATHS::Vector3 & vPosition );

      /*
       * Polymorphism.
       */

      /*
       * API.
       */
       const MATHS::Vector3 & GetPosition() const;
       void  SetPosition( const MATHS::Vector3 & vPos );
           // Set/get the point of emission.

protected:
      /*
       * Helpers.
       */

private:
      /*
       * Data.
       */
       MATHS::Vector3 m_vPosition;


}; // end class

//-------------------------------------------------------

class EmitterDirectional
: public Emitter
, public HasSpeed
, public HasDirection
{
```

```
public:
    /*
     * Constants/typedefs/enums.
     */

    /*
     * Lifecycle.
     */
        EmitterDirectional( const MATHS::Vector3 & vPos,
                            const MATHS::Vector3 & vDir,
                            float fMinSpeed,
                            float fMaxSpeed,
                            float fPerturbation = 0.0f );

    /*
     * Polymorphism.
     */

    /*
     * API.
     */
        MATHS::Vector3 GetParticleVelocity() const;
            // Gets a velocity based on the direction,
            // speed and perturbation settings.

protected:
    /*
     * Helpers.
     */

private:
    /*
     * Data.
     */
        float m_fPerturbation;



}; // end class


}
```

There are no virtual function calls required here, so it's all nice and quick. Notice that there is no 'create particle' call in the `Emitter`. The function of this object is to calculate initial values, and it does this by having ranges between which random values can be picked (if we want a single value, then we make a range of size zero). Within game code, a subclass of Emitter needs to support a non-virtual member function InitialiseParticle, where the particle type is also defined in the game code. This then uses the base emitter to calculate values to set up the particle:

```
void MyEmitter::InitialiseParticle( MyParticle * p )
{
    p->SetLife( GetLifeSpan() );
    p->SetVelocity( GetParticleVelocity() );
}
```

The class that creates and manages particles is the ParticleSystem, which is a templated object based on three parameters:

- The Particle, which you provide and which should support the *non-virtual* methods

  ```
  void Update( Time aDeltaT );
  bool IsActive() const;
  void Render( Renderer * pRenderer ) const;
  ```

IsActive() should return false if the particle has expired.

- The Emitter subclass, supporting InitialiseParticle() as described above.
- The renderer you're using as an argument to the particle Render() method.

Putting these all together looks like a bit like this:

```
namespace PRTCL
{

template<class Particle,class Emitter,class Renderer>
class ParticleSystem
{
public:
    /*
     * Constants/typedefs/enums.
     */

    /*
     * Lifecycle.
     */
    ParticleSystem( Emitter * pEmitter,
                    int       iMaxParticles );
```

```
        virtual ~ParticleSystem();

         /*
          * Polymorphism.
          */
        // Update active particles by the elapsed time.
        virtual void Update( float fDeltaT );

        // Removes all active particles, sets the age to 0.
        virtual void Initialise();

        // Renders all the (active) particles.
        virtual void Render( Renderer * pRenderer ) const;

         /*
          * API.
          */
        // Generates a number of particles. The maximum set
        // in the constructor cannot be exceeded (it will
        // silently fail if so). The return value is the
        // actual number generated.
        int Spawn( int iRequestedParticles );

        int GetActiveParticleCount() const;
        float GetAge() const;
        Emitter * GetEmitter();
        const Emitter * GetEmitter() const;

protected:
        /*
         * Helpers.
         */
          inline void elapseTime( float fDeltaT )
          {
              m_fAge += fDeltaT;
          }

          void freeActiveParticle( iterator itParticle );

private:
        /*
         * Data.
         */
          tParticleList m_ActiveParticles;
```

```
        tParticlePool m_ParticlePool;
        Emitter *     m_pEmitter;
        int           m_iMaxParticles;
        float         m_fAge;
};

}
```

Yes, the particle system is free to have virtual functions. Any instance of a
system is only updated once per game loop (or perhaps less), so a single polymorphic call will be dwarfed by the actual update of the contents. We can then
use the API and the protected helpers to fine-tune our subclassed particle
system. For instance, a particle system that continuously chucks out particles
(e.g. smoke) may look like this:

```
template<class Particle, class Emitter, class Renderer>
class ParticleSystemContinuous
: public PRTCL::ParticleSystem<Particle,Emitter,Renderer>
{
public:
    /*
     * Constants/typedefs/enums.
     */

    /*
     * Lifecycle.
     */
    ParticleSystemContinuous( Emitter * pEmitter,
                              int       iMaxParticles,
                              float     fGenRate );

    /*
     * Polymorphism.
     */
    void Update( float fDeltaT );

    /*
     * API.
     */
    // Sets and gets the maximum number of particles
    // that can be produced. You can't set more than
    // the maximum passed in the constructor.
    void SetCapacity( int iCapacity );
    int GetCapacity() const;
```

```
    // Sets the rate at which particles are replenished.
    void SetGenerationRate( float fRate );

protected:
    /*
     * Helpers.
     */
    void maintainParticleDensity( float fDeltaT );

private:
    /*
     * Data.
     */
        float m_fGenerationRate;
        int   m_iCapacity;

};
```

11.1.8 And so on

Within Cordite, there are many more components that make up the complete game. For example, a path controller that intelligently rescales Avatar walk cycle animations depending on the route direction and speed, a camera controller, or a console that allows inspection and modification of internal game state. The large majority are reusable without change; of the remainder, only one or two are so specific to this game that they are not worth recycling. With good design and careful implementation, video games can – contrary to the received mythology – be created from small, reusable building blocks, which can be extended through the familiar mechanism of polymorphism. Figure 11.16 summarises the components we have discussed.

We've split the components into three – somewhat arbitrary – levels: core, which are components that are generic and/or exist in their own right or are used in another game; intermediate, which are components written especially for Cordite but that are otherwise generic; and game, which are (somewhat loosely) classes that specialise classes in the other levels and generally glue the required behaviours together but are generally not reusable. In this example game, given the (fairly arbitrary but not unrepresentative) components we have selected for discussion, 13 of 17 components are reusable. That's nearly 77% of the components. Although it would be a big (and mistaken) assumption to make that all the components are the same size in terms of lines of code or number of bytes of object code, it is hard not to reach the conclusion that by writing games using component technologies, the overwhelming majority of component code is reusable and about half of that may exist already. Tell that to your producer!

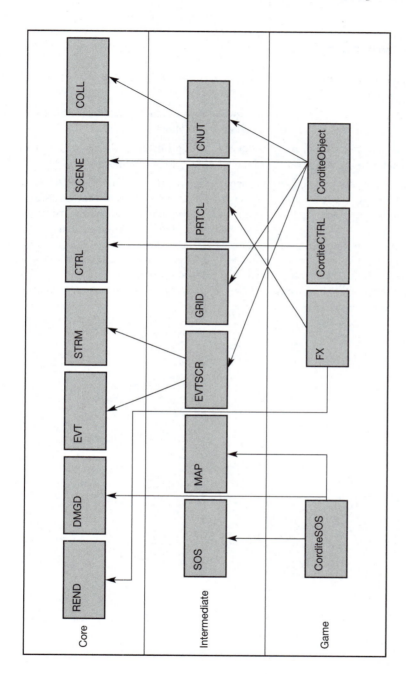

Figure 11.16
Overview of the Cordite components that we've discussed.

11.2 Summary

- Much of a game's architecture can be put together with a set of existing, reusable components.

- The components provide a framework from which specific behaviours are implemented and utilised via the mechanism of inheritance.

- The bits that cannot be put together in this way can still be written as components with the possibility of reuse in other games or applications.

- The notion that you can't do reuse in games is therefore utterly refuted. It is the author's fond wish that this is the straw that breaks the Hacker's Charter's back. However, this does not mean that game development will become easy, or a cynical, churn-'em-out process that recycles dated technology. Far from it. The intention is to stop bogging our development down with rewriting, re-debugging and retesting the 'simple' stuff, and to focus instead on utilising the increasing amounts of CPU power and RAM to push the boundaries of what we believe is possible. After all, isn't that why we're in the games business in the first place?

Appendix: coding conventions used in this book

The conventions used follow the policy discussed briefly in Chapter 3. More standards are adopted than are required by the policy, which is intended to be a useful minimum rather than a definitive maximum:

Variable scope is indicated by a single-letter prefix followed by an underscore:

g_ means a variable is global.
s_ means a variable is static – visible only in the declaring module.
c_ means a variable is a static class member.
m_ means a variable belongs to a class instance.

A *modified Hungarian notation* indicates the type of variable:

p means a pointer.
i means an integer (compiler native size).
u means an unsigned integer (compiler native size).
c means a character (eight-bit signed).
str means a nul-terminated string (or string class type).
v means a vector.
m means a matrix.
a means an instance or reference.
f means a single-precision floating-point value.
b means a Boolean value.

Publicly accessible functions and methods start with an upper-case letter. Private functions and methods begin with a lower-case letter. In both cases, names are composed of word fragments with no separators, each fragment starting with a capital letter.

So if we see the variable m_pResourceManager, we know we're dealing with a class member that points at a resource manager type. If we see iNumSprites, we are looking at a local integer counter for our sprites.

Preprocessor macros are in upper case with word fragments separated by underscores for clarity, e.g. MAX_SPRITE_NAME.

Namespaces are given names with a single short (no more than five characters) word fragment in upper case, e.g. namespace REND { /*...*/ }.

Bibliography

Abrash, M. (1994) *The Zen of Code Optimisation*, Scottdale, AZ: Coriolis.

Alexandrescu, A. (2001) *Modern C++ Design*, Upper Saddle River, NJ: Addison-Wesley.

Ammeral, L. (1997) *STL for C++ Programmers*, Chichester, UK: Wiley.

Bourg, D. (2001) *Physics for Game Developers*, Sebastapol, CA: O'Reilly.

Brown, W., Malveau, R., McCormick, H., Mowbray, T. (1998) *Antipatterns*, New York: Wiley.

Eberly, D. (2000) *3D Game Engine Design*, San Francisco: Morgan Kaufman.

Gamma, E., Helm, R., Johnson, R., Vlissides, J. (1994) *Design Patterns – Elements of Reusable Object-Oriented Structure*, Reading, MA: Addison-Wesley.

Johnstone, M. Wilson, P. (1998) The memory fragmentation problem: solved? www.cs.utexas.edu/users/wilson/papers/fragsolved.pdf/.

Lakos, J. (1995) *Large-Scale C++ Software Design*, Reading, MA: Addison-Wesley.

Maguire, S. (1993) *Writing Solid Code*, Redmond, WA: Microsoft Press.

Maguire, S. (1994) *Debugging the Development Process*, Redmond, WA: Microsoft Press.

McConnell, S. (1993) *Code Complete*, Redmond, WA: Microsoft Press.

Myers, S. (1995) *More Effective C++*, Reading, MA: Addison-Wesley.

Myers, S. (1997) *Effective C++*, 2nd edition, Reading, MA: Addison-Wesley.

Rollings, A., Morris, D. (1999) *Game Architecture and Design*, Scottdale, AZ: Coriolis.

Singhal, S., Zyda, M. (1999) *Networked Virtual Environments*, New York: Addison-Wesley.

Stroustrup, (2000) *The C++ Programming Language*, 3rd edition, Reading, MA: Addison-Wesley.

Watt, A., Policarpo, F. (2000) *3D Games: Real-Time Rendering and Software Technology*, Harlow, UK: Addison-Wesley.

Web resources

No collection of Web resources for game developers would be complete without Gamasutra: lots and lots of really useful source code, tutorials, reviews, post mortems. See www.gamasutra.com

For advanced, occasionally esoteric, cutting-edge C++ with deep insights by ANSI committee members, see www.gotw.ca/

Sweng-gamedev is a group talking C++, software engineering and project management for games, among other things. Subscribe at www.midnightryder.com/

If you're writing compilers, a scripting system or other language-related systems, and you're fine with using STL in a game, then ANTLR surpasses yacc and lex. See www.antlr.org/

For lots of info about how to write physics for games, Chris Hecker's page is a very good place to start: www.d6.com/users/checker/dynamics.htm

Index